African Intelligence Services

Security and Professional Intelligence Education Series (SPIES)

Series Editor: Jan Goldman

In this post–September 11, 2001, era there has been rapid growth in the number of professional intelligence training and educational programs across the United States and abroad. Colleges and universities, as well as high schools, are developing programs and courses in homeland security, intelligence analysis, and law enforcement, in support of national security.

The Security and Professional Intelligence Education Series (SPIES) was first designed for individuals studying for careers in intelligence and to help improve the skills of those already in the profession; however, it was also developed to educate the public on how intelligence work is conducted and should be conducted in this important and vital profession.

Counterintelligence Theory and Practice
Second edition by Hank Prunckun

Methods of Inquiry for Intelligence Analysis
Third Edition by Hank Prunckun

The Art of Intelligence: More Simulations, Exercises, and Games
edited by Rubén Arcos and William J. Lahneman

Weaponized Marketing: Defeating Radical Islam with Marketing That Built the World's Top Brands
by Lisa Merriam and Milton Kotler

Shadow Warfare: Cyberwar Policy in the United States, Russia and China
by Elizabeth Van Wie Davis

African Intelligence Services: Early Postcolonial and Contemporary Challenges
by Ryan Shaffer

To view the books on our website, please visit https://rowman.com/Action/SERIES/RL/SPIES or scan the QR code below.

African Intelligence Services

Early Postcolonial and Contemporary Challenges

Edited by Ryan Shaffer

ROWMAN & LITTLEFIELD
Lanham • Boulder • New York • London

Executive Editor: Dhara Snowden
Assistant Editor: Rebecca Anastasi
Marketing Manager: Kim Lyons

Credits and acknowledgments for material borrowed from other sources, and reproduced with permission, appear on the appropriate page within the text.

Published by Rowman & Littlefield
An imprint of The Rowman & Littlefield Publishing Group, Inc.
4501 Forbes Boulevard, Suite 200, Lanham, Maryland 20706
www.rowman.com

British Library Cataloguing in Publication Information Available

Library of Congress Cataloging-in-Publication Data
Names: Shaffer, Ryan, 1982– editor, author.
Title: African intelligence services : early postcolonial and contemporary
    challenges / edited by Ryan Shaffer.
Description: Lanham : Rowman & Littlefield, 2021. |
    Includes bibliographical references and index.
Identifiers: LCCN 2021016098 (print) | LCCN 2021016099 (ebook) |
    ISBN 9781538150825 (cloth) | ISBN 9781538150832 (ebook)
Subjects: LCSH: Domestic intelligence—Africa, Sub-Saharan—History. |
    Internal security—Africa, Sub-Saharan—History.
Classification: LCC JQ1875.A55 I63 2021 (print) | LCC JQ1875.A55 (ebook) |
    DDC 363.230967—dc23
LC record available at https://lccn.loc.gov/2021016098
LC ebook record available at https://lccn.loc.gov/2021016099

Contents

Acknowledgments

This book was guided by several people who provided important insights and encouragement. Jan Goldman, Dhara Snowden, and Rebecca Anastasi from Rowman and Littlefield were enthusiastic with the idea from the very start. They and the other Rowman staff made the process as easy and efficient as publishing an anthology can be. Harry Verhoeven encouraged me to further develop my interest about African intelligence services into what became this anthology. Kathleen Wilson provided advice about different approaches, Mwangi Njagi gave me valuable cultural and historical feedback, and Sylvia Kamene helped with field research. The anonymous reviewers' careful attention to detail pushed the book in new directions that improved the scope. I also owe a huge debt of gratitude to the authors who contributed their research to this book and to my family for their help and support.

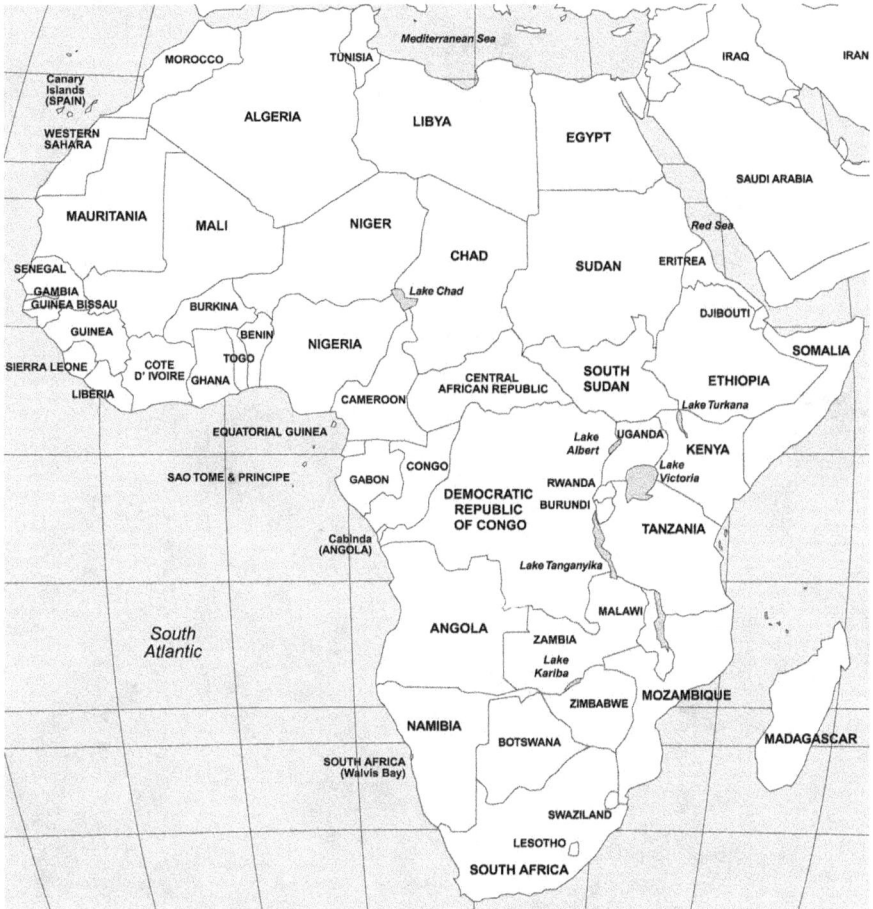

Map of Africa from the Cartographic Research Laboratory, University of Alabama.

Introduction

by

Ryan Shaffer

Africa has long been a location of geopolitical struggles. With nearly sixty countries and a population of over one billion, the great powers of the world have focused money and resources on building favorable relations with oil- and mineral-rich countries, emerging economic capitals, and geostrategic nations. The scholarship on African governments, history, international relations, and geopolitics is rich. In contrast, Africa's intelligence and security services are not as well studied. However, African intelligence services have played a prominent role in governments and in conducting intelligence collection, operations, and analysis against domestic and foreign targets. During the Cold War, the great powers competed with each other to provide aid to countries for economic reasons and acquire geopolitical influence. African intelligence services worked for, against, and with foreign intelligence services throughout that period, seeking to defend their national security interests. This activity persists, as intelligence agencies continue international relationships and have a broad range of threats to monitor.[1]

African intelligence services play a vital role in security and stability for their countries but are largely unexplored by scholars. There are some notable exceptions to this, but compared to the amount of research about U.S. intelligence, African intelligence and security services have not received anywhere near the same amount of attention. World Catalog, a worldwide database of library holdings, reveals about 300 books, chapters, articles, official documents, and media cataloged on the subject.[2] If the search is narrowed to South Africa's intelligence history, which is the most robustly researched African nation on intelligence, the search returns over 200 results.[3] In contrast, a search by subject for material about the Central Intelligence Agency reveals over 15,300 holdings.[4]

This anthology highlights the importance of exploring Africa's intelligence services with historical and contemporary perspectives to recognize their trajectories, strengths, weaknesses, targets, and customers. As African intelligence services have often been overlooked and understudied, this book argues for researching them as a key institution and actor in African history and government. Taking an academic approach to African intelligence services' colonial legacies and contemporary challenges is vital to understanding security and intelligence in Africa. Scholarly research and conclusions about intelligence contributes to the public's understanding and government policies and nongovernment organizations' work when—for example—considering international aid and partnerships, peacekeeping operations, long- and short term stability, and foreign investment. Moreover, Africans more generally should be able to learn about their intelligence services' history as well as issues of security and intelligence oversight because that knowledge can build trust and transparency with the government.

The anthology adds to the academic discourse and public understanding about Africa generally and intelligence services specifically. By examining a range of countries in Africa from different time periods, it provides the reader with insight into the challenges surrounding African intelligence services as well as the similarities and differences in how they function and the topics they monitor. The book does not aim to be a comprehensive study, as that is not possible with such a diverse continent with so many countries, cultures, ethnic groups, and histories. Rather, this anthology explores a select range of countries with attention to historical and contemporary issues, arguing the history of intelligence services is vital to any study about modern Africa.

This introduction has five parts. It begins with a brief overview of research about intelligence beyond Europe and North America broadly and the literature about African intelligence specifically. Next, it turns to the book's objective of providing a diverse collection of chapters about African intelligence services' early postcolonial and contemporary challenges. Then it explores the book's methodology, with the contributors taking different historical, legal, and political science approaches to engage with the past and present. Moving to source material, the lack of available primary sources in the traditional sense is examined as well as there is an exploration of the intentional destruction and concealment of some African intelligence records. Then the introduction details the anthology's structure by providing a brief summary of each chapter. Last, the introduction highlights common challenges and themes between the African intelligence services examined in the book and calls for further research to illuminate the important, but understudied, role of intelligence in Africa.

INTELLIGENCE OUTSIDE EUROPE AND NORTH AMERICA

Most of the scholarship in intelligence studies has centered on Europe and North America, but there are notable exceptions. This is not entirely due to Western-centric attitudes, but also because many countries do not have the declassification, oversight, transparency, and freedom of information laws that many European and North American countries have. Recent monographs about China, Japan, and Pakistan demonstrate scholarly and public interest in learning about intelligence services in regions beyond Europe and North America.[5] Additionally, academic articles cover intelligence related to less traditional states, such as the Islamic State's intelligence service and Iran's Ministry of Intelligence and Security.[6] As for Africa specifically, there are dozens of academic articles about African intelligence in *Intelligence and National Security, International Journal of Intelligence and CounterIntelligence*, and *Journal of Intelligence History*. With the notable exception of about ten articles, they are mostly about colonial intelligence, the world wars, or Western intelligence services in Africa.[7] Additional articles appear in journals that deal with broader African security topics, such as in *African Affairs* and *African Security Review*.[8] Focusing on anthologies specifically, the body of scholarship outside of European and North American intelligence is even more limited.

Scholarship largely until the end of the Cold War usually examined intelligence of other countries from the perspective of foreign activity. Indeed, often the research explored intelligence activity from the perspective of a colonial or world power in a smaller country of geostrategic importance. Such histories mostly centered around colonial or Western power as having the agency in the foreign country at key historical moments.[9] Given that colonial and wartime records were available to scholars, these publications also examined foreign governments and intelligence from the perspective of Western documents. While this was not always the case, most of the research approached the subject through Western records that were available, which could be problematic, as those records often ignored local agency and the subaltern.

There are some recent exceptions that demonstrate the scholarship moving more toward the study of lesser known intelligence agencies. Notably, *Changing Intelligence Dynamics in Africa*, edited by Sandy Africa and Johnny Kwadjo, has chapters that detail Ghana, Kenya, South Africa, Uganda, and the African Great Lakes region, written by one academic and five former government officials in Africa.[10] This book is a welcome publication, containing many insightful first-person narratives about African intelligence agencies. Additionally, *The Security Activities of External Actors in Africa* centered around African security and focused on non-African actors.[11] Specifically, the authors examined China, France, Russia, the United Kingdom, the United States, the European Union, and the United Nations as external security actors in Africa but did not explore the agency of African intelligence or security services.

There have been recent anthologies that examine intelligence beyond the "Anglosphere," but unfortunately Africa was not significantly explored. *Intelligence Elsewhere*, edited by Philip H. J. Davies and Kristian C. Gustafson, contains a good collection of chapters with insightful analysis about countries not usually studied, but the book includes just a single African country—Ghana.[12] As for *National Intelligence Systems*, Gregory F. Treverton and Wilhelm Agrell's edited volume included contributions about the future of intelligence but did not examine Africa or any developing countries or new countries' struggles to create effective security institutions.[13] Whereas, Zachary K. Goldman and Samuel J. Rascoff's anthology, *Global Intelligence Oversight*, sought to analyze global issues, but took a legal approach that focused on Anglophone alliances, Israel, and Germany, with Africa completely excluded.[14] This anthology seeks to fill the gap by directly exploring African intelligence services by building from earlier research published about intelligence in specific African countries.

OBJECTIVE

This book's objective is to introduce readers to different African intelligence services by looking at early postcolonial and contemporary challenges. It uses the term "postcolonial" broadly by examining chapters ranging from Kenya's first decade of independence to contemporary issues in Botswana and even explores Rhodesia following the Unilateral Declaration of Independence when many other African countries experienced independence with majority rule.[15] This approach highlights the wide range and complexity of historical and contemporary intelligence services in Africa. Aimed at scholars as well as students, the chapters provide case studies written by academics and intelligence practitioners. Each chapter represents work conducted with publicly available sources and does not necessarily represent the opinions of their current or former places of employment. Indeed, the chapters are the culmination of open source research and years of experience on African matters.

Readers are reminded of the rich cultural, ethnic, political, and religious diversity in Africa, which makes providing a general theory about African intelligence services challenging. Though this introduction's conclusion provides an analysis of the broad challenges and commonalities between African intelligence services, the contributions here are too specific and the countries are too diverse to develop a theory about how African intelligence operates. Africa's complexity and diversity would likely make a single intelligence theory too broad for any meaningful contribution or too narrow to be valid across the continent. This anthology, however, adds to the scholarship on African intelligence services by arguing for putting the institutions front and center in the research about African security and governments. These chapters highlight African agency in intelligence where Africans shaped and controlled intelligence and security services for their own objectives, including personal incentives of wealth and power, protecting independence, or for ensuring government stability from internal and external threats.

The anthology format was selected so readers could understand the diversity of African intelligence services in one book. Indeed, the point of the book is to take a broad approach in countries, methodologies, and time periods. There is no single African intelligence service type, but many different types shaped by diverse cultural, economic, historical, religious, and political factors. By including different approaches—such as historical, contemporary, legal, and intelligence-practitioner perspectives—in one volume, it helps readers understand the changes and continuities since colonialism. Yet, differences between the countries' intelligence services comprise only part of the story. African countries have similarities in intelligence, but also commonalities with American, Asian, and European nations. Intelligence services—despite having allegiances to their nations—share similarities in tradecraft, objectives, and evolution because they are all rooted in bureaucracy and information that have been passed internationally for centuries, notably through imperialism and other types of foreign intrusion.[16]

By exploring African intelligence and security services, this anthology provides a new understanding on the topic and encourages further research on the subject. The scholarship should consider African intelligence and security an important topic while the world powers vie for influence on the continent. Future research should analyze the transformation of African nations since the end of the Cold War, as some African governments have declassified intelligence records, instituted intelligence reforms, and embraced democratization. Studies about African intelligence are vital to understanding Africa's past, present, and future not only because of foreign interest, but also because of how African intelligence services have protected domestic power, shaped peace and conflict, and engaged in creating stability and instability in Africa.

METHODOLOGY

When examining foreign governments, especially in less studied countries and involving secretive subjects, readers face the challenge of confirmation bias. Readers often try to relate foreign institutions, concepts, and events to the ones they are familiar with. This can lead to bias when readers "mirror-image" institutions, concepts, and events according to their own cultural, social, governmental, and political experiences. The problem is compounded when dealing with intelligence services—especially historic ones—that existed in different national and international contexts. This anthology takes the approach of understanding African intelligence services in their own terms rather than providing a comparative approach. It highlights African intelligence's uniqueness in historical and contemporary terms and encourages readers to avoid confirmation bias by contextualizing the services in their own histories, politics, and cultures.

The anthology takes a broad view of what constitutes an intelligence and security service. While the United Kingdom, for example, has separate intelligence services for domestic and foreign intelligence, this form is not necessarily adopted in other countries. Consequently, African countries with smaller populations and fewer resources may have had only one intelligence service that carried out internal, foreign, and even military objectives. Moreover, some African intelligence services also had security mandates along with law enforcement functions. This was historically true in British colonies where independent civilian intelligence services were established because of growing security challenges to colonial police intelligence branches.[17] As Georgina Sinclair described: "Overhauling police intelligence systems and creating independent special branches across the British Empire did not occur until the aftermath of the Second World," which was done because the governments "were initially badly served by inadequate or non-existent police special branches as effective security and political intelligence providers."[18]

The contributors to this book were asked to consider how the legacy of colonialism impacted early postcolonial and contemporary challenges in African intelligence services. The scholarship on security and insurgency in Africa is lengthy, which has largely examined colonial subjects not directly tied to the present or leaned toward contemporary actions without providing significant distance from the past to fully analyze the events.[19] This anthology engages with the past and present by considering the changes and continuities of intelligence since colonialism while understanding contemporary challenges. Authors were encouraged to study the historical evolution of African intelligence in select cases to better understand the interactions between the past and present. The anthology's objective is not to limit the study to only history or contemporary issues, but to provide readers with an understanding of the intersection where the past and present are negotiated and produced the issues African intelligence services have faced or are facing.

Often in broader intelligence literature, studies about intelligence are usually historical or contemporary. There are several notable exceptions, but usually, the research falls into the historical or contemporary category due to the scholar's background as, for example, a historian or political scientist. Though the importance of history on the present is widely recognized, including history and contemporary issues in this anthology highlights the power of the past in shaping African intelligence specifically. This is not a teleological argument about the legacy of colonialism, but rather one to recognize the power of the past by detailing, for instance, how colonial practices of surveillance and governance were adopted and transformed during postcolonialism.

SOURCES

Scholars of intelligence face challenges in obtaining credible sources to write about a world that is secretive and difficult to analyze even with access to the proper records. Understanding intelligence in light of these sources and interpretative limitations raises interesting epistemological issues about how scholars learn about the past. Indeed, two well-qualified individuals in intelligence studies can look at the same records and come to vastly different conclusions about their meaning.[20] The research is complicated when examining intelligence in countries where governments regularly release documents and authorize and approve studies about their histories as well as allow intelligence officers to write and talk about their work. However, the challenge grows in magnitude when researching African countries where there is even more restricted access to primary sources due to laws that do not allow disclosure, where intelligence services lack meaningful oversight, or where the government tightly controls reporting and access to its intelligence and security institutions.

Archival records, official government documents, and commission reports remain necessary, but imperfect, sources for scholars.[21] In the case of former British colonies, many original records are available at the National Archives, Kew, United Kingdom. These records detail the origins and development of the British colonial intelligence services, demonstrating how interlinked the personnel were with intelligence leaders in India, for example, giving advice for establishing intelligence in Kenya; or a young British intelligence officer,

Ian Henderson, serving in Kenya during the Second World War then moving to Lesotho's intelligence service, but earned infamy as the head of Bahrain's intelligence service for thirty years.[22] Yet, official documents have their limits because analyzing intelligence organizations and history merely from intelligence files could be inaccurate. Intelligence records can be wrong or misleading depending on their original sources of the information and interpreted incorrectly without broader knowledge of the personalities or cultural, institutional, historical, and political contexts.

Official records could also be problematic because intelligence documents can contain not only redactions of important information, but also some may have been intentionally hidden from scholars and the public. In the case of the U.S. Central Intelligence Agency, declassified records, including documents about Africa, are released on its website often with redactions.[23] Whereas, other material is accessible, such as documents in the Stasi Records Agency that survived the purge of East German records, which requires researchers to petition the agency for access.[24] Furthermore, some of the Soviet Union's operational details were made available in books about the "Mitrokhin Archive," material consisting of handwritten notes made from 1972 to 1982 by Vasili Mitrokhin, a Committee for State Security (KGB) archivist who defected to the United Kingdom in 1992.[25] Mitrokhin's 2005 posthumous book, coauthored with Christopher Andrew, examined Soviet intelligence operations in the "Third World," with one of its four sections devoted to Africa.[26]

As for primary sources from the actual colonial African intelligence services, sensitive or uncomfortable documents were intentionally hidden for decades at a British government facility at Hanslope Park, United Kingdom. In 1961, the British government decided that classified and "accountable documents" that could "embarrass" the government or "compromise sources of intelligence" be destroyed or moved to the United Kingdom.[27] Despite efforts by the independent African governments to obtain records about their countries, the Public Records Office declined to provide the documents.[28] Only when former Mau Mau activists sued the British government in 2005 for atrocities committed in Kenya before independence did the existence of the records come to light. The documents were not provided to researchers with knowledge of the specific missing documents and were not given to the plaintiffs but were released in 2011 following a high court ruling.[29] The government admitted that "historical papers relating to no fewer than 37 former British colonies, amounting to more than 8,800 files in total" were "irregularly held."[30] The missing documents were not a surprise to scholars or Kenyan government officials who long suspected the British government of suppressing records, with Kenyans witnessing smoke rising from government buildings before independence and finding empty shelves where records should have been held.[31] Subsequently, histories involving intelligence in the colonies have been written using those formerly missing records.[32]

One African country where research about intelligence has proliferated because of access to primary sources is South Africa. There is a large amount of literature on South Africa's intelligence community, which is partly due to the government choosing to make remaining records available and the Truth and Reconciliation Commission publicly recording the testimonies of intelligence officers. In March 1992, the National Intelligence Service "ordered the destruction of all operational records, including records confiscated from individuals and organisations," which resulted in the systematic purging of intelligence documents throughout the country.[33] While the apartheid government intentionally destroyed forty-four tons of paper and microfilmed records, some local offices failed to carry out the order. The surviving documents have since been made available to researchers, and other records are in the personal possession of some former security officers.[34] Additionally, there are many memoirs detailing apartheid-era intelligence, including by former National Intelligence Service leaders.[35]

From these sources, academic studies on the transformations from South Africa's apartheid era to post-apartheid intelligence as well as critiques of intelligence surveillance have been published.[36] There have also been biographies about apartheid-era intelligence officers as well as collaborators and suspects.[37] More contemporary works on South African intelligence had major political impact despite the government's efforts to restrict that information. Jacques Pauw gained access to intelligence sources who revealed corruption within the State Security Agency and the broader government.[38] The State Security Agency unsuccessfully attempted to block the book from publication, making it the best-selling book in the country's history, and the book contributed to forcing President Jacob Zuma from power in 2018.[39]

Beyond South Africa, there are academic books that have examined other African nations' intelligence with primary sources, such as published memoirs and interviews. These studies include diverse historical and contemporary examples, such as research about Egyptian, Rhodesian, and Tunisian intelligence.[40] For other countries, there are some published primary sources by African intelligence officers. In the case of postcolonial Kenya, for instance, only two intelligence officers wrote memoirs in over sixty years since independence.[41] The government of Kenya, nevertheless, understood the value of documenting its intelligence history and commissioned a historian to write a history of intelligence in the country from 1887 to 1999.[42] However, the more typical published sources about African intelligence are usually memoirs from government officials who make casual or infrequent mentions about the subject, not former African intelligence officers. For example, primary source material about Uganda's State Research Bureau and Special Branch is sparse, but one of the most cited about Idi Amin's use of the government to murder opponents was written by the former minister of health who offered a few descriptions of the intelligence services.[43] Additionally, former Soviet and East German intelligence officers have published memoirs that discuss their activities and relationships with African intelligence officers.[44]

Although there is a limited number of primary sources about African intelligence compared to Europe and North America, this book offers different examples for using records and research methodologies to analyze African intelligence services. The scholars drew from a variety of archival, field, and text research for this book. Some authors made use of archives in Africa, Europe, and North America to examine documents ranging from colonial to declassified postcolonial government records. Others drew from published primary sources, such as foreign language memoirs and witness testimony from public hearings. Still others interviewed current government officials in Africa or former African intelligence officers who defected. Finally, one author served as an official government-approved observer in Liberia contributing firsthand insights. All the chapters in this book cite unique primary sources that were carefully selected to analyze a specific topic or time period involving African intelligence and national security issues.

STRUCTURE

This book is organized in chronological order to highlight the evolution of African intelligence and security services. The anthology begins with chapters that examine decolonization and independence to understand the transition away from colonialism, and then the book explores broader periods of transformation and current challenges facing African intelligence services. Each contribution was selected to explore different histories of African intelligence services and to provide the reader with a spectrum of countries and issues. The authors were requested to consider the legacy of colonialism and examine intelligence services' challenges that were unique to the African country or region. The uniting theme in the book is postcolonial and contemporary African intelligence challenges, rather than examining different countries with a single theory or research methodology. The authors took interdisciplinary approaches to help fill gaps in the intelligence studies literature by using historical, legal, and political science perspectives to understand African intelligence services. Every chapter offers a unique framework to investigate how African intelligence services operated and transformed in a given location. As a result, the authors explore the many factors, including colonial legacies and postcolonial contexts—geopolitics, international partners, political systems, legal frameworks, and governance—that influenced intelligence priorities, operations, and relations with the military and civil society. Additionally, the chapters analyze domestic use and abuse of intelligence through surveillance, human rights violations, and torture.

Each chapter examines a country or region from a different era and geopolitical context. In particular, the contributors were asked to focus on how the relevant intelligence services were shaped by colonial legacies and their roles in the government. For more contemporary cases, several authors provided recommendations for overcoming challenges where appropriate. Despite these diverse approaches, the chapters overlap by showing interwoven colonial legacies and challenges facing intelligence on the continent. Specifically, there are significant intersections between the chapters in the postcolonial foundations and Cold War context between countries.

The book has eleven chapters organized chronologically, with attention to countries with overlapping histories, groups, institutions, and external actors. The first half of the anthology explores early postcolonial intelligence services. Ryan Shaffer begins the book by highlighting the continuity and changes in Kenyan intelligence as the country moved from a colonial possession to an independent state in the midst of the Cold War. He argues that the new government largely kept the colonial structure and methods, but they were applied to an increasingly autocratic government that exercised intelligence to secure and maintain political power. Also exploring the first decade of independence in East Africa, Simon Graham focuses on the use of Cold War German rivalries to build indigenous intelligence capabilities by looking at the nexus between decolonization, intelligence, and nonalignment in Zanzibar and Tanganyika from 1962 to 1972. He shows how postcolonial intelligence in Zanzibar and Tanganyika involved a rupture from the former colonial power and how a newly independent government successfully harnessed competition from the Cold War to gain support for the newly independent country's security.

Building from this Cold War lens, Owen Sirrs describes Angola and Mozambique's transitions from being Portuguese colonies to independent nations, but argues that the Soviet Union, Cuban, and East German intelligence services had a lasting impact on the new colonies' intelligence communities. He details how Portugal, unlike France and the United Kingdom, abandoned the countries, leaving a void that the Soviet Bloc successfully exploited by shaping Angola and Mozambique's intelligence and security services. Next, Glenn A. Cross explores Rhodesia (currently, Zimbabwe) after the Unilateral Declaration of Independence, by detailing Rhodesian intelligence's responses to the growing conflict against white minority rule from 1965 to 1980. He finds that the small intelligence service had limited resources and still successfully collected actionable intelligence, but nonetheless, the intelligence service was not the key to the Rhodesian government resolving the conflict.

The anthology's second half also analyzes the legacy of colonial intelligence services, but examines a broader time period by looking at the colonial history in light of more contemporary events. Investigating a former Belgian colony, John Burton Kegel describes Rwandan intelligence following independence with attention to how regionalism and ethnicity shaped postcolonial intelligence officers' actions that ultimately destabilized the country. He argues that select officers used their positions and knowledge to undermine the Rwandan government due to regional politics and that instability unleashed ethnic forces that led to genocide. Taking a different approach, Benjamin J. Spatz and Alex Bollfrass analyze the role of intelligence in neo-patrimonial political systems, the dominant mode of governance across Africa. Drawing from fieldwork in Liberia, they describe the form, function, and transformations of the country's intelligence services and their relation to political imperatives. They find that intelligence is not inherently more politicized in neo-patrimonial systems than it is in democracies or authoritarian regimes despite neo-patrimonialism's far weaker formal institutions. Rather, intelligence in these contexts interacts with politics in different ways based on political structures, objectives, and imperatives.

Also examining a wide time period, Joseph Fitsanakis and Shannon Brophy detail the history of Sudan's intelligence services since British colonialism with attention to how the services have been used, how they operated, and the role they played in colonial and independent governments. They chart the transformation from a civilian service with an effective human intelligence network that reflected the diverse ethnic population to a more securitized system that supported an autocratic leader. Narrowing the period, Tshepo Gwatiwa and Lesego Tsholofelo explore the historical influences on the institutional design and politicization of the Directorate of Intelligence and Security (DIS) in Botswana. They argue that abuse of the service was due to legal and political "loopholes" that facilitated elites to politicize it. They also highlight the limited oversight mechanisms and lack of accountability that enabled various excesses by the DIS. They also review recent attempts at reforms as well as their prospects. Next, Kevin A. O'Brien surveys South African intelligence in both the apartheid era on both sides of the conflict and in the post-apartheid era, highlighting a number of key themes across the individuals, institutions, structures, and processes of intelligence. He argues that intelligence—as product, process, and institution—has been continuously misused, politicized, and corrupted, aside from a brief transitionary period after apartheid, with leaders of all stripes (political, service, and liberation movement) wielding the power of intelligence for narrow, often parochial, objectives rather than broader strategic ones.

The last two chapters provide legal analyses about current intelligence services to understand how laws have evolved. Ibikunle Adeakin examines the challenges facing intelligence in Nigeria following decades of military rule, with attention to intelligence laws and practice since the end of the military government in 1999. He argues that the legacy of intelligence during military rule provided the intelligence services with a lack of accountability that the government's leaders are not ready to abandon. Also looking at legal structures from a similar time period, Christopher E. Bailey analyzes constitutional and statutory law in Kenya, Uganda, and Tanzania to understand the legal frameworks in East Africa that started out having similar colonial intelligence, security, and police service structures. This comparative assessment finds that Uganda has the weakest legal structure, and Kenya, despite abuses, has the strongest and most thorough laws.

CONCLUSION

This anthology synthesizes historical and contemporary challenges and themes in African intelligence services. It argues for placing African intelligence services front and center in scholarly analyses about African security and treating African intelligence as a significant actor in governments and societies. The anthology reveals the importance of understanding African intelligence services as unseen, but vital, institutions that aid domestic and foreign governments' power and influence. The chapters demonstrate how African intelligence agencies are the secret guardians of, and sometimes, threats to, their nation's security, stability, and international alliances. Additionally, the chapters explore challenges African intelligence has faced since the colonial era and how governments have responded.

The first several chapters highlight colonial legacies and early postcolonial challenges with analysis about the role of colonialism in shaping contemporary African intelligence communities and national security, whereas the latter chapters examine intelligence in geopolitical contexts of international alliances and legal frameworks that impact national intelligence communities. All the chapters demonstrate the significance that political systems, ethnic and religious composition, and legal frameworks have in influencing intelligence collection, operations, dissemination, and targets. With roots in colonial institutions, the broader intelligence cycle and approach characteristic of North American and European intelligence is apparent in Africa, but mixed with more localized tactics and concerns.[45]

These chapters provide readers with insight into common challenges and features in African intelligence. Due to similar colonial and Cold War histories as well as generalities in autocratic governments, some of the commonalities between African intelligence services are also shared with Asian intelligence services as described by Bob de Graaff.[46] There are exceptions to any broad explanation of how African intelligence services function. Nonetheless, the chapters in this anthology highlight some broad African intelligence service challenges and features.

First, in many cases, African intelligence has served those in power, largely in autocratic and illiberal democracies. The ruling elite consider themselves to be the government, and the intelligence services have personally served the people in power by attacking political and business opposition as well as suppressing dissent. This resulted in cases where intelligence was used to violate human rights and was exercised as a tool for other abuses.

Second, the services in many countries had and have overlapping powers because of the blurring of targets (like crime and terrorism) and do not always coordinate due to issues, including bureaucratic competition and mutual suspicion. Some of this competition was by design to prevent factions of the government from becoming too strong and posing a threat to the leader. The overlap, whether intentional or not, caused problems in establishing a service's mission and defining parameters of its mandate and caused a drain on resources due to redundancies.

Third, the African intelligence agencies in this book largely relied on human intelligence (HUMINT) and foreign partnerships, rather than their own indigenous technical means to collect intelligence. The notable exceptions involve more recent technology. These include Botswana—as described by Gwatiwa and Tsholofelo—and South Africa—as noted by O'Brien—that have reported technical capabilities.[47] Some African nations harnessed foreign relations with the colonial powers to collect more intelligence, but others used Cold War competition to obtain help for intelligence collection in their national security objectives. The reliance on HUMINT created challenges in collecting reliable information from trustworthy and useful sources as well as caused problems in society by aiding the public's paranoia about who is an informant.[48]

Fourth, the intelligence services concentrated on internal and regional issues of stability, terrorism, and competition, not global or international concerns of world powers. The focus on local and regional issues is due to more immediate issues that directly impact a country's stability and alliances. This does not deny African countries' engagement with broader foreign powers and global issues, but as these countries had little influence in great power competitions, their intelligence services had more pressing security concerns. Those wider global issues were important, as they related to local and regional security anxieties. Consequently, this focus posed a challenge to African governments when they had to confront more global issues or international threats.

Fifth, the services usually had or have limited oversight largely due to weak legislatures or a lack of interest and political will. Indeed, this is a serious challenge in African countries for building public support for national security objectives and democratic institutions. The connection between a strong democracy and intelligence oversight is apparent, as unstable countries and newer democracies usually tilt the power of intelligence toward the executive leadership. Power in the hands of one person in a single branch of government facilitates corruption and abuse. Even in African countries with intelligence oversight mechanisms, there are questions about their implementation and effectiveness due to the lack of political will to investigate and punish abuses.

Sixth, the colonial histories of African countries have shaped the names, structures, strategies, and tactics of early postcolonial services, which laid the foundation for what evolved in the subsequent decades. These colonial histories include complex racial, ethnic, and linguistic relations that led to favoring particular groups and disenfranchising others, which negatively impacted the public's perception of and support for the intelligence services. Overcoming and addressing this history sometimes placed African intelligence services in difficult positions in dealing with historically marginalized populations. Some African intelligence services actually made matters worse by manipulating and attacking certain population segments, which led to large-scale violence and undermined governance.

Last, the Cold War and the end of the Cold War played an important role where African intelligence services—and, more broadly, African governments—acquired aid and support from international powers vying for influence in Africa. Foreign intervention, both during colonialism and the Cold War, posed challenges to African security and has made the civilian population and intelligence services skeptical about foreign presence in their countries. Indeed, foreign governments and interests caused a variety of challenges to African governments, with their intelligence services collecting intelligence and analyzing the intentions of foreign presence.

This book fills a gap in the intelligence studies literature by illuminating the rich and important past and present of African intelligence services. More than that, it hopes to encourage further research of African intelligence services as they become an increasingly significant institution, while powers throughout the world expand efforts to exert influence on the continent. Additionally, interest in the subject will undoubtedly grow as Africa becomes more interconnected, reflecting the establishment of institutions, such as the African Union's Committee of Intelligence and Security Services, which brings together intelligence and security leadership and enables "back channel" communication for over fifty countries.[49] As the following chapters explain, African intelligence services have faced and continue to face numerous challenges—some unique to African institutions, and others familiar to all intelligence services. These issues are vital to understanding where the institutions that protect national security in Africa have been and where they are headed.

NOTES

1. Special thanks to Mwangi Njagi of American University and Kevin O'Brien at King's College London for their feedback. For the main African international organization, see: "Background," Committee of Intelligence and Security Services of Africa, 2020. https://cissaau.org/about-cissa/background/; Lawrence E. Cline, "African Regional Intelligence Cooperation: Problems and Prospects," *International Journal of Intelligence and CounterIntelligence* 29, no. 3 (2016): 447–469.

2. The number of books under "su:Intelligence service Africa" in World Catalog, 2020. https://www.worldcat.org/search?q=su%3AIntelligence+service+Africa&&dblist=638&fq=.

3. The number of books under "su:Intelligence service South Africa" in World Catalog, 2020. https://www.worldcat.org/search?q=su%3AIntelligence+service+South+Africa+&qt=results_page.

4. The number of books under "su:Central Intelligence Agency" in World Catalog, 2020. https://www.worldcat.org/search?q=su%3ACentral+Intelligence+Agency&qt=results_page.

5. Owen L. Sirrs, *Pakistan's Inter-Services Intelligence Directorate: Covert Action and Internal Operations* (New York: Routledge, 2016); Hein G. Kiessling, *Faith, Unity, Discipline: The Inter-Service-Intelligence (ISI) of Pakistan* (New York: Harper Collins, 2017); Richard J. Samuels*, Special Duty: A History of the Japanese Intelligence Community* (Ithaca: Cornell University Press, 2019); Roger Faligot, *Chinese Spies: From Chairman Mao to Xi Jinping* trans. Natasha Lehrer (London: Hurst, 2019).

6. Carl Anthony Wege, "The Changing Islamic State Intelligence Apparatus," *International Journal of Intelligence and CounterIntelligence* 31, no. 2 (2018): 271–288; Carl Anthony Wege, "Iranian Counterintelligence," *International Journal of Intelligence and CounterIntelligence* 32, no. 2 (2019): 272–294.

7. Some of the exceptions include: Robert D'A. Henderson, "South African Intelligence under de Klerk," *International Journal of Intelligence and CounterIntelligence* 8, no. 1 (1995): 51–89; Kevin O'Brien, "Counter-Intelligence for Counter-Revolutionary Warfare: The South African Police Security Branch 1979–1990," *Intelligence and National Security* 16, no. 3 (2001): 27–59; Ulrich van der Heyden, "A Spectacular Attempt to Release Mandela from Prison under the Apartheid Regime," *Journal of Intelligence History* 19, no. 2 (2020): 184–196; Daniel E.

Agbiboa, "Eyes on the Street: Civilian Joint Task Force and the Surveillance of Boko Haram in Northeastern Nigeria," *Intelligence and National Security* 22, no. 7 (2018): 1022–1039; Patrick Peprah Obuobi, "Evaluating Ghana's Intelligence Oversight Regime," *International Journal of Intelligence and CounterIntelligence* 31, no. 2 (2018): 312–341; Brian Adeba, "Oversight Mechanisms, Regime Security, and Intelligence Service Autonomy in South Sudan," *Intelligence and National Security* 35, no. 6 (2020): 808–822.

8. For example: Tshepo T. Gwatiwa, "The Polemics of Security Intelligence in Botswana: Real or Imagined Security Threats?," *African Security Review* 24, no. 1 (2015): 39–54; Mohamed Haji Ingiriis, "Predatory Politics and Personalization of Power: The Abuses and Misuses of the National Intelligence and Security Agency (NISA) in Somalia," *African Affairs* 119, no. 475 (April 2020): 251–274. For an older example, see: James Barber, "BOSS in Britain," *African Affairs* 82, no. 328 (July 1983): 311–328.

9. For example, Richard Aldrich, Gary Rawnsley and Ming-yeh Rawnsley (eds.), *The Clandestine Cold War in Asia, 1945–65: Western Intelligence, Propaganda, Security and Special Operations* (London: Frank Cass, 2000). This was published earlier as a 1999 special issue in *Intelligence and National Security*.

10. Sandy Africa and Johnny Kwadjo (eds.), *Changing Intelligence Dynamics in Africa* (N.p.: Global Facilitation Network for Security Sector Reform and African Security Sector Network, 2009). Not for sale in print. Free online at http://epapers. bham.ac.uk/1526/1/AfricaKwadjo_-2009-_IntelligenceAfrica.pdf.

11. Olawale Ismail and Elisabeth Skons (eds.), *The Security Activities of External Actors in Africa* (New York: Oxford University Press, 2014).

12. Philip H. J. Davies and Kristian C. Gustafson, *Intelligence Elsewhere: Spies and Espionage outside the Anglosphere* (Washington, DC: Georgetown University Press, 2013).

13. Gregory F. Treverton and Wilhelm Agrell (eds.), *National Intelligence Systems: Current Research and Future Prospects* (New York: Cambridge University Press, 2009).

14. Zachary K. Goldman and Samuel J. Rascoff (eds.), *Global Intelligence Oversight: Governing Security in the Twenty-First Century* (New York: Oxford University Press, 2016).

15. The role of Rhodesia in the broader context of decolonization is complicated. Luise White writes: "On one hand, not calling Rhodesia Rhodesia was a way to show how illegitimate it was. On the other, calling Rhodesia colonial Zimbabwe served—as did talk of the decolonization of Algeria—to change its history, to return to clumsy governance and messy episodes to the normal, linear story of colony to nation." She argues it was a case of a "colony becoming independent" and demonstrates that decolonization was an uneven process. White further highlights Rhodesia challenging imperial authority. Luise White, *Unpopular Sovereignty: Rhodesian Independence and African Decolonization* (Chicago: University of Chicago Press, 2015), 2.

16. For example, see the intelligence comradery and similarities of Pakistani and Indian spymaster antagonists. A.S. Dulat, Aditya Sinha and Asad Durrani, *The Spy Chronicles: RAW, ISI and the Illusion of Peace* (Noida: HarperCollins India, 2018).

17. Georgina Sinclair, "'The Sharp End of the Intelligence Machine': The Rise of the Malayan Police Special Branch 1948–1955," *Intelligence and National Security* 26, no. 4 (2011): 460–477.

18. Ibid., 474.

19. For example: David French, *The British Way in Counter-Insurgency, 1945– 1967* (New York: Oxford University Press, 2012); James J. Hentz and Hussein Solomon (eds.), *Understanding Boko Haram: Terrorism and Insurgency in Africa* (New York: Routledge, 2018).

20. The best example of two qualified authors using similar sources, but having vastly different conclusions is the debate surrounding Adolf Tolkachev, who allegedly supplied valuable information to CIA during the Cold War. Benjamin B. Fischer, former historian at CIA, was skeptical about the evidence Tolkachev was a spy, and Nicholas Dujmovic, also a former historian at CIA, dismissed Fischer's arguments. Benjamin B. Fischer, "Tolkachev Evidence Still Skimpy," *International Journal of Intelligence and CounterIntelligence* 29 no. 4 (2016): 846–848; Nicholas Dujmovic, "The Billion Dollar Spy: A True Story of Cold War Espionage and Betrayal," *Studies in Intelligence* 60, no. 1 (March 2016): 57–59.

21. For an anthology that provides examples of archival research on intelligence, see: R. Gerald Hughes, Peter Jackson and Len Scott (eds.), *Exploring Intelligence Archives: Enquiries into the Secret* State (New York: Routledge, 2008).

22. Ryan Shaffer, "Following in Footsteps: The History of Kenya's Post-Colonial Intelligence Services," *Studies in Intelligence* 63, no. 1 (2019): 26.

23. "Library," Central Intelligence Agency, 2020. https://www.cia.gov/library/ readingroom/.

24. "About the Archive," The Federal Commissioner for the Records of the State Security of the Former German Democratic Republic, 2020. https://www.bstu.de/en/.

25. Christopher Andrew and Vasili Mitrokhin, *The Sword and the Shield: The Mitrokhin Archive and the Secret History of the KGB* (New York: Basic Books, 1999); Christopher Andrew and Vasili Mitrokhin, *The Mitrokhin Archive: The KGB in Europe and the West* (New York: Allen Lane, 1999).

26. Christopher Andrew and Vasili Mitrokhin, *The World Was Going Our Way: The KGB and the Battle for The Third World* (New York: Basic Books, 2005), 423–470. Andrew's foreword noted that the book was examined by a working group prior to publication.

27. "Cary Report on Release of the Colonial Administration Files," United Kingdom Government, February 24, 2011. https://assets.publishing.service.gov. uk/government/uploads/system/uploads/attachment_data/file/625667/cary-report-release-colonial-administration-files.pdf.

28. Ibid.

29. Mutua, et al and Foreign and Commonwealth Office, no. HQ09X02666, High Court 2012. https://www.judiciary.uk/wp-content/uploads/JCO/Documents/ Judgments/mutua-fco-judgment-05102012.pdf; "Kenyan Mau Mau uprising documents released," BBC, 6 April 2011 https://www.bbc.com/news/uk-12983289.

30. David M. Anderson, "Mau Mau in the High Court and the 'Lost' British Empire Archives: Colonial Conspiracy or Bureaucratic Bungle?," *Journal of Imperial & Commonwealth History* 39, no. 5 (2011): 712.

31. Ibid, 707; For example: Oginga Odinga, *Not Yet Uhuru: An Autobiography* (Nairobi: East African Educational Publishers, 1968), 241.

32. For example: Calder Walton, *Empire of Secrets: British Intelligence, the Cold War and the Twilight of Empire* (New York: The Overlook Press, 2013).

33. *Truth and Reconciliation Commission of South Africa Report, Volume 1* (Truth and Reconciliation Commission of South Africa, 1998), 217. https://www.justice.gov. za/trc/report/finalreport/Volume%201.pdf.

34. Jacob Dlamini, *The Terrorist Album: Apartheid's Insurgents, Collaborators, and the Security Police* (Cambridge: Harvard University Press, 2020), 14, 15. He also noted that security officers also maintain records in their personal possession. Ibid., 20.

35. Niël Barnard and Tobie Wiese, *Secret Revolution: Memoirs of a Spy Boss* (Cape Town: Tafelberg, 2015); Barry Gilder, *Songs and Secrets: South Africa from Liberation to Governance* (New York: Columbia University Press, 2013); Maritz Spaarwater, *A Spook's Progress: From Making War to Making Peace* (Cape Town: Penguin Random House South Africa, 2012); Gordon Winter, *Inside BOSS: South Africa's Secret Police* (London: A. Lane, 1981); Petrus Cornelius Swanepoel, *Really Inside BOSS: A Tale of South Africa's Late Intelligence Service (and Something about the CIA)* (Derdepoortpark: Self-published, 2008).

36. Kevin A. O'Brien, *The South African Intelligence Services: From Apartheid to Democracy, 1948–2005* (New York: Routledge, 2011); Jane Duncan, *Stopping the Spies: Constructing and Resisting the Surveillance State in South Africa* (Johannesburg: Wits University Press, 2018).

37. Eugene de Kock and Jeremy Gordin, *A Long Night's Damage: Working for the Apartheid State* (Saxonwold: Contra Press, 1998); Jonathan Ancer, *Spy: Uncovering Craig Williamson* (Johannesburg: Jacana Media, 2018); Anemari Jansen, *Eugene de Kock: Assassin for the State* (Cape Town: Tafelberg, 2015); Jacob Dlamini, *Askari: A Story of Collaboration and Betrayal in the Anti-Apartheid Struggle* (New York: Oxford University Press, 2015).

38. Jacques Pauw, *Presidents Keepers: Those Keeping Zuma in Power and Out of Prison* (Cape Town: Tafelberg, 2017); Jacques Pauw, *In the Heart of the Whore: The Story of Apartheid's Death Squads* (Halfway House: Southern Book Publishers, 1991).

39. Jacques Pauw, "The President's Keepers: The Book that Brought the House Down," *Daily Maverick*, May 21, 2018 https://www.dailymaverick.co.za/ opinionista/2018-05-21-the-presidents-keepers-the-book-that-brought-the-house-down/; Alison Flood, "South African Security Services Move to Ban Exposé of Jacob Zuma Government," *The Guardian*, November 7, 2017 https://www.theguardian. com/books/2017/nov/07/south-african-security-ban-expose-jacob-zuma-government-jacques-pauw-the-presidents-keepers.

40. For example, Glenn Cross, *Dirty War: Rhodesia and Chemical Biological Warfare 1975–1980* (Solihull: Helion and Company, 2017); Noureddine Jebnoun, *Tunisia's National Intelligence: Why "Rogue Elephants" Fail to Reform* (Washington, DC: New Academia Publishing in association with The Center for Contemporary Arab Studies, 2017); Owen L. Sirrs, *The Egyptian Intelligence Service: A History of the Mukhabarat, 1910–2009* (New York: Routledge, 2010).

41. Ryan Shaffer, "Memoirs of a Kenyan Spymaster by Bart Joseph Kibati," *Journal of Intelligence History* 18, no. 1 (2019): 110–112.

42. Mildred Ndeda, *Secret Servants: A History of Intelligence and Espionage in Kenya, c 1887–1999, A Report Submitted to the National Security and Intelligence Service of Kenya on 30th January 2006* (Nairobi, Kenya: n.p., 2006), in author possession.

43. Henry Kyemba, *A State of Blood: The Inside Story of Idi Amin* (New York: Grosset and Dunlap, 1977), 103, 112, 114, 115, 230, 231.

44. Christopher Andrew and Oleg Gordievsky, *KGB: The Inside Story of its Foreign Operations from Lenin to Gorbachev* (New York: Faber & Faber, 1991), 554, 555; Markus Wolf and Anne McElvoy, *Man without a Face: The Autobiography of Communism's Greatest Spymaster* (New York: Times Books, 1997), 255, 257, 265, 266, 279, 280.

45. For more on the intelligence cycle, see: "How Intelligence Works," United States Government, 2020. https://www.intelligencecareers.gov/icintelligence.html.

46. Due to shared colonial histories, Cold War experiences, and government systems, African intelligence has several common themes with Asian intelligence due to colonial history. Bob de Graaff's analysis of Asian intelligence examined many of these commonalities, such as the function of intelligence shaped by colonial history and government type as well as that many of the countries lack intelligence oversight. Bob de Graaff, "Elements of an Asian Intelligence Culture," in *Intelligence Communities and Cultures in Asia and the Middle East: A Comprehensive Reference*, ed. by Bob de Graaff (Boulder, Colorado: Lynne Rienner Publishers, 2020), 461–470.

47. Jane Duncan also described the origins of South African signals intelligence during the apartheid era and from the military. Jane Duncan, *Stopping the Spies: Constructing and Resisting the Surveillance State in South Africa* (Johannesburg: Wits University Press, 2018), 59, 60. Also see: Walter Volker, *Army Signals in South Africa: The Story of the South African Corps of Signals and Its Antecedents* (Pretoria: Veritas Books, 2014).

48. For a recent press example, see: Jacob Ngetich, "That Tea Girl or Watchman in the Office Could Be a Detective," *The Standard*, 8 April 2018. https://www.standardmedia.co.ke/kenya/article/2001276037/that-tea-girl-or-watchman-in-the-office-could-be-a-detective.

49. "Conference," Committee of Intelligence and Security Services of Africa, 2020. https://cissaau.org/structure/conference/; "Objectives," Committee of Intelligence and Security Services of Africa, 2020. https://cissaau.org/about-cissa/objectives/.

Chapter 1

"The More Things Change: Kenya's Special Branch during the Decade of Independence"

Ryan Shaffer

Kenya's intelligence services have played a significant role in thwarting internal and external threats to the country throughout the twentieth century. This chapter explores Kenyan intelligence and security services in the era of transition from colonialism to independence using declassified Kenyan intelligence records. It argues Kenya's postcolonial Special Branch largely continued colonial structures, but as the intelligence service was "Africanized," it increasingly became a tool of authoritarian political surveillance. It focuses on the era of Kenyan transition because the 1960s were pivotal in shaping the following decades of Kenya's intelligence collection and operations. Under one-party rule, the intelligence and security services were involved in investigating crime, international threats, and insurgencies as well as critics of the government. Only decades after independence were Kenyan's intelligence and security services professionalized with oversight and new legal frameworks to serve the country under the multiparty democratic system.[1]

This chapter draws from archives in Kenya and the United Kingdom as well as published primary sources. In particular, it analyzes declassified Kenyan intelligence, explaining how reports were shared with the Special Branch and the Office of the President. The declassified intelligence records and other sources came from the Kenya National Archives and the National Assembly.[2] The documents include handwritten intelligence reports, typed policy documents from government leaders, and Kenyan parliamentary papers and published memoirs to examine the changes and continuities of Kenyan intelligence as Kenyans established their own government. Additionally, the chapter incorporates records from the Foreign and Commonwealth Office at the National Archives in Kew. Postcolonial Kenya press was also examined, including material from *Daily Nation*'s office archives, but political pressure at the time meant newspapers rarely mentioned the Special Branch and had little value to this research.

This chapter has four sections. In the first, it examines the origins and evolution of the colonial Special Branch in Kenya. The next section explores the colonial Special Branch's structure with attention to collection methods, targets, and operations during the Emergency. The third part details postcolonial intelligence with attention to the changes and continuities of the Special Branch in the first years of independence. Last, the final section looks more broadly at the postcolonial Special Branch's intelligence, processes, targets, and foreign partners that established the way Kenyan intelligence operated in the following decades. The conclusion highlights how colonial intelligence and security service institutions played a significant role in shaping Kenyan intelligence and security, but African agency reshaped and transformed the intelligence targets and operations with the priorities of autocratic leaders.

THE FOUNDATIONS OF THE SPECIAL BRANCH IN KENYA

Formalized intelligence services have existed in Kenya for more than a hundred years.[3] As the end of British colonialism approached, intelligence structures, institutions, and methods hardened, which foreshadowed intelligence collection and operations in independent Kenya. The country's current intelligence service has roots during the Second World War era, but that formation was influenced less by international conflict and more by local colonial events. Though Kenya was under the authority of the Colonial Office in London, each separate colonial administration was responsible for organizing an intelligence community to be informed of potential threats and subversion (for Sudan, see Fitsanakis and Brophy in this volume).[4]

The Special Branch's personnel and activities in Kenya were influenced by the British Empire's decades of colonial police and intelligence in East Africa. At the start of the twentieth century, intelligence in Kenya was under the authority of the commissioner of police. Subsequently, there was a Special Branch in the Criminal Investigation Department (CID) under the director of civil intelligence (later named the director of intelligence and security and then just the director of intelligence) to collect and analyze intelligence that came from local police and other parts of the administration.[5] In 1939, the governor of Kenya, Robert Brooke-Popham, recommended the secretary of state for the colonies establish a "Special Branch" under the CID where the same person would be director of both.[6] The objective was to provide a "constant interchange of information and occasional meetings" of Kenya and neighboring territory.[7] The Special Branch planned to issue "a brief periodical appreciation on the general situation and in particular the probable attitude and possible intentions of our northern neighbour."[8] The budget to expand the CID and start the Special Branch was approved by the secretary in March 1939.[9]

The intelligence service faced challenges. In 1945, the Special Branch was placed under the control of a "specially appointed police officer," who had the title director of intelligence and security, but remained in the CID, which led to problems.[10] An official government report concluded that addressing "crime was urgent," but "the collection of political intelligence appeared less urgent, and consequently suffered."[11] To improve the situation, the Special Branch was detached from the CID and made responsible for all intelligence, security, and immigration while remaining a police service under the commissioner of police and provided reports to intelligence consumers whose responsibility involved the specific reports' contents.[12]

After the Second World War, the Special Branch remained a small organization that provided intelligence to key government stakeholders. The commissioner of police proposed expanding the Special Branch to the provinces, but only two specialist officers were appointed prior to the 1952 Emergency.[13] F. D. Corfield, a colonial government administrator in Kenya, reviewed the intelligence of this period and concluded "the machinery set up to collect information and intelligence functioned tolerably well" and the director of intelligence and security "did in fact succeed" despite "the very small staff available in Special Branch" by sending "a vast volume of reports" about "political agitators" as well as sending coverage from press and trade unions.[14] A review of the intelligence reports concluded that, while there were notable exceptions, "there was no collective assessment" of intelligence reports and the "inescapable conclusion" was "they just 'disappeared' into the Central Secretariat."[15] One notable exception was the Mau Mau movement being tracked in 1950 along with calls to improve the intelligence structure in the colony.[16]

The government's leadership had faith in the Special Branch despite intelligence gaps that quickly became major issues. In April 1951, colonial governor Philip Mitchell, who previously served as governor in Uganda and Fiji, wrote, "Kenya at the present time has by far the most competent and effective internal intelligence service that I have met in the whole course of my colonial service," believing "the work is centralized in the comparatively small directorate in Nairobi under a highly competent head."[17] However, colonial official F. D. Corfield found the lack of Special Branch activity in the Central and Rift Valley provinces meant intelligence about the Mau Mau was not collected or exploited to adequately warn leaders about the threat.[18] Last, the director of intelligence and security rarely explained the intelligence's significance to customers, and the final assessments were left mostly to the attorney general and chief native commissioner.[19]

The Mau Mau movement was largely misunderstood by authorities and emerged as a threat to the colonial government. Authorities first became aware of the movement, a secret society made up of Kikuyu—Kenya's largest ethnic group, in March 1948 and proscribed it as an illegal society by the colonial government in August 1950.[20] Yet, the Mau Mau grew in popularity, with Kenyan intelligence estimating that 250,000 Kikuyu took the Mau Mau oath by then, and colonial authorities responded with brutality.[21] Caroline Elkins's work examined the brutality of the capture, interrogation, and detention of about 1.5 million people, where she estimates 160,000–320,000 died—significantly more than official British records state.[22] It was a secretive movement perceived by authorities as unified, but was actually divided along the lines of several groups, including the Kenya African Union that sought independence.[23] British authorities wrongly believed the Mau Mau was led by Jomo Kenyatta, a former London School of Economics student who headed the Kenya African Union and was a key figure in the Kikuyu Central Association. Rather, the Mau Mau was a grassroots movement formed in response to thousands of Kikuyu residents being forced to resettle, who took an oath of solidarity against the government.[24]

The Mau Mau engaged in violence, ranging from murder and theft to attacks on the government and Africans loyal to the government. At the forefront of the battle against the Mau Mau, Elkins described, was the Kenya Police including the Special Branch, which had many "white" officers who "were a lowbrow corps of recruit" that "routinely roughed up the local Africans" according to "their racist upbringing."[25] Authorities used a combination of local informants and interrogations of suspected Mau Mau to get intelligence about their activities. Elkins described the torture of Mau Mau suspects by the Special Branch, notably at the Mau Mau Investigation Center, which included electrocution and body mutilation.[26] Regular meetings involving the Special Branch and the police were held for government policy and about suspects who would be released or transferred.[27]

The Special Branch officers' training in this period was rudimentary and lacked specific counterinsurgency education. The Special Branch consisted of people who were given basic police training and mostly tasked with investigating Mau Mau attacks and thefts.[28] Derek Franklin, who served as an assistant inspector in the Special Branch, wrote a memoir detailing his life in the organization from 1953 until his departure in 1966. After leaving East London in 1947 and joining the Kenya Police in 1953, he received training in the Rift Valley at a "basic camp" of stone huts where he learned basic law, rudimentary Kiswahili, use of small arms and fundamentals about the population.[29] In fact, a 1956 Kenya Police memorandum noted the "urgency" to establish a CID and Special Branch training center with specialized police courses because the current training was inadequate.[30]

In September 1952, destruction of agriculture and property and the killing of livestock by the Mau Mau was considered "the opening of the Mau Mau offensive."[31] That month, Evelyn Baring became governor and toured the Central Province where he met with provincial and district commissioners to assess the situation.[32] Following the murder of a loyalist African and two policemen in October, Baring made a recommendation to the Colonial Office to declare a state of Emergency that suspended various legislative and judicial roles as well as restricted freedoms.[33] On October 21, the Emergency went into effect, with Jomo Kenyatta and dozens of others getting arrested based on lists drafted by the Special Branch while homes were raided where thousands of documents were collected.[34] At the time, the "entire" Special Branch "consisted of only three European and one Asian officers with a handful of African rank and file, with its permanent personnel limited to Nairobi and Mombasa."[35]

A NEW STRUCTURE FOR KENYAN INTELLIGENCE

The Special Branch needed help to meet the demands of the Emergency. In fall 1952, the governor requested that Scotland Yard help the Special Branch in Kenya, but Percy Sillitoe, director general of the Security Service (MI5), "misunderstood" the request and thought the governor wanted MI5's assistance.[36] Sillitoe agreed to personally visit Nairobi to help.[37] In November 1952, Sillitoe and MI5 officer A. M. MacDonald traveled to Nairobi where they provided recommendations about the intelligence organization.[38] Sillitoe arrived on a Friday and left the following Tuesday with the governor accepting the proposals that morning.[39] Meanwhile, MacDonald stayed in Kenya as an security adviser to aid intelligence collection and coordinate activities, which necessitated restructuring the Special Branch that was "grossly overworked, bogged down in paper" and "housed in offices which were alike impossible from the standpoint of security or normal working conditions."[40] Additionally, "officers were largely untrained, equipment was lacking and intelligence funds were meagre."[41] Several changes were instituted, notably the establishment of the Kenya Intelligence Committee, which received information from the Provincial and District Intelligence Committee meetings at least once every two weeks and reported to the governor.[42]

The Special Branch initially produced a fortnightly intelligence product for the governor of Kenya and the secretary of state for the colonies. The summary consisted of a "general" first paragraph about the country and moved to specifics of security by district, issues by groups—such as "Europeans"—and provided a list of the numbers of surrendered Mau Mau.[43] The summary also included a review of notable press articles as well as a list of proscribed periodicals and books.[44] The products included assessments about what the information meant for the colonial leadership, such as explaining that a specific area would "likely" become a "base for intensive" Mau Mau "activity."[45]

The Special Branch improved, and in August 1953, MacDonald recommended his position be abolished because the organization went "from strength to strength."[46] Yet, as Christopher Andrew wrote, MI5 as well as Whitehall and the colonial administration "did not grasp the complexities of the rebellion."[47] Despite improved intelligence and expanded operations, gaps remained, and incorrect assessments continued.[48] As a result, the colonial government developed new ways to battle the insurgency in Kenya. Under the command of General George Erskine, a handbook for anti–Mau Mau operations was issued, laying out the Special Branch and military's roles as well as the tactics used. The document stated that the Special Branch was not designed to collect operational intelligence, but any information it obtained needed to be sent "immediately" to the "nearest" military unit or formation.[49]

The methodologies used by the Special Branch to obtain intelligence involved deception through pseudo gangs. In official records, the pseudo gang (or counter gang) method of using former Mau Mau was described as Special Branch "operations."[50] Richard Catling, commissioner of police from 1954 to 1964, wrote that the pseudo gang method did not originate in Kenya, as it "was used many years earlier in Palestine" as well as in Malaya but "achieved its widest measure of success in Kenya."[51] Notably, Special Branch officer Ian Henderson, who later led Bahraini intelligence until 1998, described joining the Kenya Police in 1945 and serving with the Special Branch during the Emergency. He was one of a "handful" of officers who was fluent in the local language, which made him instrumental in battling the Mau Mau insurgency in which he won two George Medals—a prestigious award given to nonmilitary personnel.[52]

The Special Branch lacked the military capability to fight the Mau Mau. As a result, British Army officers, such as Frank Kitson, were sent to "reinforce" the Special Branch in specific areas.[53] John Prendergast, Special Branch director from 1955 until 1958, reorganized the Special Branch during the Emergency by forming the Joint Army Police Operational Teams that consisted of the Kenya Regiment, British Army, and Special Branch officers focusing on political intelligence.[54] The Kenya Regiment's objectives in 1953 were to deny the Mau Mau secure bases, arrest them, and "provide information of Mau Mau activities and plans."[55] By May 1953, the teams were replaced by the Operational Intelligence Organisation, but this changed again in July 1955 when the Special Branch was charged with collecting operational intelligence and controlled investigation centers.[56]

While the Emergency lasted until 1959, the Mau Mau's defeat largely happened in 1956 when key leaders were killed and the violence declined.[57]

Prendergast was credited with the victory through the use of the pseudo gang strategy.[58] Meanwhile, the Special Branch remained small, and Mau Mau's attacks on the European population were limited. An internal document from 1956 discussed training and stated the number of Special Branch officers in Kenya was 423 and another 391 in CID.[59] Officially, the insurgency left 11,503 "terrorists" dead, 101 security force members (of which 63 were Europeans) and 1,819 civilians (of which 32 were Europeans) dead, though the numbers of alleged Mau Mau are undoubtedly larger.[60]

Despite the Mau Mau's defeat, the "wind of change" was coming to Kenya as the political situation shifted in favor of the Kenyan nationalists.[61] After the Emergency, the Special Branch focused on internal matters as well as issues involving border security and surveilling targets. These operations were more typical intelligence matters for a service under the authority of the police, focusing on criminal and political intelligence. Franklin, for example, was assigned to the Ethiopia border, which included collecting intelligence about "illegal crossings, the activities of Ethiopian security forces, water and border disputes and virtually any other act or incident, that could have cross-border repercussions."[62] The Special Branch also collected intelligence on internal groups, the communist countries' embassies, foreign press, and foreigners who were usually leftists.[63] Other Special Branch responsibilities included intercepting mail, vetting personnel for access to classified information, providing guidelines for classification, and recording the possession or loss of "secret" documents.[64]

POSTCOLONIAL SPECIAL BRANCH IN KENYA

After decades of struggle, Kenya achieved independence from Whitehall on December 12, 1963, but the colonial intelligence structure and methods largely remained. The new government faced internal threats to its freedom ranging from pockets of unrest and lawlessness to the Cold War and fears of communist subversion. This section explains that while the early postcolonial years saw few substantial changes to the Special Branch's organization, the intelligence personnel slowly transformed and targets shifted to the demands of the new leadership. It demonstrates how the first decade of the Special Branch under independence had a high level of continuity with the methodologies, tactics, and intelligence structure largely staying the same.

Following independence, former colonial Special Branch enemies became statesmen that the postcolonial Special Branch had to defend.[65] In the February 1961 legislative election, the Kenya African National Union (KANU) won the largest share of voters but declined to form a government unless Kenyatta was released from prison. Formed the previous year, the party was deeply divided with Kenyatta being the "glue" holding it together.[66] In August he was freed and elected to government but assured white settlers of their place in an independent Kenya.[67] During the May 1963 election—the last colonial election—KANU led by Kenyatta won the majority of parliamentary seats. The transition of power had been planned for years. Starting in 1960, several Kenyans were involved with independence negotiations in London with colonial secretary Iain Macleod to develop an interim constitution.[68]

The new government recognized the need for experienced people even if they served colonial authorities. In August 1963, Prime Minister Kenyatta ordered the identification of expatiate officers who would be asked by the independent government to continue in their roles.[69] Months later, Kenyatta gave amnesty to all political prisoners, releasing people the Special Branch had previously designated as "terrorists."[70] Minister of Home Affairs Jaramogi Oginga Odinga reflected on the government handover, explaining: "It was now our police force, our civil service, and even the chiefs were our servants, and the former attitude of hostility to an alien government had to make way for cooperation in the interests of the country."[71]

While Kenyatta and KANU controlled the government, the colonial structure of the institutions largely remained the same. According to scholars Daniel Branch and Nicholas Cheeseman, the provincial administration, founded in 1900, grew by independence, and governing was passed to local elites rather than a centralized authority.[72] They explained that the colonial governor "was empowered by its control, via the chief native commissioner, of the provincial administration," which enabled "the executive to bypass the legislature when necessary."[73] African elite with business interests were appointed to the provincial administration, and Kenyatta continued this form of governing.[74] In December 1964, the republic was founded with a new constitution that took power away from regional assemblies, making Kenyatta president of a "highly centralised one-party state" while abolishing his former post of prime minister.[75] The provincial administration was returned to "the direct control of the executive," and "the positions of provincial and district commissioners were reinstated with the Office of the President given control of appointments."[76] By the end of the decade, the provincial administration amassed a broad range of duties, including serving as "the eyes and the ears of the executive."[77]

With the government having "eyes and ears" throughout the country, the Special Branch collected intelligence through this system based on fear. The Special Branch appeared ubiquitous because its intelligence came from so many sources. Information was obtained from official channels of weekly intelligence reports and letters from senior leaders on rumors of what people said about the government, critics of the government, the press, suspicious foreigners' movements, and radio broadcasts.[78] Colonial and postcolonial

Kenya's provincial and district commissioner reports were key to providing information to the government about subversive activity.[79] This information was used against government critics who opposed the colonial power and for repressing critics of the independent government.

The last colonial director of intelligence was Mervyn Manby, who helped plan the transfer of power to the independent government and focused on quickly training senior African officers.[80] As the end of colonialism arrived, in 1960, the Special Branch stopped training European officers and concentrated on African officers.[81] Even still, certain courses offered by the Special Branch's Training School were restricted to only European officers who signed the Official Secrets Act declaration.[82] Scholar David Throup explained, "Most African members of Special Branch were deemed unsuitable for senior office, being either insufficiently educated to hold senior positions or too young and inexperienced; twelve, nevertheless, were earmarked for rapid promotion."[83] As a result, the top African recruits held senior leadership posts "after only a couple of years in the Police Force."[84]

The intelligence structure in Kenya largely stayed the same immediately after independence with several colonial officers continuing their work in the first years. Richard Catling remained commissioner of police and earlier was a colonial Special Branch officer but was, "in effect, replaced by his deputy, Lewis Mitchell."[85] Duncan Ndegwa, secretary to the cabinet and the head of civil service, explained: "Catling and even such despicable people as Ian Henderson" were requested to stay on "partly because there were no Africans competent enough to head the police force."[86] Kenyatta partly continued employing British officers because he was concerned about the Somalia *shifta* threat and decided not to change the leadership on Independence Day.[87] Bernard Hinga, a former assistant superintendent of police, became the first African head of the Special Branch, but one year later, Hinga replaced Catling as commissioner of police on December 31, 1964.[88] Ndegwa wrote that when Hinga took the position, "he basically followed Catling's management style and organisation structure" and the "language of police reports, for instance, remained unchanged."[89]

More Kenyans were appointed by Kenyatta to key intelligence and security leadership positions. Peter Ochieng Okola, who helped "establish" the Special Branch during the Emergency and recruited and trained Special Branch officers, became the first African director of the CID in 1965.[90] James Kanyotu, a then twenty-eight-year-old who joined the Kenya Police in 1960, was appointed Special Branch director, interchangeably known as director of intelligence, in January 1965.[91] The official public notice was a September 1965 listing that Kanyotu was promoted to assistant commissioner of police effective January 1, 1965—the rank established for the Special Branch director following MI5's 1952 recommendation.[92] Kenyan Army officer

Kanwal Sethi observed, "Key security institutions were headed by loyalist Kikuyus from the Kikuyu heartland of Kiambu and Nyeri, with Bernard Hinga heading the police," Ben Gethi leading the paramilitary General Service Unit and Kanyotu as Special Branch director.[93] Kanyotu led the Special Branch until January 1992, remaining a mysterious figure during his tenure, but turned to business after retiring from government and was involved in controversial deals, dying a wealthy man in 2008.[94]

After a few years, the Special Branch's rank and file started to become more aligned with the composition of the independent government as more Africans joined the police. By the end of 1965, there was a total of about 300 British police officers.[95] The new government's official policy was the "Africanization" of the civil service, which subsequently included quotas for different groups.[96] Meanwhile, the government had concerns about expatriates in the Special Branch, worried that these people knew Kenya's secrets and might take "these secrets to their countries of origin."[97] In a few years after independence, the British officers left Kenya for career and family reasons as the government required civil servants and even business owners to be Kenyan citizens.[98]

Memories of the Special Branch's brutal and bloody fight against the Mau Mau rebellion were fresh and still impacted the government. Summarizing the composition of the Kenyan government, William Attwood, the U.S. ambassador to Kenya from March 1964 to May 1966, wrote upon his departure that "a white Kenyan was still Minister of Agriculture and seventeen hundred Englishmen still worked in various branches of the Kenya Government; there was less tension between the races than before *uhuru* [independence]."[99] However, after just a few years, the police service composition changed. Notably, Ian Henderson was deported from Kenya by Odinga, minister for home affairs and vice president, who wrote that Henderson's presence in independent Kenya made the government "uncomfortable" and was "hated" throughout the country.[100] Odinga explained that Catling told him, "If Henderson goes, I go too," and the removal had the endorsement of Kenyatta.[101] Prendergast also left the country and subsequently served as director of intelligence in Cyprus and then Yemen.[102]

INTELLIGENCE REPORTS, PROCESSES, AND TARGETS

The postcolonial government targeted opponents and potential subversives using the processes and methods from the colonial era. The early postcolonial Special Branch continued the colonial procedure of circulating weekly intelligence reports from around the country. The "Special Branch Weekly Intelligence Report," referred in the records as WIR, was sent to the Office of the President by James Kanyotu, head of the Special Branch and whose title was director of intelligence. The reports spanned the previous week's activity, were numbered in chronological order, and the lead sentence notified the reader of significant activity that week. Notably, the reports delivered to the Office of the President contained summaries of events rather than analysis and overwhelmingly described domestic events. For example, report number twenty-two described a previous week's meeting as displaying a lack of unity in the ruling KANU party and Vice President Daniel arap Moi accusing Odinga and Ronald Ngala "of having been bought by American money to create disunity."[103] Other reports, such as number thirty-six, opened with an explanation about "no reported national political activity of any consequence," focusing on trade union activities, KANU district rivalries, and the Shifta War.[104]

Following the establishment of the republic, the first president circular of 1965 "made quite clear" that President Kenyatta had authority over security through the locally appointed leaders who are "directly responsible to the President's Office."[105] Specifically, the document stated that the republic's constitution "vests the executive authority of the Government in the President, provid[ing] for his authority to be exercised through officers subordinate to him" in which security matters under that authority "is exercised through the District and Provincial Commissioners, who are responsible for the peace and good government in the districts."[106]

In January 1966, a charter for the Kenyan Intelligence Committee (KIC) and Provincial and District Intelligence Committees established that all intelligence from the district is "pooled" at the committee level "in all cases" and the director of intelligence "must" be "consulted at some stage."[107] The structure of Kenyan intelligence was from top to bottom: director of intelligence, deputy director of intelligence, provincial Special Branch officer, district Special Branch officer, chief inspector, inspector, assistant inspector, senior sergeant, sergeant, corporal, and constable.[108] Answering to the Ministry of Home Affairs, the district and provincial committee's secretary was a Special Branch member, which "enabled" local information to be sent to the KIC.[109] The KIC, founded in 1953, was internally known as a "permanent and regular feature of the government" that reviewed intelligence and provided advice to the president.[110] It was dependent on the local committees for information, but the charter was modified due to changes in Kenyatta's cabinet, putting the KIC under the authority of the Ministry of Home Affairs.[111]

There are few published primary sources about the Special Branch's intelligence processes and collection during the decade of independence. The most detailed memoir from an intelligence officer was written by Bart Joseph Kibati, who was recruited after independence, spent twenty-seven years in intelligence, and rose to be second-in-command by the time he left in

1995.[112] He described key personalities, processes, and how intelligence was consumed at the highest levels. A former Mau Mau youth scout, his journey in the intelligence service began just years after independence when he was interviewed and accepted to join the Kenya Police in 1968.[113] The following year in April 1969 he attended the Special Branch Training School, where he learned about analysis, counterterrorism, espionage, and subversion.[114]

Postcolonial government leaders were consumers of intelligence who wanted to be informed about political developments. Just prior to independence, colonial Special Branch director Manby provided intelligence personally to the governor, delivering updates of political issues and press summaries.[115] This continued under the new government. Kibati described how "Kenyatta received" intelligence briefings "only from" director of intelligence Kanyotu and "Kenyatta was keen to get the final product" rather than the raw intelligence.[116] Kenyatta and his successor Daniel arap Moi also "relied heavily on the Provincial Administration and security agencies" in running the agenda so much to the point that "Provincial Commissioners had no respect for politicians including ministers," which points to problems and the push to disband the provincial administration and reform the security services decades later (see Bailey in this volume).[117]

Little is known about the functioning of intelligence at the highest levels during the 1960s as the leaders died without publishing details. However, Godfrey Gitahi Kariuki was one of the few cabinet members with knowledge of the inner workings of intelligence and security who published a memoir. He was a member of parliament from 1963 until 1983 and was appointed in 1979 by President Moi as minister of state, putting him in charge of Kenya's internal security and the provincial administration. Kariuki explained: "I was supposed to be in charge of those organs that deal with internal security," including the Special Branch and CID, but "my authority was theoretical, and far from reality."[118] For example, he wrote "the Special Branch reported directly to the President, and the department had no obligation to refer to the Minister except as a courtesy," meaning "the Minister was just a figurehead."[119] Kariuki explained, the "real power rested with the President, who hired and dismissed officers at will."[120] As for the provincial administration, Kariuki wrote he "was just a glorified personal assistant, who was expected to take action in the best interests of the President."[121]

After independence, there was a shift in intelligence priorities for collection and operations. From Special Branch officer Franklin's perspective, the leaders who had recently gained authority "started to use power for their own purposes," such as government vehicles used for personal travel.[122] The government admitted in 1967 that "fraud involving public figures and bodies" increased by twofold from the colonial era.[123] Kibati described Kenyatta as a "benevolent autocrat" who acted like "royalty" with those close to him benefiting from his position.[124] There were numerous cases of corruption by leaders of this era who went on to acquire large real estate holdings.[125] Land was significant because Kenya was an agricultural economy, and Kenyatta used his authority to acquired vast amounts of land for himself.[126]

The use of intelligence and security services against government opponents became widespread. In 1966, over two dozen by-elections were held in what became known as the "little general election" where the government intimidated opposition and their supporters. Odinga, forced from government, established the Kenya People's Union, and members of parliament who joined the new party were forced to stand for election again.[127] Meanwhile, protests were crushed, opposition campaigns were restricted, and electoral abuses occurred, with Kenyatta portraying the opponents as disgruntled Luo, a minority ethnic group.[128] In 1966, the government amended the Preservation of Public Security Act that delegated the president's power to detain people to the minister of home affairs, and amended it again in 1968, so "the detention laws were a permanent feature of life capable of being resorted to at any time rather than only in times of emergency."[129] This power was widely used in the following decades where critics or suspected critics were detained without trial. A 1971 letter to the district and provincial commissioners as well as the director of intelligence from Vice President and Minister for Home Affairs Moi explained: "There will be no more warnings to those individuals who intend to subvert the government," and that he would "take stern measures against such people."[130] In terms of elections, KANU received every vote in the December 1969 and October 1974 general elections.

There were credible rumors of the government, including the Special Branch, being involved or complicit in the torture and murders of popular figures who could be future leaders. The most notable cases were the 1965 assassination of Pio Gama Pinto, the 1969 assassination of Tom Mboya, and the 1975 assassination of Josiah Mwangi Kariuki.[131] These high-profile assassinations and the quick trials and executions of the people alleged to be behind the deaths raised questions about whether they were killed on orders from Kenyan officials for political reasons.[132] A 1975 Select Committee on Kariuki's assassination noted:

> The Committee finds it difficult to believe that the combined CID and Special Branch forces of the Kenya Police (hitherto claimed to be the best in Africa) have not been able in three months to trace the kidnappers and murders of a politician of Kariuki's "stature."[133]

Meanwhile, the Cold War was debated throughout Kenyan society and in the government. At the start, Kenyatta's cabinet was divided between supporters of the East and West, but Kenyatta was seen as pro-West.[134] Kenyatta was opposed to communism, having studied at the London School of Economics and sought to implement "African socialism."[135] In contrast, Oginga Odinga—then vice president—supported the Soviet Union and a rift between the two men deepened until Odinga resigned his post and left KANU in April 1966 to form the Kenya People's Union.[136] The government, however, was officially nonaligned with Kenyatta stating, "We rejected both Western Capitalism and Eastern Communism and chose for ourselves a policy of positive non-alignment."[137] The Special Branch warned the government about the "increasing number of young men who have been indoctrinated with the principles of Marxism-Leninism" and were willing to be violent.[138] Those educated in communist countries had difficulty finding employment, while those educated in the West readily found jobs within the government and industry.[139]

The Special Branch carefully watched Kenyans' interactions with diplomats, and the biggest concern was contact with communist embassies, rather than Western allies.[140] It was known by even the U.S. ambassador in Nairobi that communist powers were funding communist publications and institutes as well as providing weapons, which were under the watchful eye of Kenyan authorities.[141] In May 1965, diplomats were required to stay within ten miles of Nairobi or obtain permission to leave the area. Though the order was not just for communist countries' embassies, the U.S. ambassador noted that it was not "strictly enforced on the rest of us."[142] According to Special Branch officer Kibati, foreigners who were allowed in the country were carefully monitored, while Soviet diplomats were restricted to Nairobi and the Special Branch watched their movements closely.[143]

A more immediate concern to Kenya's stability was the Shifta War that occupied much of the government and Special Branch's focus on border issues immediately after independence. In November 1963, clashes increased when ethnic Somalis in Kenya's Northern Frontier District tried to secede from Kenya and become part of Somalia.[144] The roots of Somalia unification rested in decades of colonial rule where the ethnic Somalis had little trust in government and "affection towards the entity of Kenya," prompting the Northern Province People's Progressive Party and the Somalia government to oppose Kenyan rule after independence.[145] The *shifta*, Somali for bandits, were insurgents in small groups, supported by the Somalia government, engaged in ambush attacks on Kenyan soldiers and police as well as stole supplies and livestock.[146] In December 1963, the Kenyan government declared a state of emergency in the area as "the security forces took more proactive counter-*shifta* measures, and began to initiate contact with suspected *shifta* groups."[147] Kenyan officers were ordered to register Somalis with a full name, age, tribe, chief, and district along with a photograph, while information about the *shifta* was shared with the Special Branch.[148]

During the Shifta War, an intriguing document was drafted by the Special Branch titled "Report on Positive Intelligence Problems in Kenya" about a "specialist" from Israel sent to "assist" Kenya "in combating insidious foreign influences as exemplified by the Shifta war."[149] Staying in Kenya from October 12 to November 16, 1967, the specialist visited "border areas" of Somalia and Tanzania, reviewed Kenyan operations, and met with leading officials, including Kenyatta, Hinga, Moi, and Charles Njonjo. The report concluded Kenya lacked a "positive intelligence" service (defined as secret collection and research) and made several observations about the Special Branch that are quite illuminating. These included finding Special Branch officers were trained to "deal mainly" with internal security rather than "positive intelligence"; staff in the provinces is small; field units "operate on the basis of raw information only, not on the basis of intelligence"; and the Special Branch section "for processing and evaluating information is to be considered more an archives and registry centre than a full-scale research establishment."[150] The report recommended the Special Branch, for example, use "external stations in base-countries and/or target countries" and establish a "research arm" so foreign and defense policies are based on intelligence.[151]

Administrators and officers identified areas where they believed the *shifta* were and detained and punished the community. The government forced Somalis into newly built villages, a tactic borrowed from authorities during the Mau Mau uprising.[152] Kanwal Sethi, a commissioned officer in the Kenyan Army who served during the war, described how the Special Branch's intelligence "was a critical factor in operational planning."[153] The process consisted of security committees at district, provincial, and national levels for intelligence under "the ministry of internal security."[154] Whereas Daniel Opande, a Kenyan military officer, described how the military handed over captured *shifta* to the police, but intelligence sharing was a challenge because communication between "operational staff and tactical headquarters was problematic."[155] The conflict ended in 1967 when a memorandum of understanding was signed by Kenya and Somalia, with stability emerging in 1968.[156]

Kenya's intelligence service adapted to new political and international realities, which became formalized by the end of the decade. President Kenyatta had forced rivals from government, crushed dissent, successfully built international relations with the West, and thwarted a secessionist effort. Ultimately, Kenyatta officially took direct control of the Special Branch. In 1969, the Special Branch was moved directly under the authority of the Office of the President, having previously been under the Office of the Vice President and Ministry of Home Affairs (which led was by the same individual).[157] The new 1969 constitution officially gave the president even more control over police, including the Special Branch, instead of law enforcement answering to parliament.[158] In a history about the Special Branch commissioned by the National Security Intelligence Service, Mildred Ndeda explained, "The whole constitutional safeguards of the police force were absolutely and senselessly destroyed" with the constitutional amendment that put the police under the Office of the President.[159] Also in 1969, Kenyatta legalized operations through a presidential charter, which opened opportunities for the Special Branch to act against domestic and foreign threats in ways not previously sanctioned.[160] The details of these changes as well as the size and budget of Kenyan intelligence during this period remain unknown.

CONCLUSION

The Special Branch cast a long shadow over Kenyan politics and government for decades. It worked in secret to benefit the nation's security as well as the personal interests of its leaders. Effective through detentions and torture, the Special Branch became synonymous with fear in Kenya. Scholar Susanne D. Mueller wrote, "No one felt safe and no one knew when or if the Special Branch or the police would show up on their doorstep."[161] In response to criticism, former Special Branch officer Kibati justified the Special Branch's actions in the later years of its existence, writing it "had the unpleasant duty of safeguarding an unpopular regime that was constitutionally in office."[162] The colonial past and first decade of independence is key to understanding how the Special Branch came to operate, treat government critics, and earned its reputation during the latter part of the twentieth century. During the 1960s, the Kenyan government had a chance to break from the past of colonial structures and institutions, but it kept the Special Branch's structure mostly the same. Some colonial-era officers stayed for a few years, while the targets for collection, tactics, and methods largely continued and evolved. Intelligence structures established during colonialism were mostly maintained in the first decade of independence and some persist to the present. Notably the Kenya Intelligence Committee, established during the Emergency, continues to coordinate intelligence for the Kenyan government today.[163]

Under a one-party state with power concentrated in the hands of a president, the Special Branch served not only as a tool for government stability, but ensured the leaders' and party's continuity through detentions without trial and torture.[164] Stories about repression and torture under the Special Branch became more widespread as the decades progressed and people wrote about their experiences.[165] The fear of the Special Branch is what made it powerful. It was ubiquitous because people believed it was. People watched and reported on others out of fear that they would fall under suspicion if they did not. This message was also delivered at the highest level. As President

Moi told members of the only legal political party in 1978, "I know too much, more than people think I know." He continued, "Some of those who hold night meetings come to me to pay lip-service, but I remind them of their activities, to their shock."[166] It took several more decades, a multiparty democracy, parliament-led intelligence reform, and a new name for the Special Branch before Kenyan intelligence and security services could distance itself from widespread and systematic abuse. Kenya could have embraced intelligence reform in the first decade of independence, but the new governing elite chose to largely maintain the intelligence structure that just years before considered them enemies.

NOTES

1. For an overview, see: Ryan Shaffer, "Following in Footsteps: The History of Kenya's Post-Colonial Intelligence Services," *Studies in Intelligence* 63, no. 1 (2019): 23–40.

2. Special thanks to Sylvia Kamene, a local researcher in Nairobi, who provided me with a collection of primary sources.

3. For a brief overview of the history by a Kenyan intelligence director, see: Wilson Boinett, "The Origins of the Intelligence System of Kenya," in *Changing Intelligence Dynamics in Africa*, eds. Sandy Africa and Johnny Kwadjo (Birmingham, UK: GFN-SSR and ASSN, 2009), 23.

4. F. D. Corfield, *The Origins and Growth of Mau Mau: An Historical Survey, Sessional Paper No. 5 of 1959/60* (Nairobi: Colony and Protectorate of Kenya, 1960), 30.

5. Corfield, 31.

6. Letter from Governor Robert Brooke-Popham to secretary of state for the colonies Malcolm MacDonald, April 26, 1939, 1, CO 533/507/8, The National Archives (TNA), Kew, United Kingdom.

7. Letter from Governor Robert Brooke-Popham to secretary of state for the colonies Malcolm MacDonald, April 26, 1939, 2, CO 533/507/8, TNA.

8. Ibid., 2.

9. "Telegram from the Secretary of State for the Colonies to the Governor of Kenya," March 27, 1939, TNA CO 533/507/8.

10. Corfield, 31.

11. Ibid., 31.

12. Ibid., 31.

13. Ibid., 31.

14. Ibid., 31, 32.

15. Ibid., 35.

16. Ibid., 35.

17. Ibid., 36.

18. Ibid., 36.

19. Ibid., 37.

20. Ibid., 31.

21. Ibid., 31.

22. Caroline Elkins, *Imperial Reckoning: The Untold Story of Britain's Gulag in Kenya* (New York: Henry Holt and Company, 2005), xiv, xiii. For more on the Mau Mai, also see: David Anderson, *Histories of the Hanged: The Dirty War in Kenya and the End of Empire* (New York: W. W. Norton, 2005).

23. Elkins, 25.

24. Ibid., 25.

25. Ibid., 85.

26. Ibid., 87, 207.

27. "Minutes of the 21st Monthly Liaison Meeting," July 19, 1957, FCO 141/6270, TNA.

28. Derek Franklin, *A Pied Cloak: Memoirs of a Colonial Police (Special Branch) Officer* (London: Janus Publishing Company, 2006), 44, 45.

29. Ibid., 44.

30. Letter from W. Ramsbottom, Civil Secretary of Police, "Special Branch and Criminal Investigation Department Training Centre Nairobi," July 10, 1956, AH/13/260, Kenya National Archives (KNA), Nairobi, Kenya.

31. Nicholas van der Bijl, *Mau Mau Rebellion: The Emergency in Kenya 1952–1956* (South Yorkshire: Pen and Sword, 2017), 46.

32. Van der Bijl, 46.

33. Ibid., 47.

34. Ibid., 50.

35. Randall W. Heather, "Intelligence and Counter-Insurgency in Kenya, 1952–56," *Intelligence and National Security* 5, no. 3 (1990): 61.

36. Letter to Whyatt from P. Rogers, Colonial Office, October 29, 1952, CO/822/446, TNA.

37. Letter from P. Rogers, Colonial Office, October 27, 1952, CO/822/446, TNA; In his memoir, Sillitoe mentioned his 1952 visit to Nairobi but did not explain the purpose or provide details. Percy Sillitoe, *Cloak without Dagger* (London: Cassell and Company, 1955), 193. A. W. Cockerill's biography briefly discussed this. A. W. Cockerill, *Sir Percy Sillitoe: The Biography of the Former Head of MI5* (London: W. H. Allen, 1975), 188–189.

38. Christopher Andrew, *The Defence of the Realm: The Authorized History of MI5* (New York: Allen Lane, 2009), 456.

39. Ibid., 456.

40. Ibid., 456.

41. Ibid., 456.

42. Huw Bennett, "Soldiers in the Court Room: The British Army's Part in the Kenya Emergency under the Legal Spotlight," *Journal of Imperial and Commonwealth History* 39, no. 5 (December 2011): 720.

43. "Kenya Special Branch Headquarters Fortnightly Intelligence Summary no. 19/53," December 1953, CO 822/374, TNA.

44. "Kenya Special Branch Headquarters Fortnightly Intelligence Summary no. 18/53," December 1953, CO 822/374, TNA.

45. "Kenya Special Branch Headquarters Fortnightly Intelligence Summary no. 18/53," December 1953, 5, CO 822/374, TNA.

46. Andrew, 457. Also see: Corfield, 37.

47. Andrew, 457.

48. Ibid., 457.

49. *A Handbook of Anti-Mau Mau Operations* (Nairobi: EA-GHQ, 1954), 8, 9.

50. For example, Letter from Mweiga-Ngobit, Nanyuki District Officer's Office, February 11, 1956. CO 822/446, TNA.

51. Ian Henderson and Philip Goodhart, *Man Hunt in Kenya: The Termination of a Most Bizarre and Violent Terrorist Organization* (New York: Bantam, 1988), unpaginated front matter. For a comparative examination of British insurgencies where the colonies adapted techniques from previous conflicts, see: David French, *The British Way in Counter-Insurgency, 1945–1967* (New York: Oxford University Press, 2012).

52. Henderson and Goodhart, 26, 29. See actual citations: "Award of Colonial Police Medal," *The Official Gazette* (Kenya), no. 1359, October 4, 1955, 978; "Award of Bar to George Medal," *The Official Gazette* (Kenya), no. 1360, September 27, 1955.

53. Frank Kitson, *Bunch of Five* (London: Faber & Faber, 1977), 19.

54. Van der Bijl, 81.

55. Guy Campbell, *The Charging Buffalo: A History of the Kenya Regiment, 1937–1963* (London: Leo Cooper, 1986), 53.

56. Huw Bennett, *Fighting the Mau Mau: The British Army and Counter-Insurgency in the Kenya Emergency* (New York: Cambridge University Press, 2013), 54, 55.

57. Andrew, 458; David A. Percox, "Mau Mau and the Arming of the State," in *Mau Mau and Nationhood: Arms, Authority and Narration*, eds. E. S. Atieno Odhiambo and John Lonsdale (Athens: Ohio University Press, 2003), 131.

58. For example: Andrew, 458.

59. Memorandum by the Minister for Defence, "Police Department Special Branch and CID Training Centre," 1956, AH/13/260, KNA.

60. Corfield, 316.

61. For more on Prime Minister Harold Macmillan's speech, see: L. J. Butler and Sarah Stockwell, eds., *The Wind of Change: Harold Macmillan and British Decolonization* (New York: Palgrave Macmillan, 2013).

62. Franklin, 106,

63. Ibid., 136, 138, 139.

64. Ibid., 137; Letter to permanent secretaries, heads of department and provincial commissioners, December 22, 1960, PC/N2A/4/20/4, KNA. For the form: "Appendix B Security Vetting," Director or Intelligence and Security, n.d. circa, 1960, AE/24/4, KNA; G. P. Henderon, "Reference (55)," n.n., December 5, 1957, AE/24/4, KNA; "Loss of Secret Document," The Protective Security Officer, Special Branch Headquarters, October 27, 1960, S/8035, KNA.

65. After independence, the Special Branch headquarters was located at Kingsway House at the crossing of Muindi Mbingu Street and University Way.

66. Daniel Branch, *Kenya: Between Hope and Despair, 1963–2011* (Yale University Press, 2011), 7.

67. Andrew, 467.

68. Irungu Thatiah and Jane Kiano, *Quest for Liberty: Gikonyo Kiano* (Nairobi: Sasa Sema Publications, 2013), 109. There are reports MI5 secretly recorded the Kenyan guests. Calder Walton, *Empire of Secrets: British Intelligence, the Cold War and the Twilight of Empire* (New York: The Overlook Press, 2013), 269.

69. Letter, F. N. Brockett, "Retention of Expatriate Officers," Directorate of Personnel, August 13, 1963, S/5988, KNA.

70. Director of criminal investigation T. P. McBrierley, "Independence Amnesty," November 12, 1963, BB/12/48, KNA.

71. Oginga Odinga, *Not Yet Uhuru: An Autobiography* (Nairobi: East African Educational Publishers, 1968), 241–2.

72. Daniel Branch and Nicholas Cheeseman, "The Politics of Control in Kenya: Understanding the Bureaucratic-Executive State, 1952–78," *Review of African Political Economy* 33 no. 107 (2006): 18.

73. Ibid., 18.

74. Ibid., 21.

75. Branch, 15.

76. Branch and Cheeseman, 22.

77. Ibid., 23.

78. For an example of radio being monitored, see the 1965 intelligence report that mentioned "for the third consecutive week Radio Mogadishu has made no comment whatever concerning Kenya or the former NFD." "Special Branch Weekly Intelligence Report, no. 22/65," Office of the Director of Intelligence, June 3, 1965. KNA S/8035.

79. For colonial examples, see: Corfield, 73, 128–9, 136–7.

80. David Throup, "Crime, Politics and the Police in Colonial Kenya, 1939–63" in *Policing and decolonization: Politics, Nationalism and the Police, 1917–65*, eds. David M. Anderson and David Killingray (Manchester: Manchester University Press, 1992), 152.

81. Throup, 153.

82. Letter from Permanent Secretary for Defence, "Courses in Protective Security for Security Officers," August 28, 1961, PC/N2A/4/20/4, KNA.

83. Throup, 153.

84. Ibid., 152.

85. Branch, 39; Henderson and Goodhart, 29.

86. Duncan Ndegwa, *Walking in Kenyatta Struggles* (Nairobi: Kenya Leadership Institute, 2006), 320.

87. Throup, 153.

88. For example, see a letter addressed to Hinga. Letter from J. N. Oluoch to Hinga, April 13, 1964, KNA AHC/1/52.

89. Ndegwa, 321.

90. Francis K. Sang, *A Noble But Onerous Duty: An Autobiography by Former Director of Criminal Investigation Department (CID)* (Bloomington, IN: AuthorHouse, 2013), 29; Kibati, 185.

91. Mugumo Munene, "Former Shadowy Spy," *Daily Nation*, February 14, 2008, https://www.nation.co.ke/lifestyle/1190-228878-g0kgh9z/index.html; Charles Hornsby, *Kenya: A History since Independence* (New York: I. B. Tauris, 2013), 100.

92. "Promotions," *The Official Gazette* (Kenya), no. 1360, September 14, 1965, 1070. For information on the rank, see: Randall W. Heather, "Intelligence and counter-insurgency in Kenya, 1952–56," *Intelligence and National Security* 5, no. 3 (1990): 65.

93. Kanwal Sethi, *Shaping Destiny* (Victoria: FriesenPress, 2016), 203.

94. S. E. O. Bosire, *Report of the Judicial Commission of Inquiry into the Goldenberg Affair*, Republic of Kenya, October 2005, http://kenyalaw.org/kl/fileadmin/CommissionReports/Report-of-the-Judicial-Commission-of-Inquiry-into-the-Goldenberg-Affair.pdf; Caroline Njung'e, "No end in sight to resolving Kanyotu estate dispute," *Daily Nation*, October 28, 2019, https://www.nation.co.ke/news/No-end-in-sight-for-Kanyotu-estate-dispute/1056-5327200-116umy3/index.html.

95. Branch, 39.

96. Thatiah and Kiano, 202.

97. "Vote 1—Office of the President," The National Assembly, July 8, 1971, 2015.

98. Sethi described the racial issues as a factor for leaving the Kenyan military. Sethi, 216, 217.

99. William Attwood, *The Reds and the Blacks: A Personal Adventure* (New York: Harper & Row Publishers, 1967), 287.

100. Odinga, 277.

101. Ibid., 277.

102. Franklin, 85.

103. "Special Branch Weekly Intelligence Report, no. 22/65," Office of the Director of Intelligence, June 3, 1965, S/8035, KNA.

104. "Special Branch Weekly Intelligence Report, no. 36/65," Office of the Director of Intelligence, September 9, 1965, S/8035, KNA.

105. Letter from AG Provincial Commissioner Rift Valley Province, "Responsibility for the Maintenance of Law, Order and Security: President's Circular No. 1 of 1965," CA/39/1, KNA.

106. "Responsibility for the Maintenance of Law, Order and Security: President's Circular No. 1 of 1965," 2, CA/39/1, KNA.

107. Letter by KIC chair A. J. Omanga, "Charter for the Kenya Intelligence Committee and Provincial and District Intelligence Committees," Office of the Kenya Intelligence Committee, June 23, 1966, 2, CA/39/1, KNA.

108. Mildred Ndeda, *Secret Servants: A History of Intelligence and Espionage in Kenya, c 1887–1999, A Report Submitted to the National Security and Intelligence Service of Kenya on 30th January 2006* (Nairobi, Kenya: n.p.), 278. In author possession.

109. Letter by KIC chair A. J. Omanga, "Charter for the Kenya Intelligence Committee and Provincial and District Intelligence Committees," Office of the Kenya Intelligence Committee, June 23, 1966, 2, CA/39/1, KNA.

110. "Revised Charter for the Kenya Intelligence Committee and Provincial and District Intelligence Committees," Office of the Kenya Intelligence Committee, January 22, 1966, 1, CA/39/1, KNA.

111. Ibid.

112. Bart Joseph Kibati, *Memoirs of a Kenyan Spymaster* (Nairobi: Nairobi Academic Press, 2016). Also see: Ryan Shaffer, "Memoirs of a Kenyan Spymaster by Bart Joseph Kibati (Nairobi Academic Press, 2016)," *Journal of Intelligence History* 18, no. 1 (2019): 110–112.

113. Kibati, 43.

114. Ibid., 44.

115. For example, M. C. Manby, "Weekly Personal Report by the Director of Intelligence," Office of the Director of Intelligence, August 17, 1963, CO 1035/188, TNA.

116. Kibati, 187, 188.

117. Ibid., 188.

118. Godfrey Gitahi Kariuki, *The Illusion of Power: Fifty Years in Kenya Politics* (Nairobi: Kenway Publications, 2001), 79.

119. Ibid., 79.

120. Ibid., 79.

121. Ibid., 80.

122. Franklin, 141.

123. Branch, 103.

124. Kibati, 181.

125. Attorney General Charles Njonjo is a notable example because a government report later documented his misuse of power, but even the origins of that inquiry was undoubtedly politically driven by President Moi. Jean-François Médard, "Charles Njonjo: The Portrait of a 'Big Man' in Kenya," in *Neopatrimonialism in Africa and Beyond*, eds. Daniel C. Bach, Mamoudou Gazibo (New York: Routledge, 2012), 58–78. P. G. Okoth, "Njonjo Under the Microscope," *Drum*, 1985; *Report of Judicial Inquiry Appointed to Inquire into the Allegations Involving Charles Mugane Njonjo* (Nairobi: Republic of Kenya, 1984), 77–81.

126. Branch, 9.

127. Pal D. Ahluwalia, *Post-Colonialism and the Politics of Kenya* (Commack: Nova Science Publishers, 1996), 46. According to a handwritten intelligence report, Odinga was "expelled" from KANU, and "very many" people were in favor of this. "Intelligence Report," Coast Province, n.d., SF/SEC/, KNA.

128. Branch, 60.

129. Albert O. Mumma, "Preservation of Public Security through Executive Restraint of Personal Liberty: A Case Study of the Kenyan Position," *Verfassung und Recht in Übersee / Law and Politics in Africa, Asia and Latin America* 21, no. 4 (1988): 447, 448.

130. Letter from Daniel arap Moi, "State Security," Office of the Vice President and Minister for Home Affairs, June 22, 1971, KNA, CA/45/4 folder.

131. For Special Branch's connection to Kariuki's murder, see: Duncan Khaemba, "Murder Most Foul: JM Kariuki's Final 48 Hours," *The Standard*, March 12, 2020, https://www.standardmedia.co.ke/special-report/jmkariuki/

132. For example: David Goldsworthy, *Tom Mboya: The Man Kenya Wanted to Forget* (New York: Africana Publishing Company, 1982), 284; Joe Khamisi, *Looters and Grabbers: 54 Years of Corruption and Plunder by the Elite, 1963–2017* (Plano, Texas: Jodey Book Publishers, 2018), 119.

133. *Report of the Select Committee on the Disappearance and Murder of the Late Member for Nyandarua North, the Hon. J.M. Kariuki, M.P.* (Nairobi: National Assembly, 1975), 5. Also see: David W. Throup and Charles Hornsby, *Multi-party Politics in Kenya: The Kenyatta and Moi States and the Triumph of the System in the 1992 Election* (Athens: Ohio State University, 1998), 20.

134. Kibati, 202.

135. Ibid., 198.

136. Ibid., 198; Karen Rothmyer, *Joseph Murumbi: A Legacy of Integrity* (Nairobi: Zand Graphics, 2018), 141.

137. Branch, 37.

138. Ibid., 42.

139. Ibid., 42.

140. Sethi, 210.

141. Attwood, 249.

142. Ibid., 248.

143. Kibati, 202, 203.

144. Nene Mburu, *Bandits on the Border: The Last Frontier in the Search for Somali Unity* (Trenton: Red Sea Press, 2005), 138.

145. Branch, 29.

146. Daniel Opande, *In Pursuit of Peace in Africa: An Autobiography* (Nairobi: East African Educational Publishers, 2019), 53.

147. Hannah Whittaker, *Insurgency and Counterinsurgency in Kenya: A Social History of the Shifta Conflict, c. 1963–1968* (Leiden: Brill, 2015), 91.

148. Letter from H. M. Oching, "Control of Somalis," Eastern Province, July, 9, 1965, BB/12/48, KNA; Letter to Special Branch officer S. M. Katoe to the Director of Intelligence, "Surrendered Forrest Bandits," January 21, 1965, BB/12/48, KNA.

149. "Report on Positive Intelligence Problems in Kenya," n.d., circa 1967, 1. The report was written by someone identified only as "M.E." and was found in the KNA.

150. Ibid., 5.

151. Ibid., 5, 9.

152. Branch, 33.

153. Sethi, 112, 186.

154. Ibid., 113.

155. Opande, 57.

156. Branch, 34.

157. Kibati, 49.

158. "The Constitution of Kenya Act 1969," Republic of Kenya, April 1969, 105. The 1963 constitution had the Special Branch and other "specialized" police under Parliament's expenditure and inspector general of police authority. "The Kenya Independence Order in Council 1963," Kenya Gazette Supplement no. 105, December 10, 1963, 111.

159. Mildred Ndeda, *Secret Servants: A History of Intelligence and Espionage in Kenya, c 1887–1999, A Report Submitted to the National Security and Intelligence Service of Kenya on 30th January 2006* (Nairobi, Kenya: n.p., 2006), 259. In author possession.

160. Kibati, 50.

161. Susanne D. Mueller, "The Resilience of the Past: Government and Opposition in Kenya," *Canadian Journal of African Studies/ La Revue canadienne des études africaines* 48, no. 2 (2014): 339.

162. Kibati, 59.

163. Walton, 245; Defence White Paper, Ministry of Defence, Republic of Kenya, 2017, 22, http://www.mod.go.ke/wp-content/uploads/2017/05/White-Paper.pdf.

164. One notable quote in parliament was: "As of now, the Special Branch is known for torture." "Parliamentary Debates," Kenyan Parliament, December 9, 1998, 2817; "Special Branch Fights Horrors of Its Dark Past," *The Daily Nation*, October 3, 1999.

165. For example, see: *We Lived to Tell: The Nyayo House Story* (Nairobi: Friedrich Ebert Stiftung, 2003); *Amnesty International Annual Report 1988* (London: Amnesty International Publications, 1988), 48; Raila Odinga and Sarah Elderkin, *The Flame of Freedom* (Nairobi: Mountain Top Publishers, 2013), 338–343. Ngũgĩ wa Thiong'o, *Wrestling with the Devil: A Prison Memoir* (New York: The New Press, 2018).

166. "Omniscient Moi," *The Weekly Review*, November 17, 1978.

Chapter 2

Intelligence, Decolonization, and Nonalignment in Zanzibar and Tanganyika, 1962–1972

Simon Graham

On February 8, 1964, the People's Republic of Zanzibar and Pemba afforded diplomatic recognition to East Germany and then issued an unlikely request for financial, military, and logistical assistance from that same government, which was itself negotiating limited recognition.[1] Recently declassified intelligence sources from the German Federal Archives and the Stasi Records Agency shed light on the reasons for this request and, when understood through the prism of international history and alongside local activist literature, memoirs, and autobiography, locate decolonization in the context of Cold War inter-German rivalries.[2] International history also highlights circulations of people, ideas, and practices between intelligence communities in Europe, Zanzibar, and Tanganyika, which enables a rethinking of the so-called aid and trade narratives that dominate histories of decolonization in East Africa.[3] Far from relying on European states, the leaders of Zanzibar and Tanganyika, Abeid Karume and Julius Nyerere, respectively, tailored their relationships with East Berlin and Bonn, respectively, to catalyze financial, material, and educational support for developing their domestic security services before replicating the process with China and, to a lesser extent, the Soviet Union.[4] Consequently, East and, to a lesser extent, West German advisors collaborated freely with their hosts when formulating governance structures and training recruits but had limited influence over intelligence priorities, which were strictly aligned with national goals.[5] This prompts a reconsideration of postcolonial states' agency more broadly in Cold War intelligence collaborations.

This chapter is organized chronologically in three sections. The first section examines competition between East and West Germany with attention to foreign policy and intelligence concerns. It explains how anti-colonial revolutionaries co-opted East Berlin's ambition for international recognition and Bonn's Hallstein Doctrine to gain much needed material support while skirting direct allegiance with either the United States or the Soviet Union.[6] In the second section, it explores the consequences of Karume and Nyerere courting East and West Germany, respectively, for a united Tanzania, with attention to the types of assistance offered and the strategic calculations of a growing list of parties interested in the region. This interest brought Nyerere's commitment to nonalignment into conflict with moves by the United States, the Soviet Union, and the People's Republic of China to establish a foothold in Dar es Salaam. The third section provides a conclusion, summarizing the key fissures in relations between Tanzania, the Germanies, and the super-powers before explaining how Nyerere exploited Cold War competition for economic, material, and educational support.

In the background to Zanzibar's recognition of East Germany and request for support on February 8, 1964, were two events. First, Zanzibar gained independence from Britain on December 10, 1963, and within a few weeks, on January 12, 1964, the Western-backed predominately Arab government of Sultan Sayyid Jamshid bin Abdullah was overthrown by the majority African population under self-appointed field marshall John Okello.[7] Sheikh Abeid Karume of the Afro-Shirazi Party, described by *Time* magazine as "the burly, leftist strongman of the spice islands," formed the government in the ensuing tussle for control of the new state of Zanzibar.[8] Second, East Berlin had limited ability to formalize ties abroad thanks to the West German government's Hallstein Doctrine whereby Bonn refused to recognize states with ties to East Berlin. In this context, Zanzibar's decision to reach out to East Berlin meant forgoing the potential economic benefits of trade with Bonn's *Wirtschafts-wunder*, the West German economic miracle of the 1960s.[9]

The economic and political risk of the aspiring Zanzibar government soliciting support from East Germany did not dissuade Karume, and the relationship was consolidated by treaty on May 17, 1964.[10] In particular, the agreement committed both parties to expanding the collaboration begun in February 1964.[11] Zanzibar became the first state beyond the Soviet sphere to recognize East Germany and an unlikely foundational node in the East German Ministry of State Security's (Stasi) presence in Africa. This relationship persisted until the death of Karume in 1972 by which time Zanzibar was solic-iting support from both Moscow and Beijing. In the words of Markus Wolf, the long-standing chief of the Stasi's foreign intelligence directorate, the Main Intelligence Directorate (HVA), Zanzibar "chose us" and "forced itself on our attention."[12] The island was an intriguing, accidental ally of East Germany and, perhaps more worryingly for the Stasi, an unknown quantity in the net-work of newly independent African states showing sympathies for socialism.

At the same time, diplomatic relations were deepening between the main-land territory adjacent to Zanzibar, the newly independent Tanganyika, and

West Germany. Bonn had celebrated Tanganyika's independence from Britain on December 9, 1961, with a gift worth up to 250,000 Deutschmarks.[13] This gift primarily took the form of medical equipment despite efforts by the cabinet of Julius Nyerere, the territory's prime minister (1961–1962) and then president (1962–1985), to allocate the funds toward procuring a government aircraft.[14] Regardless of its substance, the diplomatic function of the gift was clear; it was, in Britta Schilling's words, "a gateway into further state relations."[15] Furthermore, the gift demonstrates that Tanganyika was in no way an accidental ally of West Germany, as Zanzibar was with East Germany, but rather, that the relationship was the product of Bonn's deliberate strategy of using a so-called *Unabhängigkeitsgeschenk* (independence gift) as an entrée to ongoing collaboration.

West German collaboration with Tanganyika initially prioritized economic development over entrenching security ties between the West German Federal Intelligence Service (the *Bundesnachrichtendienst* or BND) and the Tanganyika security apparatus, which was led by Julius Nyerere's brother, Joseph Nyerere.[16] A West German diplomatic mission was quickly established in Dar es Salaam and staffed by a group of "development experts" from Bonn.[17] This served to solidify West Germany's position in an increasingly crowded field of states, including the United States (USA), the Soviet Union, and the People's Republic of China, vying to support and influence Julius Nyerere and the ruling Tanganyika African Nationalist Union (TANU). In 1962, Bonn secured a treaty guaranteeing formal economic cooperation with Tanganyika and permission to support technical training schools.[18] West German–Tanganyika ties continued to deepen from 1962 to 1964 through educational exchanges with West Germany, the provision of teacher training, material support of small-scale industry, and limited security assistance.[19] This formed a stark contrast with East Berlin's insistence that security collaboration prefigure the extension of social and economic support to Zanzibar.

The turn of events in East Africa during 1962–1964 raises no shortage of questions about the place of inter-German competition and intelligence collaboration in the decolonization and unification of Zanzibar and Tanganyika, in general, and the formation of the states' security services, in particular. From 1962 to 1972, Abeid Karume and Julius Nyerere each leveraged inter-German rivalries not only to unpick colonial security structures by developing indigenous intelligence capacities on either side of the Zanzibar Channel, but also to bolster their own claims to the leadership of a united Tanzania. This chapter explores why outspoken anti-colonialists risked their revolutionary credentials by soliciting German support for the security institutions that had just overthrown imperial rule. This is important to understand, as it demonstrates how a calculated reversal of colonial roles underpinned collaborative securitization in Zanzibar and Tanganyika. Where tribal and ethnic divisions

had facilitated European expansionism throughout East Africa, now competition between ideological blocs for the allegiance of newly independent states
shifted power into the hands of revolutionaries like Karume and Nyerere.

A DIVIDED TANZANIA: COMPETITION BETWEEN EAST
BERLIN AND BONN

President Karume of Zanzibar requested "financial help and security advice,
particularly in the sphere of internal intelligence gathering and border protection" from Stasi chief Erich Mielke in mid-February 1964.[20] The reaction
from East Berlin was almost immediate, suggesting that the administration
was, at the very least, intrigued by the prospect of developing a relationship
with Karume. By late February 1964, East Berlin dispatched Stasi generals
Rolf Markert and Markus Wolf to Zanzibar as part of an advisory group to
assess the growing "stream of demands" from Karume and material needs
of the island while promoting friendly relations with their unexpected ally.[21]
They were joined by a small diplomatic delegation led by East German deputy foreign minister Wolfgang Kiesewetter, who remained on the island until
April 1, 1964, to consolidate the relationship with Zanzibar.[22] Two representatives of the East German National People's Army arrived in Zanzibar in early
March, shortly followed by ten Soviet military representatives.[23]

Over the subsequent years, the East Germany–Zanzibar relationship waxed
and waned and at different times included economic and military aid; cultural
and educational exchanges; and the training of intelligence, police, and diplomatic services. It formed one part of a much larger series of overlapping
interactions between East Germany and the Third World. For example, Klaus
Storkmann noted that "between 1970 and 1989 a total of 1895 persons from
fifteen states or organizations [including Zanzibar/Tanzania] were trained in
164 courses" by the Stasi.[24] However, Mielke's men on the ground initially
had an ulterior motive—to determine whether the Karume government
shared sufficient ideological affinity with the East German Socialist Unity
Party, and more broadly the Soviet sphere, to be a candidate for cultivating
similar security structures to those already in place in East Germany.[25] The
US Central Intelligence Agency (CIA) noted this uncertainty over the politics
of Zanzibar's revolutionaries in a report finalized on February 21, 1966.[26]
The CIA determined "that the Soviets and Chinese were uncertain about
the orientation of Zanzibar's new government. They may have felt that the
revolution could go either way."[27] Nonetheless, the Stasi officers in Zanzibar
became convinced that intelligence collaboration was possible and East German influence could become entrenched on the island.[28]

The Stasi's recommendation that Zanzibar was a viable partner for East Germany was made against a background of an increasingly adventurous East German foreign policy toward the Third World and, particularly, Africa during the 1960s. East German policy change was motivated by two key factors. First, East Germany sought to garner support from newly independent states to improve its standing and influence in both the socialist and nonsocialist "constellations."[29] This predominately involved financing anti-colonial national liberation movements prior to and following revolution.[30] However, the support was far from benevolent. In Hans-Georg Schleicher's words, "While solidarity rested on the general internationalist principles of socialist ideology, it served as a vehicle for the specific foreign policy interests of East Germany in its drive to achieve recognition as an equal member of the community of nations."[31] Furthermore, East German support for Karume relied on the Stasi overlooking the explicitly racial African-Arab distinction underpinning Karume's domestic security policy and applying a "lump" identity to the island's people.[32]

Second, East Germany sought to disrupt the diplomatic isolation brought about by the defining feature of West Germany's foreign policy from 1955 to 1970, the Hallstein Doctrine.[33] This was to be achieved by working through paradiplomatic entities in Africa, such as the East German "Committee for Solidarity with the People of Africa," and offering security training services along with material support to states that flaunted the doctrine, like Zanzibar.[34] East Germany's rejection of the Hallstein Doctrine complemented Karume's rejection of "imperial" Europe and created common ground for future diplomacy.[35] By March 1964, East Germany recorded that it had "the largest diplomatic establishment in Zanzibar; Ambassador Günther Fritsch headed an eleven-man staff at the embassy."[36] Just as the Soviet Union had cultivated nodes in a network of client states in Eastern Europe and Africa from 1945 to 1960, East Germany deployed this approach in East Africa in the 1960s and, initially, it met with considerable success. Nevertheless, East Germany's approach was also unique in terms of the level of autonomy East Germany claimed in pursuit of its national interests. The Stasi, particularly, were not above sacrificing Moscow's designs to benefit East Berlin, especially in relation to competition with West Germany.

The West German approach to developing security relations in East Africa was considerably simpler and more cautious than that of East Germany. Rather than using its security service to facilitate diplomacy and economic collaboration, the West German *Wirtschaftswunder* leveraged its economic and diplomatic credentials in Tanganyika to legitimize a growing security presence alongside security advisors from a range of other states. By early 1964, these credentials were significant. From 1961 to 1963, West Germany provided the

Nyerere government with a 40 million Deutschmark loan, which equated to approximately 20 percent of gross foreign investment in Tanganyika during the period.[37] West Germany was also the third largest destination for exports from Tanganyika and was the country's key supplier of precision medical and industrial technology.[38] As much as the United States had used economic investment to solidify security ties with West Germany during the late 1940s, West Germany was now adapting the premise of the European Recovery Plan (Marshall Plan) to cement its own relationship with Tanganyika.

However, West Germany's diplomatic and economic links with the Nyerere government did little to ameliorate the challenges created by the highly fluid context in which the security institutions of Tanganyika were functioning. When BND representatives attached to the West German mission in Dar es Salaam began to engage with the security apparatus in Tanganyika during 1962 and 1963, they had to contend with a local intelligence community emerging from a period of transitional governance.[39] This institutional instability was further complicated by the territory's colonial legacies, legacies that Abeid Karume had largely broken away from through revolution on Zanzibar but Nyerere was forced to confront while instigating reforms on the mainland. Scholars Thomas Maguire and Hannah Franklin highlighted that chief among these legacies were British efforts to embed Tanganyika in a Commonwealth security culture where the police Special Branch was primarily responsible for intelligence matters (see Shaffer in this volume).[40] The subsequent failure of the Commonwealth model was then driven by "pre-independence security reforms, rapid post-independence Africanization, politicized new security organs responsive to court politics, policies of non-alignment and anti-colonialism by political elites," each of which also complicated BND efforts to establish a presence in the country.[41]

Nyerere was characteristically unapologetic in his anti-colonial commitment and initially looked to Israel to support the professionalization and Africanization of the Special Branch and its successor organization, the Security Service. In spring 1963, six Israeli police and Mossad officers were assigned to train a new "intelligence unit" that operated outside of Special Branch structures and was primarily accountable to the chair of the Tanganyika African Liberation Committee, Oscar Kambona.[42] This was followed by the dissolution of the Special Branch on September 6, 1963, and increased recruitment into the new Security Service from the partisan TANU Youth League. Israel, for its part, continued to provide technical support through in-country Mossad officers under the state's "periphery strategy" until late 1964, and it was not until unification with Zanzibar that Nyerere actively courted West Germany for a contribution to Tanzanian security.[43] However, even then, the BND faced stiff competition.[44]

Between 1962 and 1964, China, the United States, and even the Soviet Union on occasion took increased interest in Tanganyika. China's policy toward Tanganyika hinged on exchanging foreign aid for diplomatic ties and contracts of service in the construction industry.[45] Karume welcomed the respect with which China appeared to treat newly independent states and its expressed commitment to nonalignment.[46] However, Chinese benevolence in East Africa also served the geostrategic interests of the People's Republic by improving its internationalist credentials in comparison to the Soviet Union and its economic credentials in relation to the United States.[47] In contrast to the concerted Chinese effort in Tanganyika, Western designs for the mainland lacked coherence. Britain grudgingly accepted that its colonial legacy largely delegitimized its influence, while the United States struggled to distinguish nationalist movements worthy of support from communist revolutions in need of suppression.[48]

Soviet collaboration with East Germany on Zanzibar was cordial, but still influenced by unresolved tensions over whether East Berlin or Moscow was to be the primary representative of the Eastern Bloc on the island. This tension played out in mainland Tanganyika where East German and Soviet efforts to court Julius Nyerere occurred almost independently of one another, despite both states looking to use foreign intelligence activities to promote diplomacy and oppose West German, American, and Chinese influence.[49] The CIA argued that the cause of this distrust was the fractious "triangular relationship" between Moscow, East Berlin, and Bonn which played out in East German efforts to gain influence in mainland Tanzania.[50] The CIA speculated that East Berlin was well aware that "Soviet vital interests [took] precedence over the interests of their East German satrapy [a province in a larger state]" and feared that Moscow would "sacrifice German Communists in order to further Soviet internal and international interests," particularly the de-escalation of tensions with a resurgent West Germany in Europe.[51] This tension between allies, along with increasingly assertive Chinese policy toward East Africa, helps to explain why both Germanies became increasingly invested in a region of limited military and economic value throughout 1962–1964. The tension is also significant because it highlights the role of competing foreign ambitions in conditioning the activities of intelligence services as the vanguard of efforts to establish diplomatic relations or, alternatively, a largely reactionary force that leveraged existing ties to support intelligence collaboration.

A UNITED TANZANIA: NEW PARTNERS AND COLD WAR TRIANGULATIONS

As the 1960s progressed, Tanzania increasingly became the site of a three-way contest for the state's ideological and economic allegiance despite close

bilateral relations developing with each of the Germanies in the first half of
the decade. Karume's initial choice to solicit East Germany was largely pragmatic: East Germany was a relatively wealthy, industrialized, anti-colonial
socialist state, but not a superpower. It capably controlled its own population and unlike West Germany was not aligned with the unification-favoring
government of Tanganyika, but rather, supported Zanzibar's independence.[52]
Likewise, Nyerere's willingness to accept economic support and, increasingly, security assistance, from West Germany among other states including
China and Canada was consistent with his policy of nonalignment. For their
part, West German representatives in Dar es Salaam were also more toler-
ant of nonexclusive security arrangements than their East German counterparts on Zanzibar. Arguably, socialism and internationalism formed two of
a plethora of anti-imperial touchstones for both the Nyerere and Karume
governments, but the governments applied their convictions to securitization
through differing forms of alliance and collaboration.[53]

On Zanzibar, Karume increasingly fanned ethnic nationalist sentiment as
a means of operationalizing his anti-imperial credentials and ultimately jus-
tifying not only revolutionary but also authoritarian policies. Nadra Hashim
explained that this resulted in many of Karume's senior ministers in the governing Afro-Shirazi Party courting other allies, particularly China.[54] Karume's
cabinet shared a well-founded fear that East Germany was complicit in
Karume's effort to strengthen his power base by establishing a capable,
personally loyal internal security service.[55] Meanwhile, the Stasi were left
attempting to secure a government that was openly "divided by contradictory
goals and interests" and skeptical of East German involvement altogether.[56]

Disunity in the Karume government was exacerbated by the formation of
the United Republic of Tanzania from the territories of Zanzibar and Tanganyika on April 26, 1964. Although little changed in relations with Dar es
Salaam until the transfer of powers in October 1964, states with diplomatic
and security interests in Tanganyika increasingly sought to influence Zanzibar as well. China, in particular, acted with calculated largesse and speed to
provide financial aid to Zanzibar after negotiations with Rashidi Kawawa,
the second vice president of Tanganyika and a political rival of Karume.[57]
By June 1964, $16 million were shared between Zanzibar and Tanganyika.[58]
This contribution was seen by many in both the Karume and Nyerere governments as preferable to East German and West German material support,
respectively.[59] Indeed, a Stasi analyst observed on April 21, 1964, that "the
government of Zanzibar [seemed to] measure states which prove their willingness to help less by words than by deeds," especially financial support.[60]

Chinese financial support for the Nyerere government flowed more freely
after unification as the diplomatic heart of the new state—namely, Dar es
Salaam rather than Stone Town in Zanzibar—became the focal point for

China's thrust into East Africa. Beijing loaned the Nyerere government an additional $28 million in June 1964, and this was quickly followed by a $70 million trade agreement that was in effect from 1965 to 1969.[61] China also competed with the Soviet Union to provide military support to Tanzania, in the form of mortars and field and air defense guns as well as twenty armored personnel carriers.[62] West Germany responded to Chinese and Soviet overtures in mainland Tanzania with a policy of accommodation and continued to build educational institutions and provide material support for industry and military training to the Tanzanian Air Force.[63] This response was mirrored by the ninety-person Canadian military training mission and aimed to preserve the existing Western presence in Dar es Salaam rather than directly compete with Nyerere's new suitors.[64]

In May 1964, Chinese arms and advisors arrived on Zanzibar in what was fast becoming a micro arms race, reflective of the Sino-Soviet split.[65] The CIA observed that "Chinese, Soviet, and East German representatives were reported to be bearing gifts to government officials, with whom they kept in close touch" in the months immediately following the revolution.[66] These gifts not only included rifles and ammunition, but an AN-2 Colt biplane and a *Solidaritätssendung*, or "solidarity shipment" of small arms and a fifty-foot patrol boat from East Germany.[67] Meanwhile, the author of the Stasi report of April 21, 1964, found Chinese ideological influence in Zanzibar to be "striking," observing that "the foreign minister of the Republic of Zanzibar, [Abdulrahman Mohamed] Babu, has an extensive collection of the writings of Mao Tse Sung [*sic*], but no writings of the classics of Marxism-Leninism."[68] This observation is corroborated by the CIA report for February 21, 1966, which contended that "the Chinese were at the forefront in this aspect of the bloc propaganda campaign. Chinese propaganda was evident everywhere—in hospitals, in the schools, in government offices."[69]

In contrast to China's assertive approach in Zanzibar, Western powers did not develop a unified policy response or initially destabilize the island, as East Berlin had feared, despite a consolidated effort by West Germany to cement its influence in Dar es Salaam. The Stasi report of April 21, 1964, concluded that "there are no strong efforts on the part of the West German government or certain [Western] monopoly groups to gain influence in Zanzibar," in part due to Karume's closure of the West German embassy earlier that year.[70] The CIA internal review of the revolution in Zanzibar corroborated the Stasi's earlier assessment of the situation.[71] It noted that "while the West stalled on recognition and further alienated Karume and the other pro-Western elements in Zanzibar by interpreting the revolution as Communist, the Soviets and Chinese moved quickly to win Zanzibar's favor."[72] Indeed, the Soviet Union and China "applauded the revolution, hastened to extend recognition to the new government, and offered to support it with arms and economic assistance."[73]

This effort was underpinned by the work of the Stasi to "strengthen the radical, pro-Communist elements in the government," like Karume.[74]

Concurrent with these developments were the tensions arising from the administrative changes brought about by unification. When the transfer of powers was completed on October 29, 1964, Karume became vice president of Tanzania and retained a legislature that could enact internal reforms for Zanzibar.[75] Zanzibar officially ceded control of diplomacy and external security matters to the Tanzanian government in Dar es Salaam. Moreover, the now Tanzanian president, Julius Nyerere, opposed collaboration with East Germany and demanded that Karume close the East German embassy on Zanzibar.[76] Stasi officers in Zanzibar emphasized this point to East Berlin, reporting that: The "union [Nyerere] government only [recognized] the West German Federal Republic as the sole representative of Germany and [did] not maintain any official connections with the East German embassy in Zanzibar."[77] West Germany echoed Nyerere's demand in an effort to maintain the integrity of the Hallstein Doctrine as an "effective warning signal" to other African states of the costs of recognizing East Berlin.[78] Hubertus Büschel largely attributed Bonn's position, a position opposed by the West German development experts initially dispatched to Tanzania, to the influence of the hawkish BND detachment in the West German embassy in Dar es Salaam.[79] He suggested that the BND understood Bonn's influence in Tanzania (both mainland and Zanzibar) in terms of a zero-sum game with East Germany and were consequently quick to oppose any measure that could be perceived as a concession.

Karume countered Nyerere's apparent allegiance to Bonn by signing a *Treaty of Friendship, Mutual Assistance and Increased Cooperation* with East Germany ostensibly on behalf of a united Tanzania on May 17, 1964, and in early 1965, an East German trade mission opened in Dar es Salaam. A consulate in Zanzibar was also retained.[80] This placed the West German foreign minister, Gerhard Schröder, in the unenviable position of having to uphold the Hallstein Doctrine by restricting engagement with Tanzania in the knowledge that China, among other states, was actively pursuing a relationship with Nyerere. Schröder ultimately responded to Nyerere's concessions to Karume and, by extension, East Germany, much as the BND had advised, by threatening to withdraw West German trainers seconded to the Tanzanian Air Force and 40 million Deutschmarks worth of military and security assistance in the hope that Nyerere would choose between the Germanies in the West's favor.[81] However, Nyerere called Schröder's bluff, and in February 1965, demanded the immediate withdrawal of all West German security personnel from Tanzania. While Schröder's threat reflects the BND's insistence on preserving the Hallstein Doctrine, the incident, and particularly Nyerere's rejection of the German ultimatum, highlights how little the BND understood of the Tanzanian commitment to nonalignment and anti-colonialism.

Infighting between Nyerere and Karume not only animated the proxy conflict between the Germanies in East Africa, but produced an awkward ideological disconnect in the newly unified Tanzanian security apparatus. Its representatives on Zanzibar were trained by the Stasi and loyal to Karume's revolution, while officers on the mainland were conditioned into nonalignment having learned their craft under British, West German, and later Canadian and Chinese instruction.[82] This disconnect was particularly concerning for East Germany, given its investment in Zanzibar's security services. North Atlantic Treaty Organization (NATO) assessments of Tanzanian unification, stolen by Stasi sources in West Germany, reveal that in early 1965, the Stasi were attempting to predict whether Karume would join Nyerere in advocating for nonalignment. The Stasi believed that as long as Karume's loyalties lay with East Germany, East Germany could use the fact that Nyerere was "counting on the personal support of Karume" for the stability of Tanzania's government to influence the mainland, even in the absence of an embassy.[83]

NATO, and particularly West Germany, was concerned by the prospect of Karume adopting a policy of nonalignment and playing a larger role in politics on the mainland. Nyerere's Western partners were skeptical that the "excesses of the revolutionary regime of Zanzibar," and particularly Karume's security apparatus, could be reconciled with Nyerere's effort to "consolidate the Union, by means of the talks and cautioning against the use of force."[84] Instead, NATO sought to "urge the Government of Tanzania to face the dangers that could result for the union from the revolutionary tactics pursued by the communists."[85] Bonn unsurprisingly echoed these calls, warning that "the politically charged situation on [Zanzibar] and the threat of communist infiltration require particular attention."[86] As Ian Speller described, West Germany increasingly saw Zanzibar as an "African Cuba" that threatened West German interests on the mainland and invited Soviet-aligned states and China to expand and ultimately monopolize influence in Tanzania.[87]

The East German intelligence community recognized the intensification of the contest for influence on the mainland. Particular emphasis was placed on the rivalry with West Germany in a report from the Stasi Main Intelligence Directorate (HVA) written in February 1965. The report cited "internal Tanganyika [mainland] documents" secretly obtained by West Germany, and then copied by HVA assets in Bonn, which "assessed the outcome of the trip by Vice-President Kawawa and other ministers to the Soviet Union, Czechoslovakia and Poland as 'extremely disappointing.'"[88] This document is significant because it foregrounds ironic circulations of intelligence through Tanzania: namely, East Germany exploiting West German espionage against its purported ally, Tanzania, to steal a classified Tanzanian report on East Germany's own allies and highlights the fraught environment in which intelligence collaboration took place. William Gray argued that "the struggle over

Zanzibar reveals just how intense the competition between the rival German states had become" as a result of Tanzania's postcolonial and increasingly global context.[89] As Tanzania left the British imperial fold, it became a more fertile site for Cold War rivalries to play out. This generated a range of new opportunities and challenges for the Nyerere and Karume governments as they engaged in securitization activities, not to mention the East German and West German intelligence services.

It was in the context of these escalating Cold War rivalries that the West German government quickly celebrated the "extremely disappointing" experience had by Julius Nyerere's representatives during their travels in socialist Eastern Europe. For Bonn, discrediting socialism in the eyes of Nyerere was the first step in undermining Karume; expelling East German representatives from Zanzibar; and thus, diminishing Soviet influence in the united state.[90] However, the East German intelligence service came to quite a different conclusion regarding their position on the mainland.[91] Unlike Bonn, the HVA argued:

> East Germany is in a favorable situation in Tanzania. With a fraction of the effort in Zanzibar, [East Germany] had a more significant influence on Tanzania than the Federal Republic [West Germany]. . . . The influence of Zanzibar on Tanganyika [the mainland] is constantly growing. In essence, the Union is not effective. . . . It must therefore be countenanced that sooner or later the developments in Zanzibar will be carried through throughout Tanzania. . . . In order to preserve West German positions in Tanzania, the Federal Government would have to make increased use of a policy of blackmail and continue to insist on the closure of the East German consulate general.[92]

The HVA assessed that the Stasi had effectively implemented East German diplomatic objectives in Zanzibar, alone and through collaboration with Karume, such that the government of Zanzibar had acted as East Germany's proxy representative to the Nyerere government. This process had diplomatically wedged West Germany between, on the one hand, Bonn's stated commitment to the Hallstein Doctrine and, on the other hand, Nyerere's commitment to nonalignment.[93] Consequently, West Germany overplayed their hand by threatening to terminate support for Tanzania in February 1965 and provoked Nyerere into ending security collaboration with West Germany. As Young-Sun Hong noted, Bonn's intransigence over the diplomatic recognition of East Germany, driven by the BND, was an effective West German tool for blunting the efforts of East Berlin and the Stasi in other parts of Africa, but it met with limited success in Tanzania.[94]

West Germany struggled to contain the influence of China in Tanzania, which increased exponentially during the late 1960s and early 1970s. For example, in one East German analysis, from September 1967, the author warned of China's growing ideological footprint in Tanzania, arguing that the "Chinese associate their military subjects with political lessons. They distribute Mao's writings (in the local language) and Mao badges. In the army camps, they also introduce Chinese films."[95] A similar report produced by the BND in May 1971 noted changes in the kind of investments made by China in mainland Tanzania. In particular, the author cited the construction of a Chinese missile observation and tracking station in Tanzania as evidence of the increased assertiveness in the region.[96] Meanwhile, the CIA interpreted China's actions as a deliberate effort to dislodge West Germany from Dar es Salaam while exposing "the Soviet Union [and its allies] before the 'revolutionaries' of the world" as a hegemon in order that China might form a compelling nonaligned alternative to the major Cold War blocs.[97]

By the late 1960s, Bonn was relatively limited in its ability to respond to the BND's concerns over China's growing interest in Dar es Salaam, given that the West German mission in Tanzania was no longer providing security assistance to the Nyerere government. This isolation even prompted Bonn to explore the possibility of establishing diplomatic relations with the Karume government on Zanzibar to retain a modicum of influence in East Africa.[98] However, recently declassified documents from East German sources on the mainland, held by the Stasi Records Agency, suggest that Bonn may have overestimated the diplomatic consequences of the 1965 ultimatum. The East German intelligence report from June 20, 1968, argued that "most of the members of the Unions [Nyerere] Government feel more strongly bound to the capitalist than to the socialist states," and cooperation with socialist states was contingent on it not leading "to any complications with Western states, particularly West Germany."[99] It was in this context that a rapprochement of sorts occurred between Bonn and Nyerere in the early 1970s, with West Germany restoring its support of medical and educational institutions in Dar es Salaam and once again accepting Tanzanian graduates into West German higher educational institutions.[100] However, China remained the primary provider of security and intelligence support to Tanzania.

Where Bonn was hamstrung in its response to the growth of Chinese influence in Tanzania, East Germany met the challenge much as it had confronted West German opposition to its presence in Dar es Salaam in 1964 and 1965. According to an HVA report from December 10, 1968, the Stasi mission in Zanzibar entreated Karume to request that East Germany be given "full diplomatic recognition by his [Nyerere's] government" despite the fact that this would once again put Nyerere "in an unpleasant position in relation to Bonn."[101] This would not only give East Germany a stronger foothold on the mainland from which to ward off Chinese influence but also had the potential to provoke further "cooling off of [Tanzanian] relations with Bonn."[102] A second report from July 15, 1969, issued a timely warning about China's growing influence because shortly after its publication, China extended a

$400 million loan to Tanzania along with an offer of material support for the construction of the Tanzania-Zambia railway.[103] By all accounts, it was these ongoing infusions of Chinese funding from 1970, far beyond anything East Germany could match, in combination with renewed interest in Zanzibar by the United States, that caused East Germany to waver in its commitment to the island and Tanzania's security.[104] However, it was ultimately the Zanzibari government itself that ended collaboration with East Berlin. On April 7, 1972, East Germany's staunchest ally, Abeid Karume, was assassinated, and his replacement Aboud Jumbe openly favored economic and security collaboration with China over East Germany. The gunfire that shattered Karume's quiet evening of cards and bitter coffee in the white-walled headquarters of the Afro-Shirazi Party also brought to an end East Germany's special relationship with Zanzibar.

CONCLUSION

Intelligence and security relations between Tanzania, its dependencies, and external supporters were fraught during the early postcolonial period from 1962 until the early 1970s. On the mainland, West Germany struggled to establish itself as an effective ally of the Nyerere government in the security sphere despite extensive economic and diplomatic investments in Tanganyika from 1962 to 1964. The BND was held at arm's length such that even at the height of East German efforts to develop a presence on the mainland in 1964 and 1965, the West German security service was restricted to supporting Bonn's military training mission. Consequently, the BND's influence on governance structures and training of TANU recruits to the Security Service was limited, and the organization never held sway over Tanzanian intelligence priorities to the extent that the East German Stasi did in Zanzibar.[105] The lack of meaningful intelligence collaboration between the states can arguably be traced to Bonn's failure to account for British colonial legacies not only in the security services, but also in Nyerere's framework for understanding Tanzania's place in the Cold War. Policies of nonalignment, Africanization, and decolonization were incompatible with the "Hallstein ultimatum" of 1965. Far from cementing West German influence in the Tanzanian intelligence community, the doctrine proved surprisingly susceptible to manipulation by Zanzibar's "silent partner," East Germany, and ultimately soured relations between Dar es Salaam and Bonn. This created space for the deepening of Sino-Tanzanian security relations and, despite renewed West German engagement with Nyerere in the 1970s, China remains a key stakeholder in the country today.

Meanwhile on Zanzibar, the relationship between the Stasi and the Karume government was intense and extensive, encompassing political, economic, and security concerns. From the Stasi's perspective, it maintained a symbiotic partnership with Karume throughout the second half of the 1960s, where the *modus operandi* was exchanging military aid and Stasi trainers for the advancement of East German interests. These trainers embedded the Stasi's approach to intelligence in the priorities and processes of Zanzibar's security apparatus even after union with Tanganyika had forced East Germany into a subsidiary role as a quasi-legitimate ally.[106] However, the East German approach differed from Joseph Stalin's effort to replicate vassal services across Eastern Europe in the 1950s in that Stasi principles, which were originally copied from the Committee for State Security (KGB), were adapted in Zanzibar to suit local bureaucratic structures, concerns, and conditions.[107] Additionally, the Stasi's involvement in Zanzibar changed the dominant narrative within the East German organization on the objectives of intelligence sharing and cooperation. Where West Germany used intelligence activities to support diplomacy in Tanzania, East Germany increasingly superimposed formal diplomatic relations over existing collaboration such that intelligence ties predated, anticipated, and facilitated wider engagement, rather than being a consequence of it.[108] Thus, while the "aid and trade" narratives that dominate histories of decolonization in East Africa resonate with West Germany's entrance into Tanganyika, they are far from representative of East German engagement with Zanzibar.

The international history of intelligence collaboration in Tanzania's early postcolonial period helps reassess the significance of security partnerships, both in terms of their role in facilitating transitional governance and as a metric of institutional decolonization. In the space of a decade, Tanzania exited the British Empire, became a divided territory in need of assistance from abroad, and finally formed a united postcolonial state negotiating the internationalization of domestic political fissures as a part of the wider Cold War conflict. British attempts to instill a so-called Commonwealth security culture in the police Special Branch at the point of independence failed primarily as a result of Julius Nyerere's unswerving commitment to a model of transitional governance defined by nonalignment and decolonization. This model welcomed Israeli, West German, Canadian, and Chinese support, but left little room for collaboration with the former colonial power. The failure was then compounded when Abeid Karume instigated the Zanzibar Revolution and sought out East German support of an explicitly anti-imperial and ethno-nationalist political program. Indeed, the formative years of the Tanzanian security apparatus on both the mainland and in Zanzibar were arguably defined by a reaction against colonial legacies, first against Britain in 1961 on

Tanganyika and 1964 in Zanzibar, then again against West Germany in 1965 when Bonn attempted to draw Nyerere in its tussle with East Berlin by invoking the Hallstein Doctrine. These incidents also highlight how postcolonial intelligence collaboration not only entailed breaking with the colonial power but also colonial practices that saw the imperial metropole's disputes played out on the imperial periphery and at its expense.

Nyerere and Karume's anti-colonial commitment did not prevent them from appropriating the imperial powers' strategies to ensure that security collaboration served their objectives. Rather than risking their revolutionary credentials, both leaders solidified them by successfully leveraging inter-German rivalries prior to unification not only to develop indigenous intelligence capacities on either side of the Zanzibar Channel, but also to bolster their own claims to the leadership of a united Tanzania. In Zanzibar, securitization flowed out of alliance with East Germany, whereas in Tanganyika it was increasingly shaped as a reaction against West German interventions. After unification, a similar pattern is evident in the emerging Cold War triangulation centered on Dar es Salaam. Leading figures in the Tanzanian government played representatives of the Western and Soviet blocs and the People's Republic of China off one another to preserve nonalignment and extract maximum financial and material support for security institutions. Nyerere and Karume and their deputies derived considerable agency from the intense ideological competition over Tanzania and used this to catalyze a calculated reversal of colonial roles through their formation and dissolution of security and intelligence partnerships.

NOTES

1. I am thankful for the Stasi Records Agency (BStU), Berlin, for providing access to key sources. Additionally, the support and advice of Professor Glenda Sluga of the Laureate Program for International History at the University of Sydney was invaluable in developing the final manuscript.

2. Jens Gieseke, *Die hauptamtlichen Mitarbeiter der Staatssicherheit: Person alstruktur und Lebenswelt 1950–1989/90* (Berlin: Christoph Links Verlag, 2010), 100; Walter Süß and Siegfried Suckut, eds., *Staatspartei und Staatssicherheit Zum Verhältnis von SED und MfS* (Berlin: Christoph Links Verlag, 1997); Daniela Münkel, *Staatssicherheit Ein Lesebuch zur DDR-Geheimpolizei* (Berlin: BStU, 2015).

3. Odd Arne Westad, *The Global Cold War: Third World Interventions and the Making of Our Times* (Cambridge: Cambridge University Press, 2007), 73–109; Gareth Winrow, *The Foreign Policy of the GDR in Africa* (Cambridge: Cambridge University Press, 1990), 176; Siegfried Schulz, "Features and Trends of East Germany's Aid and Trade with the Third World," in Marie Lavigne, ed., *The Soviet Union and Eastern*

Europe in the Global Economy (Cambridge: Cambridge University Press, 1992), 86–102; Ulrich van der Heyden, *GDR Development Policy in Africa: Doctrine and Strategies Between Illusions and Reality, 1960–1990* (Vienna: LIT Verlag GmbH & Co. KG, 2013), 38; Ludger Wimmelbücker, "Architecture and city planning projects of the German Democratic Republic in Zanzibar," *Journal of Architecture* 17, no. 3 (2012): 407–32.

4. Christopher Andrew and Vasili Mitrokhin, *The World was Going our Way: The KGB and the Battle for the Third World* (New York: Basic Books, 2005); Radoslav Yordanov, *The Soviet Union and the Horn of Africa during the Cold War: Between Ideology and Pragmatism* (Lanham: Lexington Books, 2016); Joseph Sassoon, "The East German Ministry of State Security and Iraq, 1968–1989," *Journal of Cold War Studies* 14, no. 1 (2014): 4–23.

5. For a broader discussions of the role of intelligence in the Cold War see: Michael Herman, "Intelligence Threats as Reassurance," in *Intelligence in the Cold War: What Difference Did It Make?* eds. Michael Herman and Gwilym Hughes (London: Routledge, 2013); Richard Aldrich, "Intelligence," in *Palgrave Advances in Cold War History*, eds. Saki Dockrill and Geraint Hughes (Basingstoke: Palgrave Macmillan, 2006), 21.

6. The Hallstein Doctrine was a policy of "aggressive non-recognition" pursued by West Germany from 1955 that made diplomatic relations with Bonn contingent on non-recognition of East Germany. *Ostpolitik* replaced this approach upon the signing of the Basic Treaty between the two Germanies in 1972. See: Agnes Bresselau von Bressensdorf and Elke Seefried, "Introduction," in *West Germany and the Global South in the Cold War Era*, eds. Agnes Bresselau von Bressensdorf, Elke Seefried, and Christian Ostermann (Berlin: Walter de Gruyter GmbH, 2017), 7–24. For additional information, see: Britta Schilling, *Postcolonial Germany: Memories of Empire in a Decolonized Nation* (Oxford: Oxford University Press, 2014), 122; William Gray, *Germany's Cold War: The Global Campaign to Isolate East Germany, 1949–1969* (Chapel Hill: University of North Carolina Press, 2003), 156.

7. Joachim Krüger and Hermann Schwiesau, "Zeittafel Außenpolitik der DDR," in Siegfried Bock, Ingrid Muth and Hermann Schwiesau, eds., *DDR-Außenpolitik Ein Überblick: Daten, Fakten, Personen* (Münster: LIT Verlag, 2010), 132 and Timothy Parsons, *The 1964 Army Mutinies and the Making of Modern East Africa* (Westport: Greenwood Publishing, 2003), 106.

8. Parsons, *The 1964 Army Mutinies*, 107; "*ZANZIBAR: Death at Sunset*," *Time* 99, April 17, 1972.

9. *Wirtschaftswunder* (lit: economic miracle) was a term used to refer to the rapid economic recovery and rebuilding of West Germany following the Second World War. See: Armin Grünbacher, *West German Industrialists and the Making of the Economic Miracle: A History of Mentality and Recovery* (London: Bloomsbury Academic, 2017) and Hanna Schissler (ed.), *The Miracle Years: A Cultural History of West Germany, 1949–1968* (Princeton: Princeton University Press, 2001).

10. Krüger and Schwiesau, "Zeittafel Außenpolitik der DDR," 133.

11. Ibid.

12. Markus Wolf and Anne McElvoy (ed.), *Man Without a Face: The Autobiography of Communism's Greatest Spymaster* (New York: Public Affairs, 1997), 280.

13. Schilling, 115.

14. Ibid.

15. Ibid., 117.

16. Roy Pateman, "Intelligence Agencies in Africa: A Preliminary Assessment," *Journal of Modern African Studies* 30, no. 4 (1992): 571.

17. Hubertus Büschel, *Hilfe zur Selbsthilfe: Deutsche Entwicklungsarbeit in Afrika 1960–1975* (Frankfurt am Main: Campus Verlag, 2014), 59.

18. Schilling, 117.

19. Ibid.

20. Wolf and McElvoy (ed.), 281.

21. Der Bundesbeauftragte für die Stasi-Unterlagen (BStU), "Informationsbericht über die Durchführung einer Sonderaufgabe der Regierung der DDR durch Angehörige des Ministeriums für Nationale Verteidigung in der Republik Sansibar und Pemba," MfS, HAI, Nr. 17493, April 21, 1964, 247, Wolf and McElvoy (ed.), *Man Without a Face*, 285 and Ralf Blum and Philipp Springer, "Aufstieg und Fall eines Umfehlbaren,' Der Leiter Oberst Roland Leipold und die Nachkriegsgeneration im MfS," in *Das Gedächtnis der Staatssicherheit: Die Kartei- und Archivabteilung des MfS*, eds. Karsten Jedlitschka and Philipp Springer (Göttingen: Vandenhoeck & Ruprecht GmbH, 2015), 318.

22. BStU, MfS, HAI, Nr. 17493, April 21, 1964, 247, Paul Bjerk, *Building a Peaceful Nation: Julius Nyerere and the Establishment of Sovereignty in Tanzania, 1960–1964* (Rochester: University of Rochester Press, 2015), 324 and Hermann Wentker, *Außenpolitik in engen Grenzen: Die DDR im internationalen System 1949–1989. Veröffentlichungen zur SBZ-/DDR-Forschung im Institut für Zeitgeschichte* (Munich: R. Oldenbourg Verlag, 2007), 296.

23. Klaus Storkmann, *Geheime Solidarität: Militärbeziehungen und Militärhilfen der DDR in die "Dritte Welt"* (Berlin: Christoph Links Verlag, 2012), 141.

24. Ibid., 568.

25. BStU, MfS, HAI, Nr. 17493, April 21, 1964, 246–47, Wolf and McElvoy (ed.), 283 and Roman Loimeier, *Between Social Skills and Marketable Skills: The Politics of Islamic Education in 20th Century Zanzibar* (Leiden: Koninklijke Brill NV, 2009), 466.

26. Directorate of Intelligence, *Intelligence Study: Zanzibar: The Hundred Days Revolution* (Langley: Central Intelligence Agency, 1966), 92, https://www.cia.gov/library/readingroom/docs/esau-28.pdf.

27. Ibid.

28. BStU, MfS, HAI, Nr. 17493, April 21, 1964, 246–47, Wolf and McElvoy, ed., 283 and Loimeier, 466.

29. Hans-Georg Schleicher, 'GDR solidarity: The German Democratic Republic and the South African liberation struggle', *Road to Democracy* 3, no. 2 (2008): 1071.

30. Young-sun Hong, *Cold War Germany, the Third World, and the Global Humanitarian Regime* (New York: Cambridge University Press, 2015), 147.

31. Schleicher, 1071.

32. Amrit Wilson, *The Threat of Liberation: Imperialism and Revolution in Zanzibar* (London: Pluto Press, 2013), 56.

33. Hong, *Cold War Germany*, 146.

34. Ibid.

35. Mohammed Ali Bakari, *The Democratisation Process in Zanzibar: A Retarded Transition* (Hamburg: Institut für Afrika-Kunde, 2001), 109.

36. Directorate of Intelligence, *Intelligence Study*, 92.

37. Carey Singleton, *The Agricultural Economy of Tanganyika* (Washington, DC: Regional Analysis Division— The Department of Agriculture, 1964), 52.

38. Ibid., 47–48.

39. Thomas Maguire and Hannah Franklin, "Creating a Commonwealth Security Culture? State-Building and the International Politics of Security Assistance in Tanzania," *The International History Review* (2020), 3.

40. Ibid., 7–8.

41. Ibid., 17.

42. Ibid.

43. Ibid., 3, 9.

44. Ibid., 17.

45. John Copper, *China's Foreign Investment and Diplomacy*, vol. 3 (Basingstoke: Palgrave Macmillan, 2016), 36.

46. Ibid.

47. Ibid., 37.

48. It is worth noting that the imperial history of Zanzibar differs from that of Tanganyika in that it did not fall under the rule of Imperial Germany. The island was retained by Britain under the Heligoland–Zanzibar Treaty of 1890. Thus, Karume could look to East Germany without the risk of compromising his anti-colonial credentials. See: James Olson (ed.), *Historical Dictionary of European Imperialism* (New York: Greenwood Press, 1991), 279; Elizabeth Schmidt, *Foreign Intervention in Africa: From the Cold War to the War on Terror* (Cambridge: Cambridge University Press, 2013), 24.

49. Hong, *Cold War Germany*, 36; Winrow, *The Foreign Policy of the GDR in Africa*, 65–68.

50. Directorate of Intelligence, *Intelligence Memorandum: Strains in Soviet-East German Relations: 1962–1967* (Langley: Central Intelligence Agency, 1967), 88. https://www.cia.gov/library/readingroom/docs/caesar-42.pdf.

51. Ibid., 92.

52. Julius Nyerere, "The Second Scramble," in *Freedom and unity: Uhuru na umoja: A Selection from Writings and Speeches, 1952–65* (Oxford: Oxford University Press, 1967), 204–12.

53. BStU, MfS, HAI, Nr. 17493, April 21, 1964, 251.

54. Nadra Hashim, *Language and Collective Mobilization: The Story of Zanzibar* (New York: Lexington Books, 2009), 207.

55. Ibid.

56. Jens Gieseke trans. David Burnett, *The History of the Stasi: East Germany's Secret Police, 1945–1990* (New York: Berghahn Books, 2014), 181; Jens Gieseke, *Die Mielke-Konzern: die Geschichte der Stasi, 1945–1990* (Munich: Deutsche Verlags-Anstalt, 2006), 209–15; Wolf and McElvoy (ed.), *Man without a Face*, 283.

57. Alaba Ogunsanwo, *China's Policy in Africa, 1958–71* (Cambridge: Cambridge University Press, 1974), 137.

58. Ibid.

59. Helen-Louise Hunter, *Zanzibar: The Hundred Days Revolution* (Santa Barbara: Praeger Security International, 2010), 10; Ogunsanwo, 137.

60. BStU, MfS, HAI, Nr. 17493, April 21, 1964, 251.

61. Alicia Altorfer-Ong, *Old Comrades and New Brothers: A Historical Re-Examination of the Sino-Zanzibari and Sino-Tanzanian Bilateral Relationships in the 1960s* [Thesis], Department of International History, London School of Economics, 2014, 128.

62. Altorfer-Ong, 172.

63. Schilling, 118.

64. Altorfer-Ong, 182.

65. Ibid.

66. Directorate of Intelligence, *Intelligence Study*, 84–93 and BStU, MfS, HAI, Nr. 17493, April 21, 1964, 247. https://www.cia.gov/library/readingroom/docs/esau-28.pdf.

67. Schilling, 121 and Hunter, 80.

68. BStU, MfS, HAI, Nr. 17493, April 21, 1964, 247.

69. Ibid.

70. Ibid.

71. Ibid.

72. Ibid.

73. Ibid.

74. Ibid.

75. S. Akweenda, *International Law and the Protection of Namibia's Territorial Integrity: Boundaries and Territorial Claims* (The Hague: Kluwer Law International, 1997), 38 and Godfrey Mwakikagile, *The Union of Tanganyika and Zanzibar: Formation of Tanzania and its Challenges* (Dar es Salaam: New Africa Press, 2016), 323.

76. Paul Bjerk, *Julius Nyerere and the Establishment of Sovereignty in Tanganyika* [thesis], University of Wisconsin-Madison, 2008, 270, Schilling, *Postcolonial Germany*, 122 and Nyerere, *Freedom and unity*.

77. BStU, "Einzel-Information über [title illegible]," MfS, HVA, Nr. 209, February 6, 1965, 133–34.

78. Büschel, *Hilfe zur Selbsthilfe*, 59.

79. Ibid.

80. Winrow, 65–67.

81. Altorfer-Ong, 173.

82. BStU, "Stellungnahme zum Schreiben des Ministers für Nationale Verteidigung, Genossen Armeegeneral Hoffmann, an das Mitglied des Politbüros und Sekretär des

Nationalen Verteidigungsrates, Genossen Erich Honecker, vom 20.2.1969," MfS, HAXVIII, Nr. 8369, February 28, 1969, 59.

83. Hashim, *Language and Collective Mobilization*, 207 and BStU, MfS, HVA, Nr. 209, February 6, 1965, 132–33.

84. Ibid.

85. Ibid., 136.

86. "AA B68/259, Vermerk betr. Unabhängigkeit von Sansibar, June 5, 1963," in Schilling, *Postcolonial Germany*, 121.

87. Ian Speller, "An African Cuba? Britain and the Zanzibar Revolution, 1964," *Journal of Imperial and Commonwealth History* 35. no. 2 (2007): 284; BStU, MfS, HVA, Nr. 209, February 6 1965, 133.

88. BStU, MfS, HVA, Nr. 209, February 6, 1965, 134.

89. Gray, 161.

90. Ibid., 156.

91. Schilling, 121; BStU, "Auskunft über die Wirtschaftspolitik und einige andere Maßnahmen der westdeutschen Bundesrepublik in den Ländern Schwarzafrikas," MfS, HVA, Nr. 267, 1966, 70.

92. Ibid.

93. Storkmann, *Geheime Solidarität*, 138–149 and Hannfried von Hindenburg, *Demonstrating Reconciliation: State and Society in West German Foreign Policy toward Israel, 1952–1965* (New York: Berghahn Books, 2007), 23.

94. Young-Sun Hong, "'The Benefits of Health Must Spread Among All' International Solidarity, Health and Race in the East German Encounter with the Third World," in *Socialist Modern: East German Everyday Culture and Politics*, eds. Katherine Pence and Paul Betts (Ann Arbor: University of Michigan Press, 2008), 186.

95. BStU, MfS, HVA, Nr. 228 1/2, September 29, 1967, 22, BStU, MfS, HVA, Nr. 231, December 15, 1967, 140 and BStU, "Einzel-Information über einige außen und innenpolitische Probleme Tansanias," MfS, HVA, Nr. 139, December 10, 1968, 248.

96. Erich Schmidt-Eenboom, *Geheimdienst, Politik und Medien: Meinungsmache Undercover* (Werder an der Havel: Homilius, 2004), 29.

97. Directorate of Intelligence, *Intelligence Study*, 90.

98. BStU, MfS, HVA, Nr. 131, June 20, 1968, 218–19.

99. BStU, "Einzel-Information über die Haltung Tansanias zur DDR," MfS, HVA, Nr. 131, June 20, 1968, 218–19.

100. Eric Burton, "Navigating Global Socialism: Tanzanian Students in and beyond East Germany," *Cold War History* 19, no. 1 (2019): 77–79.

101. BStU, MfS, HVA, Nr. 139, December 10, 1968, 248.

102. Gray, 160–61 and BStU, MfS, HVA, Nr. 139, December 10, 1968, 248–52.

103. BStU, MfS, HVA, Nr. 147 2/2, July 15, 1969, 327 and Paul Bjerk, *Julius Nyerere* (Athens: Ohio University Press, 2017), 80.

104. Ibid.

105. R. Gerald Hughes and Len Scott, "'Knowledge Is Never too Dear:' Exploring the Intelligence Archives," in *Exploring the Intelligence Archives: Enquiries into*

the Secret State, eds. R. Gerald Hughes, Peter Jackson, and Len Scott (London: Routledge, 2008), 13.

106. Thomas Barnett, *Romanian and East German Policies in the Third World: Comparing the Strategies of Ceauşescu and Honecker* (Santa Barbara: Praeger Security International, 1992), 121.

107. Christopher Andrew and Vasili Mitrokhin, *The Mitrokhin Archive II: The KGB and the World* (London: Allen Lane, 2005), 423–70, Stephen Lee, *European Dictatorships, 1918–1945* (London: Routledge, 2000), 91–92; Alvin Rubenstein, *Moscow's Third World Strategy* (Princeton: Princeton University Press, 1988), 184.

108. A particularly helpful discussion of the uses and limits of intelligence in diplomacy and international relations can be found in: Peter Jackson, "Historical Reflections on the Uses and Limits of Intelligence," in *Intelligence and Statecraft: The Uses and Limits of Intelligence in International Society*, eds. Peter Jackson and Jennifer Siegel (Westport: Praeger, 2005), 11–52. Also see: Krüger and Schwiesau, "Zeittafel Außenpolitik der DDR," 132.

Chapter 3

Soviet Bloc Security Services and the Birth of New Intelligence Communities in Mozambique and Angola

Owen Sirrs

António de Oliveira Salazar's dictatorship ran Portugal and its overseas empire for more than thirty years. One essential key to Salazar's longevity was an intelligence and security apparatus called the *Polícia Internacional e de Defesa do Estado* (PIDE) or the International and State Defense Police. Ironically, for Salazar's African subjects, the PIDE's legacy of extralegal surveillance, indefinite detention, torture, and "disappearances" outlasted the dictator in two of Portugal's former African colonies: Mozambique and Angola. Still, as this chapter argues, it was the Soviet, Cuban, and East German security services that had the greatest impact in shaping the new intelligence communities in both countries.

Unlike many other African states that transitioned to independence with vestiges of the old colonial security apparatus still in place, Mozambique, Angola, and Guinea-Bissau started their new lives with clean slates: the Portuguese civilian, military, and intelligence bureaucracy went home, leaving few traces of their existence behind.[1] In fact, Mozambique and Angola soon developed Leninist dictatorships that included personality cults and the fierce suppression of political dissent. Both created brutal security services with the aid of the Soviet Union's Committee for State Security (KGB) and the East Germany Ministry of State Security (Stasi) and the Cuban *Dirección General de Inteligencia* (DGI). Just as the PIDE aids us in understanding Salazar's three decades of power, so too do the *Serviço Nacional de Segurança Popular* and *Direção de Informação e Segurança de Angola* help explain why Mozambique and Angola effectively remain one-party states today.

This chapter examines the origins and evolution of intelligence communities in Mozambique and Angola. It analyzes primary sources such as memoirs by Mozambican, Soviet, and East German intelligence officers; U.S. State Department cables; press accounts; and published laws in official gazeteers to flesh out the narrative. This chapter draws heavily on Portuguese language documents, although there are also sources in Russian, German, and French. All translations were conducted by the author. The sensitive nature of the subject matter limits the number of available primary documents. For example, the Mozambique and Angola state archives currently are not accessible to scholars, particularly in the national security arena. Another limitation is the lack of primary sources dealing with the Cuban intelligence services.

This chapter is divided into three sections, each of which is organized in chronological order. The first two deal with Mozambique and Angola, respectively. The Portuguese colonial legacy, including the use of security services, is examined first, followed by the clandestine existence of the anti-colonial guerrilla movements. In both cases, the leading parties were influenced by Marxist-Leninist thought, and this laid the foundations for close ties with the security services of the Soviet Union, East Germany, and Cuba. After independence, Mozambique and Angola were afflicted by insurgency, some of which was provoked by excesses in the security services. The final section provides a comparative analysis of Mozambique and Angola's intelligence communities by highlighting how the Soviet, East German, and Cuban services left their mark on the former Portuguese colonies in Africa. Nearly fifty years after independence, Angola and Mozambique remain, essentially, one-party states. Although some security agencies were publicly disbanded or simply changed names, the old repressive apparatus still remains in place.

MOZAMBIQUE'S INTELLIGENCE AND SECURITY COMMUNITY

The *Frente de Libertação de Moçambique* (FRELIMO) was founded in May 1962 and spent most of its pre-independence existence in Dar es Salaam, Tanzania.[2] FRELIMO was an underground party from the beginning since its demands for independence and socialist ideology were incompatible with Portugal's vision of empire. It was shaped and hardened by its decades long underground struggle against Portugal.[3] FRELIMO's first leader, Eduardo Mondlane, described the impact of clandestine politics on the party in this way: "The tight police state drove all political action underground and—partly because of the difficulties and dangers involved—underground activity turned out to be the best school in which to form a body of tough, devoted and radical political workers."[4]

The FRELIMO Security Department, led by future president Joaquim Chissano, handled counterintelligence, leadership security, membership vetting, and detaining or sometimes eliminating dissident party members. It confronted a growing list of enemies ranging from PIDE (which became the

Direcção-Geral de Segurança in 1969) and Rhodesia's Central Intelligence Organisation (CIO) to FRELIMO "dissidents" and rival liberation groups.[5] The security department also functioned as a central repository of intelligence collected from Mozambican students abroad, revolutionary allies like the *Movimento Popular de Libertação de Angola* (MPLA), and sympathizers within the Portuguese political and military establishments.[6] The security department also forged close ties with the Soviet KGB and the East German Stasi residencies in Dar es Salaam, Cairo, and Algiers (for the Stasi's influence in Tanzania, see Graham in this volume). The relationship with Cuba, on the other hand, was marred at first by personality differences, although FRELIMO cadres were later trained by Havana in Cuba and Tanzania. These early connections paid dividends later on when Mozambique created its first security service with Soviet, East German, and Cuban assistance.[7]

At times, the intelligence liaison relationships created their own security problems. According to the Soviet defector, Vasili Mitrokhin, the KGB recruited a contact inside FRELIMO, codenamed TSOM, who happened to be Security Director Joaquim Chissano. In 2016, Chissano admitted to receiving training on intelligence in the Soviet Union but denied being a Soviet "spy." He explained, "Through the KGB we received money. It was not for me, but for FRELIMO—to help us carry out our intelligence and counterintelligence work for the protection of FRELIMO itself and the search for information about the other side."[8] Furthermore, FRELIMO's close ties to the People's Republic of China generated growing unease on the part of its Soviet friends in late 1960s and early 1970s.

FRELIMO's early years were marked by considerable infighting and feuds. After Mondlane was assassinated by a parcel bomb in 1969, a communist-leaning leadership emerged centered on Samora Machel, Marcelino dos Santos, and Chissano. The party also tightened up its internal security, running a "reeducation camp" in Nachingwea, Tanzania, for "dissident" members.[9] An atmosphere of suspicion and disquiet pervaded FRELIMO ranks amid never-ending calls by the leadership to exercise more "vigilance." According to the scholar, Harry West:

> People in the wrong place at the wrong time were falsely accused of espionage. Others were labeled saboteurs for taking too long to deliver a message, for breaking a piece of "military" equipment as simple as a bicycle, or for serving a commander tea that was "too hot."[10]

The precipitating cause of Mozambique's independence was the April 25, 1974 coup in Lisbon. Under the terms of the September 7, 1974, Lusaka Accord negotiated with representatives of the Portuguese junta, FRELIMO joined a transitional government that presided over Mozambique until full independence was granted the following June. The accord did not provide for elections or other public referendums: FRELIMO's "right" to absolute power was assumed by both negotiating parties.[11]

As the countdown to independence began, FRELIMO's relationship with the Soviet Bloc became more overt. In spring 1975, for example, an East German intergovernmental team traveled to Mozambique and conducted a survey of the country's needs. Among their recommendations was the dispatch of about 250 FRELIMO cadres to East Germany for training in running prisons, intelligence and counterintelligence operations, censorship, and even constitution writing.[12] One Stasi officer was impressed by what he saw: "The involved officers of the State Security Ministry—many among them with experience in other countries—encountered a politically experienced, tightly organized FRELIMO leadership."[13] The Stasi's main liaison partner in the transition government was FRELIMO's newly created *Departamento de Defesa/Serviço de Informação* (Defense Department Information Service, DD/SI). In October 1975, the DD/SI merged with FRELIMO's security department to form a new national security service.[14]

When Mozambique received its independence on June 25, 1975, there was no question that FRELIMO was the sole party in charge of the new state. Moreover, FRELIMO's Marxist-Leninist worldview anticipated "resistance from entrenched classes," and its post-independence policies virtually guaranteed that internal dissent would take place. Once in power, FRELIMO embarked on an aggressive program of land reform, property expropriations, population resettlement, press censorship, and a widely publicized assault on religion and "tribalism." Such measures spurred a massive flight of Portuguese technicians, bureaucrats, and merchants as well as a spike in inflation and near-chronic shortages in consumer goods. In the febrile atmosphere generated by FRELIMO's suspicion and paranoia, it was easy for the movement's leadership to ascribe the country's economic collapse to domestic and foreign "enemies."[15]

On October 11, 1975, the government passed a law creating the *Serviço Nacional de Segurança Popular* (People's National Security Service, SNASP). The law stipulated that SNASP would report directly to Samora Machel in his capacity as FRELIMO chairman (as opposed to his role as Mozambique president). It also described SNASP's missions—"detecting, neutralizing and fighting all forms of subversion, sabotage and acts aimed at the organs of popular power" and gave the agency expansive powers in the areas of search, seizure, arrest, and confiscation. In fact, SNASP was exempt from the penal procedure code.[16] According to a U.S. Embassy observer at the time: "Everyone here remembers the Portuguese PIDE and a cursory reading of the SNASP decree shows that a crime is virtually anything SNASP says is a crime."[17]

Not surprisingly, given their pre-independence involvement with FRE-LIMO's security department, the East Germans took the lead role in advising SNASP. According to Markus Wolf, former head of the Stasi's foreign intelligence wing, East Berlin trained more than 1,000 Mozambican security officers in organization and management, counterintelligence, border controls, VIP protection, counter-smuggling and detecting currency forgery, signals intelligence, and communications security.[18] Some Mozambique security officers trained for extended periods at the Stasi's Legal College in Potsdam.[19] For his part, SNASP's first director, Jacinto Veloso later commented that it was the Stasi advisors who pressed hardest for a single security and intelligence service modeled after East Germany's Ministry for State Security. According to Veloso, the result was a "machine that ended up giving us some headaches. A machine with well-armed military personnel, investigators and a lot of logistical and support staff that sometimes found itself in conflict with the armed forces and the police."[20]

Cultural misunderstandings and other "friction" bedeviled the SNASP-Stasi relationship. One East German observer later noted that SNASP had overinflated expectations of what the Stasi could provide in the area of technical intelligence equipment, while East German–trained police dogs did not adapt well to the climate.[21] East German surveillance cameras and listening devices tended to rust in Mozambique's notorious heat and humidity.[22] Consequently, in 1977, SNASP requested that Cuba's *Dirección General de Inteligencia* (DGI) take over some training responsibilities.[23] In fact, a distinctively DGI "imprint" was evident in SNASP's "Luta Contra Bandidos" counterinsurgency program that was centered on the creation of local militias.

From its inception, SNASP was not only at war with domestic enemies, but with the powerful intelligence agencies of South Africa and Rhodesia as well. By vigorously adopting the United Nations embargo on trade with Rhodesia in 1976 and aiding insurgents belonging to the Zimbabwe Africa National Union (ZANU), for example, FRELIMO helped bring about a proxy war that Mozambique could ill afford. In fact, the so-called *Resistência Nacional Moçambicana* (RENAMO), a creation of Rhodesia's Central Intelligence Organisation (CIO) (see Cross in this volume), plagued Mozambique long after Rhodesia became Zimbabwe.[24] When Zimbabwe became independent in 1980, a formal liaison relationship was forged between SNASP and a CIO led by the veteran ZANU security officer (and future Zimbabwe president), Emmerson Mnangagwa.[25]

A more powerful external adversary was South Africa, which exerted political, economic, and military pressure on its weaker neighbor (for South Africa, see O'Brien in this volume). During the early 1980s, Pretoria's military intelligence services maintained a large network of Mozambican spies who provided the intelligence necessary for raids by South African forces inside Mozambique. In 1980 and 1981, when tensions with South Africa were escalating, SNASP kept an anxious eye on the buildup of South African forces across the border. At the same time, acting on the principle that it was wise to keep one's enemies closer, SNASP preserved a discreet back channel with its South African counterparts that would eventually facilitate the 1984 Nkomati nonaggression accord.[26]

Escalating border wars with Rhodesia, the RENAMO insurgency, tensions with South Africa, and FRELIMO's imposition of an ideological straight-jacket on Mozambique spurred the 1980 creation of an East German–style state security ministry with SNASP director Veloso as its first chief. This new ministry assumed direct control over SNASP as well as border security, secret diplomacy, and a new neighborhood watch project called *Vigilância Popular*.[27] Created with Cuban assistance, *Vigilância Popular*'s declared goal was "neutralizing" sabotage and espionage in Mozambican residential areas and factories. A spate of laudatory domestic press articles in the late 1970s spotlighted *Vigilância Popular*'s neo-Stalinist campaign against "indiscipline, incompetence, disorganization and negligence."[28] Workers were enjoined to keep an eye on their colleagues and avoid "sentimentality" when it came to judging those who were not pulling their weight:

> The enemy adopts an attitude of humility when discovered, and there is our tendency at times to be sentimental. Our sentimental decisions lead us to great mistakes and this fact obligates us to ally with the class enemy.[29]

In March 1979, Mozambique's People's Assembly passed the "Law for Crimes against the People and the Popular State." Replete with language like "material sabotage" and "ideological subversion," the legislation codified, defined, and spelled out penalties for "high treason," "incitement," "conspiracy," "terrorism," "sabotage," "forgery," "espionage," and "rebellion." The maximum penalty for some of these crimes, including high treason and assassination attempts against state and party leaders, was death. Furthermore, Article 8 of the law stipulated that

> [e]very citizen has the duty to promptly disclose to the authorities . . . his direct or indirect knowledge of the preparation or execution of a crime . . . his knowl- edge of the perpetrator or perpetrators of a crime . . . any information in his possession which leads to the identification or capture of the perpetrator[s] of a crime against the People's Security and the Popular State.[30]

A good case can be made that harsh policies carried out by agencies like SNASP helped generate public anger against the government and provided another spur to the RENAMO insurgency.[31] In a November 1981 speech, President Machel publicly criticized SNASP and other security organs for "violating revolutionary legality." He said, "In Mozambique, we don't want a secret police . . . we don't need it." Although Machel did not provide specifics, he criticized the agency for sending people to reeducation camps without due process.[32] Several hundred SNASP officers were subsequently dismissed from the service for abusing prisoners.[33]

However, SNASP did not suffer any diminution of its powers. In fact, as the designated watchdog and enforcer of FRELIMO's ideology, SNASP relied heavily on a nationwide network of secret informers. In 1980 Security Minister Veloso revealed that the number of SNASP informers nationwide had exceeded 300,000.[34] This dramatic demonstration of secret police capabilities is even more astonishing when we consider the country's abject poverty and general lack of socioeconomic development. No doubt, Veloso's East German advisors were pleased.

Some insights into SNASP's liaison relationship with the Soviet bloc can be gleaned from a 1981 "spy case" involving the Central Intelligence Agency (CIA). From 1975 until 1981, Mozambique maintained a polite if frigid relationship with the United States despite Washington, DC's uneasiness over Maputo's Soviet bloc ties. In February 1981, this surface cordiality vanished when Mozambique expelled six "CIA agents" who were allegedly spying on Cuban and Soviet military advisors as well as the armed forces. U.S. officials denied the espionage accusations. They also insisted that the expulsions were retaliation for a failed attempt by the Cuban DGI to recruit an American diplomat.[35] The minister for state security, Jacinto Veloso, later wrote that the CIA network had been under surveillance since before Mozambique's independence. By 1980, Cuban DGI and East German Stasi advisors were pressuring him to break up the ring and expel the Americans, but Veloso resisted on the grounds that useful intelligence could be obtained through continued surveillance. Things came to a head in early 1981 when then KGB chief Yuri Andropov urged Machel to act against the Americans. Veloso believed Andropov's motivation had more to do with driving a wedge between Mozambique and the United States than with the actual merits of the case.[36]

In addition to the Stasi and the DGI, the KGB maintained a residency in Maputo and embedded a small advisory team in SNASP.[37] Although the overall tenor of the relationship was good, the KGB was overbearing at times. The Soviets, for example, had long made it clear that they were suspicious of FRELIMO's extensive pre-independence ties to the People's Republic of China. In one case, the head of the KGB liaison team approached the Mozambicans with the alarming news that he had encountered a "Chinese spy" walking the halls of the security ministry. It turned out that this "spy" was a young Mozambique national whose parents had emigrated from China decades before.[38]

Unlike Angola, which deemed it politically expedient to disband its first security service, the *Direção de Informação e Segurança de Angola* (Directorate for Information and Security of Angola) in 1979, SNASP survived under the Mozambican Security Ministry's aegis right up until July 1991 when it too was formally abolished by parliamentary decree. On August 23, 1991, a successor agency called the *Serviço de Informaçao e Segurança do Estado* (State Information and Security Service, SISE), was created to take SNASP's place. While SISE retained its predecessor's direct reporting link to the presidency, it was nonetheless forced to relinquish SNASP's controversial powers of arrest and detention.[39]

Restructuring the security service was part of a broader pattern of democratic change that swept over Mozambique with the end of the Cold War. It was also a vital piece in the October 1992 Rome Peace Agreement between FRELIMO and RENAMO that ended the sixteen-year civil war. One article of that agreement was devoted to SISE and the role it should play in Mozambique's new multiparty democracy. Indeed, the agreement reiterated that SISE's "activities and prerogatives . . . shall be confined to the production of information required by the President of the Republic" and added that "in no way may police functions be assigned to SISE."[40]

Since 1992, Mozambique's peace process has been stressed by the differing goals and objectives of the two signatories. FRELIMO still dominates the country's parliament and presidency after nearly fifty years in power. For its part RENAMO, a secretive and often brutal organization, has seen its election hopes dashed, and frustrated factions within it have returned to insurgency. SISE remains an essential organ of Mozambique's powerful presidency despite calls from parliament for greater legislative controls over the security forces.[41] Still, when measured against the expansive powers of its brutal SNASP predecessor, the fact that parliament is even debating controls over SISE is a promising sign that Mozambique's democracy has made some progress over the last thirty years.

ANGOLA'S INTELLIGENCE AND SECURITY COMMUNITY

By the early 1970s, Angola was the largest and richest of Portugal's remaining colonies. It was the world's fourth largest coffee grower, sixth largest diamond producer, and Africa's third largest oil exporter.[42] Salazar ran Angola in the same manner as he did Mozambique: a Lisbon-centered authoritarian structure that permitted no dissent. The secret police, PIDE, had maintained offices in Luanda since 1957, and it was successful in infiltrating and weakening the nascent nationalist movement.[43] According to historian John

Marcum, the PIDE's powers to "arrest and imprison anyone without charges for consecutive and indefinitely renewable blocks of time" meant that it was "the real core of political power in Angola."[44] In fact, according to Fernando Guimarães, another analyst of Angolan politics, the PIDE was so effective that the Angolan nationalists had to "resort to clandestinity and, subsequently guerrilla warfare."[45] It was in this context of regime repression and underground activism that Marxism became the dominant "political language" of much of the anti-colonial opposition.[46]

Unlike Mozambique and Portuguese Guinea, Angola's insurgency was weak and its effectiveness further diluted by three mutually hostile factions: the *Frente Nacional de Libertação de Angola* (FNLA), the *União Nacional para a Independência Total de Angola* (UNITA), and *Movimento Popular de Libertação de Angola* (MPLA).[47] The MPLA was the strongest of a weak deck. Founded in 1956, it had advantages in organization and ideology that the other two lacked. Many of its leaders had come from a small circle of Luanda mulatto intellectuals who were influenced by Marxism-Leninism thanks to close contacts with the pro-Moscow Portuguese Communist Party.[48]

The MPLA's greatest challenge was geography. After it moved its headquarters from Leopoldville in the former Belgian Congo to Brazzaville in late 1963, the movement had no direct access to the Angolan colony (except for the small Cabinda enclave). This geographical obstacle meant that the MPLA could not maintain guerrilla bases inside Angola for long.[49] Sheer distance also separated the MPLA from its most important foreign sponsors—the Soviet Union, Cuba, and East Germany. Ultimately, however, Moscow and Havana's aid proved decisive in the MPLA's 1975 seizure of power.

Portuguese communists had introduced the KGB to the MPLA leader Agostinho Neto in 1956, but it was not until eight years later, after Neto visited Moscow, that a more formal relationship was established.[50] Still, in the eleven years between 1964 and 1975, when the MPLA captured Luanda, the KGB questioned Neto's effectiveness as a leader, the MPLA's factional tendencies, and the organization's limited military capabilities.[51] These doubts were not assuaged by a 1967 Soviet "fact-finding" mission that toured the MPLA's offices in Tanzania, Zambia, and Congo-Brazzaville. As one of the participants later concluded, Neto "seemed neither warlike nor decisive. He gave no outer sign of how difficult it was to lead and organize a party."[52] Soviet material assistance to the MPLA waxed and waned according to Moscow's assessments of the Angolan situation. Some MPLA cadres, including security personnel, were trained either in the Soviet Union itself or with the aid of Soviet advisors in Congo-Brazzaville. Just as they did in Mozambique, the Soviets subcontracted parts of the Angola project to their East German and Cuban partners.[53]

East German ties to the MPLA dated back to the late 1950s when the *Sozialistische Einheitspartei Deutschlands*, (Socialist Unity Party, SED) hosted student and cultural delegations from Africa, Asia, and Latin America. By the time the MPLA had settled in Brazzaville in the early1960s, the Stasi had established close working ties with the MPLA security department. Further MPLA-Stasi cooperation was hampered by the fact that East Germany did not have diplomatic relations with Congo-Brazzaville, so meetings and training had to take place elsewhere.[54]

Cuba enjoyed a favorable reputation in the MPLA leadership on account of its own recent 1959 revolution and its continued defiance of the United States. According to Lúcio Lara, a stalwart in the MPLA leadership for decades, "We wanted Cuban instructors because of the prestige of the Cuban revolution and because their theory of guerrilla warfare was very close to our own."[55] The MPLA-Cuban link probably was forged in Algiers in 1963, and MPLA cadres certainly trained in Cuba later on.[56] The relationship was cemented when the Cuban *Dirección General de Inteligencia* (DGI) opened an embassy in Brazzaville in 1965 and a Cuban training team was dispatched to work with the Congolese Army and MPLA guerrillas.[57]

Although most of the MPLA's pre-independence existence was spent in friendly African capitals like Brazzaville, Lusaka, and Dar es Salaam, the party's propensity toward factional infighting inclined it toward what one author called a "culture of conspiracy." Fearing infiltration by PIDE, rival insurgent groups, and foreign intelligence services, the MPLA established a security department that was also responsible for vetting the loyalty of party members.[58] Finally, the security department tried to monitor events inside Angola via human intelligence networks.[59] All of this required foreign training and advice, which the Soviet bloc was happy to provide.

From the beginning, Angolan independence was contested by multiple competing insurgencies as well as the conflicting interests of outside powers like Zaire, South Africa, the United States, Cuba, and the Soviet Union. When the Portuguese lowered their flag in Luanda for the last time on November 11, 1975, they left a power vacuum in their wake. The MPLA eventually emerged victorious, but only after a bloody civil war and the assistance of thousands of Cuban soldiers.

Notably, the third law passed by the new Angolan government on November 29, 1975, created the *Direção de Informação e Segurança de Angola* (Directorate for Information and Security, DISA). Article 2 of that law defined DISA's mission in the broadest sense possible: "Defending and consolidating the independence and national unity, ensuring the revolutionary victories of the people and promoting the reeducation of elements whose actions could compromise [national] objectives." Article 3 further stipulated that DISA was intended to protect and serve the party in power: namely, the MPLA.[60]

DISA was established during a crucial phase of the civil war when the MPLA barely controlled three provinces in central Angola and Cabinda.[61] The rest of the country was contested by the FNLA (which received backing from Zaire and South Africa) and UNITA, which was directly supported by South African combat units. Consequently, DISA possessed a militarized hierarchy and a broad mandate to collect and analyze internal and external intelligence as well as wage "special operations" against domestic and foreign enemies.[62] Like its SNASP counterpart in Mozambique, DISA was granted the powers to investigate, arrest, incarcerate, interrogate, confiscate, and eliminate "political enemies" of the state and the MPLA.[63] In the first months of its existence, DISA confiscated numerous properties across Angola, some of which it retained for its own use or that of the MPLA leadership.[64] Yet the real key to DISA's power was its direct reporting authority to the new president of Angola: Agostinho Neto.[65]

One telling sign of DISA's power was reflected in the personalities and status of its first director and deputy director. Rodrigues João Lopes, a.k.a. Ludy Kissassunda, was not only DISA director but he also had a seat on the MPLA's Politburo, National Security Commission, and Council of the Revolution.[66] His deputy, the mulatto Henrique de Carvalho Santos, a.k.a. Onambwe, had a grim reputation in DISA's "torture centers" and was later mentioned as a possible heir to Agostinho Neto himself.[67]

DISA's central directorate was based in Luanda, and over time the agency also established local directorates in each of the provincial capitals as soon as they fell under MPLA control. Necessity drove DISA to focus on internal intelligence as a top priority, and its officers soon developed a "vast network of secret collaborators inside cities, towns, and villages."[68] When the FNLA's fortunes soured early in the war, DISA's primary target became UNITA, whose ranks it tried to infiltrate and manipulate.

DISA's operational directorates focused on counterintelligence, border security, battling subversion, and detecting and preventing sabotage.[69] One unique duty that was in keeping with Angola's circumstances was a DISA directorate devoted to providing security for the country's lucrative diamond fields. DISA also ran Angola's notorious "reeducation camps," which housed the MPLA's growing list of domestic and foreign enemies.[70]

East Germany's Stasi played a prominent role in creating DISA. The Stasi had experience to draw from including training Cuba's DGI and Mozambique's SNASP and, no doubt, facilitated work with the Angolans.[71] Some authors, such as Lara Pawson, detected a continuity of missions and methods between the Portuguese PIDE and DISA, but the abrupt break between Portugal and its former colony meant that it was the East Germans who shaped the new Angolan service.[72] One Angolan intelligence officer claimed that DISA was modeled after security agencies in other "socialist states," and although he does not mention the Stasi, it is clear that he had the East Germans in mind.[73]

East German advisors provided the new Angolan security service with critical assistance in technical surveillance, interrogation techniques, and propaganda.[74] The Stasi also helped train Angolan security officers at the Wilhelm Pieck Officers School in East Germany. Finally, the Stasi's Felix Dzerzhinsky Guards Regiment aided DISA and the Angolan armed forces in training and arming the Katangan militias that invaded Zaire in 1978 and South West Africa People's Organization (SWAPO) guerrillas based in Angola.[75]

There is a striking similarity between Mozambique's SNASP and Angola's DISA, when one examines the language of their enabling laws, their early doctrine, and organizational structures. This similarity stems from the East German (and, to a lesser extent, Soviet and Cuban) imprint on both agencies. Indeed, the operational model for SNASP, DISA, and their successors was the Stasi and these influences outlived the East German state itself.[76]

In addition to the Stasi, the other major foreign player in DISA's early development was the Cuban DGI. In a retrospective account that explored DISA's origins, an Angolan intelligence officer noted that DISA's staff was too small and inexperienced to handle the organization's expansive early missions and responsibilities. As a result, the Angolans relied heavily on the Cuban DGI for training and advice.[77] Several non-Cuban sources spotlight Havana's role in training DISA's "special troops," brutal interrogation practices, the monitoring of foreign embassies in Luanda, the creation of a signals intelligence (SIGINT) service, and running human intelligence networks.[78] In his memoirs, Markus Wolf, the former head of East Germany's foreign intelligence arm, paid tribute to the DGI's successes in espionage.[79] Some of those skills and expertise were evidently also passed on to the Angolans.

DISA quickly earned a notorious reputation for torture, "disappearances," and regime-sponsored terror. It instilled fear in both the MPLA ranks and the general population, but it also generated considerable anger and resentment, especially when the Angolan economy continued to shrink after independence and shortages of basic commodities became widespread.[80] Later, acute observers of the Angolan scene noted how that country's *cultura de medo* ("culture of fear") would outlive DISA's relatively brief existence.[81]

The MPLA was plagued by factional rivalries that revolved around ideology and race. By late 1976, some of these disputes were coming to a head, and the catalyst was the ambitious black interior minister Nito Alves. During a series of stormy meetings of the MPLA's Central Committee on May 20 and 21, 1977, Alves and another associate, José Van Dunem, raised a number of grievances, including that the MPLA favored whites and mulattos over blacks. While the MPLA needed to carry out an accelerated shift to socialist economic policies, DISA had to be reined in because of its human rights abuses and the corruption of its leaders, and the role of the Cubans in the security forces had to be curbed.[82]

The MPLA leadership rejected Alves and Van Dunem's pleas and put them under arrest. On May 21, Agostinho Neto told a mass audience at a Luanda stadium that both had been dismissed from the party. He said, "There cannot be any factions inside the MPLA" and "Either you are of the MPLA or you are not." Neto also publicly defended DISA, an implicit recognition that Alves' critique of this institution was resonating in some quarters. DISA was "fundamental" to the national defense, the president insisted. Any mistakes made by its officers were due to "lack of experience" and had to be forgiven.[83]

Neither the Alves and Van Dunem dismissals nor Neto's speech alleviated the simmering unrest that was about to boil over in Luanda and several other cities. On May 27, an elite Angolan unit that had been trained by the Soviets mutinied and sprang Alves and Van Dunem from prison. What followed was an intra-regime bloodbath that still haunts Angola today.

Institutionally, DISA appears to have been divided over its response to the May 27 insurrection. Most of the officers in DISA's Benguela provincial office, for example, were arrested for sympathizing with Alves and "never came back."[84] Others rallied around DISA's deputy director, Henrique de Carvalho Santos a.k.a. Onambwe, who led a "liquidation mission" against the Luanda mutineers with the critical assistance of Cuban soldiers.[85] The brutal reprisals against the coup plotters in DISA's incarceration centers makes for grim reading and is testimony to the atavistic anger that had been unleashed within the MPLA's ranks. Those who managed to survive the initial slaughter faced an uncertain future in DISA's reeducation camps where "[t]hey tried to take away all of your bad and anti-revolutionary thoughts."[86]

In the aftermath of the May 27 insurrection, DISA became an "über agency" of the Angolan presidency, enjoying all the powers normally handled by interior ministries and intelligence agencies in other countries. Much like its counterpart in Mozambique, DISA had police powers to investigate, arrest, detain, and confiscate in addition to other responsibilities such as border security, immigration, internal and external intelligence, and counterintelligence. By law it was answerable only to President Neto.[87]

DISA's already formidable authorities were further augmented and defined with the May 26, 1978, "Law on Crimes against State Security." Under this law, provisions were made for defining and punishing the following "crimes": espionage, sabotage, "incitement" or "instigation to collective disobedience," incitement to strike, and threats to foreign dignitaries and representatives as well as assassination attempts against the state leader or "supreme organs of the state." The broad categorization and definition of "state security crimes" enshrined in this law were to survive DISA's 1979 demise.[88]

By summer 1979, the MPLA's difficulties in running Angola only multiplied, despite or because of its powerful internal security forces. One formidable challenge lay in the economic arena, where an unfortunate combination of drought, war, government policies, and bureaucratic ineptitude had produced shortages of nearly everything from basic food stuffs to fuel.[89] On the battlefield, the combined might of the Cuban expeditionary forces and *Forças Armadas Populares de Libertação de Angola* (FAPLA) failed to suppress an increasingly lethal insurgency led by UNITA's Jonas Savimbi. The Cuban and Soviet program for training the FAPLA had run into innumerable obstacles and, as President Agostinho Neto lamented during a January 26, 1979, meeting with Fidel Castro, "The FAPLA needs a lot of discipline. A lot of discipline."[90]

It is still not clear what spurred the MPLA leadership to dismantle DISA in July 1979. However, this was most likely a combination of factors, including power struggles inside the regime, public discontent with secret police excesses (as enunciated by Nito Alves two years before), the economic crises detailed above, and an insurgency that was once again raising its head in the south. In any case, on July 4, 1979, DISA was dissolved and its assets, personnel, and missions transferred to a newly empowered interior ministry. Law 7/79 also created a new deputy interior minister for state security who would oversee some of the former DISA's internal security and intelligence functions.[91] As for DISA's senior leadership, Ludy Kissassunda and Onambwe were dismissed from their posts, although they retained their seats on the MPLA Politburo for a while longer. According to a declassified 1985 CIA report, Onambwe "was hated and feared by many in the regime" because of his ties to DISA and Eastern Bloc security agencies. Not surprisingly, he was also an opponent of dialogue with UNITA.[92]

According to one Angolan intelligence officer, writing from the perspective of hindsight, the post-DISA interior ministry "had a very complex structure."[93] It was a large, unwieldy amalgam of agencies and functions from border protection and national policing to protecting key infrastructure and conducting counterintelligence operations. Another problem with the 1979 reform was that it placed critical state security functions like intelligence and covert action under the interior minister rather than the presidency as previously.[94] In any case, the new arrangement did not survive President Neto's death from cancer in Moscow on September 10, 1979. Neto's successor, José Eduardo dos Santos, wanted to bring the security services under his direct control, and the result was a new organization called the *Ministério da Informação e Segurança de Estado* (MINSE).[95]

Ultimately, MINSE was a re-creation of DISA insomuch as it retained the latter's "military command" structure and the direct reporting chain to the presidency.[96] It was formally responsible for foreign and domestic intelligence collection and analysis, counterintelligence, VIP protection, and border security. MINSE also had the policing powers of arrest and detention, but its primary task was combating the UNITA insurgency. In this capacity, MINSE had direct control over specialized counterinsurgency units that identified and eliminated UNITA cadres.[97]

In some ways, successive reforms of the Angolan security service were fruitless. The Angolan economy continued to stagnate, while the UNITA threat expanded exponentially with South African backing. When a KGB delegation visited Luanda in 1981 for liaison meetings with its MINSE counterpart, some of its members were shocked by the conditions they found there. KGB officer Vadim Kirpichenko recalled, "Angola was a ruined country."[98] Consumer goods were scarce, stores were shuttered, and the Soviet "colony" was advised against leaving the Luanda city limits for security reasons. Even the KGB's government guesthouse had no running water.[99] Kirpichenko was not impressed with MINSE either. He assessed its procedures as "primitive, poor, and shoddy," while its overall performance was "very low."[100] The KGB officer did have a better opinion of MINSE's chief, Kundi Paihama, whom he had previously met in Moscow. Paihama was not only "polite, correct" Kirpichenko observed, he also was realistic about his ministry's many challenges.[101]

Nine years later, on yet another trip to Luanda, Kirpichenko noticed some improvements at MINSE. The ministry was functioning "in a more organized manner," he wrote, adding that the "professional and cultural level of Ministry employees had increased."[102] There were other developments. Kundi Paihama told the visiting KGB delegation that he was supervising secret negotiations with UNITA. Such talks were sorely needed: after decades of civil war, Angola was littered with land mines, the economy was in shambles (except for the off-shore oil sector), and the country lagged in virtually all socioeconomic indicators.[103]

However, on December 22, 1988, one dimension of Angola's interminable war came to an end with the signing of the Tripartite Agreement between Angola, Cuba, and South Africa. Under its terms, the Cubans and South Africans withdrew their forces from Angola, and Namibia was granted its independence. The end of large-scale foreign involvement was accompanied by limited progress in peace talks between Luanda and UNITA, but a real breakthrough remained elusive pending changes in the international arena that came about with the end of the Cold War.

For Luanda, the end of the Cold War ushered in a period of uncertainty and unwanted change. The Berlin Wall's fall and the end of communism in Eastern Europe followed by the collapse of the Soviet Union itself meant that the Angolan government lost virtually all of its most important foreign backers within the space of only two years. These major developments, in turn, facilitated the Angolan peace process and pushed the MPLA toward reform. On February 23, 1991, the government passed Law 2/91 that formally dissolved the dreaded MINSE. The ministry's functions, including intelligence and internal security, were parceled out among the national police and armed forces with the result being that there was no institutionalized management or oversight of the security establishment. Angolan intelligence officer Marcelino Franco later referred to this as a "deadly period of turbulence" when competing MPLA power centers fought over the remains of the former MINSE empire.[104]

Yet, the pendulum swung back in August 1993, when the Angolan government briefly returned to the model of a "super Interior Ministry" with vast powers in the areas of intelligence, policing, border control, and detention. This was only a stop gap because on March 25, 1994, the council of ministers passed another law that created the *Serviço de Informação* (Security Information Service, SINFO). SINFO represented a marked departure from its predecessors in that it was solely responsible for the collection and analysis of domestic intelligence.[105] Other internal security functions, such as arrest and detention, remained in the interior ministry. Separate agencies were created for external and military intelligence, and a new Angolan intelligence community began to take shape minus its Soviet bloc advisors.

CONCLUSION

Geography, local cultures, and the exigencies of modern nationalism aside, the similarities between Angola and Mozambique are often greater than the differences. This is especially true of their respective intelligence and security communities. Both were Portuguese colonies for centuries, and Lisbon tried to hold on to them after other European powers had vacated their African empires. Portuguese repression, including the use of a powerful secret police apparatus, meant that the expression of nationalist sentiment in Angola and Mozambique was not only clandestine in nature but Marxist-Leninist in orientation. Both FRELIMO and the MPLA developed internal security organs to protect themselves from the Portuguese and other liberation movements. Both relied on the Soviets, East Germans, and Cubans to train their intelligence and security services after independence.

Angola and Mozambique received their independence at roughly the same time due to an army-led coup in Lisbon. The new communist regimes in Maputo and Luanda used their existing ties with Soviet Bloc intelligence agencies to build powerful new intelligence and security services that dwarfed anything the Portuguese had in this field. In fact, the East German Stasi became the model for Angola and Mozambique to follow in the late 1970s and 1980s.

In both countries, the new governments faced powerful insurgencies backed by regional powers. While the foreign link to these groups is unmistakable, it should not disguise the fact that internal repression by Mozambique's SNASP and Angola's DISA often helped further galvanize existing insurgencies, in the case of Angola or spurred the creation of new ones in the case of Mozambique. It is remarkable that SNASP and DISA excesses led the political leaders of Mozambique and Angola to publicly denounce them. DISA was even disbanded and its functions eventually assigned to a new ministry for state security. A similar process occurred in Mozambique, although with a different timeline.

It is no coincidence that Mozambique and Angola discarded their East German–style security ministries at the same time that the East German state itself ceased to exist. Even more intriguing is that Maputo and Luanda created new intelligence communities where domestic, external, and military intelligence functions were divided among different agencies, and internal security functions became the exclusive preserve of police agencies and interior ministries.

Although both Angola and Mozambique now claim to be pluralistic democracies with opposition parties, freedom of speech, respect for human rights, and a free and open media, the ghosts of SNASP and DISA still haunt the present. A *cultura de medo* ("culture of fear") pervades both countries today whose ruling parties in 2020 are the same ruling parties in 1975.[106] There has been no public accounting for the abuses of the secret police and old crimes and criminals go unpunished, safeguarded by anachronistic and corrupt political systems that have a vested interest in letting the sleeping dogs lie. To truly overcome the legacy of the past, both Angola and Mozambique need more of a *cultura de abertura* ("a culture of openness"), where inquiries into the past can be safely conducted and truths discerned without fear of reprisal. South Africa's Truth and Reconciliation Commission is perhaps the most culturally appropriate and effective model for Angola and Mozambique to follow.

NOTES

1. There are several good studies on the French and British intelligence communities and their ties to postcolonial services. For example: Calder Walton, *Empire of Secrets* (New York: Overlook Press, 2013), 210–86; Jean-Pierre Bat, *La Fabrique des Barbouzes: Histoire des Réseaux Foccart en Afrique* (Paris: Noveau Monde, 2015).

2. Republic of Kenya, National Security Intelligence Service Act (1998) (repealed). Wilson Boinett, "The Origins of the Intelligence System of Kenya," in *Changing Intelligence Dynamics in Africa*, eds. Sandy Africa and Johnny Kwadjo (Birmingham, UK: GFN-SSR and ASSN, 2009).

3. Eduardo Mondlane, *The Struggle for Mozambique* (Middlesex: Penguin Books, 1970), 118, 128; Luis Serapiao and Mohamed El-Khawas, *Mozambique in the*

Twentieth Century: From Colonialism to Independence (Washington, DC: University Press of America, 1979), 124–25, 272; Christopher Andrew and Vasili Mitrokhin, *The World Was Going Our Way: The KGB and the Battle for the Third World* (New York: Basic Books, 2005), 445–46; John F. Burn, "Mozambique's Marxism has Allowances for Capitalism," *New York Times*, July 25, 1976; *João* Cabrita, *Mozambique: The Tortuous Road to Democracy* (New York: Palgrave Macmillan, 2000), 27–28, 44–45; Piero Gleijeses, *Conflicting Missions: Havana, Washington, and Africa, 1959–1976* (Chapel Hill: University of North Carolina Press, 2002), 87.

4. Mondlane, 118.

5. Jacinto Veloso, *Memórias em Voo Rasante* (Lisbon: Papa-Letras, 2007), 71; Mondlane, *Struggle*, 133–36; Serepiao and El-Khawas, 90–91, 124.

6. Veloso, 71–73.

7. Bernd Fischer, *Als Diplomaten mit zwei Berufen* (Berlin: Edition Ost, 2009), 31; Andrew and Mitrokhin, 265–66, 447; Cable from Amembassy Dar Es Salaam, "FRELIMO Pardons 240 'Traitors,'" March 18, 1975, no. 00806; Gleijeses, *Conflicting Missions*, op. cit., 87, 227; Sven Felix Kellerhoff, "Wie Markus Wolf in der Dritten Welt Faden Zog," *Welt*, September 18, 2013, https://www.welt.de/geschichte/article119990899/Wie-Markus-Wolf-in-der-Dritten-Welt-Faeden-zog.html.

8. Andrew and Mitrokhin, 445, 447; "Former Mozambican President confirms contact with KGB," *Club of Mozambique*, April 11 2016, https://clubofmozambique.com/news/former-mozambican-president-confirms-contact-with-kgb/.

9. Veloso, 65–67; Sereipiao and El-Khawas, 92–93, 132–133; Cabrita, 48–52.

10. Harry West, *Kupilikula: Governance and the Hidden Realm in Mozambique* (Chicago: University of Chicago Press, 2005), 148.

11. Mozambique History Net, "State Security: Vigilância Popular and SNASP," Dossier MZ-0155, http://www.mozambiquehistory.net/snasp.php.

12. Fischer, 112–13, 189–94; Cable from Amembassy Lourenco Marques, "Mozambique Government Officials to German Democratic Republic for Training," November 25, 1975, no. 01256; Cable from Amembassy Maputo, "Internal Stability in Mozambique," May 25, 1979, no. 00652.

13. Fischer, 113.

14. According to Veloso, FRELIMO's Defense Department/Intelligence Service became the Ministry of Defense/Intelligence Service after June 25, 1975: Veloso, 99–100.

15. Cable from Amconsul Lourenco Marques, "GPRM Intensifies Attack Against Organized Religion," October 17, 1975, no. 01120; Cable from Amconsul Lourenco Marques, "Mozambique Four Months after Independence," op. cit.; Cable from Amembassy Maputo, "Internal Stability," op. cit.; Burn, "Mozambique's Marxism," op. cit.; John Darnton, "Mozambique, with Cuban Help, is Shoring up its Internal Security," *New York Times*, June 24, 1979; Cabrita, 88.

16. Decreto no. 28/78 in *Principal Legislação promulgada pelo Governo da República Popular de Moçambique* 6, June 25, 1978, to June 25, 1979 (Maputo: Imprensa Nacional, 1979), 241–242; Conselho de Ministros, Decreto-lei 21/75, *Boletim da República*, série 1, no. 46 (October 11, 1975), 193–94, http://www.mozambique-history.net/governance/snasp/19751011_lei_de_snasp.pdf; Serepiao and El-Khawas,

162–64; U.S. Department of State, *Country Report on Human Rights Practices for 1986*, https://www.ecoi.net/en/document/1252281.html.

17. Cable from Amconsul Lourenco Marques, "Mozambique Four Months after Independence."

18. Markus Wolf, *Man without a Face* (New York: Times Books, 1997), 265. Also see: Fischer, 115–16, 119–21.

19. Jana Scholz, "Überwachungskameras *Für* Mosambik," *Portal Wissen* 2, 2017, http://irtg-strategy.de/sites/default/files/downloads/PortalWissen_02_2017_ger/index.pdf.

20. Veloso, 104.

21. Fischer, 116–17, 120.

22. Holger Catenhusen, "Wie die Stasi in Übersee spionierte," *Potsdamer Neueste Nachrichten*," August 22, 2018, https://www.pnn.de/wissenschaft/ddr-geheimdienst-im-ausland-wie-die-stasi-in-uebersee-spionierte/22916766.html.

23. Cabrita, 90; Darnton, "Mozambique, with Cuban Help."

24. For two opposing views on RENAMO's origins, see: Cabrita, *Tortuous Road*, and Ken Flower, *Serving Secretly: An Intelligence Chief on Record* (London: John Murray, 1987).

25. Veloso, 129.

26. Ibid, 133–35, 144.

27. Cable from Amembassy Maputo, "SNASP Grasps New Powers," February 8, 1979, no. 00191.

28. "Grupos de vigilância: estudar a actuação inimiga," *Tempo* no. 444, April 15, 1979, 14; "Colocar o inimigo na defensiva passive," *Tempo*, no.460, August 5, 1979, 53–54; "Reforcemos a Vigilancia Popular," *Noticias*, February 6, 1980.

29. "Colocar o inimigo na defensiva passive," 54.

30. Assembleia Popular, Comissão Permanente, "Lei dos crimes contra a segurança do povo e do estado popular," *Tempo*, no. 439, March 4, 1979, 25.

31. For example, Cabrita, 108–15.

32. S. Machel, "Ofensiva da legalidade: garantir a paz, tranquilidade e segurança," *Tempo* 579, November 15, 1981, 22–28, 37–41.

33. Department of State, *Country Report on Human Rights Practices for 1986*.

34. Benedito Luis Machava, "State Discourse on Internal Security and the Politics of Punishment in Post-Independence Mozambique," *Journal of Southern African Studies* 37, no. 3 (September 2011), 598.

35. Bernard Gwertzman, "U.S. Blames Cuba for Expulsion of 6 Americans from Mozambique," *New York Times*, March 5, 1981, https://www.nytimes.com/1981/03/05/world/us-blames-cuba-for-expulsion-of-6-americans-from-mozambique.html.

36. Veloso, 145–46.

37. Vladimir Shubin, *Cholodnaya Voina: Yug Afriki (1960–1990)* (Moscow: Goryachaya, 2017). Chapter ten provides a useful overview of the Soviet-Mozambique relationship.

38. Veloso, 195–96.

39. Stephen Chan and Moisés Venâncio, *War and Peace in Mozambique* (New York: Palgrave Macmillan, 1998), 163–64.

40. Ibid.

41. "Estatuo especial do SISE questionado em Moçambique," *Deutsche Welle*, https://www.dw.com/pt-002/estatuto-especial-do-sise-questionado-em-mo%C3%A7ambique/a-51392340.

42. Gleijeses, 233.

43. Tony Hodges, *Angola from Afro-Stalinism to Petro-Diamond Capitalism* (Bloomington: Indiana University Press, 2001), 44; Fernando Andresen *Guimarães, The Origins of the Angolan Civil War: Foreign Intervention and Domestic Political Conflict* (New York: St. Martin's Press, 2001), 31, 41; Cable from Amconsul Luanda, "Luanda Situation—0900 July 19," July 19, 1974, no. 00572.

44. John Marcum, *The Angolan Revolution, Vol I: The Anatomy of an Explosion (1950–1962)* (Cambridge, MA: Massachusetts Institute of Technology Press, 1969), 36.

45. *Guimarães*, 31.

46. Marcum, 33–37.

47. Gleijeses, 81–82, *Guimarães*, 33, 43–44.

48. Marcum, 27–30; *Guimarães*, 39, 45–46; *Hodges*, 8.

49. Gleijeses, 82, 174–75.

50. Vadim Kirpichenko, *Razvedka: Litsa i Lichnosti* (Moscow: Mezhdunarodniye Otnosheniya, 2019), 212; *Guimarães*, 60, 164.

51. Gleijeses, 243; Mitrokhin and Andrews, 446–47; Kirpichenko, 212–13.

52. Kirpichenko, 213.

53. *Guimarães*, 99, 166–167; *Mitrokhin and Andrews*, 429.

54. East Germany also provided arms and ammunition to the MPLA: "Wir haben euch Waffen und Brot geschickt," *Der Spiegel*, March 3, 1980; Wolf, 265–66; Fischer, 102–3; Gleijeses, 164.

55. Quoted in Gleijeses, 83.

56. Director of Central Intelligence, Angola Working Group, "Cuban Involvement in Angola," October 22, 1975, https://www.cia.gov/library/readingroom/docs/LOC-HAK-102-5-3-9.pdf; Memorandum from the Director of Central Intelligence to the National Security Adviser, "Cuban Involvement in Africa," June 29, 1977, https://www.cia.gov/library/readingroom/docs/CIA-RDP79R00603A002700040001-1.pdf; *Guimarães*, 136; *Gleijeses*, 244.

57. *Guimarães*, 118, 137–38; *Gleijeses*, 82, 160.

58. Marcelino *Cristóvão* Bonzela Franco, *A Evolução do Conceito Estratégico do Serviço de Inteligência de Segurança do Estado da República de Angola,* Dissertação para Mestre em Estratégia do Instituto Superior de Ciências Sociais e Politicas, Universidade de Lisboa, 2013, 17–18.

59. Ibid., 17–19.

60. Decreto-Lei no. 3/75, *Diario da Republica*, 1a Serie, no. 17, November 29, 1975.

61. Franco lists these provinces as Cabinda, Malange and Lunda. By 1976 DISA had sent teams of 4–5 men and women to most of the provincial capitals. Franco, 27–28.

62. Ibid., 22.

63. Decreto-Lei no. 3/75.

64. Lara Pawson, *In the Name of the People: Angola's Forgotten Massacre* (London: I. B. Tauris, 2016), 75; Cable from Amembassy Lisbon, "Correspondence from Luanda FSL Julio Correa," April 2, 1976; Fernando Vumby, "A trajectóra criminosa dos serviços secretos angolanos," *Pambazuka News*, March 31, 2014, https://www. pambazuka.org/pt/governance/traject%C3%B3ra-criminosa-dos-servi%C3%A7os-secretos-angolanos.

65. Cable from Amembassy The Hague, "Exchange of Information on Angola," March 9, 1978, no. 01242; Decreto-Lei no. 3/75.

66. Franco, 26.

67. Vumby, "trajectóra criminosa"; Cable from Secretary of State, "Analysis of Situation"; Cable from Amembassy Rome, "Angola after Neto."

68. Franco, 22–23.

69. Ibid., 23.

70. Pawson, 103–4.

71. Wolf, 302.

72. Pawson, 14.

73. Franco, 26.

74. Cable from Secretary of State, "Analysis of Situation in Angola"; Cable from Amembassy Rome, "Angola after Neto"; Cable from Amembassy The Hague, "Exchange of Information on Angola"; Cable from Amembassy Lisbon, "Portuguese Leaders on Angola," April 11, 1978, no. 5389; Andrews and Mitrokhin, 453–454; Francois Soudan, "L'heritage de Neto," *Jeune Afrique*, September 19, 1979, 32–34; "Wir haben," *Der Spiegel*.

75. Fischer, 92; "Wir haben," *Der Spiegel*.

76. For example, Scholz.

77. Franco, 29.

78. Ibid., 29; Cable from Secretary of State, "Analysis of Situation in Angola"; Cable from Amembassy Rome, "Angola after Neto"; Cable from Amembassy The Hague, "Exchange of Information on Angola"; Fernando Vumby, "Instrumento de tortura utilizado pela Disa polícia secreta de Agostinho Neto e pares," *Angola24Horas*, February 29, 2016, https://www.angola24horas.com/index.php/opiniao/item/5892-instrumento-de-tortura-utilizado-pela-disa-policia-secreta-de-agostinho-neto-e-pares; Memorandum from the Director of Central Intelligence to the National Security Adviser, "Cuban Involvement in Africa," June 29, 1977.

79. Wolf, 302.

80. Leonor Figuierdo, *Sita Valles: Revolucionária, Comunista até à morte* (Lisboa: Alêtheia Editores, 2014).

81. Pawson, 3.

82. Cable from Amembassy Lisbon, "Angola Insurrection: The Portuguese View," June 8, 1977, no. 4534; Pawson, 33–34.

83. Pawson, 175–76.

84. Nelson Sul d'Angola, "Membros da polícia política de Angola também foram vítimas do 27 de maio," *Deutsche Welle*, May 22, 2012, https://www.dw.com/pt-002/membros-da-pol%C3%ADcia-pol%C3%ADtica-de-angola-tamb%C3%A9m-foram-v%C3%ADtimas-do-27-de-maio/a-15958575.

85. Pawson, 35; Cable from Secretary of State, "Analysis of Situation in Angola"; Cable from Amembassy Lisbon, "Angola Insurrection: The Portuguese View."

86. Pawson, 91.

87. Decreto-Lei 3/75; Franco, 21–22, 27.

88. Decreto-Lei no. 7/78, *Diario da Republica*, no. 136, 1a Serie, May 26, 1978; Hodges, 74.

89. James Ciment, *Angola and Mozambique: Postcolonial Wars in Southern Africa* (New York: Facts on File, 1997), 61–63.

90. "Memorandum of Conversation between Fidel Casto and Agostinho Neto," January 26, 1979, Woodrow Wilson Center Digital Archive, https://digitalarchive. wilsoncenter.org/document/117941, 4.

91. Decreto-Lei no. 7/79, *Diario da Republica*, no. 157, 1a Serie, July 4, 1979, 422.

92. Central Intelligence Agency, "Angola: Prospects for MPLA-UNITA Reconciliation," February 1985, ALA-85–10017L, https://www.cia.gov/library/read-ingroom/docs/CIA-RDP86T00589R000100080008-1.pdf.

93. Franco, 30–31.

94. Ibid., 31.

95. Lei no. 7/79, *Diario da Republica*, no. 159, 1a Serie, July 7, 1980, 1010.

96. Franco, *Evolução*, 32.

97. Ibid., 32–34.

98. Kirpichenko, 217.

99. Ibid.

100. Ibid.

101. Ibid, 216.

102. Ibid., 218.

103. Hodges, 28–41.

104. Franco, 35–37.

105. Ibid., 41.

106. Pawson, 3.

Chapter 4

Intelligence in the Rhodesian Counterinsurgency

Glenn A. Cross

Rhodesia provides an important case study about the role and limits intelligence has in counterinsurgencies. Although retrospective studies of intelligence in past counterinsurgencies have a wealth of possible case studies to choose from, none—with one notable example—analyzed Rhodesia during that country's protracted counterinsurgency through the 1960s and 1970s.[1] The Rhodesian Bush War pitted the minority European settler population against a growing black nationalist insurgency, which aimed to overthrown white rule and more equitably distribute Rhodesia's rich agricultural resources. This history demonstrates the limitations of intelligence—however excellent—in waging a counterinsurgency absent popular and political support. Although highly effective, Rhodesian intelligence was not and could not have been a decisive factor in winning that counterinsurgency. Throughout the war, Rhodesian intelligence successfully penetrated the nationalist organizations, and the depth and extent of Rhodesian intelligence on the insurgent leadership, personnel, recruitment, training, and operations were excellent. Despite the success of Rhodesia in unraveling the insurgency from an intelligence perspective, Rhodesia was forced to concede political defeat in March 1980, after elections swept Zimbabwe African National Union (ZANU)'s Robert Mugabe to power.

This chapter examines the evolution as well as the effectiveness and limitations of Rhodesian intelligence during that country's long counterinsurgency from the mid-1960s to March 1980, when Britain formally granted the colony its independence to a government elected under majority rule. It argues that while Rhodesia boasted intelligence services on par with many European nations and those of South Africa despite Rhodesia's small size and limited financial resources and international sanctions, intelligence was not the deciding factor in the war. The chapter highlights how the intelligence services successfully penetrated the leadership of insurgent and opposition groups, conducted sophisticated covert actions, and maintained wide-ranging liaison relationships despite Rhodesia's pariah status in the international community. Nonetheless, the war ended with a relatively peaceful vote and transition to majority rule in contemporary Zimbabwe, demonstrating the limitations of even capable intelligence services.

The chapter makes use of published accounts, relevant Rhodesian intelligence documents, unpublished histories, correspondence, private diaries, and personal interviews with former senior Rhodesian intelligence officers as well as Selous Scout officers. For those officers not available to be interviewed in person, email correspondence was used to question them on key topics. To ensure accuracy, an early copy of this manuscript was provided to some officers with firsthand knowledge of the events and who provided valuable comments. At the end of the Rhodesian conflict in 1980, Rhodesian security forces destroyed many, if not most, of the documents related to their operations. The scale of the destruction is not known, but it is assumed to have been large. Some sensitive Special Branch and Central Intelligence Organisation (CIO) archives were secretly transferred to South African intelligence, where they remain inaccessible. An effort was underway to assemble Rhodesian military operational documents from private collections. Those papers, the Rhodesian Army Archive amounting to eleven hundred boxes, were housed at the British Empire and Commonwealth Museum until its closure. The whereabouts of the archive now are unknown.

In reassembling an accurate account of the Rhodesian intelligence services, one faces some daunting challenges. Most interviews and correspondence with surviving members of the Rhodesian intelligence services now are taking place forty years after the events took place. Memories fade, and many participants' recollections differ significantly from one another. Some are clearly biased or have personal agendas. Others are hiding key facts. Accounts were corroborated using contemporary documentation, but this was only possible in a few instances. For the most part, memories were included when they were independently supported by two or more participants.

This chapter is divided into nine sections. It begins with a historical background of colonial Rhodesia and the events that led up to the colony's Unilateral Declaration of Independence (UDI) from the United Kingdom. The second section describes the role of the British South Africa Police (BSAP) in Rhodesia's security. The next section discusses the origins of Rhodesian intelligence, followed by a description of the structure of Rhodesian intelligence organizations. The role and functions of the CIO then are laid out in detail. The chapter then examines Rhodesian covert actions and its intelligence liaison relationships. Next is a look at the effectiveness of Rhodesian intelligence given the growing insurgent threat. Last, the chapter concludes with a general examination of the enduring legacy of the Rhodesian intelligence services.

BACKGROUND

Rhodesia, now the nation of Zimbabwe, in southern Africa, was formed in 1890 by the British South Africa Company (BSAC), owned by the British entrepreneur Cecil Rhodes. Initially, Rhodesia was a proprietary colony, under the control of the BSAC, as opposed to a British Crown colony. The goal of the BSAC in Rhodesia was to profit from the colony through the extraction of raw materials. The white settlers chafed under the control of the BSAC, which levied steep charges for rail shipments and wages, resulting in a high cost of living in Rhodesia. Protests against the BSAC skyrocketed in 1902 with the death of Cecil Rhodes.[2] By 1922, settler resentment of the BSAC's practices reached a boiling point. In that year, a referendum was held in Rhodesia giving the white settler population the choice of either becoming a British colony or uniting with the Union of South Africa.[3] The referendum decided that British colonial rule was preferable, and on October 1, 1923, Rhodesia became a self-ruling British colony.[4] The Rhodesians continued under a form of self-rule—in their minds, a form of quasi-dominion status—until the early 1960s when talks began about independence.

Following British prime minister Harold Macmillan's February 1960 "Wind of Change" speech in the South African parliament, London began steps to decolonize its African possessions. Talks about Rhodesian independence stalled over the issues of majority rule. The conservative ruling Rhodesia Front party was opposed to Rhodesian independence under majority rule. At the time, the ruling whites in Rhodesia numbered only about 275,000 compared to approximately 7,000,000 Africans and other races. With talks at an impasse, the Rhodesia Front government under Prime Minister Ian Smith decided to announce Rhodesia's Unilateral Declaration of Independence (UDI) on November 11, 1965.

At first, the African nationalist parties (the Shona-dominated Zimbabwe African National Union (ZANU) and the Matabele-dominated Zimbabwe African People's Union (ZAPU) wanted Britain to intervene—with force, if necessary—to bring the rebellious Rhodesia in line and grant independence under majority rule. Britain was reluctant to use its military to invade Rhodesia to crush the rebellion, preferring to use international sanctions and diplomatic isolation to pressure the Rhodesian government. Absent any British military action, the two African nationalist parties slowly developed their own insurgent capabilities. The Rhodesian security forces crushed the early insurgent infiltrations into the country, mobilizing overwhelming conventional military superiority and highly effective intelligence resources. The dynamic in the insurgency changed in 1972 when ZANU insurgents, using Maoist guerilla doctrine, established a foothold in northeastern Rhodesia along the border with Mozambique's Tete province. The security situation in

Rhodesia further worsened in April 1974 when the Carnation Revolution in Portugal led to that country's withdrawal from Mozambique. Following the Portuguese withdrawal, the Marxist FRELIMO government allowed ZANU forces to establish bases in the country, effectively opening a 1,100 mile second front for Rhodesian insurgents.

ROLE OF THE BRITISH SOUTH AFRICA POLICE

For most of Rhodesia's history, the colonial paramilitary police force, the British South Africa Police (BSAP) was responsible for intelligence functions, which focused almost exclusively on countersubversion. Although initially a corporate security force for Cecil Rhodes's British South Africa Company, the BSAP can best be described as typical of British colonial police forces found throughout the world in the late nineteenth and early twentieth centuries. Responsible for defending Rhodesia, the BSAP was a mounted paramilitary force with police and internal security duties. In addition to law and order responsibilities, the BSAP became heavily involved in countersubversion operations as the Cold War intensified and concerns about the rise of communism grew. In Rhodesia, communist infiltration of the labor unions aroused greater concern than that of African nationalism.[5] Although the BSAP's early countersubversion focused on European trade unionists and left-leaning political parties, by the late 1950s and early 1960s, the growing politicization of the black population—largely in Northern Rhodesia and Nyasaland—caught the attention of colonial authorities.

As the nationalist insurgency grew, Rhodesian intelligence needed to evolve from a police service under the BSAP-dominated effort to one that better supported military counterinsurgency operations. The pressure forced the intelligence community away from a police mindset focused on insurgents and criminals toward an intelligence community more responsive to the growing needs of the Rhodesian military and led to considerable strains. In the end, the BSAP continued to dominate Rhodesian intelligence, Rhodesian military efforts to establish a separate intelligence capability withered, and the Rhodesian military remained dependent on the police for intelligence on insurgent activities.

ORIGINS OF RHODESIAN INTELLIGENCE

Before Britain's creation of the Central African Federation, which comprised Nyasaland (Malawi), Northern Rhodesia (Zambia), and Southern Rhodesia (Rhodesia, now Zimbabwe), Rhodesia had no official organizations responsible for national security. The BSAP operated as a paramilitary police force charged with maintaining law and order under the Police Act. In addition, the BSAP maintained only a small section—the Security Section (XB) within the Criminal Investigations Division (CID). This section consisted of two officers, who were charged with collating a monthly digest of intelligence for the commissioner of police.[6] Until the rise of African nationalism after the Second World War, few British colonies in Africa had internal security elements.[7] The Cold War competition and the resulting Soviet and later Chinese support for anti-colonial nationalist movements in Africa were the initial impetus for the creation of security elements in the colonial governments.

Rhodesia's need for an intelligence service became apparent with the rise in African nationalist violence in the mid-1950s, notably with the Mau Mau uprising in Kenya, and the emergence of violent African nationalism in Rhodesia during the early 1960s (for Kenya, see Shaffer in this volume). The country lacked direct experience with intelligence operations and did not have a formal intelligence organization, while most threats to national security from subversion or terrorism were dealt with by the BSAP as criminal matters. Yet, some BSAP officers had intelligence experience acquired during their service in the British Army during the Second World War. Rhodesians also had some counterinsurgency experience serving in Kenya and Malaysia. Consequently, Rhodesians who developed a counterinsurgency/counterterrorist strategy turned to the British model of Malaysia that was later adapted for use in Kenya.

With the available resources, Rhodesia's intelligence organizations, for the most part, were formed from elements belonging to the BSAP. The Rhodesian government turned to the BSAP to lead the intelligence community in the face of the terrorist threat because of Salisbury's emphasis on a predominantly police response to the mounting security crisis (lessons of Malaysia and Kenya), the dominant role of the BSAP's Special Branch in intelligence collection and established network of informants, and the overwhelming reliance on police officials to staff Rhodesia's intelligence organizations. The reliance on a police force, the BSAP, as the central intelligence organization and on police officers to fill most other key intelligence roles in Rhodesia meant that Rhodesian intelligence focused more heavily on policing than military operations.

With the formation of the Central African Federation (merging Northern Rhodesia, Southern Rhodesia, and Nyasaland) in 1953, the BSAP—as the colonial police force—remained responsible for policing Southern Rhodesia. The newly formed Rhodesian Army's minor role in internal security was limited to supporting the BSAP, if needed, to maintain law and order.[8] Under the federation, intelligence coordination was handled by the Federal Intelligence and Security Bureau (FISB), but intelligence collection was controlled by each of the three territorial police forces.[9] The FISB was headed by a British Security Service (MI5) official, Basil Maurice "Bob" de Quehan, who also had served in the BSAP. In 1951, de Quehan arrived in Salisbury as the MI5 liaison officer, becoming the head of the FISB in 1954, and resigning from MI5 in 1956. Thus, for two years (from 1954 to 1956), de Quehan was both a serving MI5 officer and the head of the FISB.[10] According to Bill Crabtree, a former head of the BSAP Special Branch, de Quehan's only responsibility was to coordinate intelligence for the federation on the basis of information he received from the BSAP and the other two territorial police organizations.[11] The intelligence produced by the FISB was intended to alert the federal government to threats to its interests as a whole. Given de Quehan's ties to MI5, FISB intelligence almost certainly was also shared with London.[12] Crabtree also claimed that the FISB occasionally exceeded its mandate, resulting in a considerable duplication of effort, misunderstandings, and embarrassment.[13] The officers in the BSAP delighted in surveilling and reporting on the activities of FISB agents.[14]

In 1958, Sir Edgar Whitehead became the prime minister of Rhodesia. Of all of Rhodesia's prime ministers, Whitehead was the one who demonstrated the greatest interest in intelligence issues.[15] On becoming prime minister, Whitehead found considerable shortcomings in Rhodesia's intelligence system and sought to overhaul it. He tasked several officials to form a study group to develop recommendations for reforming the intelligence system. The study group turned to British intelligence experts for their advice.[16]

In 1960, British Prime Minister Harold Macmillan gave his famous "Winds of Change" speech before the South African parliament, marking the beginning of Britain's decolonization of its African territories. With decolonization, the Central African Federation (CAF) ceased to exist at the end of 1963 with the independence of two of the constituent colonies, Northern Rhodesia (Zambia) and Nyasaland (Malawi), the following year under majority rule. The status of Southern Rhodesia, which was self-governing since 1923 remained undetermined, largely due to the hesitance of the white minority to relinquishing the reins of government to majority rule. With the demise of the CAF, the FISB, as ineffectual as it had been, ended as well. The legacy of the FISB in Southern Rhodesia (after 1964 known as Rhodesia) was mixed. FISB officers were viewed with suspicion, but the Rhodesians recognized the need for a central intelligence organization.

In January 1961, the BSAP acted on the recommendation of Sir Roger Hollis, then director general of MI5, and began efforts to create the Special Branch.[17] In July 1962, the BSAP established the Special Branch (SB), which was designed to be a security element entirely separate from any other division in the BSAP, including the CID.[18] The first head of the BSAP's Special Branch was Bill Crabtree, a career BSAP officer in CID, who staffed the SB with "a handful" of officers and others from the ranks of the BSAP.[19]

The 1962 Rhodesian elections brought the Rhodesia Front party to power, which resulted in a renewed interest in plans to reform the intelligence services. Rhodesian Prime Minister Whitehead, formed a working group—comprising senior civil servants and service heads—to review the work of the earlier study group on intelligence to formulate recommendations on internal security.[20] This ministerial-level group experienced difficulties coping with intelligence reform. Few, if any of the group's members, had any understanding of the role of intelligence in national security or what structure or organizations were needed in confronting the challenges to Rhodesian security.[21]

During the discussions about intelligence reform, the military remained intractably opposed to the BSAP's continued control of intelligence. As Crabtree recounted,

> For reasons best known to themselves, perhaps because they possessed no effective intelligence corps of their own and may have been a little envious of the Police role in that field, the Military was adamantly opposed to the control of intelligence remaining in the hands of the BSAP.[22]

Although Crabtree may be correct in judging the military's opposition was based on jealousy, at the same time, the Rhodesian military almost certainly concluded that police control of intelligence would not serve the military's needs. Crabtree suggested that the lack of a military intelligence service resulted in the military's jealousy of the BSAP's domination of intelligence.[23] On December 31, 1963, Rhodesia formally created the Central Intelligence Organisation (CIO) to direct the nation's intelligence collection and analysis efforts. The creation of the CIO was classified, and the organization formally was a department within the Office of the Prime Minister. According to CIO director general Kenneth Flower,

> In discussion with government law officers and Gerald Clarke, the Secretary to the Prime Minister, it was considered preferable for CIO to operate under a Prime Minister's Mandate rather than seek legislation in Parliament. The Mandate was signed by [Rhodesian Prime Minister Winston] Field in October 1963 and issued to Ministers and Head of Ministries.[24]

In establishing the CIO, the then director general of the new organization, Kenneth Flower—with very little understanding of intelligence—started from scratch. Flower, a veteran BSAP officer, began studying several other foreign intelligence organizations in search for a model. He quickly focused on the British intelligence organizations—especially the Secret Intelligence Service (MI6) and the Special Branch—because he believed that British intelligence was the best in the world. As Flower recounted in his autobiography,

> The most compelling fact that I could put down was that British Intelligence works in spite of mistakes and relies to some extent on the Briton's well-known

flair for improvisation. The British have acquired experiences through being first in the field; they insist on quality, not quantity, in their personnel; they provide a thorough training; they demand an exceptionally high standard of integrity and dedication to duty from those who serve them.[25]

In discussions with British authorities, Flower recounts that his British contacts, including the head of MI6, emphasized that the Canadian system (i.e., the Royal Canadian Mounted Police) would be best for Rhodesia to emulate.[26] The British recommendation likely was based on the similarities in mission and organization between the two services, both being tasked with national security missions as well as national policing. The British also opposed the idea of integrating the Rhodesian Special Branch with the CIO. They believed the head of the Special Branch would have difficulty wearing two hats— reporting to both the CIO director general and the commissioner of police.[27]

Flower also looked at the French and Portuguese intelligence systems but discounted their usefulness. As he recounted in his memoirs, Flower believed that these intelligence services were overly personality driven and too overshadowed by their militaries to be truly effective.[28] In the end, Flower concluded that the British intelligence system was the most useful model for Rhodesia. Although he had examined the Soviet and American intelligence communities, he found the Soviet system to be ruthless and efficient but too authoritarian for Rhodesia. As for the American intelligence community, he did not comment on why he believed it was less suited to Rhodesia.[29]

INTELLIGENCE STRUCTURE

The Rhodesian intelligence structure grew from a single police-dominated entity in the early 1960s to a more complex intelligence community comprising police, foreign intelligence collection, covert action, and military elements by the mid-1970s (Figure 4.1) as the insurgency grew. The size of Rhodesian intelligence increased as did the sophistication of its capabilities. This expansion largely took place in response to the growing insurgent threat. Although certainly more capable with the integration of imagery and signal intelligence as with human intelligence tools, Rhodesian intelligence, especially in the later years of the counterinsurgency, became plagued with interservice rivalries that threatened its effectiveness. Throughout the Rhodesian counterinsurgency, the CIO dominated Rhodesian intelligence.

On October 31, 1963, the Rhodesian Prime Minister Winston Field authorized the creation of the CIO in response to growing concern that Rhodesia's security situation would deteriorate following the independence of Northern Rhodesia and Nyasaland.[30] Following Rhodesia's UDI in November 1965,

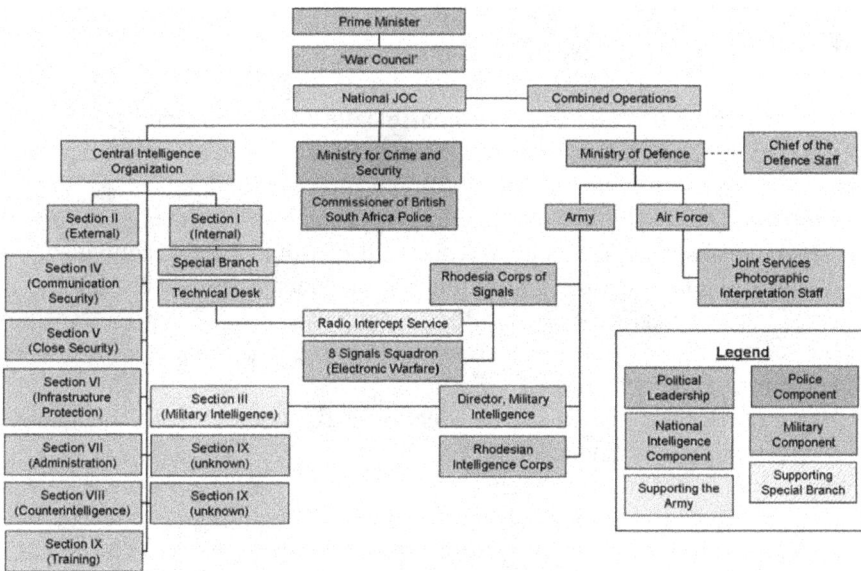

Figure 4.1 Organization of Rhodesian Intelligence Community, c. 1977–1980

a nascent African insurgency developed that seriously threatened the white-dominated government by 1976. Established on December 31, 1963, the CIO formed the overall umbrella for all of Rhodesia's intelligence components.[31]

The CIO was largely staffed by police officers from the BSAP's Special Branch with some remnants of the FISB serving in Branch II. The BSAP's domination of the CIO was inescapable; all three top positions in the CIO—director general, deputy director general (Internal), and deputy director general (External)—were all occupied by senior BSAP officers. Administration and budget issues also were handled by the BSAP. Organizationally, the CIO consisted of eleven sections (Figure 4.2):

- Branch II (External): The External Section, headed by retired BSAP officer Ken Leaver, was responsible for all intelligence collection operations conducted outside Rhodesia, including foreign liaison. The section also operated specialist analytical divisions, producing strategic intelligence analyses for the Rhodesian leadership.[32] This section—modeled after Britain's MI6—operated clandestinely out of stations in which Rhodesia had diplomatic representation. Branch II also focused on overseas political activities, propaganda, and psychological operations, including disinformation. The branch received intelligence from foreign liaison services in South Africa, Portugal, Francophone Africa, and anti-communist Middle Eastern governments.[33]

- Branch III: Military Intelligence Section, headed by the director of military intelligence and the director of air plans.[34]
- Branch IV: Government Telecommunications Agency was the communications security organization responsible for encrypting and decrypting government communications and manufacturing secure communications devices and equipment.
- Branch V: The Close Security Section was charged with the physical security of government dignitaries. This section would be the equivalent of the U.S. Secret Service. Most training for officers in Branch V came from Rhodesian Special Air Service (RhSAS) instructors.
- Branch VI: The Government Protective Service was mandated to protect key infrastructure facilities.[35]
- Branch VII: The Administration Section was responsible for personnel, transportation, and finance.
- Branch VIII: Counterintelligence.
- Branch IX: Training. This section operated the training school and was responsible for instruction in intelligence collection, tradecraft, surveillance, countersurveillance, safe house operation, and source handling.[36]

DETAILS OF CIO BRANCHES I, II, AND III

Branches I, II, and III played important, but distinct roles. Branch I was synonymous with the BSAP Special Branch and reported to the officer commanding, Special Branch. Importantly, the Special Branch had a longer history of intelligence collection, so it was allowed to operate both inside and outside Rhodesia's borders to fulfill its intelligence collection mission. Yet, it drew on the Criminal Investigation Division (CID) for manpower.[37] Headed by the director, Internal (DIN), the Internal Section was formed when the BSAP Special Branch's intelligence collection and analysis functions were integrated into the CIO. Led by veteran BSAP officer Bill Crabtree until 1970, Branch I was responsible for collecting intelligence used to identify and target insurgents inside Rhodesia, penetrating African nationalist groups in the country, identifying white dissidents, and operating against counterintelligence threats from hostile foreign intelligence services. Dual-hatted, the head of Branch I served as director general (Internal), reporting to the head of the CIO and as a deputy commissioner of BSAP reporting also to the head of the BSAP.

When the Special Branch was integrated into the CIO, Flower ordered it to cease all foreign intelligence activities, but he admitted that this decision damaged Rhodesian intelligence collection.[38] In his memoirs, Flower conceded that he allowed the Special Branch to continue its foreign intelligence collection activities.[39] Crabtree claimed, that in discussions with Flower, Crabtree argued that control of CIO liaison functions should remain with the Internal Section. Crabtree described telling Flower that he had established close, personal ties with the intelligence services of Portugal and its colonies, the remaining British colonies in Africa, and South Africa. Crabtree argued these ties should remain "in police channels."[40] Flower and Crabtree reached a compromise that allowed them to jointly handle foreign liaison exchanges.[41]

According to a former Special Branch officer, Henrik Ellert, the Special Branch suffered from a lack of credibility with Rhodesian-born Prime Minister Ian Smith, who reportedly distrusted the largely British-born Special Branch senior leadership. Smith preferred information from his Rhodesian-born district commissioners over what he heard from the Special Branch.[42]

By October 1977, the Special Branch consisted of the following desks: A desk[43] (nationalism [A1] and terrorist [A2]), C desk (European affairs), D desk (technical), E desk (protective security and vetting), F desk (administration and training), G desk (commercial and industrial intelligence), Z desk (Selous Scouts), and GC desk (ground coverage).[44] Desks typically were staffed by between eight and twelve officers and members, usually headed by a detective superintendent with three to four detective inspectors, and the remainder made up of noncommissioned members. One exception was the Z desk, which was commanded by Chief Superintendent Michael McGuinness with two superintendents as deputies. Formal intelligence training for Special Branch officers was nonexistent; what was taught was learned on the job and typically modeled on MI5.

The Special Branch desks were operationally involved in intelligence. Notably, these included the European desk, the nationalist and terrorist desks (later combined to form the A desk), the Special Branch liaison to the Selous Scouts (Z desk), technical (D desk), and ground coverage (GC desk). The European affairs desk arguably had the oldest origins, tracing back to the early Security Section with its emphasis on countersubversion. The C desk, likely named because the emphasis was on countering communist subversion and left-wing agitation, largely focused on the labor unions in Rhodesia.[45] The desk also monitored left-wing and right-wing political parties, religious organizations, academics, media representatives, and foreign diplomats in Rhodesia. Left-wing activities by students and faculty at the University of Rhodesia were closely tracked.[46] In monitoring foreign diplomats, concern was not only about their potential contact with dissident organizations, nationalist parties, but also as a counterintelligence threat. Henrik Ellert, a former Special Branch officer assigned to the European desk, described it as needing

> to report on all aspects of the security threat from Europeans, to obtain intelligence on a wide variety of subjects including the activities and workings of

neighboring police forces, security and intelligence organs, armies, and air forces, economic intelligence, the University, religious targets, and both left- and right-wing organizations. . . . Primary targets on the left included individuals or subjects active in political and social organizations perceived as being in support of or sympathetic toward African nationalist aspirations.[47]

Little is known about Rhodesian counterintelligence operations due to the lack of available records. One possibility is that Rhodesia's lack of international recognition limited the number of foreign diplomats and intelligence officers stationed in the country. One documented example involves Special Branch surveillance of post office boxes in Salisbury used as dead drops first by the MI6 and later by the Central Intelligence Agency (CIA) which led to the arrest of two CIA assets, John Roger Nicholson and Alfred Trevor Gallagher, in Salisbury.[48] Based on the number of keys issued for the target post office box, many more individuals likely used that drop to communicate with the CIA. The CIA officer involved was the declared liaison to CIO, Irl Wilson Smith, who left Rhodesia shortly after the arrests took place.[49]

The nationalism desk was primarily concerned with collecting intelligence on African nationalist groups. Until 1972, the Special Branch had an excellent record of domestic human intelligence (HUMINT) operations, including penetrations of the leadership of Zimbabwe African National Union (ZANU) and Zimbabwe African People's Union (ZAPU).[50] The successful penetration provided the Special Branch with advanced warning of insurgent infiltration attempts. In most cases, Rhodesian authorities intercepted the insurgent bands before they had an opportunity to launch any attacks. Crabtree explained,

> The Special Branch succeeded in penetrating both ZAPU and ZANU at all levels and seldom were we not prewarned of "enemy" incursions—once a group of terrorists had been infiltrated we were able to plot their subsequent movements almost day by day.[51]

Likewise Andrew Field explained, "The penetration of African Nationalist movements remained very active right up to the end of the war. ZANU's internal wing, the Peoples Movement, was thoroughly infiltrated by the Special Branch source network right up to April 1980."[52] Almost certainly, the Special Branch maintained well-placed sources within the leadership of both ZANU and ZAPU as well as other African political parties active in Rhodesia. The problem was with agent handing, briefing, and debriefing when most of these sources were in foreign countries outside the easy reach of Special Branch operators.

The terrorist desk focused on combating the activities of insurgent groups operating in Botswana, Zambia, Tanzania, and later, Mozambique.[53] Much of the intelligence obtained by this desk was from detailed interrogations of captured insurgents. The terrorist desk also ran agent operations inside the insurgent organizations, which provided invaluable intelligence on leadership intentions and plans. The desk collected extensive detailed information on the numbers, location, training, equipment, morale, and activities of insurgents. Little has been written due to limited records describing the Projects Section, which was ostensibly part of the terrorism desk. According to former Special Branch officer Ellert, the Projects Section was created to make immediate operational use of the intelligence collected by the terrorist desk.[54] The project section was headed by Detective Inspector Vic Opperman and was based at an old house inside the Braeside Police Camp in Salisbury and at a farmhouse on Retreat Farm outside Bindura. The farm became the focal point for Operation Favour, a program to enlist and provide rudimentary training to African youth for an armed auxiliary force to combat the increasing number of insurgents.[55]

Z desk—perhaps more commonly referred to as SB Selous Scouts—was a group of roughly a dozen Special Branch officers assigned as liaison officers to the Selous Scouts.[56] Under the command of Chief Superintendent Michael McGuinness, this unique element typically reported through McGuinness directly to CIO director general Flower. With the advent of the Selous Scouts and the need to return "turned terrs" for operations, those assigned as liaison officers worked closely with the Selous Scouts, handling most terrorist interrogations, collecting intelligence, and providing intelligence support to Selous Scout operations. SB liaison officers often conducted interrogations in the field and at the Selous Scout forts to collect intelligence useful in furthering Selous Scout operations. These officers focused largely on tactical intelligence support to internal Selous Scout operations. The information came from prisoner interrogations, which began immediately after the captured insurgent arrived at the Selous Scout "fort" while the prisoner was still feeling the emotional impact of his capture. The commander of the Selous Scouts, Lt. Colonel Ron Reid-Daly claimed that nine times out of ten, prisoners revealed all the information they had as soon as the interrogation began.[57] The Special Branch also exploited documents, weapons, and pocket litter found on the insurgents killed in combat by security forces. Ellert explained:

> Items of personal belongings, note-books, and documents were carefully examined and from these the Special Branch was able to build up accurate records of guerilla names, identity of sector and detachment personnel. In the early days, the note-books turned up extremely important information giving both the real name and Chimurenga non-de-guerre and weapons serial numbers. Other note-books revealed the location of hidden arms caches and details of contact men in villages.[58]

In contrast to the tactical focus, strategic intelligence about insurgents or information useful for external operations typically was passed to Combined Operations (COMOPS), which was responsible for directing and coordinating the operations of the Rhodesian security forces.[59] The SB liaison officers also reportedly participated in the distribution of doctored materials developed as part of the Rhodesian chemical and biological weapons (CBW) effort.[60]

As for the technical desk, it was responsible for the operational targeting/ direction of Z3, which were sources known as "THETA" and "GAMMA." THETA involved mail interception addressed to specific Special Branch targets, while GAMMA was the collection of radio signals and targeted monitoring of telephone calls. For much of the insurgency, GAMMA and THETA focused on monitoring white dissidents suspected of ties to the African nationalist political parties ZAPU and ZANU.[61] Located in Salisbury, Z3 typically reported directly to the provincial Special Branch officer (PSBO) for Salisbury and Mashonaland. These operations relied heavily on the cooperation of the Post Office's Special Investigation Branch (SIB).[62] Intelligence obtained from mail monitoring was aided by the Universal Postal Union (UPO) agreeing that all mail destined for what was the Federation of Rhodesia and Nyasaland be channeled through Salisbury. Due to a UPO oversight, the agreement stayed in place after UDI. Consequently, mail from Eastern European countries destined for Zambia and Malawi still went through Rhodesia. Interception of this mail proved useful in identifying insurgents trained in Eastern Europe as well as their family members in Rhodesia and mistresses in Zambia.[63] GAMMA collection (radio intercepts and telephone monitoring) took place at Special Branch headquarters. Those who worked this knew the monitoring station as "The Black Box" or simply "The Box." Linkage from the main post office telecom switching board to SB headquarters was set up with all monitored lines connected to reel to reel tape recorders. The Box also housed teleprinters that intercepted number-coded transmissions from local embassies.[64]

Last, the BSAP's uniformed duty branch ran a low-level intelligence effort dubbed "ground coverage" beginning in the early 1960s. Crabtree detailed how he sought to introduce the Kenyan experience with "ground coverage," a system of emplacing low-level informants in rural areas to report on operations of local activists or insurgent groups.[65] Ground coverage employed uniformed African constables operating out of district stations to maintain contact with villagers and run informants in rural African communities inside Rhodesia.[66] These efforts provided useful intelligence about the support for insurgents among local populations and alerted the Rhodesian security forces to the location of insurgents. The failure of Rhodesian authorities to detect insurgent success in winning the battle for the "hearts and minds" of the rural African population in northwestern Rhodesia resulted in the collapse of the ground coverage network of rural informants in that region by the end of 1972.[67] As the African population's support swung away from the white-minority government toward the nationalist parties, the Special Branch's network of village informants in rural areas dried up, and Special Branch officers often relied on more physical "coercive" means to obtain information, further alienating the rural population against the government.[68] However, the Special Branch's network of informants in urban areas remained consistently productive throughout the conflict.

As the foreign intelligence arm of the CIO, Branch II operated in the same way as most HUMINT services would, focusing on HUMINT asset recruitments and developing liaison relationships with foreign intelligence services.[69] Branch II also oversaw covert action (including propaganda, disinformation,[70] assassinations, and sabotage) and sanctions-busting activities.[71] In all of these areas, it was relatively successful for such a small service with very limited resources in terms of manpower and money. The CIO's Branch II had extensive HUMINT networks operating in the "frontline" states of Zambia, Botswana, Mozambique, and Angola. Notably with a relatively sizable English-speaking population of European descent in Zambia, Branch II operated relatively free in the country, and many white Zambians actively supported CIO operations inside Zambia.[72]

Communication with agents in Zambia was simple: blacks living in Zambia merely crossed the border into Rhodesia, and whites in Zambia often passed intelligence to the CIO over the telephone.[73] Those operations included the wide-scale penetration of Zambian institutions including the Zambian intelligence service, political institutions, and military, and at least one successful assassination—that of ZANU national chairman Herbert Chitepo in 1975.[74] The CIO also mounted successful operations against the Soviet and Chinese embassies in Lusaka, Zambia.[75] In contrast, CIO operations in Mozambique reportedly were hampered by the limited number of Portuguese speakers available to the CIO. Branch II was led by Kenneth Leaver, a career BSAP officer who had been the FISB deputy director under Basil de Quehan. Following the breakup of the federation, Leaver took a post in Rhodesia's then newly formed Central Intelligence Organisation, becoming its director (designation, DEX or director, External) of Branch II.[76]

Branch III was the Directorate of Military Intelligence. Military intelligence was a vital but overlooked resource. Until 1973, the Rhodesian military did not have a national-level military intelligence capability.[77] Before its creation, a Rhodesian military officer was assigned to the CIO as the director of military intelligence (DMI). He was a liaison with the CIO and served as a referent on military issues.[78] Military intelligence was confined to junior officers or enlisted men (often, reservists) serving at company, regimental, or brigade level. Under this arrangement, the military intelligence personnel almost always were outranked and overruled by more senior Special Branch representatives.[79] The lack of emphasis on military intelligence was a major weakness in the Rhodesian intelligence structure. One reason that Rhodesia

did not develop a military intelligence capability sooner was strong opposition from the Rhodesian Treasury and the CIO. They argued that a military
intelligence department was unnecessarily expensive and duplicative.[80] In the
short period between the inception of Rhodesian military intelligence and the
transition to majority rule in 1980, Rhodesia's military intelligence failed to
become a major player in the country's intelligence community.

In 1973, the Rhodesian Army established the Directorate of Military Intelligence (DMI), led by the director, Military Intelligence, who was appointed
by the Rhodesian army commander, but was under the operational control of
the CIO director general. The DMI focused on external military intelligence,
largely derived from Rhodesian signals intelligence (SIGINT) and imagery
intelligence (IMINT) efforts.[81] It was largely created to remedy the inadequa-
cies of entirely relying on policemen, as with the Special Branch, to collect and
interpret intelligence, according to one former Rhodesian Intelligence Corps
member.[82] From its outset, the DMI was plagued with several problems. First,
it was staffed largely with inexperienced territorial (reservist) officers who
lacked a basic understanding of intelligence collection or analysis. Second, the
Special Branch leadership, anxious to preserve its dominance within the Rhodesian intelligence community, refused to cooperate with the DMI, although
some joint Special Branch/RIC cooperation did occur at local levels.[83] Last,
the army undercut the DMI by continuing to rely on the Special Branch for
intelligence.[84] As commander of the Selous Scouts Reid-Daly explained:

> The Special Branch regarded Rhodesian Military Intelligence [MI] with disdain.
> This was because of MI's amateurism, lack of experience and the poor quality
> of their officers. The latter was due to the fact that officers who showed little
> promise in commanding men were posted sideways, into Military Intelligence.[85]
> They relied exclusively on hand-me-downs from the Special Branch.[86]

One former BSAP officer, Andrew Field, suggested that the failure to develop
an effective military intelligence capability to serve the army and air force's
operational requirements does not lay at the feet of any interservice rivalry
with the BSAP or CIO. Field argued that the failure to develop an effective
military intelligence capability was caused by the inability of the Rhodesian
military to appreciate the need for military intelligence. If the military leadership valued intelligence, they could have built an intelligence collection and
analytic capability at the unit level.[87] However, the Rhodesian military leadership had no understanding of intelligence's value or how it could be exploited
operationally. Rhodesian military training failed to address the value of intelligence and how intelligence was collected or used.

In early 1978, Reid-Daly approached army commander General Hickman
and suggested the creation of a Special Forces Intelligence Center (SFIC) to

combine the Special Air Service and Selous Scout intelligence sections with officers from the Rhodesian Intelligence Corps. Reid-Daly described:

> General Hickman was enthusiastic over the concept which I had recommended, and particularly the Special Forces Intelligence Centre I envisaged, which was an amalgamation of the Special Air Service's and Selous Scouts' Intelligence Sections souped up by officers of the Army Intelligence Corps.[88]

This would have largely excluded Special Branch officers from Selous Scout operations. By August 1978, efforts had been made to construct a large operations room and staff quarters and to assign necessary personnel. Yet the plan collapsed after only seven weeks when the Special Branch opposed the concept, believing the creation of a Special Forces Intelligence Center usurped their intelligence role. As a senior Special Branch liaison to the Selous Scouts wrote in an October 1978 memorandum:

> It is constantly stressed to me by Colonel Reid-Daly that it is not his intention to over-ride Special Branch responsibilities, but I cannot see what else he is doing by having this organization. It is constantly stressed to me also that the SFIC intend only to concern themselves with military matters for dissemination on a National basis. I find this difficult to believe as the SFIC Selous Scouts internal set-up encompasses all those responsibilities presently covered by Special Branch. Further, tactics do not change so rapidly that a whole new organisation has to be created to collate and disseminate them. There are good points in the overall concept of the SFIC and I in no way wish to denigrate the whole organization, I only wish to point out that the aspects in the SFIC concerning the Selous Scouts is a duplication of effort and has become virtually a take-over of the Special Branch role in the Selous Scouts.[89]

The chief of the defense staff and the director general of the CIO added to the debate by voicing concerns about the creation of a new intelligence center given the multiplicity of existing intelligence elements and the likely unnecessary duplication of effort. Reid-Daly complained that "piles of intelligence . . . lay gathering dust, because there were no people to process it."[90] In contrast, a scholar of the Rhodesian conflict, J. K. Cilliers, described how the demise of the SFIC and subsequent reassignment of personnel to the DMI was a boon for the Rhodesian intelligence community.[91]

Complementing the nascent military intelligence efforts, the Rhodesian Intelligence Corps (RIC) was established in 1975 to fill the long-ignored need for an indigenous military intelligence capability. Commanded by Rhodesian army colonel John Redfern, it reported through the Rhodesian Army chain of command and did not answer to the CIO.[92] The RIC's creation was likely in response to the perception that Special Branch intelligence did not effectively

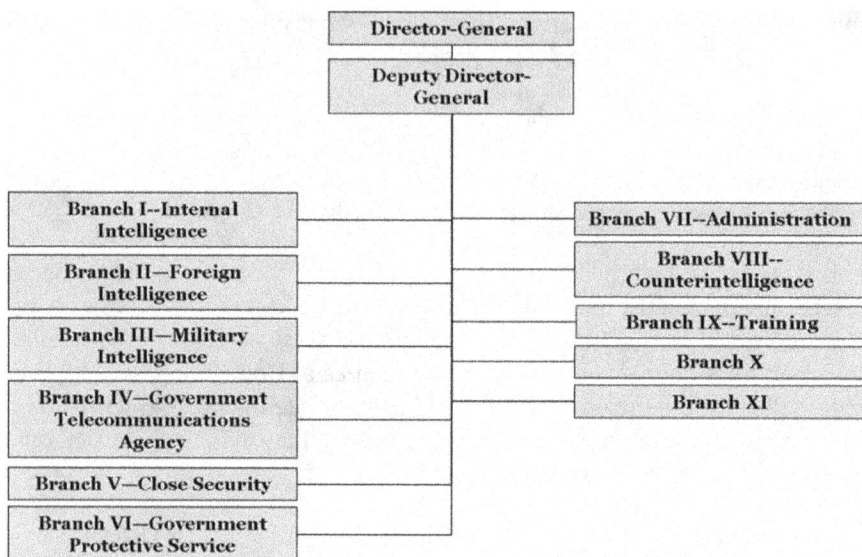

Figure 4.2 Structure of Rhodesian CIO.

support military operations requirements. As one former RIC member, J. R. T. Wood, stated: "One mistake was to leave the intelligence requirements to the Special Branch personnel who, untrained in military intelligence, did not assist the military planning cycle."[93] A small number of joint Special Branch/RIC teams collected operational intelligence, but most Rhodesian Special Branch members had a low opinion of the RIC in general.[94] Generally regarded as staffed by poor-caliber territorial officers who were part time, the RIC's only notable contribution to counterinsurgency operations was the production of small-scale topographical maps of Rhodesia and basic research. Little Special Branch intelligence was shared with the RIC.[95]

COVERT ACTION

Rhodesia's covert action capabilities consisted of propaganda operations and direct action against opponents inside and outside Rhodesia. Rhodesian direct-action resources rested exclusively in the Rhodesian Special Air Service (SAS) and the Selous Scouts. The CIO planned and carried out what is probably the most successful direct-action operation conducted in the conflict. That operation involved the March 1975 assassination of the military head of ZAPU, Herbert Chitepo, with a car bomb hidden beneath his Volkswagen Beetle detonating when he attempted to start the car. Zambian authorities concluded that the assassination was part of a leadership struggle in ZAPU, resulting in widespread arrests of ZAPU members in Zambia. Many Rhodesian sources have written accounts of the CIO's involvement in the assassination. Despite these admissions, some remain convinced that the assassination was carried out by others inside ZAPU.[96] The Selous Scouts also conducted assassinations of internal targets and launched a bombing campaign prior to the 1980 elections to discredit insurgent political parties.[97]

One significant CIO propaganda operation was the use of a clandestine radio station (Voz da Africa Livre—the Voice of Free Africa) to broadcast Portuguese-language anti-FRELIMO programming into Mozambique. To transmit the Voz da Africa Livre broadcasts nightly, the CIO tasked the Rhodesian Broadcast Corporation to recondition a large transmitter, "Big Bertha," inherited from the Portuguese when they abandoned Mozambique.[98] The radio station broadcast reports of a fictitious insurgent group fighting to overthrow the Marxist FRELIMO government of Mozambique. By 1975, the CIO formed an actual Mozambique resistance, the Mozambican National Resistance (MNR)—a.k.a. *Resistência Nacional Moçambicana* (RENAMO)—against FRELIMO (see Sirrs in this volume).[99] The MNR was wholly a Rhodesian creation funded by South African intelligence and continued to wage a vicious civil war against the FRELIMO government until 1992. Despite the 1992 end of the Mozambique civil war, clashes between FRELIMO and RENAMO have occasionally continued until a 2017 truce. The creation of RENAMO is one of the regrettable legacies of Rhodesia's counterinsurgency efforts.

LIAISON

The vast bulk of Rhodesia's foreign intelligence was derived through liaison arrangements—often very informal after Rhodesia's UDI—with several foreign intelligence services. Despite the lack of international recognition for the Rhodesian government, the CIO's liaison relationships were essential to the service's foreign intelligence collection. With Rhodesia's limited financial and personnel resources, close ties to friendly liaison services served as an important force multiplier for Rhodesian intelligence.

The CIO's Branch II focused its liaison efforts on developing close intelligence relationships with South Africa's Bureau of State Security (BOSS) and Portuguese services (the *Polícia Internacional e de Defesa do Estado* [PIDE], renamed *Direcção-Geral de Segurança* in 1969). Informal liaison—often based on long-standing personal ties—existed with several other services, including British intelligence (MI6 and MI5), the French *La Direction Générale de la Sécurité Extérieure* (DGSE), Italian and Greek services, the United States' Central Intelligence Agency (CIA), and even Zambian intelligence on issues of mutual interest.[100] The CIO's continuing contact with Britain's intelligence services resulted from CIO head Kenneth Flower's personal ties to senior members of both British services.[101] The CIO station in Paris—headed by CIO officer Max Dumas—was charged with maintaining ties to both the French DGSE and the Italian service. Dumas cultivated close ties with both Alex de Marenches (head of the DGSE) and General Michelli (director of the Italian Security Service).[102] DGSE head de Marenches had a close affinity for Rhodesia, having lived briefly in the country. Rhodesian intelligence received nearly all its information on the external support for the insurgent armed wings, including ZANU's Chinese-backed Zimbabwe African National Liberation Army (ZANLA) and Eastern bloc–backed ZAPU's Zimbabwe People's Revolutionary Army (ZIPRA), from the CIA, MI5, or other Western intelligence services via liaison channels.[103]

EFFECTIVENESS

No matter how effective or professional an intelligence service is in recruiting and running sources, developing technical capabilities, building liaison relationships, intelligence itself does not win wars or end insurgencies. Intelligence is necessary, but insufficient on its own. Intelligence has the potential to shorten wars and aid decisive victories, but only if the political and military leadership have the willingness and capability to use the intelligence effectively. The Rhodesian intelligence services during the counterinsurgency demonstrate that success is not dependent solely on collecting intelligence and running operations. Rather, the Bush War's end was because the government's position was increasingly untenable, especially given US and UK pressure on South Africa to cut arms and fuel supplies to Rhodesia. At the same time, the neighboring African frontline states were pressuring insurgent groups to come to the negotiating table to resolve the conflict. After four months of negotiations, all sides signed the Lancaster House Agreement in London on December 21, 1979, effectively beginning a ceasefire. Elections were held in March 1980, and an independent Zimbabwe became a reality on April 18, 1980, ending fifteen years of insurgency.

The Rhodesian strength in HUMINT operations provided remarkable successes early in the conflict, but these early gains evaporated as the tide of support among Rhodesia's African population swung to the insurgents.[104] The BSAP's ground coverage intelligence collection failed to counter the threat that subversion posed to the rural African population, and the intelligence networks built up over the years by the BSAP in northeastern Rhodesia were dismantled by ZANLA within weeks. Following ZANLA's subversion of the African populace in the region, the BSAP never could reestablish its informant network, necessitating the Selous Scouts. While the Selous Scouts and their SB liaison officers produced large volumes of intelligence on insurgent groups, these successes did not replace the intelligence capability lost when ground coverage collapsed. Rhodesian intelligence also failed to warn the government about the growing cooperation between FRELIMO and ZANU that eventually led to a second front in the insurgency and provided ZANU's military arm with operating bases in Mozambique.[105]

One explanation put forward by Andrew Field, a former long-serving Special Branch officer, was that Rhodesia's intelligence elements continued throughout the war to produce crucial intelligence, but the intelligence consumers failed to use the intelligence provided. These consumers, chiefly the military, did not act on or understand the value of the information.[106] As Field described,

> When the sabotage campaign changed to an insurgency campaign and then finally into a low intensity war, perhaps all elements involved in combating these threats had reacted a little too slowly especially to tactical change based on the valuable intelligence that was being gleaned at the time.[107]

This situation, in part, may be due to a lack of intelligence training in the Rhodesian military officer corps with little emphasis placed on the correct use of intelligence.[108]

Rhodesian intelligence services' experience was marred by interservice rivalries and lack of cooperation that damaged its effectiveness. As the Rhodesian security situation deteriorated, the Rhodesian intelligence structure devolved into personal fiefdoms. Often, these fiefdoms pursued narrow institutional or personal agendas at odds with other elements of the Rhodesian intelligence community. The Rhodesian intelligence services also were marred by suspicions about the loyalties of their leaders.

Another problem that reduced the effectiveness was the lack of any systematic intelligence cycle to use more recent American terminology. The intelligence cycle is a process by which policymakers (i.e., political and military leaders) convey their prioritized intelligence needs to the intelligence service for collection.[109] Collection against those priorities is conducted, and raw intelligence is then provided to analysts for evaluation and assessment. Next, analysts produce intelligence reports from a wide variety of sources, and those assessments are provided to the intelligence consumers, usually policymakers. The objective is to provide timely and actionable intelligence to those who need it. Yet, in the Rhodesian example, a system of communicating political and military leadership intelligence was lacking. The CIO produced monthly and quarterly appraisals of the security situation based on the information collected, but it is not clear how responsive these were to the consumers' needs or how that information was used. In fact, CIO director general Flower's memoir portrayed Rhodesia's political leaders as likely to discount CIO assessments as unduly pessimistic.

In terms of operational capability, Rhodesian intelligence could not compensate for the limited military manpower available to the country. Although Rhodesian intelligence generally could identify the insurgent groups operating inside Rhodesia, the Rhodesian military often was unable to deploy to the region before the insurgents had moved. Added to the difficulty facing the Rhodesian Security Forces, insurgent groups operating inside Rhodesia avoided contact with government units whenever possible. Instead, the insurgents preferred to attack softer targets (e.g., European farmhouses, lone vehicles traveling on the roads, schools, missions) and to lay mines.

Although Rhodesia developed a capable intelligence service, the police-dominated intelligence structure likely was better suited to counterterrorism than a rapidly growing insurgency. Rhodesia's counterinsurgency would have been better served if it had a professional military intelligence service dedicated to providing actionable, timely intelligence to the elements of the armed forces. While acknowledging the lack of adequate military intelligence, Selous Scout commander Reid-Daly chafed at the Special Branch stranglehold over intelligence and its use. Reid-Daly complained that the Special Branch control over intelligence prevented his unit from acting on critical information in a timely manner. His frustration led him to undertake disastrously rogue intelligence missions.[110]

LEGACY

The Rhodesian intelligence services have left a damaging legacy that endures today in Zimbabwe and in neighboring countries. Most notably, the CIO outlived Rhodesia and continues today in post-independence Zimbabwe. In 1980, the new government of Zimbabwe asked Rhodesian CIO director general Kenneth Flower to remain as head of the CIO under Zimbabwean prime minister Robert Mugabe.[111] Several other European CIO officers remained in senior CIO positions for several years, leading the organization through turbulent times as well as integrating intelligence officers from the insurgent groups, notably ZANLA. One example of a former Rhodesian officer who continued to have a senior leadership role in the new CIO is BSAP chief superintendent Danny Stannard, who headed CIO's Branch 1 (Internal) from independence until 2000 when he immigrated to the UK. At least initially, these officers served to shape the ethos and direction of the CIO in Zimbabwe. Nonetheless, the Zimbabwe CIO evolved into a wholly different organization.

Although Flower sought to ensure the Rhodesian CIO was above partisan politics, the Zimbabwean CIO became a tool of the ruling ZANU political party, one largely serving to protect the rule of Robert Mugabe and his supporters. In protecting Mugabe's personal ambitions, there are reports that the Zimbabwe CIO is a repressive tool, engaging in arbitrary arrests, illegal detention, and torture of political opponents and regime dissidents.

Another legacy of the Rhodesian CIO was its involvement in the internal affairs of neighboring states. The CIO played a key role in the long-standing civil war in Mozambique, which only reached a stable cease-fire in 1992. The Rhodesian CIO had created RENAMO, which engaged in a brutal insurgency against the ruling FRELIMO forces. Until 1980, the Rhodesian CIO funded, equipped, trained, and directed RENAMO so that Mozambique's long and painful conflict was a direct legacy of the Rhodesian CIO.[112] Rhodesia's Special Branch, largely in the person of Chief Superintendent Michael McGuinness, also had a hand in supporting Malawi's Special Branch, a central player in President-for-Life Hasting Banda's oppressive autocratic regime.[113]

Last, many members of Rhodesian intelligence at the time of independence went south to join South Africa's intelligence organizations. Along with former members of Rhodesian special forces, they planned and participated in covert operations aimed at destabilizing the newly independent Zimbabwe. These operations included sabotaging the Zimbabwean air force at its Thornhill Air Base, involving the loss of several warplanes and the destruction of a key munitions depot. Other operations included car bombings and murder, largely of African National Congress members in Zimbabwe.[114] Several, mostly from the Selous Scouts and one former Special Branch member, went on to join South Africa's notorious Civil Cooperation Bureau, which targeted opponents of the apartheid government. The Special Branch operations, run out of the Selous Scout fort at Bindura, arguably became the model for South Africa's Vlakplaas, site of a Security Police counterterrorism interrogation and execution facility (see O'Brien in this volume).[115]

NOTES

1. Bruce Hoffman, Jennifer Taw, and David W. Arnold, *Lessons for Contemporary Counterinsurgencies: The Rhodesian Experience* (Santa Monica, CA: RAND Corporation, 1991). https://www.rand.org/pubs/reports/R3998.html. I thank the following individuals for their comments and suggestions regarding this research. Among the former BSAP SB members are included Roger Capper, Andrew Field,

Winston Hart, Michael McGuinness, Keith Samler, and David Willis. Among the former Rhodesian Intelligence Corps members are John Redfern and Dr. Richard Wood. Statements here represent the author's personal views and do not represent the position of the U.S. government.

2. Harold Nelson et al., *Area Handbook for Southern Rhodesia*, DA Pam 550–171 (Washington, DC: US Government Printing Office, 1975), 23.

3. Nelson, 4.

4. Ibid., 27.

5. Andrew Field, email communication with the author, July 25, 2007.

6. Bill Crabtree, *Came the Fourth Flag* (Lancaster, UK: Scotforth Books, 2002), 188.

7. Those few British territories with internal security elements were located in the Far East.

8. Rhodesia and Nyasaland Army (RNArmy).

9. Ken Flower, *Serving Secretly: An Intelligence Chief on the Record* (London: John Murray Ltd., 1987), 11.

10. Philip Murphy, "Creating a Commonwealth Intelligence Culture: The View from Central Africa 1945–1965," *Intelligence and National Security* 17, no. 3 (2002): 133.

11. Crabtree, 201.

12. Andrew Field, email communication with the author, July 25, 2007.

13. Crabtree, 201.

14. Ibid. 223.

15. Flower, 11.

16. Flower, 12.

17. Crabtree, 199.

18. BSAP memorandum, "Organisation and Function of Special Branch and CIO," October 11, 1977, 2.

19. Crabtree, 199.

20. Ibid.

21. Flower, 15.

22. Crabtree, 222.

23. Ibid.

24. Flower, 16.

25. Ibid.

26. Ibid.

27. Ibid., 13.

28. Ibid., 15–16.

29. Ibid., 16.

30. BSAP memorandum, "Organisation and Function of Special Branch and CIO," October 11, 1977, 3.

31. Ibid.

32. Flower, 17.

33. J. R. T. Wood, "There Never Was Enough Intelligence: The Role of Intelligence in the Rhodesian Counter-Insurgency Campaign, 1962–1980," unpublished paper (n.d.), 3.

34. Military Intelligence Directorate (MID)—not generally referred to as Branch III. DMI (director of military intelligence) and DAI (director of air intelligence) were under operational command of DG CIO for intelligence and under administrative command of the commanders of the army and air force, respectively.

35. Ibid.

36. The roles of CIO Branches X and XI remain unidentified.

37. J. R. T. Wood, "There Never Was Enough Intelligence: The Role of Intelligence in the Rhodesian Counter-Insurgency Campaign, 1962–1980" (n.d.), 3.

38. Crabtree, 225.

39. Flower, 17.

40. Crabtree, 225.

41. Ibid.

42. Ellert. 15.

43. The Rhodesian Special Branch did not have a "B desk."

44. BSAP memorandum, "Organisation and Function of Special Branch and CIO," October 11, 1977, 2.

45. Andrew Field, email communication with the author, July 25, 2007.

46. Henrik Ellert, "The Rhodesian Security and Intelligence Community 1960–1980," in Ngwabi Bhebe, Terence O. Ranger, eds., *Soldiers in Zimbabwe's Liberation War* (London: John Curry 1995), 95.

47. Ellert, 89.

48. "Journalist Pleads Guilty in Rhodesia," *New York Times*, December 10, 1969. https://www.nytimes.com/1969/12/10/archives/journalist-pleads-guilty-in-rhodesia.html; "Consul in Rhodesia Denies U.S. Link to Espionage Case," *New York Times*, January 6, 1970, https://www.nytimes.com/1970/01/06/archives/consul-in-rhodesia-denies-us-link-to-espionage-case.html; Ellert (1989), 125.

49. David Willis, email communication with the author, April 26, 2020.

50. Flower, 105.

51. Crabtree, 241. Crabtree explained: "Indicative of our invasion of their hierarchy; once whilst on business in London, I was able to make a covert personal contact with one of ZAPU's most militant leaders and in the confines of my hotel room (during which much beer was consumed) in an atmosphere of amicability, I was able to extract from him invaluable information on the future intentions of his party."

52. Andrew Field, email communication with the author, July 25, 2007.

53. Ellert, 93.

54. Ibid., 94.

55. Ibid., 95. Operation Favour was the attempt to train and equip the Security Force Auxiliaries (SFA) made up of the militias belonging to the various UANC factions following the 1978 Internal Settlement.

56. Keith Samler, email communication with the author, April 26, 2020.

57. Reid-Daly, 105.

58. Ellert, 30.

59. Keith Samler, email communication with the author, April 26, 2020. BSAP Assistant Commissioner Michael Edden led a National Interrogation Team that was

tasked to conduct interrogations and exploit intelligence collected following external raids.

60. Ellert, 94. He wrote, "Initiatives undertaken by the Terrorist Desk in this regard included the use of sophisticated explosive devices installed in radios and the use of poisoned clothing which was then delivered to guerrilla units by informers and agents employed by their SB runners."

61. Keith Samler, email communication with the author, April 26, 2020. According to Andrew Field, while Z3 was the exclusive domain of the C Desk, most of the Special Branch stations had a Z3 source functioning (See Andrew Field, email communication with the author, July 25, 2007).

62. BSAP/2, personal communication with the author, March 4, 2005.

63. David Willis, email communication with the author, April 26, 2020. Willis wrote, "The Universal Postal Union had agreed that all mail destined for what was the Federation of Rhodesia & Nyasaland be channeled through Salisbury. Due to a UPO oversight, the agreement stayed in place after UDI. As a consequence mail from Eastern European countries destined for Zambia and Malawi still went through Rhodesia. This was very handy for correspondence, particularly mail to Zambia and Rhodesia from Hungary. Some ZIPRA members who had spent time in Lusaka before being sent for training in the communist bloc had developed amorous relationships with Zambian residents. They kept in touch with their sweethearts and talked about their life and activities in Eastern Europe. They identified themselves and surprisingly members of the ANC's Umkhono we Sizwe. In a number of instances mail to their wives or families in Rhodesia came in the same bag. We had a field day fully identifying them."

64. Ibid.

65. Crabtree, 207.

66. Andrew Field, "GC Desk: Ground Coverage," undated paper.

67. J. K. Cilliers, *Counter-Insurgency in Rhodesia* (London: Croom Helm, 1985), 221.

68. Torture, mutilations, massacres, and other atrocities became an increasingly common practice by both sides in the conflict especially as the insurgency intensified during the late 1970s.

69. CIO Branch II officers were posted to Athens, Paris, Lisbon, Pretoria, Washington, Libreville, and Lourenco Marques. See Ellert, 99.

70. Within CIO's Branch II was the Directorate of Psychological Warfare (DPW), which was responsible for planning and execution of all government psychological warfare operations including propaganda and disinformation campaigns as well as take defensive measures against foreign propaganda and disinformation efforts. See BSAP memorandum, "Organisation and Function of Special Branch and CIO," October 11, 1977, 5–6.

71. Cilliers, 219.

72. Although Ellert does not describe the race of the individuals involved, he claims that Rhodesian intelligence was very successful in recruiting sources inside the Zambian intelligence service, Zambian police, and all branches of the Zambian

military. Rhodesian intelligence even recruited a woman, who worked in the registry of the Zambian intelligence service. The woman reportedly provided classified Zambian intelligence materials to the Rhodesians for several months. Ellert, 92.

73. Hoffman, et al., 33–34.

74. Despite numerous admissions of responsibility for Chitepo's assassination, some debate still lingers. For more information, see: Luise White's *The Assassination of Herbert Chitepo: Texts and Politics in Zimbabwe* (Bloomington, Indiana: Indiana University Press, 2003). For descriptions of the CIO's role in Chitepo's assassination, see Ken Flower, *Serving Secretly: An Intelligence Chief on the Record* (London: John Murray Ltd., 1987), Peter Stiff, *See You in November* (Johannesburg, South Africa: Galago Publishing, 1985), and David Martin and Phyllis Johnson, *The Chitepo Assassination* (Harare, Zimbabwe: Zimbabwe Publishing House, 1985).

75. Hoffman, et al., 33.

76. Andrew Field, https://www.wikitree.com/wiki/Leaver-217.

77. Andrew Field in email communication with the author, July 25, 2007. He wrote: "In March 1965 General Putterill instructed Colonel West to set up the Directorate of Military Intelligence (DMI) within the organization of the CIO specifically to assist the CIO with its intelligence functions." This function described by Field likely refers to the liaison position in the CIO.

78. Cilliers, 223.

79. Ibid., 224–25.

80. Hoffman, et al., 28.

81. Military Intelligence Directorate (MID and Director of Military Intelligence (DMI). (See note 4).

82. Wood, 195.

83. Cilliers described this as a generalization, because in DMI he did not experience any refusal to cooperate. Cilliers, 226.

84. Hoffman et al., 29.

85. This statement is based on a subjective dislike by the author for certain individuals. Brig. F. G. D. Heppenstall (DMI 1973–74) and Brig. P. J. Hosking (DMI 1975) both commanded at platoon, company, battalion, and brigade level. Col. J. L. Redfern commanded at platoon and company level and may be the object of the author's statement for subjective reasons.

86. R. F. Reid-Daly, *Pamwe Chete: The Legend of the Selous Scouts* (Johannesburg: South Africa: Covos-Day, 1999) 69.

87. Andrew Field, email communication with the author, July 25, 2007.

88. R. F. Reid-Daly as told to Peter Stiff, *Selous Scouts: Top Secret War* (Alberton, South Africa: Galago Press, 1983), 487.

89. Memorandum from Superintendent Keith Samler to Officer Commanding Special Branch, "Selous Scouts: Special Branch Involvement," XYS 8777/7, dated October 26, 1978.

90. Reid-Daly, 304.

91. Cilliers, 232.

92. John Redfern, email communication with the author, June 25, 2020.

93. JRT Wood, "Countering the Chimurenga: The Rhodesian Counterinsurgency Campaign 1962–80," in Daniel Marston and Carter Malkasian, eds., *Counterinsurgency Modern Warfare* (Oxford: Osprey Publishing, 2008), 192.

94. BSAP/2, personal communication with the author, November 22, 2004.

95. David Willis, email communication with the author, May 11, 2020.

96. See: Luise White, *The Assassination of Herbert Chitepo: Texts and Politics in Zimbabwe* (Bloomington, Indiana: Indiana University Press, 2003). For descriptions of the CIO's role in Chitepo's assassination, see Ken Flower, *Serving Secretly: An Intelligence Chief on the Record* (London: John Murray Ltd., 1987); Peter Stiff, *See You in November* (Johannesburg, South Africa: Galago Publishing, 1985); David Martin and Phyllis Johnson, *The Chitepo Assassination* (Harare, Zimbabwe: Zimbabwe Publishing House, 1985).

97. Namely that of Rev. Arthur Kanodareka in 1978 and Edson Sithole in 1975. Glenn Cross, *Dirty War: Rhodesia and Chemical Biological Warfare, 1975–1980* (Solihull, UK: Helion and Co, 2017).

98. Ellert, 69.

99. Hoffman et al, 36.

100. Hoffman et al., 34.

101. Flower, 30–31.

102. Crabtree, 234.

103. Hoffman et al., 34.

104. In his stinging criticism of the performance of the Rhodesian intelligence services, Reid-Daly wrote:

"I have made no mention of any advance intelligence on terrorist activities and intentions provided to the army before any large-scale terrorist incursion was made. The reason for that is simple: there was none. The Central Intelligence Organisation, whose explicit task was the acquisition of such intelligence, had failed dismally. . . . Military officers, particularly those in the Special Forces, were acutely conscious of the fact that, apart from the Sinoia incursion, the security forces had received no advance warning of any crossings. This was shown by the large-scale crossings of terrorists that led to operations *Nickel* and *Cauldron*. In his book, *Serving Secretly* Flower makes much of the fact that he had seasoned the terrorist organizations with a sprinkling of informers who kept him abreast of their intentions. If in fact they did, Flower was remarkably slow to pass this intelligence to the military, as is borne out by the fact that from *Operation Nickel* onwards there was not a single occasion in which the CIO gave the military precise advance information of any terrorist incursions into Rhodesia." Reid-Daly, *Challenge*, 163.

105. Cilliers, 220.

106. Andrew Field, email communication with the author, July 25, 2007.

107. Ibid.

108. Cilliers, 223.

109. "Intelligence Works," 2020, https://www.intelligencecareers.gov/icintelligence.html.

110. Notable was the one involving Rhodesian helicopter pilot turned Selous Scout, Mike Borlace, who was sent on a covert reconnaissance mission to scout ZAPU/ZIPRA targets in the Zambian capital Lusaka. For Borlace's account of this ill-fated mission, see https://www.mikeborlace.com/about-mike-borlace. Chief Superintendent Michael McGuinness had a very different account of the reasons for the failure of the Borlace mission.

111. Flower served as the head of the Zimbabwe CIO from 1980 until his death in 1987.

112. The Rhodesian CIO is not solely responsible for the Mozambique conflict. After Zimbabwean independence, South African assumed sponsorship of RENAMO.

113. Discussions with McGuinness. Also see Henrik Ellert and Dennis Anderson, *A Brutal State of Affairs: The Rise and Fall of Rhodesia* (Harare, Zimbabwe: Weaver Press, 2020), 200.

114. Phyllis Johnson and David Martin, *Apartheid Terrorism: The Destabilization Report* (London: James Currey Ltd., 1989), 67.

115. Robin Binckes, *Vlakplaas: Apartheid Death Squads 1979–1994* (Barnsley, UK: Pen & Sword, 2018), 15. Vlakplaas as the brainchild of South African police colonel (later Brigadier) J. J. Viktor, who had been attached as a liaison to the Rhodesian Special Branch at Bindura under Chief Superintendent Michael McGuinness. At the time of Zimbabwean independence, McGuinness arranged for much of the material at Bindura to be transferred to Viktor at Vlakplaas. (Discussions between author and McGuinness). McGuinness and Viktor maintained a longstanding relationship long after McGuinness relocated to South Africa in 1980. (see Henrik Ellert and Dennis Anderson, *A Brutal State of Affairs: The Rise and Fall of Rhodesia* (Harare, Zimbabwe: Weaver Press, 2020), 198.)

Chapter 5

The Role of the Forces Armées Rwandaises Intelligence Services and Parallel Power Structures during the Rwandan Struggle for Liberation

John Burton Kegel

From July 1, 1962, onward, when Rwanda gained its independence, the Rwandan intelligence services played a significant role in destabilizing the government, undermining peace negotiations, and creating the environment for the 1994 genocide. Although much has been written about the genocide, there are two gaps in the historiography of the period leading up to this cataclysm. The first is the presidency of Juvénal Habyarimana from 1973 to 1994.[1] The second is the four-year civil war from 1990 to 1994, known as the Rwandan Struggle for Liberation, which shaped the context of the genocide.[2] In taking an intelligence studies perspective, this chapter chips away at these gaps by uncovering the largely unexplored internal politics of the Rwandan army—the *Forces armées rwandaises* (FAR)—as well as the role of the country's intelligence services.

A group of well-organized officers within the FAR had a significant impact on Rwanda's trajectory. After Habyarimana's plane was shot down on the evening of April 6, 1994, these officers and troops loyal to them systematically killed everyone who might replace him as president, including designated prime minister of the Broad-Based Transitional Government (BBTG) Agathe Uwilingiyimana, chief justice of the supreme court Joseph Kavaruganda, and the leaders of the moderate opposition parties. Although we do not definitively know who shot down the plane—possibly the extremist officers within the FAR or a Rwandan Patriotic Front (RPF) commando—this is beside the point. It was the murder of the moderate Rwandan political establishment that ushered in the genocide. General Roméo Dallaire, the leader of the United Nations Assistance Mission for Rwanda (UNAMIR), explained:

> In just a few hours the Presidential Guard had conducted an obviously well-organized and well-executed plan—by noon on April 7 the moderate political

leadership of Rwanda was dead or in hiding, the potential for a future moderate government utterly lost.[3]

These senior officers have been identified by researchers and by the International Criminal Tribunal for Rwanda (ICTR). Most of them, like Colonel Theoneste Bagosora and Lieutenant Colonel Anatole Nsengiyumva, were from Rwanda's northwest. Though they were not the only people involved in organizing and orchestrating the genocide, their role was particularly important. Considering UNAMIR's military weakness and mandate, the FAR was the critical organization that could have stopped the genocide before it got underway. As Rwanda's army, the FAR had the necessary intelligence service, weapons, troops, and organization to stop the ethnic militias, such as the *Interahamwe* and *Impuzamugambi*, from killing Tutsis in the streets of Kigali and later throughout the country. However, these officers ensured that the FAR supported and protected the ethnic militias and even participated in the killings.

The active and diverse Rwandan political opposition was mirrored by a multitude of positions within the FAR officer corps itself. Previous studies about the fractures within the FAR have mainly focused on the latter years of the war and especially the start of the genocide.[4] This superficially appears to be correct, as the genocidal ideology of the extremists had, by that time, coalesced the FAR into two distinct camps: moderates who were opposed to the killings and extremists who were carrying them out. However, national and interorganizational politicking had a long history in the Rwandan armed forces, called the *Garde nationale* from 1962 to 1973, and the FAR from 1973 to 1994. For example, military intelligence was involved in several successful or attempted coup d'états. It was also actively involved in the creation and maintenance of patronage networks within the army.

This chapter is based on research conducted for my PhD, "The Road to Genocide: A History of the Rwandan Struggle for Liberation," and draws on the same source material. Most of the archives relevant to the intelligence agencies (Ministry of Defense and Office of the President) were scattered or destroyed during the genocide. What little remains is practically inaccessible for researchers, held under lock and key in Rwanda. However, various intrepid journalists and international institutions have collected the scattered material. The most important among these is the International Criminal Tribunal for Rwanda (ICTR), which has both evidence and court testimony available via its website. Linda Melvern also found several documents written by the FAR when she visited Rwanda just after the genocide: they are available at the University of Wales in Aberystwyth, and many have also found their way onto the ICTR website. Generally, documents drawn up by the pre-1994 Rwandan government are written in French. The translations in this text are my own, and the original French can be found in the endnotes. Another excellent repository for primary source material on Rwandan history is the France Genocide Tutsi website database, with over ten thousand documents arranged chronologically.

Besides documents created by the Rwandans, there are invaluable reports and testimonies by the diplomatic corps in the country. The American, British, and Dutch cables used in this paper are from the U.S. National Archives and Records Administration (NARA) in Washington, DC; the National Archives at Kew, London; and the *Nationaal Archief* in the Hague, respectively. Several other archives hold key material on Rwanda between 1990 and 1994 but remain firmly closed to researchers. The most important among these are the French and Belgian military archives. Both countries had military assistance agreements with Rwanda and were the premier foreign supporters of the Habyarimana government. It is safe to assume that these relationships also extended to their intelligence services.

This chapter argues that the Rwandan intelligence services played a crucial role in the events leading to the genocide. It demonstrates how extremist officers, using their positions within military intelligence, undermined both the FAR's fighting power and the multiparty government that had negotiated a peaceful conclusion to the war, thus creating a conducive environment for genocide. This chapter is divided into seven sections, the first half of which explore Rwanda's precolonial and colonial history with attention to the origins of regionalism. This also includes an overview of President Grégoire Kayibanda's rule from 1962 to 1973, the 1973 coup d'état in which President Habyarimana seized power, and the challenges within the FAR. The second half analyzes important phases of the civil war that led to the 1994 genocide, the introduction of multiparty democracy, the peace process, and the collapse of stability. The conclusion highlights key themes, including the role of interethnic competition, which centered on regionalism.

INTRODUCTION TO RWANDAN HISTORY

The Nyiginya Kingdom, the forebear of the Rwandan state, was probably founded around the 1650s.[5] From its heartland between the Nyabarongo and Akanyaru Rivers, it steadily expanded until 1895, by which time it controlled Rwanda's modern borders. Though the Nyiginya king, also known as the *Mwami*, was the kingdom's technical ruler, it would be incorrect to see Rwanda as a fully centralized state during this period. The authority and reach of the court waxed and waned according to the ability of the *Mwami*. Several provinces that fell within the sphere of influence of the kingdom were never fully integrated.

Things changed with the arrival of Europeans toward the end of the 1800s. Eager to protect his realm from the horrors of the advancing Congo Free State to the west, the young *Mwami* Musinga, also known as Yuhi V, signed a treaty with Imperial Germany, which was advancing into Central Africa from its base on the East African coast. This turned Rwanda into a German protectorate. With German help, Musinga incorporated and consolidated the peripheral regions which had, until then, escaped the court's authority. The most important among these were several independent Kiga states in the north of Rwanda. The alliance between court and colonizer was one of convenience: the young Musinga needed the Germans to help consolidate his rule, while the Germans could not hope to exercise any influence in Rwanda without the help of the court. Following the First World War, Rwanda became a League of Nations mandate administered by Belgium. The arrival of the Belgians showed that the amicable relationship between the court and the colonists was not a given, and Musinga was deposed in 1931. He was replaced by Mwami Mutara III, who was more to the liking of the Belgian authorities.

The categories "Hutu" and "Tutsi" existed before colonization, but they denoted socioeconomic status rather than ethnicity. Generally, a "Tutsi" was connected to the court, or else (and sometimes also) a cattle-herder or a warrior, while a "Hutu" might be a porter, a servant, or a farmer.[6] However, the categories were fluid, intermarriage existed, and a Hutu who acquired cattle might become a Tutsi and vice versa. There were also checks and balances on the power of the *Mwami*, who was always a Tutsi: "while the *Mwami* had theoretically unlimited power, three chiefs divided responsibility on each of Rwanda's hills. Each chief had a separate portfolio for agriculture, pastoral herding, or taxes, and one of these chiefs was always Hutu."[7] When the Germans and Belgians arrived, they did not understand the nuances of this system and imposed their own system instead.

Building on pseudoscientific social Darwinist ideology, Western colonial anthropologists posited that the Tutsi were an ancient people descended from the biblical figure of Ham, who had traveled from Ethiopia and conquered Rwanda. As such, they perceived the Tutsi as naturally superior to the Bantu Hutu. Consequently, a system was created in which the Tutsi aristocracy retained much of their traditional privileges but lost their political power. They could still levy workers and demand tribute from their mostly Hutu clients, but it is the Belgians who had the final approval in the appointment of a "chief." In addition to their control over political power, the Belgians regularly demanded labor for infrastructural work and forced farmers to grow certain cash crops like coffee. The combined traditional dues to the Tutsi aristocracy and demands made by the colonial authorities placed an enormous strain on most of the ordinary population. As historian Alison des Forges explained, "Many Rwandans saw Belgian rule as the beginning of the 'time of the whip.' Hutu bore its sting most often, but Tutsi suffered from it occasionally as well."[8]

As the prospect of independence arose in the late 1950s, "the electoral salience of ethnic labels" became increasingly clear to Rwanda's newly legal political parties.[9] It was understood that Rwanda, a United Nations Trust Territory, would become independent on the one person, one vote principle. The mostly Tutsi court and aristocracy hoped to preserve their power but realized this would be difficult as Hutu made up 80–85 percent of the population. Political parties organized along ethnic lines were formed on both sides. Tensions rose and exploded in 1959 when a period of civil war, known as the Social Revolution, led to the monarchy's overthrow. In the resulting conflict that lasted until 1964, the Hutu seized power and genocidal violence against the Tutsi forced most to flee to the surrounding countries.

NORTH-SOUTH FRACTURES IN THE DOMINANT HUTU COALITION

Following the 1959–1964 Social Revolution, Rwanda could best be described as a dictatorship of the majority.[10] The British diplomat J. S. Bennett wrote:

> Parmehutu [President Kayibanda's political party] today is the only organised political force in Rwanda. There are in the country no unions. There is no intelligentsia or bourgeoisie class. There is no press. . . . Rwanda must be considered a one party state.[11]

After decades of Tutsi and Belgian rule, so Parmehutu's thinking went, it was now the turn of the Hutus to rule the country. In what remains one of the best histories of Rwanda, scholar Gérard Prunier explained the official ideology as: "Hutu were the silent demographic majority [85% of the population], which meant that a Hutu controlled government was not only automatically legitimate but also ontologically democratic."[12]

However, it would be incorrect to assume that ethnicity alone could ensure unity. President Kayibanda was from the south-center of the country, and it was not long before Rwandans from the north, who were also Hutu, started accusing him of regionalism. This geographical resentment was felt on both sides. As Filip Reyntjens explained, "The report of the 1964 parliamentary commission notes in [the southern town of] Butare 'a certain frustration, which feeds a vague southern resentment against the center-north axis.'"[13] However, the overriding feeling was a belief that Kayibanda's south-central home region was profiting from independence, while the north was being denied investment from the national coffers. A second major area of friction between north and south involved patronage based on land rights. Following the Social Revolution, the north likely believed it would regain a measure of the political independence lost during the early stages of colonization. As the eminent historian René Lemarchand wrote, "The thrust of their 'revolutionary' efforts in the 1950s aimed at turning the clock back to the golden age of pre-Tutsi days."[14] During the colonial period, the position of patron in certain specifically precolonial Kiga/Hutu patron-client relationships (*ubukonde*) had been taken over by Tutsi connected to the monarchy. As most of the Tutsi had been driven out or eliminated during the Social Revolution, powerful northern lineages expected that they would once again take on the role of patron. However, this directly opposed the view of President Kayibanda and those in the center and south of the country who believed that such patron-client relationships were incompatible with egalitarian and socialist principles.[15]

In 1967, three years after the Parliamentary Commission had mentioned the existence of tensions between the north and the south of the country, an ambitious young officer from the north tried to seize power. Lieutenant Joachim Maramutsa, who was nicknamed "the First Consul" by Belgian military assistants, planned for the Ruhengeri police to march on Kigali, the capital of Rwanda. When they arrived, the Kigali police and Maramutsa's company of soldiers would join the coupists, and together they would move on the president's residence. However, the last-minute withdrawal of the Kigali police and the lack of support among the army led to the coup's failure.

The lack of support for Maramutsa's coup among the high command of the *Garde nationale*—the then military—is notable, considering it was mostly made up of northerners. The most important among them was Major Juvénal Habyarimana, who had been made minister of defense by President Kayibanda in 1965. Others included Major Alexis Kanyarengwe and Habyarimana's brother-in-law, Commander Pierre-Celestin Rwagafilita. It is unknown why they did not support the lieutenant, although several possibilities come to mind. First, Kayibanda had shown these men trust by allowing their rise through the ranks. It appears likely that the president knew how the north felt and tried to co-opt the region by allowing some of its sons to take important positions. Second, Rwanda was on a reasonably steady trajectory following the Social Revolution, and maintaining that stability was key to ensuring the county's economic growth. Third, if other groups were entertaining thoughts of a coup, personal ambition might have motivated their lack of support for the young lieutenant.

Rwanda's steady course was abruptly disturbed when problems in neighboring Burundi spilled over the border in 1972. President Kayibanda was unable to stop this, and the country soon faced the prospect of imminent armed conflict with both Burundi and Uganda. To make matters worse, the Belgian government made it clear that the *Garde nationale* would not be able to count on its continued support in case of war.[16] Habyarimana, who was now minister of defense, probably understood that he would have to act if he wanted to save Rwanda and his cherished *Garde nationale* from destruction. However, it is unclear who was responsible for removing President Kayibanda. Most say it was President Kayibanda who invited Habyarimana to his house under false pretenses with the intention of assassinating him. According to this theory, the would-be assassin missed his mark and allowed Habyarimana to get away. After fleeing to Camp Kanombe, where there was a large contingent of sympathetic Belgian military assistants, Habyarimana directed his counterattack against the president. By July 5, 1973, he was in control of the country.

THE FAR BETWEEN 1973 AND 1990

From 1973 onward, the Rwandan intelligence services were made up of three distinct organizations. The only civilian intelligence agency was the *Service Central de Renseignements*, also known as the *Sûreté de l'État*. In 1980, its budget made up roughly 1 percent of state expenditure.[17] The other two intelligence organizations were run by the General Staffs (G2 sections) of the FAR and the Gendarmerie, respectively, both of which came under the Ministry of Defense. The Rwandan Gendarmerie was comparable to its French equivalent, an independent branch of the armed forces that acted as a paramilitary police force responsible for maintaining law and order within the country.

The responsibilities of these three services were poorly defined. Both the *Sûreté de l'État* and the FAR G2—best described as military intelligence—carried out operations inside and outside Rwanda. The most important of these, especially in the late 1980s, was keeping an eye on Rwandan exiles and refugees in Uganda and Burundi. While it is normal for military intelligence to watch for external threats, its internal role was, in this case, less appropriate. Indeed, from the outbreak of war in October 1990 onward, but probably even before, Rwanda's military intelligence was also involved in the repression of internal dissidents. Often, it did so in conjunction with the Presidential Guard Regiment. Although the latter was not officially part of the intelligence services, it had a close relationship with both military intelligence and the *Sûreté de l'État*. For example, Pascal Simbikangwa held the roles of head of the *Sûreté de l'État* while simultaneously being a captain in the Presidential Guard. Other commanders of the *Sûreté de l'État*, like Major Lizinde, who headed the service between 1973 and 1979, also had military backgrounds. As such, it would be incorrect to see the *Sûreté de l'État* as a civilian organization. Finally, the G2 of the Gendarmerie had the extensive remit of internal security, including criminal intelligence and counterterrorism, but very little is known about the organization.

The 1973 coup d'état did not have positive consequences for the FAR. At the core of its problems lay the mutual relationships and conduct of its officers. Officers, and elite units like the Presidential Guard and the Para-Commando Battalion, came to be recruited almost exclusively from the country's northwest. The lack of external armed threats between 1973 and 1990 left officers with little to do. When Belgian military technicians were withdrawn from the chain of command, the esprit de corps of the colonial times slowly disappeared. In the best-case scenario, officers spent their time vying for privileges and competing for positions. In the worst case, undoubtedly encouraged by the fact that the 1973 coup had put political power within the grasp of military men, they plotted to seize power themselves. These dynamics led to two important affairs.

In 1980, Colonel Kanyarengwe and Major Lizinde started preparing to launch a coup. Both were key supporters during the 1973 coup and had initially been rewarded. Kanyarengwe had become minister of the interior, while Major Lizinde was the head of the *Sûreté de l'État*. However, when they were sacked in 1979, they decided to act.[18] One of their preparatory moves was to approach Lieutenant Colonel Bagosora in the hope he might join them. Bagosora would later be one of the main planners of the 1994 genocide, and his testimony before the ICTR gives an interesting glimpse into the workings of his mind. After admitting to the court that he did not warn President Habyarimana that the two officers had approached him, he explained:

I refused to participate in that coup d'état, because in my opinion, it was not warranted. It was just after the 1978 presidential election, and President Habyarimana had been elected by over 90 per cent of the population. . . . The reason they gave me did not suffice for me to get involved in the coup d'état. . . . I posed a condition to them, which I knew they were not going to fulfil . . . that they had to secure the agreement of Colonel Mayuya, who was a commanding officer of Kanombe camp, as well as the paracommando battalion. I knew full well that Colonel Mayuya was not going to accept. He was my friend, as well as the friend of the president. I knew that.[19]

Word of the attempted coup by Kanyarengwe and Lizinde soon got out. The latter was jailed in Ruhengeri, while the former managed to escape to Tanzania.

Eight years later, Colonel Stanislas Mayuya was assassinated. According to an anonymous ICTR witness:

Prior to the death of Colonel Mayuya, there was a, sort of, indiscipline in one of the companies of the paracommando battalion. Colonel Mayuya had been sick and had been taken to Belgium. He was operated on, treated and brought back, and he found that there was a rumour circulating that he had been poisoned.

And while convalescing, he opened an inquiry himself. And while he was questioning people, the NCO [non-commissioned officer] who had circulated the rumour fled outside the country, and those who were suspected were taken to justice. And in the meantime, Colonel Mayuya was assassinated and the chief of staff decided to dissolve the unit in which that rumour had been circulating [3 company].[20]

It is commonly believed that Mayuya was being groomed by President Habyarimana as a potential successor, much to the anger of the *Akazu*, an elite patronage network around first lady Kanziga.[21] Scholar Gérard Prunier noted, "Colonel Serubuga, one of the most powerful *Akazu* members, organized Mayuya's murder. The sergeant who actually pulled the trigger was later murdered in jail and the prosecutor in charge of the file was murdered during the inquiry."[22] Giving testimony before the ICTR, Laurien Uwizeyimana, professor at the National University of Rwanda, said that he believed that the soldiers who investigated the assassination found out that it had been committed by people close to Habyarimana, but the president "did not dare to act against the murderers, and it was the investigators who were gaoled."[23]

Both these events are of Byzantine complexity and shrouded in mystery. But they show the poisonous atmosphere among the upper echelons of the FAR. In an intelligence report just before the outbreak of the Rwandan Struggle for Liberation, Anatole Nsengiyumva, then head of military intelligence, wrote that:

This ill [regionalism] NEVER disappeared from the country. It is currently in full swing. It is sometimes "NORTH-SOUTH", or else "GISENYI-RHENGERI", or else "BUGOYI-BUSHIRU" . . . the NORTH-SOUTH problem is currently being exploited by certain minds who always want to create disturbances. The demands of "Southerners" are still UNCLEAR, although they consider themselves victims of a certain injustice towards people of the south. . . . From the point of view of the "Northerners" the regime is instead courting the people of the SOUTH, who are insatiable and UNGRATEFUL, while those of the NORTH are victims of this situation. They believe they should have more than they receive at present.[24]

ORIGINS OF THE WAR

On October 1, 1990, the children of the refugees who had fled between 1959 and 1964 returned to Rwanda by force. Deserting from the Ugandan Army— the country where they had grown up and played a key role in President Yoweri Museveni's rise to power—they crossed the frontier and revealed themselves to the world as the Rwandan Patriotic Front (RPF). The armed wing of the RPF, the Rwandan Patriotic Army (RPA), quickly swept away the

FAR at the border and marched on Kigali. However, the untimely death of the RPA's inspirational leader, Fred Rwigyema, and the intervention of Zairian and French troops on the side of the government of Rwanda swung the tide of battle. By the end of October, the RPF was in retreat. Under the leadership of Paul Kagame and a highly able and experienced high command, the RPA regrouped in the jungle-clad Virunga Mountains. From there, it waged an increasingly effective campaign against the FAR.

The outbreak of war should have unified the FAR officer corps in the face of a clear external enemy. However, the opposite occurred. Between October 1990 and early 1991, dozens of officers were arrested, seven of whom were court-martialed in July 1991.[25] Majors Sabakunzi and Mutambuka were arrested on October 2, 1990, and accused of conspiracy. According to James Gasana, who became minister of defense in 1992, Sabakunzi had uncovered insurance fraud by a FAR captain, who had promptly turned the situation around and accused the major of conspiracy.[26] Gendarmerie Lieutenant Colonel Uwihoreye was charged with cowardice and conspiracy because he had disobeyed an order to execute the prisoners of the jail he commanded as it was being overrun by the RPA.[27] Others who faced the court on various charges, including failure to carry out orders, were Commanders (Emmanuel) Habyarimana, Munyagatanga and Kanamugire. While these officers were all acquitted, they lost their salary and were not allowed to rejoin the FAR.[28] According to former Rwandan minister of defense James Gasana:

> The botched management of this war situation disorganized the FAR and reduced its performance. Deputy chief of staff Colonel L. Serubuga, sometimes in complicity with Colonel E. Sagatwa, took advantage of the war to marginalize officers from the south, such as Colonel Rwanyagasore who died in a mysterious accident, and Majors A. Nteziryayo, Sabakunzi and F. Niyonsaba. He also took the opportunity of exposing to mortal danger brilliant young rival officers from the north, feared for their more developed sense of the state, for their popularity among the troops . . . such as Lieutenant Colonel D. Nsabimana and Major Rwendeye.[29]

Gasana argued that the established officers from the northwest were prepared to carry on playing regional politics to maintain their own positions, even if this meant that the FAR would be less effective when fighting the RPA. Just a few months later, a group of officers from Byumba—in the north of Rwanda but outside the northwestern regions where power was concentrated—addressed the president directly. In a bold letter, they wrote:

> Major Emmanuel Mugabo and Major Evariste Nyampame were sidelined from their career through incomprehensible transfers carried out arbitrarily and in an illegal manner. Some others, such as Commander Gaspard Mulindahabi and Commander Godfroid Butare, who were summarily dismissed on the eve of

their retirement, Captain Pierre Canisius Hitimana, Lt. Evariste Bizimana, as well as Second Lt. Mukuralinda, were arbitrarily and illegally sidelined in very confusing circumstances, clearly motivated by hatred. . . . Lt. Colonel BEM Anselme Nkuliyekubona and Major BEM Gaspard Mutambuka were arbitrarily arrested and detained respectively for more than two years and more than 11 months and finally released without any formal charges being brought against them, before they were dumped on the street.[30]

To make matters worse, when officers were sidelined, arrested, or fired, they were often also ostracized. The letter explained that these men and their families now "live in a situation of total material isolation and are deprived of their elementary social rights."[31] Even those who had distinguished themselves against the RPA were not spared this treatment:

Commander BEM Emmanuel Habyarimana, who was illegally and arbitrarily arrested, although he had proven his qualities on the battlefield during almost the entire month of October 1990 in Mutara. . . . Your excellency, we believe that it is within your authority and power to find a remedy to this situation . . . which is only bringing shame to our country. Also we would like to point out that Byumba is not the only prefecture that has suffered from such injustice at all levels both within the Military and the Civil Service.[32]

These internecine rivalries likely had a debilitating effect on the FAR. The officers bickered among themselves instead of forming a united front against the RPA, which was growing stronger by the day. Though incontrovertible evidence has yet to be discovered, it is highly likely that these rivalries would have impacted morale and battlefield operations leading to incidents such as commanders withholding supplies or support from those other regions or else refusing to take orders from their nominal superior.

THE INTRODUCTION OF MULTIPARTY DEMOCRACY

On April 7, 1992, the first multiparty government of Rwanda was sworn in. President Habyarimana and his political party, the *Mouvement révolutionnaire national pour le développement* (MRND), had been forced to make this concession in the face of pressure from several quarters. Between January and March 1992, the RPA had inflicted a series of important defeats on the FAR. At the same time, the Rwandan internal opposition was becoming increasingly vocal. Badly needed international financial support for the Habyarimana presidency came with obligations. Even France, whose president had close personal ties with Habyarimana, insisted that some democratization was necessary. Unwilling to hold elections, the president appointed Dismas

Nsengiyaremye, a member of the *Mouvement démocratique républicain* (MDR) opposition party, as the country's new prime minister.

This marked the first time since the 1960s that political parties operated freely in Rwanda. The MDR was the main "Hutu" opposition party and drew its inspiration from President Kayibanda's legacy. In contrast, the *Parti libéral* (PL) was a more urban and inclusive party that counted several important Tutsi among its members. The *Parti social-démocrate* (PSD) was strong in the south and an inclusive party on the ethnic issue with a socialist outlook. Indeed, it was one of the most cohesive opposition parties before the genocide. Finally, there was the president's party, the MRND. These parties had varied approaches to the RPF. Both the PL and the PSD were prepared to negotiate an end to the civil war with the RPF and to give the RPF a role in the postwar dispensation. The MDR was split on the issue. Though Prime Minister Nsengiyaremye was prepared to negotiate, talks with the RPF were anathema to most of the MDR and MRND.

The effect of multipartyism on the FAR officer corps provided yet another opportunity for internal division. Bagosora described the situation years later at the ICTR:

> What I could see was that . . . officers had to remain apolitical. It is obvious that they had relationships. Officer of the centre and south since they had family members they were in a political environment of the opposition, it could be said that they were close to the opposition on account of the prevailing environment at the time. Northern officers, since they had family members, relatives, and brothers, who were members of parties like the MRND, it could be said they were close to the MRND party. . . . I can mention Rusatira, Léonidas. It was said that he was close to the MDR. Personally, I thought he was close to the RPF. . . . Ndengeyinka, about him it was said he was close to the MDR. . . . Rutayisire was close to the PSD. He was the brother in law of Minister Gatabazi who himself was a member of the PSD.[33]

Bagosora's distrust of his colleagues is still evident, years after the events. He is convinced that some of them collaborated with the RPF against the FAR. Rusatira, a full colonel himself, explained: "At the time the extremists were blackmailing everyone, even the army. Calling an officer, whatever his rank, a traitor . . . was enough to destabilise him. You had to do everything to make sure you were not classified with the traitors."[34] This is the point where parallel command structures grew within the FAR. Anatole Nsengiyumva, the intelligence chief quoted earlier, was a firm MRND supporter. He wrote in a July 1992 intelligence report:

> In my previous memo, I talked about a subversive movement led by the *Parti Liberal* and some members of other opposition parties. . . . Commander Donat

Habimana has been recruited by the PL and was said to be the leader of the team in Gisenyi. . . . [He] often attends meetings one of which was held in Lando's house. . . . Warrant Officer Ndoli . . . received a Mazda car offered by Lando-ald Ndasingwa (the car belongs to him). It is now driven by former Corporal Rurangwa of the Recce Battalion.[35]

The report names several other units and sections that he believed were infiltrated by the PL and then described the RPF's covert activities. Yet, it never linked the two. What becomes clear is that these soldiers were being followed by the military intelligence services not because they were a threat to the FAR but because they did not support the MRND. He further explained:

> Our soldiers have been contacted by the PL and by other opposition parties, and they are involved in demobilizing good soldiers. Those identified as such should be dismissed from the Rwandan Armed Forces [FAR]. I will strive to find tangible evidence. . . . Major Ngirumpatse and Ntezilyayo should be kept on a close watch. The G4 service of the RASH should be streamlined, because it has been infiltrated by Major Ngirumpatse. The case of Commander Donat Habimana should be followed up closely, while Commander Bahizi should be closely watched.[36]

The introduction of multiparty politics and a power-sharing cabinet also had profound implications for the intelligence services. As part of the arrangement, the *Sûreté de l'État* was broken up. Its external intelligence department was attached to the Ministry of Defense, while its internal intelligence department was attached to the Prime Minister's Office, held by the MDR. However, although the *Sûreté de l'État* technically no longer existed, a new organization appeared—it is unclear if it was rebranded or if it was newly founded. This *Service de sécurité* contained former members of the *Sûreté de l'État* and was most certainly involved with Rwanda's internal affairs. This reorganization created havoc within the intelligence community. As minister of defense James Gasana explained, "With the partisan politization of the administration, the officials of these services pass on more information to their parties and political allies than to their superiors. . . . The breakup of the intelligence service was already an important source of instability."[37]

JAMES GASANA AND THE ARUSHA NEGOTIATIONS

The position of FAR officers who had been in service since 1962 was largely secure until the 1992 swearing-in of the new multiparty government. Their regional background ensured their continued promotion, and many held important positions. Colonel Laurent Serubuga was chief of staff of the FAR, and Colonel Pierre-Celestin Rwagafilita, his counterpart in the Gendarmerie. Lieutenant Colonel Anatole Nsengiyumva was head of the G2 (military intelligence) in the General Staff, and Colonel Bagosora headed various commissions. However, the battlefield losses against the RPA and their well-known opposition to negotiations put them in a difficult position.

One of the most important members of Prime Minister Nsengiyaremye's cabinet was minister of defense Gasana. An MRND supporter, Gasana had already been minister of agriculture, livestock, and the environment but was known as an honest and effective operator. Perhaps because he was from Byumba rather than from the northwest, he had a realistic view of the war. Like Nsengiyaremye, he was convinced that a negotiated solution was the best option. At the same time, he was well aware that a strong FAR would ensure the multiparty government held a good hand at the negotiation table. For him, a strong FAR was one in which there was no regionalism.

An obvious step to achieving these goals would be to change the FAR and the Gendarmerie's high command. Gasana was soon presented with the perfect opportunity to set his plans in motion. On June 6, 1992, the RPA launched an offensive that captured Byumba, one of northern Rwanda's most important cities. This clear defeat meant that President Habyarimana and the French military advisers assigned to the FAR agreed that a change was needed. Serubuga and Rwagafilita, who were both from Gisenyi, were retired and replaced by the more moderate and capable Colonels Déogratias Nsabimana and Augustin Ndindiliyimana, from Ruhengeri and Byumba, respectively. Gasana also wanted to sack two other members of the Akazu: Colonels Bagosora and Sagatwa. However, the president disagreed and intervened, saving their careers. Though Bagosora was technically retired, he was allowed to stay on within the Ministry of Defense as the minister's private secretary ("directeur de cabinet").

The older officers launched a concerted effort to undermine Gasana when he took office. Just two days after he started in his new position, chief of staff, Colonel Serubuga was caught red-handed while trying to divert operational information that should have been shared with Gasana.[38] On March 25, 1992, the former head of the Rwandan courts-martial, Colonel Anselme Nshizirungu, visited the Belgian ambassador to warn him that a group of officers close to the president were the "brains" behind several massacres of Tutsi that took place that same month.[39] These killings aimed to escalate ethnic tensions, which was the opposite of Prime Minister Dismas's objective. Anselme named two members of the Presidential *Service de sécurité*, its chief, Colonel Elie Sagatwa, and former *Sûreté* boss, Captain Pascal Simbikangwa, and the head of the military intelligence service, Anatole Nsengiyumva, as part of the ringleaders.

Supporting Prime Minister Nsengiyaremye and minister of defense Gasana on the quest for a negotiated peace was foreign minister Boniface Ngulinzira. By July 1992, this triumvirate brokered the first ceasefire that held and started negotiations on the postwar dispensation with the RPA, in Arusha, Tanzania. The talks were complicated because of the many interests involved on the Rwandan government's side. President Habyarimana had to balance the increasingly radical officers of the old guard on the one hand and the mul-tiparty government on the other. He did not want to end up like Kayibanda before him, and a coup by the extremists was not a far-fetched proposition. Indeed, rumors of this had been circulating since at least 1991. On August 15, the French military attaché Colonel Bernard Cussac had reported that an attempt might come from "young officers who can no longer stand the geo-graphical recruitment imposed by the staff of the FAR and the incompetence of its leaders" or from those who were afraid of losing "their advantages and prerogatives."[40] However, Habyarimana did not want to give power to a dem-ocratic multiparty government either. Consequently, the Rwanda delegation's message at the Arusha negotiations was mixed. Nsengiyaremye, Gasana, and Ngulinzira tried to make progress but were kept in check by several soldiers sent by Habyarimana to keep an eye on things. Jean-Christophe Belliard, one of the French observers at the negotiations, recalled:

> I worked a lot with Ngulinzira who listened to me. But I also knew that Ngu-linzira was powerless. It was not him who took decisions. The real decisions were taken elsewhere. We could see that Kanyarushoki [the Rwandan Ambas-sador to Uganda, who also played a key role throughout the Arusha negotia-tions] was continually slowing things down and playing for time, while the third person, Bagosora, did not speak but seemed to think a lot. I had the sense that a lot of things got decided at his level.[41]

REMOVING THE MINISTER OF DEFENSE

As the negotiations moved forward under increasing international pressure, the extremist officers acted. On January 20, 1993, the *Alliance des militaires agacés par les séculaires actes sournois des Unaristes* (AMASASU), literally the "Alliance of soldiers annoyed by the age-old sly actions of the Unaristes," announced its existence in an open letter to the president.[42] The acronym was probably the inspiration for the name, as *Amasasu* means "bullets" in Kin-yarwanda. The group's objective was ensuring the Hutu would always remain in control of Rwanda and that the achievements of the Social Revolution of

1959–1964 would not be undone. The group proposed to reach their objective in a sinister manner:

> We know, as you do Mr. President, that we are fighting on the borders of our country whilst on the inside there are individuals who support our aggressors publicly and with impunity. If these blackmailing *Inyenzi* start the war once again, how do you plan on preventing us from teaching these inside traitors the lesson they deserve? After all we have already identified the most virulent among them and we shall act with the speed of lightning![43]

Undoubtedly, the AMASASU's core consisted of intelligence officers from the military intelligence section of the FAR General Staff (G2) led by Nsengiyumva. After a road accident in March 1994, a document was found in the car of chief of staff Nsabimana with a list of 331 people who were considered accomplices of the RPF. According to Andre Guichaoua, one of the premier historians on Rwandan politics, this kill-list was specifically made for AMASASU by Nsengiyumva.[44] Gasana's name appears on the first page.

The minister of defense was in an extremely difficult position. Normally, a threat against the life of a minister of defense would be handled by a country's intelligence and security services. Yet, in this case the threat came from the head of military intelligence. Meanwhile, the atmosphere in Rwanda was deteriorating rapidly. There were several assassinations of prominent politicians and further attempts thereof. Though these killings cannot with certainty be attributed to AMASASU, they demonstrated that no one was safe—a feeling that Nsengiyumva and his colleagues undoubtedly used when they threatened Gasana. Then on May 18, 1993, the popular MDR politician Emmanuel Gapyisi was shot dead in front of his house. He had been one of the rising stars of his party, and his death reverberated throughout the country.

When the mandate of Prime Minister Nsengiyaremye's multiparty government ran out on July 16, 1993, President Habyarimana replaced him and foreign minister Ngulinzira with other opposition politicians. Four days later, and only six months after the announcement of AMASASU's existence, Gasana found the situation untenable. After ensuring his family was safe in Switzerland, he wrote a letter of resignation that explained he was

> compelled to [resign] because of the persistent threats and sabotage that I face in my current duties. These threats which place me and my family in a permanent state of insecurity are the work of an anonymous political-military group which has named itself "AMASASU" and whose aims remain obscure.[45]

One week later, MRND stalwart Dr. Casimir Bizimungu privately told the U.S. ambassador to Rwanda that "if Gasana cannot protect himself we are all threatened."[46] Indeed, the promotion of known *Akazu* member Augustin

Bizimana as the new minister of defense signaled that the moderates' time was over. The removal of the Nsengiyaremye-Gasana-Ngulinzira triumvirate came at a critical moment for Rwanda. On August 4, 1993, when the Arusha Accords were signed, the three who had most contributed to the negotiations' success on the side of the government of Rwanda were no longer in power. Filling their positions were either well-meaning but ineffective moderates or extremists. After August, the atmosphere in Rwanda steadily deteriorated. Several influential politicians were assassinated, and the swearing-in of the Broad-Based Transitional Government—without which the rest of the Arusha Accords could not be implemented—was delayed several times. By April 1994, Rwanda was on a knife's edge.

Following the April 6, 1994, downing of President Habyarimana's plane, an enormous power vacuum appeared. The aircraft carried not only the president, but also the FAR chief of staff Nsabimana. In the ensuing chaos, Colonel Bagosora took control of the country and began eliminating the political opposition. The elite units of the FAR—the Presidential Guard, the Para-Commando Battalion, and the Reconnaissance Battalion—were mostly made up of soldiers from the northwest who readily followed his orders. When moderate officers like Colonel Marcel Gatsinzi tried to intervene, their orders were simply ignored. With the political opposition eliminated and the moderate elements within the FAR neutralized, nothing could prevent the *génocidaires* from killing 800,000 people. The genocide was eventually stopped three months later in July 1994 after the RPF had advanced from their strongholds in the north and defeated the FAR as well as the ethnic militias following heavy fighting.

CONCLUSION

While select FAR officers acted on April 6, 1994, to take control of the country, the groundwork for their genocidal success was already laid by the Rwandan intelligence services. Throughout the war, they used their privileged position to systematically block the advancement of their colleagues who were not from the northwest. When the multiparty government challenged this strategy, elements closely linked to the military intelligence services played a key role in forcing moderate minister of defense James Gasana out of power.

A study of Rwandan intelligence not only provides important insights into the country's history and the genocide, but also reveals broader lessons about intelligence. Regarding the role of ethnicity, the key takeaway is that regionalism can be an important driver of conflict within mono-ethnic power structures. Although the Tutsi were excluded from holding positions of power within Rwandan intelligence structures, the ruling coalition fractured along regional lines, as Northwesterners tried to monopolize the rents of state. The regional rivalry had deep precolonial roots and had been latent while the newly independent republic was consumed by a civil war along ethnic (Hutu-Tutsi) lines. However, when the Hutu emerged as the dominant group in the new political dispensation, and the enemy that had united them was no longer a threat, the latent regional rivalries flared up.

Regarding the role of intelligence and policymakers, the FAR intelligence officers' ability to undermine an internationally supported multiparty government demonstrates that special attention must be paid to the role of intelligence communities when switching from a single-party dictatorship to a multiparty democracy. Without clear chains of command and adequate oversight, they can turn state resources against a legitimate leadership. It also points to the importance of independent military and civilian intelligence services engaged in healthy competition. Had the *Sûreté de l'État* been a legitimate civilian organization, it might have detected the negative influence of the ethnically extremist and regionally exclusive FAR officers within the Rwandan military intelligence services. As for the goals of intelligence, the FAR officers' focus was not on immediate national security threats during a war, but on regional rivalries. This undermined the fighting power of their comrades in the field and eventually led to a position in which the RPA was militarily dominant. This is a clear example of intelligence used for self-interest, which directly contradicts national security objectives.

NOTES

1. Though it must be noted that the recent book by Andrew Wallis gives an excellent description of several important aspects of Habyarimana's rule. Especially the importance of patronage networks: *Stepp'd in Blood: Akazu and the Architects of the Rwandan Genocide against the Tutsi* (Winchester UK: Zero Books, 2018).

2. This chapter is based on my dissertation, "The Road to Genocide: A History of the Rwandan Struggle for Liberation," University of Kent, Canterbury, 2019. Regarding Rwanda's two civil wars since independence, this work refers to the first as the Social Revolution (1959–1964) and the second as the Rwandan Struggle for Liberation (1990–1994). Both names have political connotations; they are the names used by the respective victors of the wars.

3. Roméo Dallaire, *Shake Hands with the Devil* (London: Arrow Books, 2004), 232.

4. Alison Des Forges, "Expert Witness Report of Dr Alison Des Forges: In the Trial of Bagosora, Nsengiyumva, Kabiligi and Ntabakuze before the ICTR" (unpublished). This is a good starting point for an analysis of the days before and after April 6, 1994. Another useful account is Filip Reyntjens, *Rwanda: Trois jours qui ont fait basculer l'histoire* (Bruxelles: Institut Africain-CEDAF, 1995).

5. Jan Vansina, *Antecedents to Modern Rwanda: The Nyiginya Kingdom* (Madison: University of Wisconsin Press, 2004), 207.

6. Ibid., 134–35. There is a vast literature on the Hutu-Tutsi categories, their historical origin, and meaning. Besides Vansina, some of the more important are Catherine Newbury, *The Cohesion of Oppression: Clientship and Ethnicity in Rwanda, 1860–1960* (New York: 1988, Columbia University Press); David Newbury, "Precolonial Burundi and Rwanda: Local Loyalties, Regional Royalties," *The International Journal of African Historical Studies* 34, no. 2 (2001), 255–314; Alison L. Des Forges, *Defeat is the Only Bad News: Rwanda under Musinga, 1896–1931* (Madison: University of Wisconsin Press, 2011); James J. Carney, *Rwanda Before the Genocide: Catholic Politics and Ethnic Discourse in the Late Colonial Era* (Oxford: Oxford University Press, 2014).

7. Carney, 14.

8. Des Forges, *Defeat is the Only Bad News*, 183.

9. Carney, 48.

10. From: J. S. Bennett, Bujumbura To: West and Central African Department, "Elections in Rwanda," July 28, 1964, FO 371/181948, JN 1018/2, The National Archives (TNA), Kew, United Kingdom.

11. Ibid.

12. Gérard Prunier, *The Rwanda Crisis: History of a Genocide* (London: Hurst, 1997), 80.

13. Filip Reyntjens, *Pouvoir et Droit au Rwanda: droit public et évolution politique, 1916–1973* (Tervuren: Musée Royal de l'Afrique Centrale, 1985), 487; "Le rapport de la commission parlementaire de 1964 note à Butare 'un certain complexe de frustration, qui nourrit un vague ressentiment du sud contre l'axe centre-nord."

14. René Lemarchand, "Rwanda: The Rationality of Genocide," *Issue: A Journal of Opinion*, 23, no. 2 (1995): 8–11, 9.

15. For more information, see: Reyntjens, 493.

16. From: U.S. Embassy, Brussels To: Secretary of State, "Belgium may withdraw military technical assistance from Rwanda," June 28, 1973, ADD: Electronic Telegrams, 1973, U.S. National Archives and Records Administration (NARA), Washington, DC, United States of America; "Belgian Diplomats Fear Burundi Clash With Rwanda Force," *New York Times*, May 17, 1973, 10.

17. "Government Budget of 1980," Rwanda National Archives Digital Repository.

18. Wallis, *Stepp'd in Blood*, 92.

19. Transcript of Tuesday, November 15, 2005. Cross-examination of Théoneste Bagosora. *The Prosecutor v. Bagosora et al.* ICTR-98-41-T, 54–56.

20. Transcript of Thursday, October 20, 2005. Testimony of Witness LE1. *The Prosecutor v. Bagosora et al.* ICTR-98-41-T, 36–37.

21. Wallis, *Stepp'd in Blood*, 137–146.

22. Prunier, 87. The importance of Mayuya is emphasized by the fact that Camp Kanombe, one of Rwanda's biggest military bases, was renamed Camp Colonel Mayuya in his honor. He was in command of the base when he was murdered there. Transcript of Monday, September 18, 2006. Testimony of Aloys Ntabakuze. *The Prosecutor v. Bagosora et al.* ICTR-98-41-T, 13. Additional information on Mayuya can be found in Transcript of Tuesday, October 25, 2005. Testimony of Theoneste Bagosora. *The Prosecutor v. Bagosora et al.* ICTR-98-41-T, 49–59.

23. Transcript of Monday, November 27, 2006. Testimony of Laurien Uwizeyimana. *The Prosecutor v. Bagosora et al.* ICTR-98-41-T, 8.

24. From: Anatole Nsengiyumva To: "N042/G2.2.0.," May 22, 1990, File 1990/ Planning, Linda Melvern Rwanda Genocide Archive, University of Wales (LMRGA-UoW), Aberystwyth, Wales. "Ce Mal N'a JAMAIS disparu de ce pays. Actuellement, il bat son plein. Tantôt 'NORD-SUD', tantôt c'est 'GISENYI-RHENGERI', tantôt 'BUGOYI-BUSHIRU' . . . Le problème 'NORD-SUD' est actuellement exploité par certains esprits qui veulent toujours semer des désordres. Les revendications des 'Sudistes' NE sont toujours PAS claires, mais ils se jugent victimes d'une certaine injustice vis à vis des gens du SUD. . . . Pour les 'Nordistes' le régime courtise plutôt les gens du SUD insatiables et NON reconnaissants, tandis que ceux du NORD sont victimes de cette situation. Ils jugent qu'ils devraient avoir plus qu'ils N'obtiennent actuellement."

25. From: Swinnen To: belext bru, "Sitrep 19–20–21/07/91," July 22, 1991, France Genocide Tutsi (FGT), http://www.francegenocidetutsi.org/.

26. James K. Gasana, *Rwanda: du parti-État à l'État-garnison* (Paris: L'Harmattan, 2002), 159.

27. From: Swinnen To: belext bru, "Sitrep 19–20–21/07/91," July 22, 1991, France Genocide Tutsi (FGT), http://www.francegenocidetutsi.org/

28. Ibid.

29. Ibid., 66–67. "Le cafouillage dans la gestion de cette situation de guerre dés-organise les FAR et réduit leur performance. Le chef d'état-major adjoint, le colonel L. Serubuga, parfois en complicité avec colonel E. Sagatwa, profite de la guerre pour marginaliser les officiers du Sud, tels que le colonel Rwanyagasore qui périra dans un mystérieux accident, les majors A. Nteziryayo, Sabakunzi et F. Niyonsaba. Il en profite également pour exposer à la mort les jeunes officiers rivaux brillants du nord, redoutés pour leur sens de l'Etat plus développé, pour leur popularité au sein des troupes, et surtout pour le soupçon des intentions de putsch, tels que le lieutenant-colonel D. Nsabimana et le major Rwendeye."

30. From: Major Nyampame, Amicale de Byumba To: His Excellency the President of the Republic of Rwanda, Kigali, "Amicale de Byumba," October 22, 1991. "Exhibit Number: P431A, Date Admitted: 9–11–2006 (English Translation)," *The Prosecutor v. Bagosora et al.* ICTR-98-41-T.

31. Ibid.

32. Ibid.

33. Transcript of Monday, Thursday, October 27, 2005. Testimony of Theoneste Bagosora. *The Prosecutor v. Bagosora et al.* ICTR-98-41-T, 28.

34. Wallis, *Stepp'd in Blood*, 268.

35. From: Nsengiyumva To: Chef EM AR 'Sûreté intérieure de l'Etat', July 2, 1992. "Exhibit Number: P20(b), Date Admitted: November 11, 2002 (English Translation)" *The Prosecutor v. Bagosora et al.* ICTR-98-41-T, 1.

36. Ibid., 3.

37. Gasana, *Rwanda: du parti-État*, 108; "Avec la politisation partisane de l'administration, les fonctionnaires de ces services transmettent plus d'informations a leur partis et a leur allies politiques qu'a leurs chefs. . . . L'éclatement des services de renseignements constituait déjà une source importante d'instabilité."

38. Gasana, *Rwanda: du parti-État*, 103; see also Transcript, November 27, 2002, Examination-in-Chief by Ms. Mulvaney of Witness ZF. *The Prosecutor v. Bagosora et al.* ICTR-98-41-T, 23–26.

39. From: Swinnen, Belgian Embassy, Kigali To: belext bru "Getuigenis van rwandees officier over politieke toestand," March 25, 1992, FGT. Swinnen spells the name as "Nhizirungu," though the correct spelling seems to be "Nshizirungu".

40. Colonel Cussac To: Armées Paris "Situation militaire et renseignements divers," August 15, 1991, FGT. "Soit d'une action, menée par une partie de l'armée et particulièrement par de jeunes officiers qui ne supportent plus le recrutement géographique imposé par l'Etat-Major des FAR et l'incapacité de ses dirigeants. Soit, plus vraisemblablement, d'une action d'intoxication, menée par l'armée, pour durcir les positions du gouvernement qu'il voit se diriger vers la démocratie, au risque de faire perdre, aux caciques du régime, leurs avantages et prérogatives."

41. U.S. Holocaust Museum and The Hague Institute for Global Justice. *International Decision-Making in the Age of Genocide: Rwanda 1990–1994: Annotated Transcript.* The Hague. June 1–3, 2014, 1–26.

42. UNAR was the 1950s and 1960s vintage royalist party. It strongly supported the Mwami and was mostly made up of Tutsis. In this sense, Unaristes as meaning RPF—which was considered to be a Tutsi organization.

43. From: AMASASU to: His Excellency the President "Creation of AMASASU," January 20, 1993. "Exhibit Number: P3D1(b), Date Admitted: 78–09–2002" *The Prosecutor v. Bagosora et al.* ICTR-98-41-T.

44. André Guichaoua ed., *Les crises politiques au Burundi et au Rwanda (1993–1994)* (Paris: Karthala, 1995), 662.

45. André Guichaoua, *From War to Genocide: Criminal Politics in Rwanda 1990–1994*, trans. Don E. Webster (Madison: University of Wisconsin Press, 2015), 88. Annexes "Resignation of James Gasana," http://rwandadelaguerreaugenocide. univ-paris1.fr/minister-of-defense-james-gasanas-resignation-from-office-and-flight-abroad-on-20-july-1993/.

"Je me sens contraint de prendre cette décision en raison des menaces persistantes et des actions de sabotage dont je fais l'objet dans mes fonctions actuelles. Ces menaces qui me placent, ainsi que ma famille, dans une situation d'insécurité permanente sont l'œuvre d'un groupe politico—militaire anonyme qui s'est donné pour nom 'A.M.A.S.A.S.U.' et dont les visées restent obscures."

46. From: Flaten, U.S. Embassy, Kigali To: Secretary of State, Washington, DC, "the MDR vs. the MDR," July 26, 1993. Department of State FOI, https://foia.state. gov/Search/results.aspx?searchText=Rwanda&beginDate=&endDate=&publishedBeginDate=&publishedEndDate=&caseNumber=.

Chapter 6

Intelligence and Political Power in Neo-Patrimonial Systems: Theory and Evidence from Liberia

Benjamin J. Spatz and Alex Bollfrass

The fortunes of intelligence services and political leaders are often intertwined, their collusions and collisions rarely without significant political consequence.[1] Academic research into these relationships' effects on governance have been thorough and insightful, but focused on only a sliver of the times and places in which spies and political leaders have been in contact.[2] Like with any intelligence topic, the absence of historical data—namely, the rare access to files of secret services—shapes the questions that can be convincingly answered. As a result, the field skews toward the relatively open American and British intelligence experiences, limited by declassification schedules to the periods before and during the Cold War. Indeed, with important exceptions, the best research about the political dimensions of intelligence addresses the historical experiences of globally powerful twentieth-century Western democracies and Soviet Union autocracy, which are unrepresentative of broader phenomena. Insofar as a theoretical program has emerged, conceptual frameworks about intelligence have been shaped by these parochial contexts.

An additional limitation in the literature is that preferred definitions of—and explanations for—politicization are entangled. Even the most judiciously conceptualized and rigorously empirically tested model of politicization as "the manipulation of intelligence to reflect policy preferences" conveys a theory of its purpose.[3] This imperils the concept's ability to contribute to understanding intelligence-politics interactions beyond the immediate historical context in which they were developed.

As the field of intelligence studies works toward a more rigorous theorization, one important building block is gaining better knowledge about the political dimensions of individual intelligence communities.[4] Canvassing states beyond the Cold War context suggests that the patterns of interactions

143

between intelligence and politics is understudied in an empirically common type of governance structure—neo-patrimonial states, where formal and informal institutions have merged and personal power dominates the bureaucracy. Such systems are often lumped under the imprecise categories of "fragile states," "competitive authoritarian systems," or "political marketplaces," but no matter the nomenclature, neo-patrimonial modes of governance centrally feature wielding state resources and institutions as the currency of politics.[5] Studying these systems promises to contribute directly to the broader politicization literature.

This chapter explores the current theoretical constructs in the context of Liberia to explain and interpret the political role of intelligence services. It argues that in neo-patrimonial systems, where formal institutions are tied to the interests of the elite, intelligence will be used as a political weapon to ensure the leader maintains power and internal competitors remain disadvantaged. This makes neo-patrimonial intelligence institutions—and even intelligence as a product—subject to a fundamentally different logic than either the Western democratic apolitical ideal or the regime-defense objective of security services protecting single-party autocracies. This chapter reveals the analytical dangers of importing the often implicit assumptions that typically frame analysis of Western security services. The goals and rules of the game are different, and therefore, political institutions—including intelligence institutions—should be seen to serve slightly different ends.

The chapter begins with a review of the literature on the politicization of intelligence in Western anglophone democracies and then uses studies about the services in single-party authoritarian contexts to help understand intelligence beyond these contexts. Next, it turns to the conceptual exploration of the political dimensions of Liberian intelligence to surface elements of intelligence politics. The empirical discussion is grounded in the political realities of elite politics. The conclusion takes stock of the further avenues for intelligence studies research that open up when examining the relationships of intelligence and politicians in novel geographic, historical, and political contexts.

Methodologically, the chapter's empirical analysis derives from data obtained from fieldwork by one of the authors (Spatz), including original English language documents from Liberia's intelligence services. It also relies on that author's participant observation as the arms expert on the United Nations Panel of Experts on Liberia, the independent body appointed by the United Nations secretary general to monitor, investigate, and report to the United Nations Security Council on compliance with, and violations of, the United Nations sanctions regime imposed on Liberia as well as other relevant issues of peace and security in Liberia and the subregion as mandated. This experience provided access and insight into issues pertaining to

Liberia's elite politics and its institutional structures, including that regarding intelligence entities. No privileged information is included.

POLITICS AND INTELLIGENCE

Scholars differ about whether domestic or international political variables shape a state's intelligence apparatus. In one view, the balance of foreign and domestic threats to a state, regime, or a particular leader's security shapes intelligence structures. For example, some comparative work has proposed that the *external* threat environment reduces the incentives for, and likelihood of, top-down politicization.[6] Competing work on the origins and roles of intelligence services in domestic politics suggests that forces *inside* the state explain the operation of intelligence services better than the external environment. Comparative research about the origins of intelligence organizations argues they are typically formed in response to domestic threats.[7] This line of inquiry concludes that once in existence, they continue to be shaped more strongly by domestic factors than external threats. For instance, Amy B. Zegart's analysis of the United States' national security agencies found that they are the product of bureaucratic and political incentives and forces "not rationally designed to serve the national interest."[8] Even the relatively clear division between foreign and domestic intelligence in the West has been a function of historical contingency and what would probably be called coup-proofing in other contexts.

Other work suggests that intelligence politics may well be shaped by a combination of domestic and international variables. Steven David coined the term "omnibalancing" to describe how some states must devise interrelated survival strategies at both the domestic and the international level.[9] This view is echoed in the intelligence literature, such as Christopher Andrew, who argues from empirical observation "that the determination of one-party states to destroy all opposition has a major influence on their foreign as well as domestic intelligence operations."[10] Whichever direction the causation runs, intelligence agencies have always been inherently political actors and foreign and domestic intelligence have always overlapped, sometimes to the point of indistinguishability.[11]

POLITICIZATION FROM ABOVE AND BELOW

Inquiries into the "politicization" of intelligence consumes a large proportion of the literature's attention in anglophone contexts. This section explores how the concept has been used to describe or warn against a variety of phenomena.

It has mostly appeared as a dependent variable and occasionally serves as an independent variable to explain a bad assessment. These conceptualizations assume that intelligence services, left to their own devices, would be constrained only by resources in their ability to produce more accurate assessments or effectively operate against enemies of the state.

Concepts of politicization are divided by whether the hypothesized cause of politicization originates from within the intelligence community (bottom-up) or the policymaking leadership (top-down). Beginning with the latter, Joshua Rovner developed the "oversell" model of top-down politicization to explain this "pathology." The model specifies two necessary conditions for politicization to occur: First, policymakers must be publicly committed to a policy and second, a "critical constituency" must emerge against which the policymaker will seek to mobilize intelligence.[12] Assessments of foreign governments are especially vulnerable to politicization because they can be interpreted as evaluations of how well political leaders are representing the national interest. The model was developed specifically for democracy, but its application to other systems with elite competition is evident. Whenever policymakers compete for an audience's approval, they will be incentivized to use intelligence as a "signal that policymakers have access to special information and, as a consequence, are in the best position to make decisions on how to act."[13] Consequently, politicization is a threat to the effectiveness and competence of the intelligence services.

Taking a different approach, Glenn Hastedt offered another view of top-down politicization, illustrating a division between the "soft" and "hard" varieties. "Soft" politicization uses what Hastedt described as "non-coercive means," such as "deliberate attempts to alter the assumptions underlying an analysis, the decision rules by which an analysis moves forward, and the institutional setting within which these deliberations occur."[14] To qualify as its "harder" counterpart, there must be "deliberate attempts to coerce analysts into adopting a certain set of assumptions or conclusion or in the extreme overruling analysts and imposing a conclusion on the analysis."[15] In a challenge to scholars, soft politicization is less visible in the historical record than its hard counterpart.

This scholarship helps in understanding the politics of intelligence in the United Kingdom, United States, and perhaps all Five Eyes countries. However, it is doubtful whether the concept even extends to other Western European nations. There, absent meaningful legislative oversight, intelligence services are more likely to be the private domain of the executive. Moreover, the reverse is possible in a Western democratic context. Intelligence services may even pose a threat to the executive when an intelligence service sees itself as a guardian of the regime or specific leader, higher than the government. In a "hard" form of bottom-up politicization, if a given government does not combat perceived domestic subversion with sufficient vigor, the agency may act to remove it, as has happened in Italy.[16] "Softer" forms of bottom-up politicization have been observed and categorized.[17]

INTELLIGENCE IN SINGLE-PARTY STATES

These "hard" bottom-up politicization phenomena, as well as the methods used to defend against the threats emanating from spy chiefs to political leaders, have received attention in historical accounts and some comparative research about "coup-proofing" in autocratic states.[18] By gathering information and conducting clandestine activities against threats to the regime, intelligence agencies can potentially provide a critical service to autocratic leaders: keeping elite politics noncompetitive. At the same time, that collected knowledge can be a source of power that threatens autocratic leadership.

From an inductive historical perspective, Andrew argued that it is difficult to overstate the importance of intelligence services in these governance structures:

> Modern intelligence systems have changed the nature of authoritarian regimes and with it the workings of the international system. The one-party state, the most malign political innovation of the twentieth century, depended on the creation of new intelligence agencies with an unprecedented ability to monitor and suppress dissent in all its forms. Though it is, of course, impossible to reduce the history of Stalin's Russia, Hitler's Holocaust, Saddam Hussein's Iraq or Kim Jong-Il's North Korea simply to the history of their intelligence and security services, all were heavily dependent on those services. The centrality of their intelligence communities to the functioning of one-party states and their systems of social control is frequently underestimated even in otherwise excellent political histories.[19]

In a single-party regime, the power to staff the state and thereby to shape its decisions is vested in a political party that may range from revolutionary to reactionary.[20] The majority of states that historically fit this description have been Marxist-Leninist in orientation. Contemporary China is a particularly salient expression of a party in firm control of a state and even the country's economy. The Soviet Union was the most powerful state with this form of government and forcefully achieved the replication of its governance model in states of the Warsaw Pact. In the Soviet model, intelligence services were specifically deputized to serve the governing party as its "sword and shield." Indeed, the Committee for State Security (KGB) leaders also became party secretaries. Of course, even this simultaneous top-down and bottom-up politicization could not, in the end, preserve the regime.

Past coup-proofing arrangements seem to have backfired in several instances by reducing the effectiveness of intelligence services. For instance, Saddam Hussein did not permit his intelligence analysts to collect data freely on the internet, which deprived him of a potential second opinion about his personal judgment that the United States was a smaller threat to his regime than Iran.[21] As a result, he remained safe from internal challenge, but nevertheless lost control of the Iraqi state. Consequently, in a noncompetitive regime, intelligence may be more likely to excel in operations than analysis and be thoroughly politicized from the top down.

THE LIBERIAN CASE OF NEO-PATRIMONIALISM

Politicization has been treated as an aberration worthy of study for democracies and accepted as an inherent feature of autocratic regimes. Less attention has been paid to the many states governed by other models. Liberia provides an important case study where the intelligence service exists within the context of neo-patrimonial governance, where formal and informal institutions are fused, personal power permeates the bureaucracy, and where tools of the state (especially those related to the security arena) are wielded for personalized political ends, mainly to gain and sustain political power.

Liberia is a good case for conceptual exploration. The country's experience of violent neo-patrimonialism and regionalized civil war is unique and extreme in the specifics, but shares abstract features with many other African nations. Like Liberia, most African countries do not have global geopolitical objectives or project power to shape or disrupt the geopolitical order.[22] Rather, they are integrated into geographic regions of influence. Even—or especially—conflicts that are labeled as "intrastate" are, in fact, internationalized/regionalized.[23] Liberia's intelligence service reflects this reality. The concerns can be understood as concentric circles, where the primary focus is on the domestic; if and when regional and geopolitical elements become priorities, it is because these outer-ring issues connect directly back to internal domestic politics.

Liberia is an excellent case study due to the variety of government types and conflicts it has experienced. Indeed, Liberia's intelligence services experienced extreme top-down politicization of intelligence as a single-party state (until 1980), under the military dictatorship of Samuel Doe (1981–1990) and the authoritarian but democratically elected Charles Taylor (1997–2003), who ruled during periods of repression and regionalized civil war; the democratic peacetime leadership of Ellen Johnson-Sirleaf (2005–2017) exhibited far less extreme politicization of intelligence.[24] However, elements of top-down politicization remain, which helps illuminate continuities and discontinuities across multiple governments in very different circumstances.[25]

This analysis finds instances of top-down politicization and coup-proofing but also that the intelligence bureaucracy was often but a minor subject of such politicization. Indeed, this is one of the key findings—the Liberian intelligence services become politicized at certain moments in relation to the key variables and most pressing issues of elite politics (i.e., how to remain in power, often through the targeted use of political finance and coercion). When these issues were not at play, the intelligence service was largely left alone. In these instances, the National Security Agency (NSA)—Liberia's primary intelligence service—carried out its bureaucratic mission with relative professionalism. This is true across time and regime types. This chapter argues that any formal institution in these contexts is likely wielded according to the interests of elite power—that is, intelligence and intelligence structures will be used as a political tool to enhance the leader's grasp on power and/or to undermine real or perceived competitors.

INTELLIGENCE SERVICES, VIOLENT NEO-PATRIMONIALISM, AND POLITICAL POWER

Most intelligence services in Africa are embedded in systems of neo-patrimonial governance. Accordingly, this chapter uses neo-patrimonialism simply to describe the de facto form and function of formal and informal institutions in these contexts (i.e., fused), which make sense of how power is *actually* exercised and provides the context within which intelligence is politicized. This chapter does not use neo-patrimonialism or any related concepts as an explanatory variable and cautions scholars from doing so.[26]

Neo-patrimonialism takes many forms—just as there is no one-size-fits-all type of democracy or authoritarian regime—and is often defined in contrast to the bureaucratic state. Indeed, in these systems, not only do the commonly held assumptions about the dominance of a Weberian bureaucratic state not hold, but they are often inverted. Rather than a professional bureaucracy applying impersonal rules to rational bureaucratic processes, personal power permeates—and usually dominates—the public sphere. Members of the political elite are the main actors who "try to maximize personal security, wealth and power . . . within the calculus of opportunities and constraints that patronage politics provides."[27] Oversight mechanisms, accountability structures, and formal (democratic) institutions and practices (e.g., elections) may exist, but are often insubstantial, subordinate to elite personal power. Beyond these general features, this chapter draws specific definitional elements from the "political marketplace," a modern form of neo-patrimonial governance where political power itself is a commodity; "gaining and maintaining power is the primary objective. . . . Loyalty is bought and sold. Transactions among elites are material, often violent, and usually zero-sum."[28]

These channels for gaining and maintaining power help us to understand how and when intelligence might be politicized. Turning to the case study, the subsequent sections describe the emergence of Liberia's intelligence service, the competition among the many entities with intelligence functions, and the ways in which intelligence has been politicized over time.

ORIGINS AND EVOLUTION OF LIBERIA'S INTELLIGENCE SERVICE

Liberia's unique history sets it apart from those African countries colonized by a European power, but it is still best understood as a settler colony.[29] The short version of Liberia's founding history is that freed slaves from the United States established a colony between British Sierra Leone to the north and French Cote d'Ivoire to the south, which they declared an independent nation in 1847. Intended to be a nation governed by free black people for free black people, this never made it into practice. Indeed, the so-called Americo-Liberian settlers created a political system that ensured their dominance through the subjugation of the indigenous population. They instituted a form of indirect rule to co-opt local chiefs and leaders in the service of maintaining order and collecting taxes and supported the extractive system with a colonial militia, which they later renamed the Liberia Frontier Force (the progenitor of the Liberian Army).[30] As late as 1931, some practices were "scarcely distinguishable from slave raiding and slave trading."[31] The Americo-Liberian oligarchy ruled their "state" like the plantations they left behind, absent racial differences and with them on top this time, until 1944. In that year, the incoming president William Tubman began forging Liberia's modern state—an autocratic, extractive, patronage-based system, held together in part by an extensive spy network.

The spies were called public relations officers (PROs), one of many positions Tubman created to extend his patronage network across Liberia, and they had no duties aside from being his eyes and ears.[32] They assiduously kept tabs on the population with barely a nod to secrecy; given Liberia's dense social networks, everyone knew they were being watched. This had a twofold effect to both ensure any domestic threats were identified and dealt with and also instilled such a sense of fear among the citizenry that citizens begin to check themselves, akin to the impact of Soviet-era informant networks on dissident activity. Indeed, this was a social network put toward the purpose of political intelligence, not an intelligence entity as such. And it was fully personalized: the PROs reported directly to President Tubman, in a perfect example of the fusion of formal and informal institutions of control.[33]

Tubman had other formal and informal human sources as well as multiple formal institutions focused on intelligence collection, mostly understood as gathering information on citizen activities. There were at least eight entities that had some form of an intelligence function: the National Intelligence and Security Service (NISS), National Bureau of Investigation (NBI), Special Security Service (SSS), Executive Action Bureau (EAB), and public relations officers (PROs) as well as the Office of National Security, National Police Force, and the Armed Forces of Liberia (AFL). All reported directly to him. In this way, he maintained power from 1944 to 1971 by keeping the security sector fragmented and ensuring he knew more than anybody else at any given time. This set the tone for how intelligence was used for the majority of Liberia's history—for personalized political purposes.

External patrons were important too. Tubman joined together this personalized governance system "through a comprehensive intelligence network connected to the Central Intelligence Agency" (CIA).[34] Not incidentally, Liberia was the CIA's primary foothold in Africa at the time and throughout the Cold War.[35] Even though U.S. reliance on Liberia waned as the geopolitical environment changed, Liberia's need for U.S. support did not.[36] The United States was critical to shoring up the administrations of Tubman (1944–1971), Doe (1980–1990), and Sirleaf (2006–2017). Presidents who antagonized the United States came to regret it, including Tolbert (1971–1980), Taylor (1997–2003), and Doe, whose stay in power was enabled by the United States until they withdrew support toward the end of his repressive administration, leading to his fall. Liberia's institutions reflect their historic association with the United States and the special relationship between the two countries. The United States was always the first place where Liberia looked for international support, and this led to many security cooperation partnerships, which in turn impacted the structure of Liberia's intelligence entities in similar ways to how European colonial legacies impacted their former colonies in Africa.

COUP-PROOFING ACROSS DECADES OF VIOLENCE AND SOCIAL TURMOIL

Lurking behind Tubman's efforts to personalize, fragment, and decentralize Liberia's security services was one very real threat: coups. Tubman worried about them for twenty-seven years, and his successor, William Tolbert, was brutally murdered in a 1980 coup led by the young AFL soldier Samuel Doe.[37] Doe allegedly faced thirty-eight coup or assassination attempts during his decade as dictator—an average of nearly one every three months of his rule—and he was ultimately murdered by a former AFL soldier in 1990, causing Liberia's state to collapse.[38] From 1990 through 1997, there was effectively no central government, as regionalized civil war ebbed and flowed. Nearly a dozen armed groups emerged over this period, whose leaders feared assassination at the hands of other groups as well as from within their own ranks. The many elite killings and mysterious deaths during this time were assumed to be political assassinations.[39] Four successive interim governments later, Charles Taylor, the most dominant political actor of the 1990s and leader of the armed group the National Patriotic Front of Liberia (NPFL), was elected president in 1997. This paused the war, briefly, before widespread violence overtook Liberia again from 2000 to 2003. Taylor was convicted by the Special Court of Sierra Leone in 2012 of eleven counts of war crimes and crimes against humanity for his role in Sierra Leone's violent conflict. By the time of Taylor's conviction, Ellen Johnson-Sirleaf had just won reelection and was trying to shore up Liberia's hollowed-out bureaucracy, but was always aware of the fate of her predecessors: two of the last three had been brutally murdered in office, and no elected Liberian leader had left office willingly or alive since Edwin Barclay in 1944.[40] As a result, Liberia's political leaders recognized they faced particular dangers, and they all took various steps to ensure their safety by personalizing, fragmenting, and decentralizing the security services.

Liberia's intelligence service—and intelligence as a product—was swept along by this current. In this case, form followed function: intelligence was focused on domestic threats. This continues to have path-dependent institutional implications. Intelligence was used in service of domestic political ends. Institutional structures supposedly meant to collect, analyze, and disseminate intelligence were never empowered to stand on their own.

To illustrate this point, the following narrative—organized chronologically by administration—describes the many entities that had an intelligence function from Doe's administration to the present. Despite mandates enshrined in legislative acts, these many entities are characterized by overlapping roles and responsibilities that change as a function of the relationship between its leadership and the president (i.e., a close relationship with the president gives one power far beyond what might be found on paper).[41] The point is not to dwell on the many names or roles of specific institutions, but to recognize how intelligence (a product) and intelligence collection (as part of the bureaucracy)—that cut across the security services and even civilian entities not tasked with security—was fragmented, decentralized, and encouraged to compete for the president's favor. Moreover, they were also mostly forced to be self-sustaining and needed to generate operational funds, at times through predation. Keeping networks separate and in competition limited the ability of any individual from gaining too much knowledge, which could lead to a coup or other threat to the leadership.

THE DOE YEARS, 1980–1990

From the moment Doe took power in the bloody coup of April 12, 1980, he saw coups in the shadows. His fear only grew with time. He killed more than fifty perceived competitors, many of whom were alleged to have plotted or attempted coups, including more than half of the seventeen enlisted men who staged the coup with him. As Doe became more paranoid and violent, he carved the existing security institutions into at least fourteen distinct security entities, including military, intelligence, and police.[42] Each reported directly to Doe and competed for his favor and reported on one another's activities. The AFL had pride of place as Doe's institutional home, launchpad to power, and his protector until the end. Contrary to its stated mission, the de facto function of the 6,300 soldiers was to maintain domestic order. Within the AFL there were nine operationally distinct entities, each of which would collect information, sometimes by design, and at other times in an ad hoc manner.

Mirroring the US military, the AFL was designed with a G-2 intelligence unit. However, it did not operate like a military unit. Their primary function was to conduct surveillance and undertake the work of a secret police, often in plain clothes. Doe's G-2 penetrated civilian state institutions, including the judiciary, the civil service, and state-owned corporations as well civil society organizations.[43] In this, G-2 competed directly with the National Security Agency (NSA) and the Ministry of National Security (MNS). Under Doe, the MNS came to occupy a place as a small, but powerful unit, with some elite operatives who also played a secret police role, conducting surveillance, tailing and investigating dissidents, and infiltrating organizations perceived to be anti-Doe. The NSA did the same. This amounted to a fearsome array of intelligence entities that Doe used to support his military grip on power.

THE TAYLOR YEARS, 1997–2003

The constellation of security entities in Liberia under Taylor reflected his experiences and particular style. He never trusted the AFL since he launched his rebellion to topple Doe, so, once in power, he sidelined the military as best he could. Militias and newly created special units took on primary responsibility for security. They were led by those who had proven themselves loyal during the many years of war. The two most powerful entities were the Special

Security Service (SSS), led by Benjamin Yeaten, Taylor's primary enforcer and longtime ally, and the Anti-Terrorist Unit (ATU), led by Taylor's son, Chuckie. Rounding out the formal state security apparatus were an additional six entities: AFL, Liberia National Police (LNP), the LNP's Special Operations Division (SOD), which was at least somewhat operationally separate from the rest of the LNP, the Executive Mansion Special Security Unit (SSU), the NBI (Taylor reinstated it in 1998), and the NSA. Various other "special units and irregular militias" were also used, including the Navy Rangers, Navy, Delta Force, Wild Geese, Man Moving Man Dropping, Demus Force, Jungle Lions, the Small Boys Unit, and Special Operation Strike Force as well as even more amorphous entities in rural areas.[44] Additionally, there were "regular and irregular security units . . . frequently operated autonomously and engaged in looting and extortion; many had serious human rights abuse records."[45] Yet, the intelligence services did not. In particular, "the NSA has not figured prominently among the list of organizations accused of violations by the major international human rights organizations or the U.S. State Department since the election of President Taylor in 1997."[46]

Intelligence organizations focused on three areas. The first relates to violent threats and warfare, including rebel activity within Liberia and the connections to the subregion, which were Taylor's most pressing concerns. As a result, intelligence for these issues was primarily handled by the militia and security services closest to him and most directly involved in the actual war effort (i.e., SSS, ATU, and Navy Rangers, as opposed to the NSA). The second relates to perceived political challenges and internal dissidents, including human rights activists, journalists, and opposition politicians. This was also a serious concern for Taylor. All intelligence services were involved in surveillance and monitoring of these actors, and there were many documented instances of beatings and other forms of political violence coercion. The NSA largely avoided being singled out for such behavior, but was involved in some high-profile arrests, including that of the auditor general in 2000 on suspicion of dissidence.[47]

The third issue was economic crimes, which is where the NSA operated somewhat independently of Taylor, at least on issues that were not core to political business. Political finance was the glue that held together Taylor's system of control—needed to finance the war effort, keep allies onside, and so on—and some, but not all, of this political finance came from illicit activities or ones that skirted legality. The NSA never investigated financial issues linked to Taylor, but they did pursue unconnected cases regarding graft, bribery, and misappropriation of funds. Two high-profile cases included corruption at Liberia's National Security and Welfare Corporation and similar issues related to the Cavalla Rubber Corporation.[48] Since these issues were, in relative terms, outside of the core issues related to Taylor's personal and administration survival, the NSA could operate with some amount of independence from political pressure.

THE SIRLEAF YEARS, 2006–2017

When Sirleaf came to power, she had a deep distrust of Liberia's security services, especially the previously armed entities, given her personal experiences during Doe's repressive regime and the many years of war. She inherited Liberia's many fragmented security services and sought to keep them under control, off the streets, and without weapons. She disbanded the AFL (pending full vetting and training overseen by the United States), and all militias were demobilized during the 2003–2005 transitional period after Taylor stepped down and went into exile. Even so, there were fifteen entities with some form of security function on paper: the Ministry of Defense, Bureau of Immigration and Naturalization (later renamed Liberia Immigration Service or LIS), Drug Enforcement Agency (DEA), Special Security Services (later renamed the Executive Protection Service or EPS), Customs—Financial Security Monitoring Division, Ministry of National Security, Forestry Development Authority Police, Liberia National Police, Liberia Petroleum Refining Company Security Force, Liberia Seaport Police, Liberia Telecommunications Corporation Plant Protection Force, Monrovia City Police, Roberts International Airport Base Safety, National Bureau of Investigation, and the National Security Agency.[49]

As a reformer with a belief in government bureaucracy, Sirleaf sought to rationalize these entities. Some were eliminated altogether (e.g., Forestry Development Authority Police, Liberia Telecommunications Corporation Plant Protection Force, Monrovia City Police), and others were merged: the NBI and MNS were subsumed by the NSA, which, once again, became Liberia's primary intelligence entity. However, intelligence collection and covert operations were still undertaken by many institutions. Then, as now, Liberia's abundant security institutions had a line item for covert operations in official budgets. This included purely civilian and non-paramilitary entities like the Ministry of Justice.[50]

During this period the NSA was led by Sirleaf's stepson, Fumba Sirleaf, who was one of only two cabinet-level officials to retain their position through her entire twelve-year tenure (the other was Minister of Defense Brownie Samukai).[51] The NSA operated as a combined, and beefed-up, Federal Bureau of Investigation and Central Intelligence Agency, with responsibilities for both internal investigations and broader intelligence collection. Unlike the past, there were few instances of harassment of political opponents, civil society members, or journalists by all security services. U.S. security cooperation, which had all but stopped in the late 1980s, resumed and later produced some impressive results. Among the most prominent was a sting jointly conducted by the U.S. Drug Enforcement Administration (DEA) and the Liberian NSA, led by Fumba Sirleaf, that resulted in the arrest and conviction of drug traffickers attempting to move over four thousand kilograms of cocaine with a street value of over $100 million from Latin America through Liberia and into Europe and the United States. After the arrest in 2010, the acting director of the DEA said that "unprecedented cooperation from the highest levels of government in Liberia helped expose drug smuggling and corruption that led to indictments of African, Colombian, and Russian traffickers."[52]

Notwithstanding such successes, there are instances of apparent politicization. Fumba Sirleaf was accused of using his perch to strengthen his mother's political position. She in turn was accused of allowing him to run the NSA without proper oversight; in fact the minister of justice resigned during 2014 in protest of being blocked from investigating alleged financial improprieties at NSA.[53] A more mundane example shows how criminal convictions that came from intelligence work were politicized in times of political need. In Cote d'Ivoire during 2010, then president of Cote d'Ivoire, Luarent Gbagbo, refused to step down after losing an election, sparking violent conflict. He hired Liberian mercenaries and militants with cross-border ties to support his cause. One group killed seven United Nations peacekeepers as well as many more civilians and Ivorian security soldiers.[54] Thirteen individuals were ultimately arrested in Grand Gedeh County, based in part on high-quality work from the NSA in cooperation with other security entities. In June 2014, these individuals were convicted and sentenced to life in prison.[55] In 2017, an election year, Sirleaf pardoned four of the convicted individuals based on pressure from their politically connected patrons as a gesture of "reconciliation."[56]

CONCLUSION

Examining the politics of intelligence in the context of Liberia's neo-patrimonial governance reveals several conclusions. First, intelligence is not necessarily more politicized in neo-patrimonial systems than other forms of governance and, in fact, may be less so. The point is that it is politicized *differently* based on fundamentally different political structures, goals, and imperatives. In Liberia, on the one hand, we saw that intelligence has been gradually becoming less political. This speaks to a certain process of bureaucratization of intelligence and the move away from overt and violent competition among elites for control over state power levers. It seems that relative apolitical isolation has enabled Liberian intelligence to operate with greater effectiveness (from a Western perspective of formal institutions) and that intelligence services were spared more direct interference because they were seen as less important than the main coercive tools of the state, with a remit marginal to the core interests of most leaders. However, that independence ended abruptly when intelligence was seen as a valuable commodity in inter-elite competition. This shows that indeed, intelligence has remained a central part of elite political competition. Only the terms of the competition have changed.

Second, leaders in neo-patrimonial systems deploy the intelligence services as part of coup-proofing strategies in ways similar to their counterparts in highly bureaucratized autocratic single-party systems. However, the roots of the ruling party are never as deep, and leadership turnover does not lead to a fundamental restructuring of intelligence organizations.

Third, the specific features of intra-elite politics in neo-patrimonial systems inherently make intelligence organizations politically salient. This is its own creature, not a middle way between democracy and autocracy. In the Liberian context, neither the wholesale politicization of autocracy nor the top-down and bottom-up political pressures in the Western intelligence world are likely to be compatible donors of insightful theoretical concepts. As a result, progress in comparative intelligence studies could benefit from conceptualizing a broader set of variables to describe the relationship between political leaders and intelligence officers.

Finally, there is a broader point on how to contextualize, understand, and assess intelligence services and intelligence as a product in neo-patrimonial systems. Generally, scholarship on intelligence tends to find whichever service it is studying to be deficient. This review of Liberian intelligence produced a refreshingly positive portrait of professional intelligence capabilities being leveraged in advance of the national interest—under difficult circumstances and with key exceptions. However true, this framing represents a bias toward a certain type of Western institutional professionalism, which might be analytically limiting. The normative lens obscures the deeper political purposes for which intelligence is used and politicized. Detached assessment of the actions (and inactions) of intelligence services and the use of intelligence, based on the political circumstances and imperatives facing members of the elite in neo-patrimonial systems, can more readily reveal these deeper political forces at work and make legible these systems to outsiders. Put specifically: intelligence should be assumed to be one of many moving parts in broader struggles among members of the elite for political control. This can help scholars and the public better understand how, when, and why intelligence is—or might be—politicized and promises to open up the relationships of spies and politicians in the geographic, historical, and political contexts that constitute the majority of cases across time and around the world.

NOTES

1. The authors thank Lea Schaad for exceptionally diligent research assistance.

2. This is by no means meant to suggest that the quest for insight into the intelligence dimension of the Cold War should be concluded. Many critical questions remain unanswered. See Michael Herman and Gwilym Hughes, eds. *Intelligence in the Cold War: What Difference Did It Make?* (New York: Routledge, 2013).

3. Joshua Rovner, *Fixing the Facts: National Politics and the Politics of Intelligence* (Ithaca: Cornell University Press, 2011), 29.

4. Matthew Crosston, "Bringing Non-Western Cultures and Conditions into Comparative Intelligence Perspectives: India, Russia, and China," *International Journal of Intelligence and CounterIntelligence* 29, no. 1 (2016): 110–31.

5. Steven Levitsky and Lucan Way, *Competitive Authoritarianism: Hybrid Regimes after the Cold War* (New York: Cambridge University Press, 2010). Alex de Waal, *The Real Politics of the Horn of Africa: Money, War and the Business of Power* (Malden, MA: Polity, 2015).

6. Uri Bar-Joseph, "The Politicization of Intelligence: A Comparative Study," *International Journal of Intelligence and CounterIntelligence* 26, no. 2 (2013): 347–69.

7. Michael Herman, *Intelligence Power in Peace and War* (Cambridge: Cambridge University Press, 1996).

8. Amy B. Zegart, *Flawed by Design: The Evolution of the CIA, JCS, and NSC* (Stanford: Stanford University Press, 2000).

9. Steven David. "Explaining Third World Alignment." *World Politics* 43 (1990): 233.

10. Christopher Andrew. "Intelligence, International Relations and 'Under-Theorisation'," *Intelligence & National Security* 19, no. 2 (2004): 177–78.

11. For a popular account, see Adam Zamoyski, *Phantom Terror: Threat of Revolution and the Repression of Liberty 1789–1848* (Glasgow: HarperCollins UK, 2014).

12. Joshua Rovner, *Fixing the Facts: National Politics and the Politics of Intelligence* (Ithaca: Cornell University Press, 2011), 37. A critical constituency is "any domestic group with the ability to damage the policy objective or political future of the policymaker." Ibid, 13.

13. Ibid, 47.

14. Glenn Hastedt, "The Politics of Intelligence and the Politicization of Intelligence: The American Experience," *Intelligence and National Security* 28, no. 1 (2013): 10.

15. Ibid.

16. Matteo Faini, "The US Government and the Italian Coup Manqué of 1964: The Unintended Consequences of Intelligence Hierarchies," *Intelligence and National Security* 31, no. 7 (2016): 1011–24.

17. Stephen Marrin, "Rethinking Analytic Politicization," *Intelligence and National Security* 28, no. 1 (2013): 32–54.

18. Sheena E. Greitens, "Coercive Institutions and State Violence under Authoritarianism," Dissertation, Harvard University, 2013. https://dash.harvard.edu/bitstream/handle/1/11125991/Greitens_gsas.harvard_0084L_10871.pdf?sequence=3.

19. Andrew, 176.

20. Paul Brooker, *Non-democratic Regimes* (London: Palgrave Macmillan, 2014), 40–41.

21. Kevin M. Woods, *Iraqi Perspectives Project: A View of Operation Iraqi Freedom from Saddam's Senior Leadership.* (Suffolk: United States Joint Forces Command Joint Center for Operational Analysis, 2006): 11.

22. Outliers are Libya's nuclear, chemical, and biological weapons ambitions and sponsorship of terrorism under Qaddafi and Egypt's role in the Middle East.

23. Noel Twagiramungu, Allard Duursma, Mulugeta Gebrehiwot Berhe and Alex de Waal. "Redescribing Transnational Conflict in Africa." *Journal of Modern African Studies* 57, no. 3 (2019): 377–91.

24. The dichotomy that sorts regimes into either democracies or non-democracies inaptly captures the nuance of the state in Africa, the role and structure of formal and informal institutions, and state-society relations. See further Steven Levitsky and Lucan Way, *Competitive Authoritarianism: Hybrid Regimes after the Cold War* (New York: Cambridge University Press, 2010).

25. Bottom-up intelligence politicization did not appear to be a meaningful phenomenon in Liberia. Politicization in this section refers to the top-down, political leadership-led variety.

26. See further: Thandika Mkandawire, "Neopatrimonialism and the Political Economy of Economic Performance in Africa: Critical Reflections," *World Politics* 67, no. 3 (2015): 563–612.

27. William Reno "Patronage Politics and the Behavior of Armed Groups." *Civil Wars* 9, no. 4 (2007): 326.

28. Benjamin Spatz, "Political Marketplace Framework: Sanctions in the Political Market," Conflict Research Programme, November 26, 2019. See further Alex de Waal, *The Real Politics of the Horn of Africa: Money, War and the Business of Power* (Malden, MA: Polity, 2015).

29. On Liberia as a settler colony, see: Mike McGovern, "Rebuilding a Failed State: Liberia," *Development in Practice*, 15, no. 6 (2005): 760–66. This chapter argues that Liberia can be studied alongside states with European colonial legacies.

30. Mahmood Mamdani, *Citizen and Subject: Contemporary Africa and the Legacy of Late Colonialism* (New Jersey: Princeton University Press, 1996), 87. The Liberia Frontier Force performed both military and police functions; no intelligence functions as such. See further: Timothy D. Nevin, "The Uncontrollable Force: A Brief History of the Liberian Frontier Force, 1908–1944," *The International Journal of African Historical Studies* 44, no. 2 (2011): 275–97.

31. League of Nations, "The 1930 Enquiry Commission to Liberia," *Journal of the Royal African Society* 30, no. 120 (1931): 280.

32. Martin Lowenkopf, *Politics in Liberia: The Conservative Road to Development* (Palo Alto: Hoover University Press, 1976).

33. Tubman funneled $1 million to the PROs by the late 1960s. See further: Lowenkopf. This was a significant amount of money given that Liberia's total national expenditures in 1968 barely topped $42 million. World Bank Report No. AW-5a, May 26, 1969. http://documents1.worldbank.org/curated/en/937491468269990593/text/multi0page.txt.

34. Niels Hahn, "US Covert and Overt Operations in Liberia, 1970s to 2003," *Air and Space Power Journal-Africa and Francophonie* 5, no. 3 (2014): 19–47.

35. See further: Benjamin J. Spatz, "Cash Violence: Sanctions and the Politics of Power, and Peace." Dissertation, Tufts University, 2020; Niels Hahn, *Two Centuries of US Military Operations in Liberia: Challenges of Resistance and Compliance* (Maxwell Air Force Base: Air University Press, 2020). Thomas Jaye, *Issues of Sovereignty, Strategy, and Security in the Economic Community of West African States (ECOWAS) Intervention in the Liberian Civil War* (Lewiston: Edwin Mellon Press, 2003), 86.

36. During the Cold War, Liberia was the site of the CIA's primary listening post and also the United States' Omega navigational station for coordinating and guiding transatlantic military and civilian air traffic. Both technologies become obsolete over time. Niels Hahn, *Two Centuries of US Military Operations in Liberia: Challenges of Resistance and Compliance* (Maxwell Air Force Base: Air University Press, 2020).

37. Tolbert sought to ensure his own personalized control of the security services when he took power in 1971. He dissolved the NISS altogether and, in 1974, merged the EAB and the NBI into a new entity—the National Security Agency. He took power away from the AFL, which he mistrusted, gave more to the police, and came to rely more heavily on the Executive Mansion Guard. He also created the Ministry of National Security to oversee all security-related matters, which reported directly to him through the Office of President and was led by his son-in-law.

38. Stephen Ellis, *The Mask of Anarchy: The Destruction of Liberia and the Religious Dimension of an African Civil War* (New York: NYU Press, 1999), 63.

39. Spatz, 2020.

40. President William Tubman died in office in 1971.

41. It should be noted that most if not all countries have multiple entities that include intelligence functions and that even in the most developed and most bureaucratic political systems there are overlapping mandates among intelligence entities. This is not *necessarily* "bad" or reflective of design flaws.

42. Bill Berkeley, *Liberia: A Promise Betrayed: A Report on Human Rights by Bill Berkeley* (New York City: Human Rights First, 1986), 31; William Reno, *Warlord Politics and African States* (Boulder: Lynne Rienner, 1998), 84.

43. Berkeley, 32–35.

44. Cook, Nicholas, "Liberia: 1989–1997 Civil War, Post-War Developments, and U.S. Relations," *Congressional Research Service*, 2003, 14–15.

45. Ibid.

46. "Liberia: Information on the Role of Liberia's National Security Agency (NSA) Since the Election of Charles Taylor as President in 1997," United States Customs and Immigration Services, March 28, 2001. https://www.uscis.gov/archive/ric-query-liberia-28-march-2001.

47. "Liberia finance official held on dissidence charge," Reuters, August 18, 2000. http://www.cnn.com/2000/WORLD/africa/08/18/liberia.arrest.reut/.

48. Liberia: Information on the role of National Security Agency (NSA) since the election of Charles Taylor as president in 1997 United States Customs and Immigration Services.

49. David C. Gompert, Olga Oliker, Brooke Stearns, Keith Crane, and K. Jack Riley, *Making Liberia Safe Transformation of the National Security Sector* (Santa Monica, CA: RAND Corporation, 2007). https://www.rand.org/content/dam/rand/pubs/monographs/2007/RAND_MG529.pdf.

50. The Ministry of Justice technically oversees the NSA, LNP, DEA, and LIS, but all have their own budgets and largely operate independently.

51. His name is sometimes spelled Fombah.

52. "U.S., Liberia Join Forces in Operation Relentless," United States Drug Enforcement Agency, June 1, 2010. https://www.dea.gov/sites/default/files/divisions/nyc/2010/nyc060110p.html; Also see: Yudhijit Bhattacharjee, "The Sting: An American Drugs Bust in West Africa," *The Guardian,* March 17, 2015. https://www.theguardian.com/world/2015/mar/17/the-sting-american-drugs-bust-liberia.

53. James Giahyue, "Liberia justice minister quits, says president blocked investigation," *Reuters,* October 14, 2014. https://www.reuters.com/article/uk-liberia-politics/liberia-justice-minister-quits-says-president-blocked-investigation-idUK-KCN0HW17A20141007.

54. "Final report of the Panel of Experts on Liberia submitted pursuant to paragraph 5 (f) of Security Council resolution 2025 (2011)," United Nations Panel of Experts, S/2012/901, December 4, 2012. https://undocs.org/S/2012/901.

55. Associated Press, "Liberia sentences 13 to life for border raids," *AP News.* June 18, 2014. https://apnews.com/article/bd4983cea99d42caac61bbe4d316b079.

56. Rodney Sieh, "Ellen Pardon of Grand Gedeans Heralds Reconciliation in Liberia," *Front Page Africa,* January 4, 2017. https://frontpageafricaonline.com/news/2016news/sirleaf-s-pardoning-of-four-grand-gedeans-heralds-reconciliation-in-liberia/.

Chapter 7

The Sudanese Intelligence Services between Continuity and Disruption

Joseph Fitsanakis and Shannon Brophy

Few countries have experienced the entire spectrum of dramatic political shifts seen in Sudan from the 1890s to today. This chapter examines the intense interaction between Sudan's politics and its intelligence establishment and explains how this interaction has shaped both Sudan's intelligence services and the nation's tempestuous political journey. The sections that trace the evolution of Sudanese intelligence over the past 130 years show that, in the case of Sudan, the development of the intelligence services retained a considerable degree of autonomy from the rest of the state bureaucracy, including the nation's leadership. To some degree, this allowed the intelligence apparatus to distance itself from the tumult of Sudanese politics, which included far-reaching—and invariably violent—ideological shifts over time. The latter have ranged from anti-colonial nationalism to pan-Arabism and Marxism and from Islamism to the type of autocratic personalism that is typically associated with modern-day North Korea. What is notable throughout that turbulent history is that organized political actors eventually resorted to supplanting the nation's formal intelligence system, by setting up informal intelligence mechanisms, which operated in parallel with the nation's established intelligence services. Thus, by the late 1970s, when the government forcibly brought the intelligence apparatus under direct military control, ending Sudan's decades-long tradition of civilian-led intelligence, the country's intelligence service was but a shell of its former self. However, the rebuilding of the intelligence system along autocratic lines by an increasingly despotic leadership contributed to its own demise. The intelligence bureaucracy regained its autonomy from the state and, by the late 2010s, was in a position to challenge its political patrons, with momentous results. The ongoing Sudanese Revolution of 2018–2019 is but the latest stage in this convoluted, yet highly didactic, intelligence microcosm.

The sources used in researching this chapter can be separated into three sections, in accordance with the broad historical periods in the evolution of Sudanese intelligence. The first period relates to the British colonial era, which lasted until 1956. For this period, information from published sources was collected and compared against documents in two major record collections. The most important of those is the Sudan Archive at the University of Durham, which contains documents from administrators in the Sudan Political Service during the Anglo-Egyptian Condominium (1898–1955), and includes the "Sudan Intelligence Reports" subset. The other record collection used was the colonies and dependencies document collection in the British National Archives, especially the "War and Colonial Department and Colonial Office: Africa" subset. Documents in this collection come from the Colonial Office, the Dominions Office, the Commonwealth Relations Office, and the Commonwealth Office. The majority of the material in these archives is open for consultation, and much of it is available online. The second period encompasses Sudan's postcolonial era, which started in 1956. For this period, the authors consulted documents in the Freedom of Information Act Electronic Reading Room of the United States Central Intelligence Agency (CIA) and the Transparency and Freedom of Information Releases database of the United Kingdom's Foreign and Commonwealth Office (FCO). Additionally, they consulted documents that are available in the Virtual Reading Room of the U.S. Department of State, especially the subsets from the Bureau of African Affairs and the United States Agency for International Development. For the third period, which began with the coup d'état of 1989, the authors consulted declassified documents made available by the CIA, the U.S. Department of State, the FCO, and the United Nations Official Document System as well as the United Nations Digital Library and International Court of Justice. For this period, the authors also made ample use of online media reports in the Arabic language as well as information from interviews with Sudanese defectors with direct knowledge of, and experience in, intelligence operations by the Sudanese government from 2006 to 2015.

What is missing from these accounts—and consequently from the present chapter—is the internal deliberations of Sudanese intelligence officials after 1964, when contacts between the Sudanese state and the British and American governments were significantly reduced, as well as information from the period of Islamization of the intelligence services from 1989 to 1999. That was also the period when the Sudanese intelligence services developed extensive connections with international militants, such as Ilich Ramírez Sánchez (known by the nom de guerre "Carlos the Jackal") and Osama bin Laden. Accounts of that period remain fragmented and lack details. The same can be said for the years between 2005 and 2010, when Sudanese intelligence entered a period of rapprochement with American intelligence agencies in the context of Washington's "global war on terrorism." Almost no documents relating to the relationship between Sudanese and American intelligence after the terrorist attacks of September 11, 2001, have been declassified by either the Sudanese or the U.S. governments. Last, information relating to the period after the secession of Sudan's southern regions, and the establishment of South Sudan, remains incomplete, while the Sudanese Revolution that erupted in 2018 is still in process, resulting in contested and often incoherent information on these developments.

The chapter is organized chronologically into ten parts, which center on consequential moments in the history of Sudanese intelligence. It proceeds by first exploring the formation of Sudan's intelligence apparatus under the Anglo-Egyptian Condominium. It then moves to the decay and fragmentation of the British-run Sudanese intelligence system's human intelligence networks during the interwar period. Turning to the security reform of 1935, the chapter analyzes how the colonial intelligence apparatus was transformed in the lead-up to independence. Moving to the postcolonial Public Security Organization, the chapter then examines the role of intelligence in the securitization of Sudanese politics, followed by its marginalization in the 1960s. Next, it details the gradual Islamization of the State Security Organization and its subsequent rapprochement with U.S. intelligence agencies—primarily the CIA. Then it explores South Sudan's secession and the formation of the General Intelligence Service, with attention to the changing political nature of the service. The chapter next describes Sudan's intelligence characteristics, by highlighting the role of government, ethnic diversity, and the shift away from civilian intelligence. Last, the conclusion summarizes the current state of Sudan's intelligence and provides recommendations for improving and professionalizing the service.

SUDANESE INTELLIGENCE UNDER THE ANGLO-EGYPTIAN CONDOMINIUM

The character of the Sudanese intelligence services is the product of continuity and disruption in almost equal measure. Much of the disruption the region experienced in the late modern era is rooted in the *Turkiyya* period that began in 1820 and in the Anglo-Egyptian period that followed it. When the British unseated Sudan's Ottoman masters in the late 1800s, they found there "the rudiments of a modern state" with elementary transportation and communication systems.[1] They relied on these to govern a diverse region, whose northern half was largely Arabized and Islamic, while its southern was inhabited by tribes that followed animist principles enmeshed with Christian beliefs. These differences deepened under British rule and continue to shape Sudanese intelligence institutions today.

In the 1880s, in an effort to solidify its power over water-dependent Egypt, Britain sought to extend its control southward, along the Nile River.[2] It was there, in what is today northern Sudan, that British forces encountered the *Mahdiyya*, a caliphate ruled by Muhammad Ahmad bin Abdullah. In 1881, Ahmad had proclaimed himself the *"Mahdi"* (المهدي, "divinely guided one") and declared holy war against infidels. By 1885, his army had overpowered the Ottoman-Egyptian forces and captured Khartoum, establishing what became known as the Mahdist state.[3] Subsequently, it was defeated by Anglo-Egyptian troops in 1899 and replaced with the Anglo-Egyptian Condominium, a political term that signifies joint control of a territory by two or more countries. This new entity embodied the amalgamation of Egypt and Sudan into a single administrative constituency under the British Crown, with Egypt serving as the junior partner.[4]

The Condominium government introduced early elements of intelligence in the service of the state in Sudan. Their architect was Major—later General—Sir Francis Reginald Wingate, who in 1899 headed the British-run Egyptian Intelligence Department. A fluent Arabic speaker and author of the 1891 book *Mahdiism and the Egyptian Sudan*, Wingate has rightly been described as "the doyen of Victorian intelligence officers."[5] In the 1890s, he used his familiarity with Egypt's southern frontier to mount an extensive surveillance effort against the Mahdist state. His undertaking resulted in the creation of "a remarkable intelligence network" consisting of Ababda tribesmen opposing the Mahdi.[6] Drawing on detailed assessments of the *Mahdiyya*, Wingate's network determined that the self-proclaimed caliph was strongly opposed by commercial traders and dissenting Sunni leaders. The size and complexity of Wingate's intelligence apparatus was truly "unique [among] small colonial warfare" campaigns of the period.[7]

After 1899, as governor general of Sudan, Wingate continued to cultivate his extensive intelligence network of anti-Mahdists. The latter were gradually incorporated into a tiered system of paid informants, forming the foundation of the collection apparatus of British intelligence throughout Sudan. These informants were handled by British and Egyptian officers, many of whom spoke Arabic or other native languages, and—like Sudan's colonial administration as a whole—came from both military and civilian backgrounds.[8] Their primary mission was to facilitate clandestine functions in support of the decision-makers of the Sudan Political Service (SPS), a small and highly centralized corps d'elite, modeled after its direct bureaucratic predecessor, the Indian Civil Service. By 1956, when it was dissolved, the SPS had come to be easily "regarded as the elite of British African administrations, if not the prize jewel in the imperial service."[9]

The SPS's reputation can be partly attributed to the efficacy of Wingate's surveillance network. The latter was institutionalized throughout Sudan "far earlier than other African colonies, where such institutions were not created until after World War II."[10] Wingate's spies initially worked in a nondescript section of SPS, but in 1908 formed the Criminal Investigation Department (CID). By 1910, when it was placed under the new Intelligence Department, the CID had formed relationships with police units throughout Sudan. These were highly militarized in ethos and tactics and focused on criminal and political policing.[11] In 1915, the Intelligence Department was renamed Public Security Department (PSD) and placed under the Office of the Civil Secretary. Its officers focused on internal dissent, but the onset of the First World War quickly prompted the prioritization of security threats posed by expatriate Europeans in Sudan.[12] At the same time, the PSD's view of anti-colonial activity in Sudan was perceived as Egyptian instigated, prompting it to work closely with colonial authorities in Cairo after 1915.[13]

The structure and functions of British intelligence in colonial Sudan cannot be easily delineated. As Martin Thomas explains, since colonial administrations were primarily "animated by problems of internal security. . ., the entire bureaucratic apparatus of imperial administration . . . contributed to state surveillance of the subject population."[14] The totality of the British administration in Sudan performed loosely termed intelligence functions aimed at safeguarding the colonial state and its interests. This, Thomas points out, blurred the traditional distinctions between civilian and military intelligence and between internal and external intelligence activities. Furthermore, ever since Wingate's time, the British colonial system in Sudan had been cognizant of the limitations of direct military rule. It devised a model of monitoring and controlling indigenous politics through alliances with local tribes and religious sects.[15] The PSD's intelligence networks mirrored and oftentimes spearheaded the formation of these alliances, some of which dated back to pre-*Mahdiyya* times. They were formalized with the use of PSD subofficers, who handled local agents and informants.

DETERIORATION OF HUMINT AND EXTERNAL THREATS AFTER THE FIRST WORLD WAR

In the interwar years, British intelligence tackled the perceived influence of Russian Bolshevism and the resurgence of Mahdism in Sudan.[16] The latter was led by Sayyid Abd al-Rahman, son of the original Mahdi. Neo-Mahdism, as it was called, formed the basis of the Umma Party, which survives as a political force in modern-day Sudan.[17] The PSD responded to neo-Mahdism by intensifying human intelligence (HUMINT) collection on nationalist and religious groups, as well as on labor unions. On the analysis side, PSD products from the period demonstrate a consistent preoccupation with these actors, while also featuring an impressive assemblage of economic, demographic, and environmental data.[18]

Neo-Mahdist activities strongly reinforced the preexisting hesitance of colonial administrators to trust natives with security-related information. This bolstered the PSD's centralization, especially after the Egyptian Revolution of 1919, and had both tactical and strategic effects on its structure and operations.[19] On the tactical level, centralization increased the threshold of loyalty that informants had to demonstrate before joining the organization. As successful candidates grew scarce, reliable informants became fewer. Consequently, the organization's clandestine functions suffered prior to the White Flag revolt of 1924 and continued to decline subsequently.[20] By 1936, when the colony underwent an extensive administrative overhaul, the PSD's HUMINT network was a far cry from Wingate's early creation.

On the strategic level, the rise of neo-Mahdism accelerated PSD planners' tendency to structure their HUMINT networks on a heavily segmented view of tribal and ethnic groupings. The service had always been a willing accomplice in the "southern policy" of the SPS, which deliberately amplified preexisting communal differences between Sudan's northern and southern regions.[21] By the mid-1920s, British intelligence had become deeply knowledgeable of the country's ethnic mosaic, which is among Africa's richest. Consequently, PSD divisions reflected ghettoized tribal constituencies, with a notable overrepresentation of riverine Arabized Nubians, such as the Shaigiya and the Ja'alin. Members of these tribes grew accustomed to populating the PSD's junior administrator and regional handler ranks. Many were graduates of British-run educational institutions, primarily the Gordon Memorial College that was established in 1902. At the same time, informant networks in northern Sudan consisted mostly of anti-Mahdist herders, whose collaborationist links with the British dated to the Wingate era.[22] Meanwhile, PSD counterintelligence functions centered on keeping pro-Mahdist elements out of its junior administrator and informant ranks, due to constant fears of anti-British conspiracies.[23] As a result, counterintelligence functions were redoubled after the mutiny of 1924 by the United Tribes Society, which later evolved into the White Flag League (جمعية اللواء الأبيض).[24]

By the 1920s, the PSD had acquired a bureaucratic identity that appeared more cohesive than those of most government agencies in Sudan, including the police services.[25] It was also relatively detached from supervision and operated with distinct autonomy from the rest of the state mechanism.[26] However, PSD planners had to contend with the budgetary restrictions of the interwar period, which became widespread during the depression of the 1930s. These setbacks were compounded by the logistical challenges posed by the sheer territorial size of Sudan.[27] Attempts to modernize the service were rare and faced stiff bureaucratic resistance. When it did occur, modernization typically came in response to existential challenges to the state's authority.

During the interwar period, the PSD categorized such existential challenges as neo-Mahdist, Arab-nationalist, or Bolshevist. The administration adopted a hardline stance against neo-Mahdist uprisings, such as the Nyala revolt of 1921 and the White Flag revolt of 1924. In September 1921, intelligence reports were sent to Tenant McNeill, the British inspector of Southern Darfur, warning that neo-Mahdist forces were gathering in the Nyala district with the aim of rebelling against the government. These were led by Abdullahi Suheini, who had declared himself the *"nabi isa"* (بي عيسى), or "Prophet Jesus."[28] Three days later, Suheini led over 6,000 armed men to an attack on Nyala, in what became known as the biggest rebellion in the history of colonial Sudan. Although it did not succeed, the Nyala revolt "fully revived the old fear of a large-scale religiously-inspired revolt" among colonial administrators.[29] Such fears deepened following the 1924 White Flag revolt, when Sudanese military officers led by Ali Abdul Latif and Abdullah Khalil openly called for an end to British rule and unification with Egypt. Having pledged allegiance to Egypt's king Fuad, the rebels organized anti-colonial rallies throughout northern Sudan, culminating in a mutiny by Sudanese military officers, which was violently suppressed.

These revolts were intensely studied by PSD analysts, who correctly concluded that Sudanese nationalists were pro-Arab secularists and, unlike neo-Mahdists, did not challenge the British on religious grounds.[30] Nationalists were almost exclusively Arabized northerners, many of whom were British educated. Their goals were clandestinely supported by the Egyptians, who aspired to dominate Sudan after an eventual British withdrawal, especially after 1922, when Egypt ceased being a British protectorate.[31] The inevitable discord between the British colonial state and the increasingly unruly Egyptians reached a boiling point in 1924, when Sir Lee Stack, governor general of Anglo-Egyptian Sudan, was assassinated by Egyptian nationalists in Cairo. In response, Britain summarily expelled all Egyptian officials from Sudan. This further degraded the PSD's intelligence collection capabilities, which relied on Arab-speaking and British-educated Egyptian junior administrators. The revolts also prompted a change in the PSD's leadership, such as Charles Armine Willis being dismissed from the post of PSD director in 1926. The move signaled the end of the service's attempts to coax the nationalist and neo-Mahdi movements. Willis's replacement, Reginald Davis, saw them as existential threats to the colony that had to be crushed without delay.[32]

It is important to note that the PSD's primary focus was external threats to the colony, mostly from rival European powers. That emphasis intensified following the rise of Bolshevism and the establishment of the Soviet Union, a development that reinforced the PSD analysts' refusal to view anti-colonial efforts as purely domestic. The standard PSD view was that anti-imperialist activities in Sudan were encouraged, funded, and in some cases, even armed, by Soviet agents in Italy and Egypt.[33] That outlook reflected the broader view of British intelligence that "Bolshevik influence was responsible for much of the unrest that characterized the post-war world."[34] Recent research dismisses that view as "too general and unsubstantiated," and led by "an element of make believe."[35] Nevertheless, the preoccupation with Bolshevism furthered the PSD's internationalization by bolstering its cooperation with British intelligence in London. Additionally, through its ties with the Colonial Office, the War Office, and the Committee of Imperial Defence, the PSD continued to cultivate "a certain foreign focus, more akin to the concerns of military intelligence."[36]

The internationalization of Sudanese security caused the PSD to neglect internal affairs.[37] By the early 1930s, the service embodied the limitations of the colonial state as a whole. Its administrative layers consisted largely of outsiders, few of whom spoke Arabic or other local languages. Inevitably, they relied on junior administrators and informers whose ideological commitment to the colonial project was tenuous. Their questionable allegiance prevented the PSD from maintaining its clandestine functionality with consistency.[38] Amid this operational stagnation, the PSD—much like the SPS as a whole—became contested space for rival tribal groupings within its ranks. With the prospect of independence looming, sectarian tensions among ethnic factions inside the organization began to flare up, as rival groups positioned themselves with an eye to dominating politics post independence. Essentially, as scholar Willow Berridge has explained with reference to the Sudanese Police Force, security agencies "became a means by which the colonial state's agents could use the state [to further their political agendas], just as much as the state could use them."[39] Although not as intense as in other SPS components, these rivalries further hampered the PSD's operational efficiency.

THE SECURITY REORGANIZATION OF 1935 AND THE ROAD TO INDEPENDENCE

The last major reorganization of the Sudanese intelligence apparatus prior to independence happened in 1935. The impetus was twofold: curtailing anti-colonialism and addressing regional challenges posed by the Second Italo-Ethiopian War.[40] Political policing was prioritized in the PSD and was led by a new department, known as the Special Branch. Its agents came mostly from Wingate's old CID, which had led political policing since 1908. Special Branch agents focused on domestic nationalist and leftist organizations, including the Graduates' General Congress, the trade unions, and after 1946, the Sudan Movement for National Liberation and the Sudanese Communist

Party (SCP).[41] It also focused on Sudanese supporters of the Egyptian Movement for National Liberation and on Sudanese dissidents abroad.[42] The PSD set up a Public Security Branch and a Press and Propaganda Section. The former took over military intelligence responsibilities, focusing on pro-fascist activities in neighboring Ethiopia, while the latter monitored the local Arab press and operated a pro-government radio station.[43] Following the administrative reorganization of the colony in 1936, the PSD appointed representatives of these branches in all nine Sudanese provinces. However, intra-agency communication with the provinces remained fragmented.

By the early 1940s, the Sudanization of the SPS was in full speed with nearly three quarters of administrators drawn from northern Sudanese tribes.[44] Severe funding restrictions caused by the war effort forced the colonial state to devolve powers to local tribal councils. This gave shape to a policy of "native administration" that was seen as "a laboratory for self-government."[45] The postwar years, by which time the tribal councils had formed a legislative assembly, found the PSD operating in siege conditions. Located in the margins of society at large, the service functioned in political and cultural isolation. It had lost many of its covert capabilities and informant networks, in a process that Ahmed Ibrahim Abushouk describes as "the gradual breakdown of the collaboration mechanism."[46] The service was also paralyzed from fear of infiltration by nationalists and was almost exclusively preoccupied with counterintelligence.

After 1950, major developments happened in quick succession. In 1953, Egypt rescinded its role as a protector of Sudan and agreed with Britain to supervise self-government in the colony for a trial period. In 1954, a temporary government emerged out of the legislative assembly in Khartoum. By that time, the British were too weak to intervene in the struggle for power among Sudan's major political groupings—namely, the neo-Mahdist Umma Party, which dominated western Sudan, and the northeast-based National Unionist and Popular Democratic parties. These forces represented Arabized northern riverine tribes, which had entered the colonial administration after 1924 as a result of the Crown's expulsion of Egyptian officials from Sudan.[47] The Arabs promoted a vision of uniform national identity based on their interests, in which "Arab nationalism and the British colonial mindset converged."[48]

THE PUBLIC SECURITY ORGANIZATION AND THE SECURITIZATION OF POLITICS

The main challenge to the northern-dominated government came from mutinies by disaffected southerners. These evolved into large-scale popular mobilizations that assumed the characteristics of a mass movement and eventually sparked the First Sudanese Civil War.[49] Its formative stages, beginning with intermittent guerilla warfare in the mid-1950s and the rise of the Anya-Nya insurgency (تمرد الأنيانيا) in 1962, shaped the institutional character of the postcolonial Sudanese intelligence apparatus. The first southern mutinies began before 1956, when the British handed over power to a five-member native Sovereignty Council. A quick succession of prime ministers from northern parties ended in 1958, when power was transferred to a thirteen-member military council under Sudan's first president, Ibrahim Abboud. The junta's goals were maintaining power in the hands of northern-dominated elites, stabilizing the economy, and finalizing a constitution.[50]

It was during that transitional period that the British-administered PSD was renamed Public Security Organization (PSO, جهاز الأمن العام) and placed under the Ministry of the Interior. The PSO's core was the old PSD Special Branch, which traced its lineage to Wingate's CID—Sudan's political police since 1908. Its mission remained largely unchanged, namely to monitor dissent against the state, primarily from southerners and trade unions. The pre-1956 focus on Arab nationalism was replaced with counterintelligence operations against communist bloc countries.[51] By 1960 the activities of the Anti-Imperialist Front and its primary patron, the outlawed SCP, had become the PSO's main focus. The SCP had considerable power in the Trade Union Federation of Sudan, which was another major PSO intelligence target. The agency also created a special unit to monitor communist organizing in the Railway Workers' Union, Sudan's most formidable syndicalist body.[52] Much intelligence collection concerned the Sudan Gezira Board Tenants' Union, a communist stronghold south of Khartoum.[53] This operational emphasis on leftist activities facilitated a continuing relationship between the PSO and the British Embassy in Khartoum.[54] British intelligence shared information on regional activities by communist bloc agents and in turn received information about the SCP. Meanwhile, the collaborative mechanism of the old PSD continued to form the backbone of the PSO's informant networks in the provinces, especially in the south.

A high degree of accord between the PSO and the state should not be assumed. Their relationship was marred by mistrust. Sudan's new rulers, many of them former pro-independence activists, saw the PSO as embodying the vestiges of British colonialism. After all, it was not long ago that it had targeted them as enemies of the state. Mistrust ran both ways. The transitory nature of early Sudanese administrations, and their manifest ineptitude at statecraft, rendered them dangerously unreliable in the eyes of intelligence officials. The latter kept their distance. They "continued to prioritize their social and familial relationships over their work" and did not view themselves as conduits of state power.[55] Consequently, the government's ability to use the PSO to further its security strategies was limited, even during the military junta from 1958 to 1964. However, the PSO did participate in the overall securitization of Sudanese politics. This trend was visible mostly in the south, where by 1962, many of the original mutineers of 1956 had organized themselves into a guerrilla army, the Anya-Nya. The rebel group "lacked a central command and a cohesive political ideology" but became progressively lethal after receiving substantial training and material support from Israel.[56]

Scholars have noted the considerable continuity between British and Sudanese administrations in the field of counterinsurgency. The term denotes the fusion of political, psychological, informational, and military measures aimed at defeating challenges to a state's authority by non-state violent actors.[57] Indeed, Khartoum's military campaign in the south bore all the hallmarks of British state violence.[58] As the southern insurgency grew, the coerciveness of the endemically authoritarian Sudanese state focused on combating the Anya-Nya's rhetoric, as expressed by its political wing, the Sudan African National Union. The latter was outlawed, while its international divisions, notably the Southern Sudan Front and the Southern Sudan Liberation Movement, were closely monitored by the PSO. The agency did not directly participate in criminalizing the opposition, which became a mainstay of Sudan in the 1960s. It did, however, help suppress secessionist voices in southern provinces where its informant networks largely paralleled and supplemented the state's enforced Arabization and Islamization campaigns. These networks were "modeled on similar efforts by the Anglo-Egyptian Condominium Government . . . to keep track of the population in northern Sudan prior to independence."[59]

CONTINUING MARGINALIZATION OF THE PUBLIC SECURITY ORGANIZATION

Gradually, civil war politics came to dominate every facet of life in Sudan, forcing a reconfiguration of Sudanese state institutions, including the intelligence services. The impasse of the "southern problem" culminated in October 1964 when Abboud's junta collapsed. The crisis prompted a merger of leftists and disaffected military officers, who formed the United National Front and pushed for a civilian government, which came to be led by the Umma Party. The new government represented a neo-Mahdist movement known as "the Ansar" but also included elements from the now legalized SCP and other leftist groups. Its impact on the PSO was immediate, as the leftists pushed for transparency and reform in the police and security services. Most senior PSO leaders were replaced with officials from outside the agency, a historic first. Additionally, a leftist coalition took control of the Interior

Ministry, under which the PSO operated, and declassified the agency's files on student leaders, trade unionists, and other activists.[60] The files' publication sparked public outrage and led to the purge of dozens of mid-level PSO officers in the first months of 1965.

The leftist-inspired reforms proved ephemeral, as the new government underwent a split between the Ansar and secular forces. Almost immediately, the SCP returned to underground work, while the constituent assembly in Khartoum, now under the firm control of the Ansar, embarked in a "law and order" program.[61] Its central pillar was the re-intensification of counterinsurgency operations in southern Sudan. The PSO's participation in that project was limited. The agency had failed to create a viable network of informants in the south, while its intelligence output attracted little attention by Ansar leaders. Having spent decades in the labyrinth of Sudanese politics, Ansar functionaries had learned to build their own networks of intelligence operatives. Unlike the PSO officers, these operatives could be guaranteed to share the ideology of the Ansar. Therefore, the PSO's role in the years of the Ansar can be characterized as one of increasing marginalization, bordering on obscurity.

In May 1969, the secularists struck back against the Ansar, as the newly formed Free Officers Movement deposed the government. It replaced it with a Revolutionary Command Council chaired by Colonel Ja'afar Nimeiry, a left-leaning pan-Arabist who enjoyed support from sections of the SCP. The new regime outlawed political parties, dissolved the National Assembly, and suspended the constitution. It also sought to reconfigure state institutions along socialist and pan-Arabist doctrines. First among them were the security services and the military. Given the marginal status of the PSO, it is perhaps unsurprising that the regime ignored its existence and proceeded to build its own intelligence service, the National Security Organization (NSO, جهاز الأمن القومي). Unlike the PSO, whose intelligence officers had been trained by the British as far back as the 1920s, the NSO was staffed by political appointees. A major criterion for their hiring was their ideological devotion to the regime's communist and pan-Arabist principles.[62] Moreover, NSO personnel came from the military, not from law enforcement, as had been the case with the PSO. By 1971, many NSO officers had received Soviet training in military intelligence, while a significant portion were card-carrying SCP members.

Similar to the PSO, the NSO had dual domestic and external functions. Unlike the PSO, which operated under the Ministry of Interior, the NSO reported directly to Nimeiry. More importantly, the NSO was given arresting and prosecutorial powers, which rivaled and often exceeded those of the police.[63] Within a year, the NSO had eclipsed the PSO in both size and scope. It was also highly centralized: unlike the PSO, which disseminated intelligence to a variety of government consumers, the NSO channeled information solely to the Revolutionary Command Council, which included the heads of the military. However, its activities in nonmetropolitan areas were limited and could not be compared to the PSO's intelligence network. The latter, though far from perfect, was considerably more extensive and stable than the NSOs. The new agency demonstrated its inexperience in July 1971 by failing to anticipate the communist coup that temporarily deposed Nimeiry and assumed power in Khartoum for several days.[64] Nimeiry's return after the failed coup signaled a new round of purges in the military, security, and intelligence agencies, during which pro-communist employees of the NSO and the PSO were dismissed.[65]

In 1976, another failed coup, this time by Libyan-backed Ansarists led by the exiled former Prime Minister Sadiq al-Mahdi, convinced Nimeiry that a repurposing of Sudanese intelligence was necessary to keep himself in power. He carried out a further round of purges in the PSO and the NSO and in 1978 merged what was left of them into a new agency, the State Security Organization (SSO, جهاز أمن الدولة). Nimeiry's placement of his trusted vice president, General Umar al-Tayyib, as head of the SSO, signified the beginning of the end of civilian control over Sudanese intelligence. The absolute demise of civilian control came in 1979, when Nimeiry summarily dissolved the Ministry of the Interior, under which the old PSO had operated.[66] Aside from militarizing the intelligence services, Nimeiry effectively eliminated the role of law enforcement, which had led Sudanese domestic security for nearly a century (for a comparison with Nigeria, see Adeakin in this volume). By that time, the civil war had subsided following the signing of the 1972 Addis Ababa Agreement and the granting of autonomy to southern Sudan. Correspondingly, the intelligence services had scaled back operations in the south, focusing instead on communist and Ansarist threats to Nimeiry's reign.

THE STATE SECURITY ORGANIZATION AND THE RISE OF ISLAMISM

Facing increasing opposition from Islamic revivalists, Nimeiry proposed a national reconciliation by moving the nation toward Islam and, in 1983, proclaimed sharia as the law of the land. However, this move failed to appease his religious opponents and agitated the non-Muslim south. In combination with his unilateral violation of the Addis Ababa Agreement, Nimeiry's turn to Islam sparked the Second Sudanese Civil War. The resurgence of war in the south, coupled with rising neo-Mahdist discontent in the north, posed massive logistical challenges for the SSO, which was already crippled by recurring purges under Nimeiry's rule. Eventually, neo-Mahdist dissatisfaction blended with widespread economic discontent to fuel the April 1985 coup d'état that ended Nimeiry's reign. It was led by his minister of defense, Field Marshal Abdel Rahman Swar al-Dahab, who sought to facilitate multiparty elections. During his brief rule, Marshal al-Dahab disbanded the SSO and reinstituted the Ministry of the Interior, which Nimeiry had shut down in 1979.[67]

Termed "the April *Intifada*" by its supporters, the coup led to the elections of 1986, in which nearly half of the country's population failed or refused to participate due to the raging civil war. Still, the election as prime minister of Sadiq al-Mahdi, great grandson of the original mahdi of 1881, inaugurated Sudan's third period of parliamentary rule.[68] The new leader was supported by the Umma Party, but also by the National Islamic Front (NIF), a formerly underground movement consisting of supporters of the failed coup of 1976. It was led by Dr. Hassan al-Turabi, an influential Islamic scholar who favored the imposition of a theocracy.[69] There were significant differences between the Umma Party and the NIF, which carried over into the intelligence field. In 1988, the unstable governing coalition enacted a new National Security Law, which ratified Marshal al-Dahab's dissolution of the SSO three years earlier. It also instituted a new intelligence agency, the Sudanese Security Apparatus (SSA, جهاز أمن السودان), under the Ministry of the Interior. By that time, however, both the Umma Party and the NIF had copied the method of the Ansar in the 1960s and had built their own informal intelligence networks. These were largely composed of former SSO officers, who had been left jobless when Marshal al-Dahab had disbanded the service.[70]

ISLAMIZATION, RAPPROCHEMENT WITH THE CIA, AND VIGILANTISM UNDER OMAR AL-BASHIR

On June 30, 1989, the uneasy alliance between the Umma Party and the NIF ended abruptly when military officers led by General Omar al-Bashir staged a coup d'état with the support of the NIF and al-Turabi. Over the next decade, al-Turabi oversaw the "top-down" Islamization of Sudanese society.[71] Under his direct supervision, the SSA returned to the days of the Ansar and was reformed along Islamist lines. It was also renamed National Intelligence and Security Service (NISS, جهاز الأمن والمخابرات الوطني) and headed by Nafi Ali Nafie, a hardcore Islamist who openly favored using torture on dissidents. It was during that tumultuous period that the NISS developed international contacts with Islamist organizations, including Palestinian Islamic Jihad, Palestinian HAMAS, Lebanese Hezbollah, the Islamic Courts Union in Somalia, and Egypt's Gama'at al-Islamiyya. Additionally, increasing numbers of NISS officers were trained by Iran. The agency sheltered senior Islamist figures in Khartoum, including al-Qaeda cofounder Osama bin Laden and many of his supporters.[72] These developments prompted the U.S.

Department of State to condemn the NIF for "harbor[ing] international terrorist groups" and include Sudan on its list of State Sponsors of Terrorism in 1993.[73]

The NISS's Islamization came to a halt in 1999 when al-Turabi and the NIF were ousted from power in a palace coup orchestrated by al-Bashir and his political platform, the National Congress Party (NCP).[74] While nominally retaining the Islamist character of the state, the NCP effectively supplanted the NIF. The state's Islamist character was gradually abandoned and replaced with progressively cultlike public displays of devotion to al-Bashir. Al-Bashir thus crafted "a personalist autocracy that tied the fortunes of . . . the security apparatus to his continued rule."[75] By 2006, the NISS was acting as al-Bashir's personal political police, while also performing counterterrorism and foreign-intelligence tasks. Al-Bashir's growing reliance on the NISS is evidenced by his budgetary priorities: it has been estimated that security-related spending amounted to as much as 70 percent of the state's annual expenditures in 2016.[76]

The terrorist attacks of September 11, 2001, presented the NISS with an opportunity to seek a rapprochement with its American counterpart, the CIA. Sudan began detaining foreign Islamists soon after the attacks. This led to a period of direct collaboration between the NISS and the CIA. Notably, in 2005, the American agency flew the director of the NISS, Major General Salah Abdallah, also known as "Gosh," to Washington for talks.[77] Around that time, the CIA began training the NISS for the agency's support in combatting al-Qaeda. Partly through its rapprochement with the CIA, the NISS grew stronger, quickly becoming "the most powerful wing of the government in Sudan."[78] Like its institutional predecessors, the agency continued to be staffed with members of Sudan's riverine Arabized tribes.[79] However, as Sudanese civil society began to challenge al-Bashir's regime in the later years of his reign, the dictator relied less on tribal affiliations and increasingly on personal loyalty. According to one observer, "[A]nyone [perceived as being] active against the government could be targeted and detained regardless of tribal and ethnic affiliation."[80]

Under al-Bashir, the NISS constantly engaged in widespread human rights abuses. This included routine arbitrary detention and systematic torture of perceived enemies of the state. From 1999 to 2009, NISS operations were officially governed by the National Security Forces Act (NSFA), which granted its officers immunity from prosecution for actions taken "in the course of their work."[81] The NSFA offered no formal method of reporting misconduct by NISS personnel, and citizens refrained from doing so, fearing reprisals.[82] But the era of lawlessness of the NISS began in 2005, when al-Bashir's regime entered a war for its very survival. In January of that year, the Sudanese government succumbed to concerted international pressure and signed the Comprehensive Peace Agreement (CPA), also known as the Naivasha Agreement. The CPA effectively ended the Second Sudanese Civil War after twenty-two years of conflict. It also authorized the United Nations (UN) to hold an independence referendum in southern Sudan, which would almost certainly lead to the division of the country and the establishment of South Sudan. The southern regions were home to the majority of Sudan's crude oil deposits, which provided most of the regime's income. It follows that Khartoum saw the prospect of losing access to those deposits as nothing short of catastrophic, given that oil's contribution to the country's national exports exceeded 80 percent. By 2011, income from oil exports accounted for 50 percent of Khartoum's overall revenue. Three-quarters of those came from oil deposits in Sudan's southern regions.[83]

Seeing the impending referendum as an existential threat, al-Bashir directed the NISS in 2005 to place the UN and France—the leading advocates of the CPA—at the top of its target list. French and UN diplomatic personnel in Sudan were targeted in extensive espionage operations that mobilized the entirety of the NISS apparatus.[84] These often included the coercive recruitment of locals with proximity to foreign diplomats. These locals were usually forced, often under threat of torture, to act as unwilling NISS informants and access agents, in places like the Khartoum International Airport and the offices and homes of foreign diplomatic personnel in Khartoum, Juba, and elsewhere. The facilities and personnel of the UN Mission in Sudan were also targeted. Around the same time, al-Bashir replaced NISS director Nafie with another unreconstructed Islamist, Mohammed Atta al-Moula, giving him carte blanche to disregard even the most basic human rights in pursuit of the service's mission.

In 2009, when the international community voiced grave concerns about human rights in Sudan, the government instituted the new National Security Act (NSA), which changed the country's human rights landscape overnight. The NSA authorized the NISS to operate as a vigilante force, affording its officers complete "immunity from civil and criminal liability for acts conducted in the course of their duty or in good faith," including "those of torture and rape."[85] Within days, large numbers of Sudanese began to disappear in a complex network of NISS-administered prisons. Foreign observers remarked with alarm that the NISS was systematically detaining perceived enemies of the state for over one hundred days without charge or even judicial review.[86] In 2015, the Sudanese government brazenly incorporated the 2010 NSA into the country's interim constitution, prompting Amnesty International to conclude that "though the NISS has for the last decade perpetrated human rights violations with impunity, its current human rights violations have reached unprecedented levels."[87] Well-informed observers in Europe noted that arbitrary detention and torture, "including acts of rape and sexual violence," had become "systematic tools of obtaining intelligence" and that their perpetrators had been granted "almost complete impunity" by the government.[88] Even the White House, which had previously worked closely with the NISS, banned the service's former director, Gosh, from entering the United States, citing "credible information" that he "was involved in torture during his tenure as head of NISS."[89]

The NISS's unrivaled power under al-Bashir sprang from its ability to maintain wide networks of informants "in nearly every government agency, rural village, and urban neighborhood."[90] Human rights observers have described in detail the process by which NISS prisoners were routinely released "to gather information [and] eventually rearrested and tortured for more information. Often this process repeated itself, with prisoners being released then re-detained in a 'cat and mouse' pattern."[91] In 2010, the U.S. Department of State documented the standard process by which Sudanese security forces attempted to "compel [prisoners] to act as NISS informers . . . as a condition for their release," adding that prisoners were "questioned, reportedly tortured, and asked to become informants."[92] Intimidation, blackmail, and torture were standard elements of the NISS's agent-recruitment methodology and were used for decades to build the service's networks of agents throughout Sudan. The vastness and complexity of these networks is difficult to fathom but is perhaps aptly illustrated by reports that the service even had agents embedded in other government agencies, including the police and the military.[93] According to some sources, as much as 25 percent of Sudan's population was employed by the NISS as informants "in some way or another" between 1999 and 2016.[94]

SOUTHERN SECESSION, THE SUDANESE REVOLUTION, AND THE FORMATION OF THE GIS

The CPA referendum led to the establishment of South Sudan and the loss of three quarters of Sudan's oil reserves. The loss of oil revenue has been the determining factor of Sudan's ongoing economic crisis. It resulted in an unparalleled devaluation of Sudan's currency and extremely high living costs. By 2016, the country was faced with having to completely restructure its economy away from the oil sector to establish some semblance of stability.[95] In late 2018, al-Bashir imposed a series of emergency austerity measures aimed at preventing economic collapse, cutting subsidies for basic goods, restricting imports, and monetizing the oil deficit. These caused inflation to exceed 70 percent and oil reserves to quickly decrease.[96] Unable to withdraw money from banks, many Sudanese could not access basic foodstuff. The threat of socioeconomic collapse forced al-Bashir to reduce wages for government employees, including NISS personnel—a move that drastically reduced the power he held over the agency. Additionally, the dictator could no longer promise economic stability to Sudan's civil society in exchange for loyalty.

Peaceful anti-austerity demonstrations began in December 2018 in eastern Sudan and quickly spread to Khartoum. They soon turned into anti-government protests with demonstrators accusing al-Bashir of mismanaging the economy and committing war crimes and crimes against humanity.[97] By early 2019, the protests showed no signs of slowing down with participants openly calling for al-Bashir's removal from office. The security forces responded to the protests by using excessive violence, including firing live ammunition, which resulted in more than one hundred deaths between December and April 2019. These incidents inflamed the protests, instead of stopping them and prompted what was initially a fragmented and disorganized movement to coalesce under the Forces of Freedom and Change (FFC), an umbrella group of forces aiming to overthrow al-Bashir.[98] These included the Sudanese Professionals Association, the No to Oppression against Women Initiative, the National Consensus Forces, the Sudan Revolutionary Front, and others. Participants signed the Freedom and Change Charter, which called for the government's removal, transition to democracy under a civilian government, and the disbandment of the NISS.[99] In an attempt to pacify the FFC and preserve its dominance in cash-strapped Sudan, the military and the NISS joined the FFC and overthrew al-Bashir in April 2019.[100] Gosh, Sudan's former NISS chief under al-Bashir, is broadly credited with organizing the coup.[101]

After ousting al-Bashir, Gosh's forces took power and announced the creation of a Transitional Military Council (TMC), whose aim was to hold multiparty elections within two years under the supervision of the security forces. However, protesters remained in the streets, insisting that their original demand of civilian rule be met.[102] The TMC continued to crack down on protests, resulting in as many as one hundred deaths of demonstrators. Following months of talks between the TMC and the FFC, accompanied by peaceful and non-peaceful protests, the two bodies agreed to a power-sharing deal, which resulted in the Sovereignty Council.[103] It consists of six civilians and five generals but is intended to transition to civilian leadership following multiparty elections.[104] The Sovereignty Council fulfilled a major protestor demand: namely, the dissolution of the NISS and the resignation of its director under the TMC, General Abu Bakr Dumblab. The service was liquidated and replaced with a new organization, the General Intelligence Service (GIS, جهاز المخابرات العامة). But NISS personnel refused to give up their posts as instructed. On January 14, 2020, NISS personnel staged an armed mutiny in several cities, seizing NISS buildings and opening fire on government forces. They were eventually pushed back by the military, and their leaders surrendered following negotiations. Gosh was blamed for this last stand of the then dissolved NISS.[105] General Jamal Abdul Majeed, with a background in military intelligence, was appointed director of the GIS, and tasked with building a new organization that would be "more professional in protecting the country and safeguarding its national security against very complicated threats."[106]

CHARACTERISTICS OF THE SUDANESE INTELLIGENCE APPARATUS

Among the most notable characteristics of the Sudanese intelligence apparatus is the very extent of its timeline. By as early as 1820, the region's conquerors were forced to confront its complex tribal, ethnic, and religious composition. It compelled them to diversify their intelligence collection to survive. In doing so, they cultivated operational contacts with an impressive multitude of constituents. By the time British forces arrived in their area, they relied on Egyptian-Ottoman middlemen to build HUMINT networks whose richness mirrored that of native populace. Consequently, at the outbreak of the First World War, the maturity and sophistication of Sudanese intelligence stood unmatched among European dominions worldwide.

Although its beginnings were undoubtedly militarized, British-led intelligence in Sudan should not be viewed as a military enterprise. On the contrary, it developed a distinct civilian identity within the wider corpus of colonial administration. The latter participated in broad intelligence-oriented tasks to protect the colonial state. However, the core mechanism of political policing remained concentrated within the Intelligence Department, which saw itself as distinct from the military. The theme of political policing has not left Sudanese intelligence. Its civilian culture gradually faded, until it was wholly extinguished in 1979 by Nimeiry. It has never returned.

That the esoteric ethos of Sudanese intelligence should have survived for over two decades following Sudan's independence is hardly surprising, given the bureaucratic cohesion of the service under British rule. The riverine Nubian tribes that dominated the service after 1924 retained control following independence and contributed to the prioritization of northern-Arabized interests in the new Sudan. They were not, however, controlled by the country's leadership in any meaningful way. On the contrary, the transient nature of Sudan's rulers—elected or otherwise—offended the intelligence services' strong belief in permanence and kept them at a safe distance from the upper echelons of power.

The contradiction between an autonomic intelligence service and a succession of highly autocratic regimes is apparent. Autocratic governments tend to prioritize domestic challenges to their authority, which results in their reliance on extensive intelligence mechanisms. In the case of Sudan, such mechanisms were built by party structures and operated alongside the state's official intelligence apparatus. By the late 1960s, the latter had fallen into obscurity, from which it emerged nearly two decades later, when it was usurped by Nimeiry. The price of its resurgence was high, as it was forced to forfeit what was left of its independence.

The enforced Islamization of the service during the 1990s extinguished the last vestiges of its colonial ethos. Moreover, it turned the service into an appendix of an increasingly tyrannical regime. Yet it would be a mistake to search for deep parallels between Sudan and other personalist systems of rule—such as with North Korea, where the state superstructure has been far more durable. Sudan, with its highly contested seat of power, and the ephemeral nature of its governing administrations over the years, is markedly different. Thus, even in the darkest days of al-Bashir's regime, the intelligence establishment assisted in the imposition of totalitarianism primarily as a means of safeguarding its own bureaucratic interests. When these could no longer be guaranteed, the intelligence service joined the coup d'état that toppled the dictator. Throughout that turbulent process, there has been no evidence that the Sudanese intelligence services are ideologically committed to the establishment of democratic canonical practices in the country.

CONCLUSION

The many critics of the Sudanese intelligence establishment rightly focus on its human-rights record, which is, even by the most lenient of accounts, abysmal. Nevertheless, these abuses are but the cruelest manifestations of deeper institutional flaws, which date back to British rule. Indeed, the very establishment of the service in 1899 embodied the securitization of politics. The criminalization of the opposition in post-independence Sudan effectively prolonged British colonialism with tasked intelligence administrators who had a set of familiar duties. In recent years, the forces of progress, in the form of the FFC, have inched closer to implementing consequential change more than at almost any other period in the country's history. In moving forward, pro-democracy leaders must see to it that the new constitution codifies the outright prohibition of political policing without exclusions.

Ever since independence, successive generations of rank-and-file officials have sought to entrench the intelligence services to ensure their permanence amid the turbulence of Sudanese politics. This method, which scholars of bureaucracies call "displacement," allowed the intelligence services to demarcate their institutional interests from those of the state.[107] This is how bureaucratic institutions often seek to survive in highly unstable political environments. Yet, institutional endurance should not be an end in itself and should not supersede the principle of public service. With the GIS's establishment, the Republic of Sudan has an extraordinary opportunity to reintegrate the intelligence service into the nation's governing apparatus with the goal of safeguarding the path to democracy. Doing so successfully requires that the GIS is rendered answerable to far more than just the highest echelons of the government. It also requires that control of its functions is shared between the executive and legislative centers of power. Furthermore, administrative and financial transparency must be built into the very structure of the new organization, so as to guard against the recurrence of some of Sudan's darkest days.

Last, the informant networks of the now defunct NISS must be abolished, and those that are not must be normalized and regulated as a matter of urgency. Their continuing existence in their present state is highly destabilizing and offers the fastest way for the GIS to revert to its predecessor's methods of operation. Not only should these extensive networks be abolished, but society at large must be offered verifiable assurances that the surveillance state built by al-Bashir has eclipsed. A state-supported model of transitional justice, perhaps incorporating elements of the 1992 "Truth Commission" in Germany, should be considered. Moreover, the use of informants and other agents for domestic purposes should be prohibited for cases other than those that are criminal or insurrectional in nature.

The 2019 revolution sparked a limited process of lustration throughout Sudan. However, the view that a clear line of demarcation can separate the old NISS from the post-revolution GIS is fantastical. Consequently, the implementation of a lengthy and enduring program of democratization, possibly a resemblance of the de-Ba'athification of Iraq or the de-Francoisation of Spain, must take center stage within the new GIS. Still, in light of the January 2020 putsch against the TMC, further attempts by the old NISS guard to regain power should not only be assumed, but expected. It follows that GIS planners should prioritize intelligence collection relating to attempts by the military and security forces to derail the process of democratization. If it is prolonged and sincere, this new emphasis could expunge the dark legacy of Sudanese intelligence and establish trust between the new GIS and the emerging civil society at the dawn of what could be the nation's first lasting age of democracy.

NOTES

1. Mohammed Nuri El-Amin, "Britain, the 1924 Sudanese Uprising, and the Impact of Egypt on the Sudan," *The International Journal of African Historical Studies* 19, no. 2 (1986): 235.

2. Per Olav Reinton, "Imperialism and the Southern Sudan," *Journal of Peace Research* 8, no. 3/4 (1971): 241.

3. Catherine Jendia, *The Sudanese Civil Conflict, 1969–1985* (Bern: Peter Lang, 2002), 19.

4. Hasan Qasim Murad, "British Involvement in the Sudan," *Pakistan Horizon* 31, no. 4 (1978): 68–69.

5. Edward M. Spiers, "Intelligence and Command in Britain's Small Colonial Wars of the 1890s," *Intelligence and National Security* 22, no. 5 (2007): 664.

6. Spiers, 664; Ahmed Ibrahim Abushouk, "The Anglo-Egyptian Sudan: From Collaboration Mechanism to Party Politics, 1898–1956," *Journal of Imperial and Commonwealth History* 38, no. 2 (2010): 211.

7. Spiers, 679.

8. J. A. Mangan, "The Education of an Elite Imperial Administration: The Sudan Political Service and the British and the British Public School System," *The International Journal of African Historical Studies* 15, no. 4 (1982): 672.

9. Robert Collins, "The Sudan Political Service: A Portrait of the Imperialists," *African Affairs*, 71, no. 284 (1972): 293.

10. Willow Berridge, "Sudan's Security Agencies: Fragmentation, Visibility and Mimicry, 1908–89," *Intelligence and National Security*, 28, no. 6 (2013): 848.

11. Martin Thomas, *Empires of Intelligence: Security Services and Colonial Disorder after 1914* (Berkeley: The University of California Press, 2008), 16.

12. John Fisher, "British Responses to Mahdist and Other Unrest in North and West Africa, 1919–1930," *Australian Journal of Politics and History* 52, no. 3 (2006): 347.

13. Thomas, 108.

14. Ibid., 14.

15. Abushouk, 209.

16. Hassan Ahmed Ibrahim, "Imperialism and Neo-Mahdism in the Sudan: A Study of British Policy towards Neo-Mahdism, 1924–1927," *The International Journal of African Historical Studies* 13, no. 2 (1980): 214.

17. Hassan Ahmed Ibrahim, *Sayyid 'Abd Al-Raḥmān Al-Mahdī: A Study of Neo-Mahdīsm in the Sudan, 1899–1956* (Boston: Brill Academic Publisher, 2004), 106.

18. Thomas, 29.

19. Muddathir Abdel Rahim "The Development of British Policy in the Southern Sudan 1899–1947," *Middle Eastern Studies* 2, no. 3 (1966): 227.

20. Berridge, "Sudan's," 850.

21. Kamal Osman Salih, "British Policy and the Accentuation of Inter-Ethnic Divisions: The Case of the Nuba Mountains Region of Sudan, 1920–1940," *African Affairs* 89, no. 356 (1990): 417.

22. Abushouk, 53.

23. Fisher, 347.

24. Abushouk, 212.

25. Willow Berridge, "'Guarding the Guards': The Failure of the Colonial State to Govern Police Violence in Sudan, ca. 1922–1956," *Northeast African Studies* 12, no. 2 (2012): 12.

26. Berridge, "Sudan's," 849.

27. Edward Grierson, *The Death of the Imperial Dream: The British Commonwealth and Empire 1775–1969* (New York: Doubleday, 1972), 4.

28. Ibrahim, "Imperialism," 216.

29. Ibrahim, *Sayyid 'Abd Al-Raḥmān Al-Mahdī*, 66.

30. Fisher, 351.

31. Jendia, 38.

32. Gabriel Warburg, *Islam, Sectarianism and Politics in Sudan since the Mahdiyya* (Glasgow: University of Wisconsin Press, 2003), 88.

33. Mohammed Nuri El-Amin, "The Role of International Communism in the Muslim World and in Egypt and the Sudan," *British Journal of Middle Eastern Studies* 23, no. 1 (1996): 29. Mohammed Nuri El-Amin, "The Sudanese Communist Movement: The First Five Years," *Middle Eastern Studies* 32, no. 3 (1996): 182–84.

34. Fisher, 347.

35. Fisher, 359. Mohammed Nuri El-Amin, "Was There an Alliance between the Watanist (Nationalist) Party, International Communism and the White Flag League in the Sudan?" *British Journal of Middle Eastern Studies* 19, no. 20 (1992): 182.

36. Thomas, 17.

37. Berridge, "Sudan's," 846.

38. Ibid., "Sudan's," 849, 853.

39. Berridge, "Guarding," 22.

40. Thomas, 140.

41. Lewis H. Gann, "The Sudan," in *World Communism: A Handbook, 1918–1965*, Witold S. Sworakowski (Stanford: Hoover Institution Press 1973), 412.

42. El-Amin, "The Sudanese," 22; Berridge, "Sudan's," 851.

43. Berridge, "Sudan's,"851.

44. Thomas, "Empires," 133.

45. Chris Vaughan, "Reinventing the Wheel? Local Government and Neo-Traditional Authority in Late-Colonial Northern Sudan," *International Journal of African Historical Studies* 43, no. 2 (2010): 256.

46. Abushouk "The Anglo-Egyptian," 227.

47. Jendia, 49.

48. Øystein H. Rolandsen, and Cherry Leonardi "Discourses of Violence in the Transition from Colonialism to Independence in Southern Sudan, 1955–1960," *Journal of Eastern African Studies* 8, no. 4 (2014): 611.

49. Matthew LeRiche and Matthew Arnold, *South Sudan: From Revolution to Independence* (New York: Oxford University Press, 2013), 1.

50. Jendia, 59.

51. Berridge, "Sudan's," 854.

52. Gann, "The Sudan," 412.

53. John A. Cookson, Howard J. John, Archibald G. MacArthur, Jean McEwen, Wyatt MacGaffey and Mildred C. Vreeland, *United States Army Area Handbook for the Republic of Sudan* (Washington, DC: US Government Printing Office, 1964), 389.

54. Berridge, "Sudan's," 854.

55. Ibid., 857.

56. Øystein H. Rolandsen and Nicki Kindersley, "The Nasty War: Organised Violence during the Anya-Nya Insurgency," *Journal of African History* 60, no. 1 (2019): 102.

57. David Kilcullen, *Counterinsurgency* (New York: Oxford University Press, 2010), 1–16.

58. Rolandsen and Leonardi, 610.

59. Rolandsen and Kindersley, 93.

60. Berridge, "Sudan's," 860.

61. Jendia, 69.

62. Berridge, "Sudan's," 855.

63. Ibid., "Sudan's," 854.

64. Mawut A. M. Guarak, *Integration and Fragmentation of the Sudan: An African Renaissance* (Bloomington: AuthorHouse, 2011), 181.

65. Berridge, "Sudan's," 856.

66. Ibid., 856.

67. Willow Berridge, *Civil Uprisings in Modern Sudan: The 'Khartoum Springs' of 1964 and 1985* (London: Bloomsbury Publishing, 2015), 175.

68. Berridge, *Civil Uprisings*, 82.

69. Willow Berridge, *Hasan al-Turabi: Islamist Politics and Democracy in Sudan* (New York: Cambridge University Press, 2017), 211.

70. Berridge, "Sudan's," 861.

71. Heather Sharkey, "Arab Identity and Ideology in Sudan: The Politics of Language, Ethnicity, and Race," *African Affairs* 107, no. 426 (2007): 21.

72. Suliman Baldo "Radical Intolerance: Sudan's Religious Oppression and Embrace of Extremist Groups" (Washington, DC: Enough! Project, 2017): 17.

73. Philip C. Wilcox, "Patterns of Global Terrorism, 1994" (Washington, Office of the Coordinator for Counterterrorism, United States Department of State, 1995, https://fas.org/irp/threat/terror_94/index.html.

74. Diana Childress, *Omar Bashir's Sudan* (Minneapolis: Twenty-First Century Books, 2010): 50.

75. Mai Hassan and Ahmed Kodouda, "Sudan's Uprising: The Fall of a Dictator," *Journal of Democracy* 30 no. 4 (2019): 92.

76. Hassan and Kodouda, "Sudan's," 92.

77. Cameron Hudson, "Removing Sudan's Terrorism Designation: Proceeding with Caution" (Washington, DC: The Atlantic Council, 2020). https://www.atlanticcouncil.org/blogs/africasource/removing-sudans-terrorism-designation-proceeding-with-caution.

78. Olivia Warham, *The Sudanese National Intelligence and Security Service* (London: Waging Peace, 2011): 1.

79. International Crisis Group, "Sudan: Major Reform or More War" (Brussels: Crisis Group Africa Report, no 194, 2012): 23–24.

80. Danish Immigration Service, *Sudan: Situation of Persons from Darfur, Southern Kordofan and Blue Nile in Khartoum* (Copenhagen: Ministry of Immigration, Integration and Housing, 2016): 77.

81. Amnesty International, *Agents of Fear: The National Security Service in Sudan* (London: Amnesty International Publications, 2010).

82. GAN Integrity, "Sudan Corruption Report" (New York: GAN Integrity, 2016): 2.

83. Kabbashi M. Suliman, *Understanding and Avoiding the Oil Curse in Sudan* (Cairo: Economic Research Forum, Working Paper No. 735, 2012): 30.

84. Statements by Sudanese defectors who were forced to participate in NISS intelligence-gathering operations targeting France and the United Nations. On file with author.

85. Priscilla Nyagoah, "Sudanese National Intelligence and Security Service Empowered to Violate Human Rights" (London: Amnesty International, March 19, 2015): 2. See also: Danish Immigration Service, 9–13; Warham, 1.

86. Home Office, "Country Information and Guidance. Sudan: Failed Asylum Seekers" (London: Government of the United Kingdom, August 2016): 7.

87. Home Office, "Country," 7.

88. Redress Nederland, "Torture in Sudan: Justice and Prevention" (Amsterdam: African Centre for Justice and Peace Studies, April 25, 2019): 2.

89. Jeff Stein, "CIA Training Sudan's Spies as Obama Officials Fight over Policy," *Washington Post*, August, 30 2010; "US Bans Former Sudan Security Chief Ghosh over Torture," Agence France Presse, August 15, 2019.

90. Hassan and Kodouda, "Sudan's," 93.

91. Warham, 3.

92. US Department of State, *Human Rights Report: Sudan* (Washington, DC: United States Government, 2010): 6.

93. Hassan and Kodouda, "Sudan's," 100.

94. Danish Immigration Service, 46.

95. "السودان في الاقتصادية الأزمة" *Al Jazeera*, March 15, 2012, https://www.aljazeera.net/programs/economyandpeople/2012/3/15/ الأزمة-الاقتصادية-في-السودان.

96. "المستوى يقفز السودان في التضخم" *Al Arabiya*, March 15, 2020, https://www.alarabiya.net/ar/aswaq/financial-markets/2020/03/15/التضخم-في-السودان-يقفز-لمستوى-70-.

97. "وخلفياتها أسبابها بالسودان مظاهرات" *BBC*, January 2, 2019, https://www.bbc.com/arabic/middleeast-46723441.

98. Ahmad Fadl, "بالتخريب اليسار تتهم والحكومة السودان احتجاجات قتلى حصيلة ارتفاع" *Al Jazeera*, January 21, 2019, https://www.aljazeera.net/news/politics/2019/1/22/ احتجاجات-السودان-ضحايا.

99. "والتغيير الحرية إعلان" (Khartoum: Sudanese Professionals Association, n.d., accessed June 30, 2020). https://www.sudaneseprofessionals.org/إعلان-الحرية-والتغيير/.

100. Ismail Azzam, "احتجاجات السودان.. لماذا كلّ هذا الصمت العربي والدولي؟" *Deutsche Welle*, January 2, 2019, https://www.dw.com/ar/a-46932026/احتجاجات-السودان-لماذا-كل-هذا-الصمت-العربي-والدولي.

101. "بالسودان "التمرد" وراء بالوقوف المتهم الغامض المخابرات رجل قوش صلاح" *BBC*, January 15, 2019, https://www.bbc.com/arabic/middleeast-51125758.

102. "ناجح تفاوض بعد المخابرات عناصر تمرد انتهاء بالسودان" *Deutsche Welle*, January 14, 2019, https://www.dw.com/ar/a-52005761/السودان-انتهاء-تمرد-عناصر-المخابرات-بعد-تفاوض-ناجح.

103. "السودان في تتواصل الاحتجاجات.. أخرى جثث على العثور بعد" *Al Jazeera*, July 1, 2019, https://www.aljazeera.net/news/politics/2019/7/1/السودان-مظاهرات-أم-درمان-المجلس.

104. "المتورطين ينتظر ما هذا.. السودان في "مخابراتي" انقلاب" *Al Arabiya*, January 15, 2020, https://www.alarabiya.net/ar/arab-and-world/sudan/2020/01/15/ النائب-العام-السوداني-يجب-محاكمة-مرتكبي-التمرد-عاجلا.

105. "ناجح:تفاوض بعد المخابرات عناصر تمرد انتهاء بالسودان" *Deutsche Welle*, January 14, 2019, https://www.dw.com/ar/a-52005761/السودان-انتهاء-تمرد-عناصر-المخابرات-بعد-تفاوض-ناجح.

106. Mahmoud Mourad, "Sudan Appoints New Intelligence Chief in Wake of Failed Revolt," Reuters, January 16, 2020, https://www.reuters.com/article/us-sudan-security-revolt/sudan-appoints-new-intelligence-chief-in-wake-of-failed-revolt-idUSKBN1ZF2FE; "بالسودان ؤالمخابرات الأمن جهاز' اسم تغيير .يحله مطالبات وسط"، Anadolu Agency, July 29, 2019, https://www.aa.com.tr/ar/الدول-العربية-وسط-بحله-مطالبات-بالسودان-والمخابرات-الأمن-جهاز-اسم-تغيير1544569/.

107. Howard P. Greenwald, *Organizations: Management without Control* (Thousand Oaks: Sage Publications, 2008), 367.

Chapter 8

Civilian Intelligence Services in Botswana: Colonial Legacies and Politicization of the Directorate of Intelligence and Security

Tshepo Gwatiwa and Lesego Tsholofelo

Intelligence in Botswana must be understood as intertwined with the state-making and nation-building process. The idea of statehood is a contested phenomenon that involves among other things balancing imported or Western ideas of statehood with traditional notions of governance, justice, and identity.[1] These have implications for how governmental institutions are formed and operated. Although Botswana was not a colony de jure, it inherited many colonial remnants. Upon independence in 1966, Botswana inherited a colonial constitution as well as a civil service corps that was predominantly European.[2] While the process of indigenizing the civil service and security services was fraught with complex ethnicization and outright corrupt pedantry, this process was relatively forgiving in Botswana.[3] Yet, the effect of benignly divergent interests including within the ruling party defined the way different state resources are deployed to give the ruling party a dominant place in society.[4] An explanation of this phenomenon through an intelligence studies lens is lacking in the academic discourse.

Botswana is a noteworthy case study to understand this process for several reasons. Botswana has been one of Africa's most stable democracies—if not the most stable—alongside Mauritius.[5] It has also avoided the infractions that have interrupted political and governance trajectories of various states for almost half a century.[6] This relative stability remained in place despite various structural idiosyncrasies and imperfections that characterize the political system in Botswana.[7] It is these idiosyncrasies that make this analysis relevant. The most notable is the formation and institutionalization of security institutions, such as the Directorate of Intelligence and Security (DIS), to provide an understanding of intelligence operational cultures and approaches to national and international security. While such analysis cannot be exhaustive, it can capture a fraction of the political, legal, and social contexts of the operations of critical security institutions.

This chapter contextualizes the DIS's belated formation and institution-alization in one of Africa's thriving democracies. It argues that the DIS's operational culture and approach during 2008–2018 must be understood in its historical, legal, and social contexts. This analysis explores three critical phases in Botswana's relatively long period of state-making and nation-building. The first is the colonial period during which Botswana was a pro-tectorate of the United Kingdom. The second is the early postcolonial period during which the relatively new government experimented with or diced dif-ferent factors of state-making and nation-building. The third period involves the post–Cold War period during which Botswana adjusted to changes in domestic and international systems. Within these three phases, the chapter identifies three critical factors that will help to understand the directorate: threat perception, intelligence governance, and operational culture. These three factors explain the characteristics that have—correctly or incorrectly—defined the intelligence directorate in the eyes of the public.

This chapter proceeds in four parts. The first part is an analytic framework that articulates the notion of intelligence individualization. It then links this notion to the literature on the democratic oversight of intelligence services. The second part situates intelligence personalization and abuse in an African context and highlights Botswana's specificities. This provides the reader with the political context of the referent legacy of the directorate. The third section discusses reports of major intelligence abuses by examining acts of subversion, intellectual repression and intimidation, surveillance, and other controversies. The fourth part examines prospects of intelligence reform by assessing the vulnerabilities lent by the constitution and Botswana's political systems as well as the Intelligence Act.

CONTEXTUALIZING BOTSWANA'S INTELLIGENCE GOVERNANCE AND OPERATIONS

The controversies that have surrounded the DIS's first decade relate to gov-ernance and perceived politicization. The basis for such a discussion needs to be juxtaposed against Botswana's system of governance—one of Africa's thriving democracies. The country's relative success with democratic gover-nance is partly attributed to a "competent bureaucracy and limited interfer-ence from political leadership."[8] Within that system is the concept of a neutral civil service that is expected to be "apolitical, impartial and professional and able to serve successive governments with equal loyalty."[9] Indeed, the Public Service Act forbids civil servants from taking part in active politics.[10] DIS employees form part of the wider civil service. Furthermore, the Intelligence and Security Act itself forbids partisanship on the part of the DIS and its officers, consequent to sections 5(2) and 16(1), respectively. Thus, ideally, any violation of this bureaucratic rule must be viewed suspiciously as a form of politicization of the civil service. Yet, it is difficult to reconcile ideals and application of this principle due to the nature of intelligence work and the difficulties that accompany it, which are challenges in Africa and beyond.

THE STATE AND PERSONALIZATION OF INTELLIGENCE AGENCIES IN AFRICA

Intelligence abuses are commonplace in Africa, especially in authoritarian and hybrid regimes. Although the number of democracies has increased in Africa since the end of the Cold War, several countries still grapple with abuse of the security and intelligence institutions, which are used for regime preservation.[11] Indeed, some governments use intelligence services for regime preservation within and outside their borders.[12] Notably, Uganda and Rwanda use intelligence organizations for political subversion and covert operations that have little to do with national security. Whereas Rwanda and Zimbabwe show that domestic repression usually involves disruptive methods that most of these governments used during liberation struggles that they transposed into the post-independence state security architecture and culture (for Rwanda, see Kegel in this volume).[13]

There is also deep personalization and sometimes outright politicization in using intelligence and security services in other African nations. This can be explained by understanding the historical context. First, the politicization of intelligence services is a result of patronage among cadres in liberation movements. For instance, South Africa (see O'Brien in this volume) and Zimbabwe grafted former liberation commanders and officers—alongside remnants of the then racist white minority regime of Ian Smith (see Cross in this volume)—into the new military and intelligence structures.[14] The comradeship between or across these groups blurred the lines between politics and civil service. Illustratively, between 2008 and 2013 a group in Zimbabwe formed the so-called Joint Military Commission (JMC) that exclusively and extensively used intelligence services to prop up the President Robert Mugabe regime after fraudulent elections.[15] Ironically, the same group removed Mugabe from power in 2017 mainly relying on the personalized use of intelligence services.[16]

Second, intelligence politicization evolved out of mutual endearment as elitism of compradors grew within African states. For instance, in the process of Africanization, the Kenyan (see Shaffer in this volume) and the Tanzanian intelligence services (see Graham in this volume) replaced British senior civil servants with native civil servants with shared ethnicity or political affiliation.[17] Similarly, former Zairian dictator, Joseph Mobutu, co-opted ethnic and personal allies to oversee a heavy-handed use of intelligence services against perceived opponents.[18] More recently, President Yoweri Museveni in Uganda promoted his son to the rank of lieutenant general three years after promoting him to major general in charge of the Ugandan Special Forces, which controls military intelligence.[19] This culture of nepotism and personalization partially explains intelligence abuse in Africa. The antecedent intelligence abuse in Botswana arose from similar circumstances: a buddy system consisting of an amalgam of technocrats and political elites working to protect their interests in the process of state-making and nation-building.[20]

THE EVOLUTION OF SECURITY INTELLIGENCE IN BOTSWANA

It is necessary to contextualize early twentieth–century intelligence in what eventually became the state of Botswana to understand the DIS. This does not imply that all the practices have translated into present practices, but it provides an important background that shaped the political, legal, and operational linkages and habits that have survived different phases of Botswana's state-making and nation-building.

Politicization of Botswana's intelligence services dates to its earliest days. It was not until 1923 that formalized intelligence activities took root in Botswana (then Bechuanaland Protectorate) under the auspices of the United Kingdom.[21] At the time, intelligence collection requirements mostly centered around pan-Africanist activities in Southern Africa, which the colonial authorities considered a threat to the establishment. In the early 1950s, the Bechuanaland Protectorate Special Branch came into being, employing plainclothes officers, most of whom were former policemen.[22] According to historian Neil Parsons, the intelligence reports were filed under eight headings: "Reports on Meetings, Movements of Prominent Members of Tribes, Attitudes of Public towards Government, African National Congress (ANC), Communications, Motor transport, General and Cattle."[23] Based on these topics, perhaps except for the ANC, the colonial authorities were mostly concerned about domestic threats that were also political in nature.

The intelligence services broadened their mandate when the liberation struggle intensified in the early 1960s. Between 1961 and 1964, the intelligence services began concentrating on the activities of apartheid South African and South West African (now Namibia) refugees and political activists some of whom were transiting the Protectorate to Tanganyika (present-day

Tanzania).[24] It should be noted that this does not imply that the intelligence services expanded their mandate and operational ambit beyond the borders. Indeed, the threat perception remained mostly domestic. The regional and/ or international threats were important only if they affected the strategic ambitions of the colonial establishment, which was somewhat collapsing and preparing to hand power to a new domestic administration.

By independence in 1966, Botswana's national security threats still focused inward. Perceived security threats comprised, among other things, communism and communist-inspired activities, pan-Africanist activities, and labor unions as well as opposition by local chiefs who resented the erosion of their traditional powers.[25] These threats reflected the empirical realities of state-making and nation-building in the then nascent state. However, it is surprising that the security briefing prepared for then incoming Prime Minister Seretse Khama in August 1966 did not include the threat posed by apartheid South Africa.[26] For the most part, and perhaps understandably, Botswana was not institutionally and politically disposed to focus on South Africa for several reasons. First, Botswana did not have an army until 1977.[27] Thus, even if Botswana's senior government officials were concerned by apartheid South Africa, they did not have the institutional means to confront South Africa. Second, the scale of South Africa's aggression in Botswana was lower compared to Namibia, Angola, and Zambia.[28] Historical evidence shows that even the South African Bureau of State Security (BOSS) agents assigned to Botswana mostly focused on intelligence gathering without any resort to the type of covert activities they employed in Lesotho, Namibia, and Angola.[29] Although there were attacks against South African exiles in Gaborone and Francistown, they were comparatively of low intensity and sporadic subversive acts.[30]

The structuring and mandating of the postcolonial intelligence services provided a defining path for Botswana's security intelligence services. In 1968, the newly elected government of Botswana issued a new charter stipulating the duties of the Botswana Police Special Branch (SB). This charter had three main duties for the intelligence: 1) security intelligence, 2) protective security, and 3) counterespionage.[31] Security intelligence entailed coverage of subversive movements, organizations, and individuals, while protective security was concerned with protection of information, operations, vital points, and personnel. The third duty focused on foreign intelligence organizations that operated within or against the government. The SB also had the responsibility of close personal protection of the president and vice president as well as visiting foreign dignitaries. Even though the head of the SB reported to the police commissioner, he also had direct access to the president of the republic for sensitive briefings.

While the issuing of the SB charter indicated a seeming departure from the erstwhile branding of domestic dissent as national security transgression, it did not stop the surveillance of those groups. This is especially true, given that intelligence, as referred to in the charter, included subversive movements. According to scholar Peter Gill, the term "subversion" if not properly qualified can mean anything, including political and labor movement's activities that are both lawful and peaceful. This ambiguity is known to have been widely abused in such countries as Canada and the United States, where the McDonald Commission from 1977 to 1980 found that the Royal Canadian Mounted Police (RCMP) had unlawfully targeted political groups under the guise of subversion, resulting in the excision of intelligence work from the RCMP and establishment of the Canadian Security Intelligence Service (CSIS).[32] Similarly, the Church Committee investigated the American intelligence services as well as the Federal Bureau of Investigation (FBI) in the United States for violations of U.S. citizens' rights.[33] Likewise, in Botswana, revelations in recent years have suggested that the SB was guilty of similar transgressions, including the surveillance of former opposition leader, Kenneth Koma.[34] Koma was reportedly kept under surveillance from the early days of party formations in Bechuanaland throughout his political life.[35] A former government minister, David Magang, recalled incidents in 1981 and 1993 when the SB surveyed one of the ruling Botswana Democratic Party (BDP) factions that was out of favor with the party's leadership.[36] The SB monitored meetings involving BDP functionaries canvassing for support for their preferred candidates, which was a normal democratic activity. This not only demonstrates the entrenched culture of politicization of intelligence, but also the extent of this politicization: monitoring of opposition and dissenting factions within the ruling party.

The nature of intelligence governance and operations changed in the 1990s. In 1998, the SB morphed into the Security Intelligence Services (SIS). While there had been slight alterations to the mandate of the SB over time since the charter was issued in 1968, the 1998 move was in essence a change in name only with no major shifts from the core mandate.[37] One notable earlier change was the passage of the 1986 National Security Act, which sought to address such military incursions due to military harassment at the hands of apartheid South Africa.[38]

In the mid-1990s, there had been discussions within the Botswana security establishment to set up an independent intelligence organization.[39] The rationale behind this was, among other things, that the security environment had evolved globally. The SIS was also finding it increasingly difficult to forge partnerships with their international counterparts on account that they were effectively a police service. The discomfort of foreign partners sharing intelligence was due to providing information likely to be used for policing or prosecutorial purposes, which could compromise sources, and made the SB's partners reluctant to share and collaborate.[40] However, owing to fears of loss of power occasioned by the jettisoning of the SIS from the BPS, some senior police officers apparently stalled the process.[41] It was not until the mid-2000s that the process regained the momentum culminating with the tabling of the Intelligence and Security Service (ISS) Bill in November 2006.

POLITICS AND THE LAW IN THE CREATION OF THE DIS

The founding of the Directorate of Intelligence and Security (DIS) can also be traced to changes in Botswana's politics in the late 1990s. Then President Ketumile Q. J. Masire introduced what would be known as "automatic succession"—a system that enables an incumbent vice president to automatically assume the presidency upon the incumbent president's departure.[42] Automatic succession was introduced when two-term presidential limits and democratization became popular in Africa.[43] In this system, a successor assumes the presidency a year and half before the general election. Presidents Festus Mogae and Ian Khama as well as the current president, Mokgweetsi E. Masisi, benefited from this process in 1998, 2008, and 2018, respectively. To some analysts, automatic succession was simply an insertion of traditional Tswana chieftaincy succession into modern politics after a considerable lull.[44] Others posit that Masire introduced automatic succession because the DeBeers Company, which controls the diamond-reliant economic sector, bought him out of the presidency.[45] Whatever the motive for automatic succession, it gave President Ian Khama time to design and create the DIS with his own preferences while he served as vice president.

The DIS's envisaged operational mandate was left unchecked before the ISS Act (hereafter, the act) became law. The act gave state intelligence officers powers to use force and intrusive means to search without a warrant. Prior to this act, the right to use arms was limited to the police and the army. Apart from powers to arrest without a warrant, section 24 of the act provides complete immunity for all intelligence officers and auxiliary operatives.[46] This was in addition to the complex and dubious nature of the rationale behind the DIS as well as its operational mandate about whether it should focus on domestic or external security threats.[47] Consequently, this meant that DIS officers could operate with impunity.

The act provided broad and ambiguous powers to the director general (DG). Sections 6, 7, and 8 of the act give the DG unlimited powers. Section 6(2) virtually gives the DG considerable power over the directorate by granting the incumbent onus of its "direction, control, administration and expenditure."[48] Contrast this with, for instance, the powers conferred on the police commissioner and the DG of the Directorate on Corruption and Economic Crime (DCEC), wherein their respective acts provide for "command, superintendence, direction and control of the service"[49] and "direction and administration of the Directorate."[50] The control over "expenditure" is an anomaly in Botswana's governance system, as state expenditure is typically controlled by a revenue department that is accountable to the accountant general.

The lack of accountability to the accountant general partially led to DG Isaac Kgosi's 2018 ouster, 2019 arrest, and current trial over mismanagement of state funds. Although the act mentions oversight committees and councils, it does not decentralize power within the agency. For instance, although section 8(4) calls for the creation of divisions of the directorate for "efficient management, administration and control," it still completely leaves that to the prerogative of the DG. Furthermore, section 7 limits the DG's consultation to a small circle comprising the president and a few senior security officials singularly appointed by the president. This legal framework explains why two people effectively controlled the DIS.

These loopholes were structurally weaponized by a set of personal networks at the upper echelons of security intelligence. Kgosi ran the DIS based on a friendship that had fledged between him and President Ian Khama since their military days. According to a retired intelligence officer, Kgosi was not among the crème de la crème of the military intelligence during his military career.[51] His rise to the rank of colonel in the military and later to the apex of the DIS was mostly based on his personal acquaintanceship to Khama.[52] This is in contrast to his successor, Peter Magosi, who, although is equally a political appointee—by virtue of provisions of the act—rose through the ranks in the BDF Special Forces as well as military intelligence.[53] Kgosi's appointment undermined effective governance. Khama also appointed relatives to the DIS Tribunal, which was created by the act to address public grievances.[54] Consequently, the DIS evolved in a politicized and personalized environment without independent oversight, where it mainly served the interests of a few elites. This resulted in several operational controversies that revolved around an occlusion of threat perception and politicization.

POLITICIZATION OF THREATS AND OPERATIONS, 2008–2018

This section describes instances of intelligence personalization and abuse between 2008 and 2018. Most cases were attributed to the DIS, but there were a few instances in which the directorate acted in concert with other services, such as police and military intelligence. In those instances, the Botswana Police Service or the Botswana Defence Force issued guarded press releases or public statements. Meanwhile, Kgosi sporadically responded to the press via telephone, especially when reports affected his or President Khama's image.

Without a radical departure from the immediate postcolonial epoch, Botswana's domestic threats are perceived to mainly emanate from within the country. Tertiary student uprisings are perceived as a threat to national security, especially for a relatively quiet nation with a small population. This dates to the late 1970s, but especially to the protests in the 1990s. In 1994, University of Botswana (UB) students started a strike that led to riots that then spread to an urban village (Mochudi), resulting in a national security crisis. At the time, a state radio journalist announced that a missing child— Segametsi Mogomotsi—had been abducted for voodoo/*muti* rituals at a certain house at Bontleng—a township in Gaborone. UB students immediately marched in protest to Bontleng and later proceeded to Mochudi, which is also the capital of Kgatleng District.[55] This resulted in widespread and protracted riots in Kgatleng, resulting in the president declaring a state of emergency. Different forms of demonstrations (from peaceful to violent) persisted at UB. This culture of protest spread to newer universities, such as the Limkokwing University of Technology.[56] In all these cases, the intelligence agencies, including DIS, infiltrated mass student gatherings to quell possibilities of future insurrections.

Labor groups and opposition movements also rank among perceived threats to Botswana's national security. Different administrations used the Special Branch to infiltrate unions and labor movements.[57] Correspondingly, labor unions have become vocal over the last few years. In April 2011, the labor union umbrella body, the Botswana Federation of Public Sector Unions (BOFEPUSU), organized a nationwide strike that lasted three months, demanding a 16 percent salary increment—the first of its kind. It affected the economy and essential services and spilled over to schools, as students also rioted protesting the absence of teachers. The protestors fought the police in Molepolole, Ramotswa, Otse, and Gaborone.[58] Opposition politicians expressed solidarity with the protesters by calling for regime change, much to the ire of the government.[59] The government was mostly concerned with the growing power of the unions that had incited members of the "essential services" category of workers to join the strike.[60] The strike brought the economy to a standstill for three months and was viewed as a national security issue. The government responded by amending the list of essential services to include about two-thirds of the civil service, which weakened the strike.[61]

It is reasonable to argue that Botswana's domestic security threats are not necessarily new but have evolved over time. Most national security issues derive from the perceptions and behavior of those in power.[62] While labor movements have always been viewed as a possible source of instability, this perception has intensified. These various security threats—formerly considered futuristic and remote—have, under the DIS, now gained serious attention. The issue is whether these threats warranted the need for a civilian intelligence agency. The answer is both yes and no. Yes, because domestic threats might not always be divorced from external threats and as such need to be handled by an intelligence agency with a broad legal mandate, such as the DIS. No, because the creation of the DIS was flawed and posed the risk of heightening and aggravating security threats that have always existed. The formation of the DIS did not eradicate the functions of military and police intelligence, and the mandate of domestic threats legally falls within the juris-diction of the police. Yet it appears that the main problem was perhaps lack of clarity of roles especially between the police and the DIS. As for the military intelligence, their mandate is quite clear: it supports the protection of the country's territorial integrity. Therefore, it follows that military intelligence is solely concerned with supporting that mandate. What about the overlaps? For instance, on the role of the DIS in organized crime, the question then arises as to what constitutes such crime to the extent that the police can leave it to the DIS? Moreover, there is the issue around potentially subversive elements like labor movements and political groups. It remains an empirical conundrum as to who should take the lead between the DIS and the police and who should take the lead in monitoring them and for what purposes.

RAMPANT NEGATIVE PUBLIC PERCEPTIONS OF THE DIS

The DIS has been accused of various but unsubstantiated abuses of power, which were perceived as an infringement of long-standing democratic tradi-tions. However, these accusations are worth summarizing hereunder because they highlight nationwide sentiments that gradually led to Kgosi's ouster and Magosi's mandate to reform the organization.[63] There were accusations of intellectual repression and harassment as well as a perception that Khama disliked any form of opposition and criticism. As a result, the new directorate was perceived to monitor and intimidate intellectuals, journalists, and tertiary students.

Chief among this were allegations of student torture during strikes. The student mass demonstration in 2008 led by an offspring of the then largest opposition parties called "The Movement against Student Suppression—Botswana National Front" (MASS-BNF) claimed that DIS officers harassed them.[64] However, these claims were routinely denied by law enforcement agencies. There were also press reports regarding communication surveil-lance of those opposed to the government of the day. Surveillance is not an anomaly, even in mature democracies.[65] Kgosi was accused of abusing provisions of the ISS Act to monitor those opposed to the Khama regime. Indeed, section 22 of the ISS Act requires the DIS make a court application to undertake such activities. In 2010, the then registrar and master of high court stated that courts were "inundated with applications" from the DIS to intercept phone calls.[66] This implies that the DIS acted within the law in this regard. However, the media frequently reported public perceptions and fears over sustained intrusive monitoring of those perceived to be anti-government in those days.

The abovementioned issues, although widespread and having somewhat influenced the change of leadership, were never thoroughly investigated by the press and other researchers. Most of the press reports were hyperbolic. However, due to the absence of functional and effective oversight structures like the Intelligence Tribunal as established by the ISS Act, these allegations remained uninvestigated. To this end, the perceptions continue. Therefore, this shows that perceptions can heavily influence politics and dynamics of intelligence governance and operations. It is thus imperative to provide a discussion of the need for intelligence reform and oversight in Botswana.

INTELLIGENCE REFORM AND OVERSIGHT

The DIS was established without credible oversight. DIS leadership appointments and accountability are the prerogative of the president.[67] Consequently, President Khama did not have to consult parliament on his appointment of Isaac Kgosi as head of the DIS in 2008. This is due to a contradiction between the constitution and the act. In principle, section 46 of the constitution gives the president absolute powers to appoint leaders in the civil service. That is why Khama did not consult the then leader of opposition, Otsweletse Moupo, on this appointment as required by section 31(3) of the act.[68] Although this section also mandates the creation of an Appeals Tribunal, there was none until the DIS was widely criticized and consequently Khama appointed relatives, friends, and party associates to the tribunal. This anomaly should be understood in the broader context of Botswana's democracy.

The weakness in democratic oversight of the DIS emanates from Botswana's type of democracy. Although scholar Charles Fombad describes Botswana as a hybrid of British parliamentary and U.S. presidential systems, in reality it is a presidential democracy where political power is concentrated in the presidency.[69] Parliament has a ceremonial role whereby it rubber stamps presidential or cabinet decisions.[70] Parliament is inherently weakened by section 46 of the constitution, but this has been worsened by a system of patronage and institutional weakness, which has been in place since the 1980s.[71] For instance, the Parliamentary Committee on Intelligence and

Security (PCIS) has, throughout its existence, failed to hold the DIS accountable because the act does not lay out its modalities for oversight. Furthermore, the idea of parliamentary oversight on intelligence was still destined to fail on two other counts.

The PCIS is undermined by its structural and operational mandate in the Intelligence Act. First, the act outlines the selection of the committee—by the president in consultation with the speaker of the National Assembly and leader of opposition—but skews it toward the ruling party. Section 39(1) mandates the creation of a nine-person committee with a quorum of five, with a caveat in 39(4) that "relative to its size reflect the numerical strengths of the political parties represented in the National Assembly." This means that the PCIS would predominantly consist of BDP legislators, which rendered it less credible, given (a) the BDP quorum and (b) Khama's strong preference for sycophancy. Second, the committee was not empowered to be independent and publicly accountable. Section 40(1) mandates the PCIS report directly to the president as opposed to parliament. This does not qualify as democratic oversight because the president effectively heads all intelligence committees, which makes him the nucleus of all accountability. Moreover, Section 40(2–3) gives the minister for security vetting powers over the publication of the PCIS report, which they have never produced. That is why leading opposition parliamentarians declined to serve in the PCIS, believing it to be ceremonial.[72] The idea of oversight remained elusive even though there were three committees that seemed amenable to provide internal democratic governance of the intelligence service.

The Intelligence Act also failed to establish credible internal oversight through the three committees to give a semblance of democratic balance. Sections 25–30 created three key committees—the Central Intelligence Committee (CIC), National Intelligence Community (NIC), and the Intelligence and Security Council (ISC). However, these committees were relatively weak and played an advisory role. According to sections 26 and 28, the CIC and NIC exist to advise the president and DG, respectively. There is little evidence the ISC—with its budgetary, operational, administrative, and judicial powers— ever convened. A few days before he was fired, on May 2, 2018, DG Kgosi, told the Parliamentary Accounts Committee (PAC) that he was not accountable to anyone including the president of the republic.[73] Such a statement by a DG was the starkest indictment on DIS security governance and oversight as well as summed up the basis of a legacy of state terrorism and poor governance that had occurred for a decade.

On the other hand, the judiciary played a tangential oversight role for those ten years, which existed in two areas. First, there was an appearance of judicial oversight because section 22 of the Intelligence Act states that the powers of entry, search, and seizure must be authorized by a senior magistrate or judge of the high court. This qualifies as a form of judicial oversight, despite its soft nature. To its credit, for the most part the DIS reportedly applied for court orders in adherence to this legislation. According to the then registrar of the high court, in 2010, the court was "inundated" with applications for warrants from the DIS.[74] Nevertheless, most of the DIS's activities were enabled by section 22(3), which states that the DG or any authorized officer can exercise powers of arrest, search, and seizure if "the special exigencies of the case so require." Without clarification of these special exigencies, the act virtually gives the DG the ability to circumvent judicial declination for a warrant. This loophole potentially encourages intelligence personalization and abuse since it does not require the DG to provide justification to a court of law *ex post facto*.

Second, there was supposed to be a tribunal to handle complaints. According to section 31, the tribunal should be headed by a retired judge or legal practitioner qualified to serve at the level of the high court judge. President Khama appointed his relatives and party functionaries to the tribunal before it ebbed into oblivion.[75] In addition, the president may appoint two other people, one of whom must have knowledge of intelligence matters.

Yet, section 32 shows the impotence and irrelevance of the tribunal. It explicitly states that the tribunal shall not inquire into any complaints that are the subject of judicial proceedings, "prejudicial to national security," and those considered "frivolous . . . vexatious or . . . not made in good faith." Moreover, the tribunal cannot examine a complaint unless it first submits a written notice to the DG. This raises questions as to whether the tribunal is for the public or an extension of the DIS. As regards to investigations, any complaint can be dismissed as baseless remarks. For instance, this implies that if an activist or politician filed a complaint, the tribunal could dismiss it without a fair hearing or investigation because they had to seek the acquiescence of a DG who is a political appointee of the president.

Furthermore, that a tribunal run by an equivalent of a judge cannot act alongside a national court creates a dilemma for prospective plaintiffs. They have to choose between approaching a politicized tribunal and directly suing the DIS. The Intelligence Act basically renders the tribunal useless by enabling it to hide behind the national security lexicon. As G. M. Malebang argued, the concept and practice of national security are not clearly defined, heavily militarized, not understood by the ordinary citizen, and courts have failed to adequately interpret the National Security Act of 1986.[76] This enables the tribunal and the executive to stonewall complaints under the pretext of national security because it is very difficult for an ordinary person to prove intelligence misuse. The required reciprocity between the tribunal, the DIS DG, Office of the President, and cabinet prior to an investigation suggests that the tribunal would inherently be politicized. In this instance, courts of law are the best recourse for the aggrieved—as demonstrated by Philip Tlhage and others who successfully sued the DIS for millions of pula.

Prospects of reform and oversight following the dramatic events insti-gated by President Masisi, who assumed office in April 2018, are cosmetic and political. Merely three weeks into his new post, President Masisi fired Kgosi and replaced him with his rival and former colleague Brigadier Peter Magosi.[77] However, Masisi has never publicly spoken about the DIS nor a possible review of the Intelligence Act. Yet, at the time of writing in 2020, Masisi is requesting the parliament to approve an amendment of the Financial Intelligence Act (FIA) to bequeath him with the powers to appoint the direc-tor general of the FIA—previously, a prerogative of the minister. The Office of the President addressed the public outcry by stating that the cabinet only sought to align the FIA with the current sweeping powers of the president as stated in the constitution.[78] This suggests that Masisi has no genuine inten-tions to reform intelligence oversight in Botswana.

Moreover, changing DIS leadership was more about settling scores rather than instituting operational and oversight reforms. By 2018, there were politi-cal rivalries involving politicians and their favorite senior security officials that placed Masisi and Kgosi in opposing camps. It was Kgosi who con-vinced President Khama to overlook his younger brother, Tshekedi Khama, as successor in favor of Masisi. Yet, by the time Masisi became president he was closer to Tshekedi Khama (who had contemplated employing Brigadier Peter Magosi as head of the new wildlife intelligence unit). Moreover, both disliked Kgosi, whom they considered too powerful. As Masisi distanced himself from Kgosi by publicly stating that "Batswana are not free," he worked closely with two retired generals (one of whom is his brother) to fire Kgosi for abuse of office. The new DIS director, Peter Magosi, was brought in to give the institution a new form and direction.[79] To his credit, Magosi addresses the public and answers questions from reporters at press confer-ences.[80] Nonetheless, Masisi—who wields power to enact reform—has been mute on internal reform, as stated in sections 25–30, restructuring the tribu-nal, reviving the PCIS, or broadening democratic oversight of the DIS. In the absence of full reform, addressing this limited oversight would indicate no genuine intentions for establishing intelligence oversight.

CONCLUSION

This chapter examined civilian intelligence in Botswana by tracing its evolu-tion from the colonial era to the present. It explored the abuses of the intel-ligence services and argued that the DIS's institutional culture from 2008 to 2018 must be understood in relation to the historical, legal, and social contexts in which intelligence emerged and operates in. Indeed, these broader historical, legal, and social issues highlight key aspects of intelligence in Botswana. These include that intelligence has been historically used to aid the powerful in government and utilized to undermine the political opposition as well as critics of the government. The chapter also described the close relationship the DIS has with the police, military, and other sectors of the government because, in part, the DIS lacks a clear mandate and can operate with impunity. Next, it showed that Botswana intelligence has used technical surveillance to go after genuine security threats as well as government critics. Furthermore, the chapter explained how the intelligence services have largely focused on internal and regional security issues. Additionally, it explored how and why Botswana lacks meaningful intelligence oversight due to political and legal shortcomings. Last, the chapter highlighted how the 1990s with the end of the Cold War provoked a rethinking about intelligence in Botswana, which led to the establishment and current status of the DIS.

NOTES

1. Amy Niang, *The Postcolonial African State in Transition: Stateness and Modes of Sovereignty* (Lanham: Rowman and Littlefield, 2018).

2. Gloria Somolekae, "A Brief History of the Botswana Public Service," *Public Administration and Policy in Botswana*, eds. Kempe R. Hope and Gloria Somolekae (Cape Town: Juta & Co. Ltd, 1998), 24.

3. C. R. Pratt, "The cabinet and presidential in Tanzania: 1960–1966," in *The State of the Nations: Constraints on Development in Independent Africa*, ed. M. Lofchie (London: University of California Press, 1971), 105–6; Crawford Young and Thomas Turner, *The Rise and Decline of the Zairian State* (Madison, Wisconsin: University of Wisconsin Press, 1985); Christian John Makgala, "History and Perceptions of Regionalism in Botswana, 1891–2005," *Journal of Contemporary African Studies* 27, no. 2 (2009): 225–242.

4. Amy R. Poteete, "Is Development Path Dependent or Political? A Reinterpretation of Mineral-Dependent Development in Botswana," *Journal of Development Studies* 45, no. 4 (2007): 544–71; Amy R. Poteete, "Electoral Competition, Factionalism, and Persistent Party Dominance in Botswana," *Journal of Modern African Studies* 50, no. 1 (2012): 75–102.

5. A. Cook and J. Sarkin, "Is Botswana the Miracle of Africa? Democracy, the Rule of Law, and Human Rights versus Economic Development," *Transnational Law & Contemporary Problems* 19, no. 453 (2010–2011): 453–89.

6. C. M. Fombad, "The Separation of Powers and Constitutionalism in Africa: The Case of Botswana," *Boston College Third World Law Journal* 25, no. 2 (2005): 301–42; Mpho Molomo, "Electoral Systems and Democracy in Botswana," in *40 Years of Democracy in Botswana, 1965–2005*, ed. Z. Maundeni (Gaborone: Mmegi Publishing House, 2005), 29–49.

7. Dithapelo L Keorapetse, "'Monopoly Politikos': An Account of a De Facto One-Party State and Lack of Regime Change in Botswana," in *Regime Change and Succession Politics in Africa: Five Decades of Misrule*, eds. Maurice N. Amutabi and Shadrack W. Nasong'o (Oxon: Routledge, 2013), 217–38.

8. Kenneth Dipholo, "The Humiliation, Persecution and Politicization of Civil Servants," *Sunday Standard*, July 10, 2016. https://www.sundaystandard.info/the-humiliation-persecution-and-politicization-of-civil-servants-by-the-political-leadership-is-bringing-botswana-to-its-knees/.

9. Marylin Reid, "Politicization of the Australian Public Service: Social and Environmental Issues" (MA Thesis, University of Tasmania, 2012).

10. According to Section 5 of the act, no public servant shall "(a) publicly speak or demonstrate for or against any politician or political party; (b) be an active member of, nor hold office in, any political party; (c) publish his or her views on political matters in writing; or (d) hold a parliamentary seat or hold a political office in any local government body, except where the office is held ex officio."

11. George B. N. Ayittey, *Africa Betrayed* (New York: St. Martin's Press, 1992).

12. Ivan M. Ashaba and Gerald Bareebe, "Frenemies for Life: Has the Love Gone between Uganda and Rwanda?" *African Arguments*, December 4, 2017. http://africanarguments.org/2017/12/04/frenemies-for-life-has-the-love-gone-between-uganda-and-rwanda/.

13. Smith Janet and Beauregard Tromp, *Hani: A Life Too Short* (Johannesburg: Jonathan Ball, 2009).

14. Eliakim M Sibanda, *The Zimbabwe African People's Union, 1961–87: A Political History of Insurgency in Southern Rhodesia* (Trenton, NJ and Eritrea: Africa World Press, 2005), 244.

15. The Joint Military Commission comprised the then minister of intelligence, Emmerson Mnangagwa, then commander of the Zimbabwe Defence Force, then air marshall Perence Shiri and other top security elites; Tendi Blessing-Miles. "State Intelligence and the Politics of Zimbabwe's Presidential Succession," *African Affairs* 115, no. 459 (2016): 203–24; Tendi Blessing-Miles, "Robert Mugabe's 2013 Presidential Election Campaign," *Journal of Southern African Studies* 39, no. 4 (2013): 963–70.

16. Ed Cropley, "Special Report: Meet the Man behind Zimbabwe's 'Crocodile' President," *Reuters*, December 30, 2017. https://www.reuters.com/article/us-zimbabwe-mnangagwa-generals-specialre/special-report-meet-the-force-behind-zimbabwes-crocodile-presiden%E2%80%A6.

17. Pratt, *The State of the Nations*, 105–6.

18. Young and Turner, *The Rise and Decline of the Zairian State*.

19. AFP, "Museveni's Son Denies Plan to Succeed Him," *Daily Nation*, June 24, 2013. https://www.nation.co.ke/news/africa/Uganda-presidents-son-denies-plan-to-succeed-father/1066-1892904-nt0gmkz/index.html; Angelo Izama, "The Queen of Uganda's Museveni Dynasty," *Foreign Policy*, February 24, 2016. https://foreign-policy.com/2016/02/24/the-queen-of-ugandas-museveni-dynasty/.

20. Makgala Christian John and Mokganedi Z. Botlhomilwe, "Elite Interests and Political Participation in Botswana, 1966–2014," *Journal of Contemporary African*

Studies 35, no. 1 (2017): 54–72; Boga T. Manatsha and Keshav L. Maharajan, "'Fancy Figures and Ugly Facts' in Botswana Rapid Economic Growth," *Journal of International Development and Cooperation*, 15, nos. 1–2 (2009): 30, 37–39.

21. Monageng Mogalakwe, "Deconstructing National Security: The Case of Botswana," *Sacha Journal of Politics and Strategic Studies* 3, no.1 (2013): 12–27.

22. Neil Parsons, "Intelligence Reporting in Colonial Botswana," *University of Botswana History Department*, 1999, unpublished paper.

23. Ibid.

24. Ibid.

25. Mogalakwe, "Deconstructing National Security," 19.

26. Ibid, 19.

27. Richard Dale, "The Politics of national security in Botswana: 1900–1990," *Journal of Contemporary African Studies* 12, no. 1 (1993): 40–56, 46.

28. Janet and Tromp, *Hani*.

29. Terry Bell and Dumisa B. Ntsebeza, *Unfinished Business: South Africa, Apartheid, and Truth* (London and New York: Verso, 2003), 112.

30. Godfrey Mwakikagile, *Botswana: Profile of a Nation* (Dar es Salaam: Continental Press, 2010), 20–21.

31. Author interview with former senior official of the now defunct Security Intelligence Service (SIS), predecessor to DIS, May 29, 2013.

32. Peter Gill, *Policing Politics: Security Intelligence and the Liberal Dramocratic State* (Oxon: Frank Cass, 1994), 104–5.

33. Ibid, 116.

34. Tshireletso Motlogelwa, "Intelligence Service Without 'Intelligence',"*Mmegi*, December 5, 2008, http://www.mmegi.bw/index.php?sid=1&aid=68&dir=2008/ December/Friday5.

35. David Magang, *The Magic of Perseverence* (Cape Town: CASAS, 2008), 471.

36. Ibid, 388, 593.

37. Author interview with former senior official of SIS, *op cit*.

38. Gabriel Malebang, "National security policy: the case of Botswana" (MA thesis, University of the Witwatersrand, 2009).

39. Author interview with former senior official of SIS, *op cit*. According to this officer, the BPS's SIS, and BDF's military intelligence were directed to look into the modalities of a stand-alone intelligence agency.

40. Author interview with former senior official of SIS, *op cit*.

41. Ibid.

42. Kenneth Good and Ian Taylor, "Unpacking the Model: Presidential Succession in Botswana," in *Legacies of Power: Leadership Change and Former Presidents in Africa*, eds. Roger Southhall and Henning Melber (Sweden: Nordic Africa Institute, 2006), 53.

43. Baturo Alexander, *Democracy, Dictatorship and Term Limits* (Ann Arbor: The University of Michigan Press, 2014): 30–40.

44. Maundeni Zibani, "Succession to High Office: Tswana Culture and Modern Botswana Politics," in *40 Years of Democracy in Botswana, 1965–2005*, ed. Zibani Maundeni (Gaborone: Mmegi, 2005) 93; Crowder Michael, Jack Parson, and Neil

Parsons, "Legitimacy and Faction: Tswana Constitutionalism and Political Change," in *Succession to High Office in Botswana: Three Cases*, ed. Jack Parson (Ohio Athens: Ohio University Center for International Studies, 1990).

45. Makgala and Botlhomilwe, "Elite Interests and Political Participation," 64.

46. Intelligence and Security Services Act, 2008.

47. See: Tshepo Gwatiwa, "The Polemics of Security Intelligence in Botswana: Real or Imagined Threats?" *African Security Review* 24, no. 1 (2015): 39–54.

48. Section 6 (2) of the Intelligence and Security Services Act, 2008.

49. Section 4 (1) of the Botswana Police Act, 1979.

50. Section 4 (2) of the Corruption and Economic Crime Act, 1994.

51. Author interview with retired intelligence officer, Francistown, Botswana, July 19, 2016.

52. Staff Writer, "Kgosi-Khama Relationship; Most Feared Duo Back Together," *Mmegi*, June 22, 2018, http://www.mmegi.bw/index.php?aid=76373&dir=2018/june/22.

53. David Baaitse, "Kgosi to Magosi: Run of the Mill," *The Weekend Post*, May 8, 2018, http://www.weekendpost.co.bw/wp-news-details.php?nid=5139.

54. Yvonne Ditlhase, "Khama Inc.: All the President's Family, Friends and Close Colleagues," *Mail & Guardian*, November 2, 2012. https://mg.co.za/article/2012-11-02-00-khama-inc-all-the-presidents-family-friends-and-close-colleagues.

55. Ornulf Gulbrandsen, "The Discourse of Ritual Murder: Popular Reaction to Political Leaders in Botswana," in *Beyond Rationalism: Rethinking Magic, Witchcraft and Sorcery*, ed. Bruce Kapferer (New York and Oxford: Berghahn Books, 2003), 217–19.

56. Staff Writer, "Protesting Limkokwing Students Arrested," *Botswana Gazette*, April 10, 2013, http://www.gazettebw.com/?p=221.

57. Ketumile Q. J. Masire, *Memoirs of an African Democrat: Very Brave or Very Foolish?* (Gaborone, BW: Palgrave Macmillan, 2006).

58. Outsa Mokone and Spencer Mogapi, "Molepolole Riots Blamed on Intelligence Failure," *Sunday Standard*, May 2011. http://www.sundaystandard.info/article.php?NewsID=10756&GroupID=1.

59. Staff Writer, "Political Solidarity," *Mmegi*, April 21, 2011, http://www.mmegi.bw/index.php?sid=1&aid=449&dir=2011/April/Thursday21.

60. According to the Section 49 of the Trade Disputes Act these include: emergency, security, financial, railways, sewerage, energy, vaccines, electric, and health services.

61. Office of the President, "MLHA Press Release on the Amended List of Essential Services," 2011, http://www.gov.bw/en/Ministries--Authorities/Ministries/State-President/Office-of-the-President/Tools--Services/NewsPress-Releases/Amended-List-of-Essential-Services/.

62. Barry Buzan, Ole Waever and Jaap de Wilde, *Security: A New Framework for Analysis* (Colorado: Lynn Rienner Publishers, 1998), 24–29. In this subsection, the authors defined the concept of "securitization" involving the process of how an issue moves from the periphery to the [near]nucleus of security through politicized speech acts by the state or non-state.

63. These do not reflect the views of author, nor is it a tacit endorsement of these reports.

64. Tshireletso Motlogelwa, "DIS Speaks Out on Torture," *Mmegi*, February 17, 2009, http://www.mmegi.bw/index.php?sid=1&aid=6&dir=2009/February/Tuesday17.

65. Todd Paul and Jonathan Bloch, *Global Intelligence: The World's Secret Services Today* (London: Zed Books, 2003), 35–37.

66. Isaiah Morewagae, "DIS Applications to Intercept Phones Overwhelm Courts—Claim," *Mmegi*, May 19, 2010, http://new.mmegi.bw/index.php?sid=31&aid=2454&dir=2010/May/Wednesday19.

67. Ian Khama, inaugural speech, Gaborone, Botswana, April 1, 2008.

68. Aubrey Lute, "Who is watching the spies?" *The Botswana Gazette*, November 25, 2008, http://www.gazettebw.com/index.php?option=com_content&view=article&id=2012:who-is-watching-the-spies&catid=18:headlines&Itemid=2.

69. Charles M. Fombad, "The Separation of Powers and Constitutionalism in Africa: The Case of Botswana," *Boston College Third World Law Journal* 25, no. 2 (2005): 301–42; Kenneth Good and Ian Taylor, "Botswana: A Minimalist Democracy," *Democratization* 15, no. 4 (2008): 750–65.

70. Mpho Molomo, "Electoral systems and democracy in Botswana," in *40 Years of Democracy in Botswana, 1965–2005*, ed. Zibani Maundeni (Gaborone: Mmegi, 2005), 29–49.

71. See: Christian Von Soest, "Stagnation of a 'Miracle': Botswana's Governance Record Revisited," *GIGA Working Papers* no. 99 (2009): 1–34, 7–14; Catharina Groop, "Controlling the Unruly Agents—Linkages between Accountability and Corruption within the Executive Structures of Botswana," *Journal of Contemporary African Studies* 35, no. 1 (2017): 34–53, 40, 43–47; Christian John Makgala and Mokganedi Z. Botlhomilwe, "Elite Interests and Political Participation in Botswana, 1966–2014," *Journal of Contemporary African Studies* 35, no. 1 (2017): 54–72.

72. Lesego Tsholofelo. "A Critical Evaluation of the Intelligence Oversight Regime in Botswana" (MA Thesis, Brunel University, 2014), http://www.e-ir.info/2014/03/03/a-critical-evaluation-of-the-intelligence-oversight-regime-in-botswana/.

73. Nicholas Mokwena, "Kgosi's Carte Blanche Powers," *The Botswana Guardian*, April 20, 2018. http://www.botswanaguardian.co.bw/news/item/3166-kgosi-s-carte-blanche-powers.html.

74. Morewagae, "DIS applications to intercept phones." May 19, 2010. http://new.mmegi.bw/index.php?sid=31&aid=2454&dir=2010/May/Wednesday19.

75. Lute, "Who is watching the spies?"

76. Malebang, "National Security Policy," 75–78.

77. Sunday Standard Reporter, "Kgosi Fired as DISS Director," *Sunday Standard*, May 2, 2018. https://www.sundaystandard.info/kgosi-fired-dis-director; Sunday Standard Reporter, "Inside the Black Op to Oust Kgosi," *Sunday Standard*, May 6, 2018 http://www.sundaystandard.info/inside-black-op-oust-kgosi.

78. Botswana Television (BTV) news bulletin, Gaborone, Botswana, June 14, 2018.

79. Online Editor, "Magosi Wants to Reform the Notorious DIS," *Sunday Standard*, April 1, 2019. https://www.sundaystandard.info/magosi-wants-to-reform-the-notorious-dis/.

80. Online Editor, "DIS New Head Promises Fresh Start at the Intelligence Agency," *Sunday Standard*, May 27, 2018. https://www.sundaystandard.info/dis-new-head-promises-a-fresh-start-at-the-intelligence-agency/.

Chapter 9

Knowledge Is Power, but Power Corrupts: Reassessing the Role of Intelligence in South Africa's Wars, Politics, and Society, 1965–2020

Kevin A. O'Brien

In October 1994, South Africa's Government of National Unity (GNU)—the first post-apartheid government—released its *White Paper on Intelligence*, the first of its kind. Within its pages, the authors espoused a "philosophy of intelligence" for the first time that would guide all dimensions of national, economic, social, and even personal security in the new era. Connected directly to the country's new constitution, this "philosophy of intelligence" was a first in major industrialized societies, reflecting the new South Africa's desire to learn from the experiences of both Western and non-Western intelligence communities and histories—for both positive and negative lessons— and stake a new position on how "intelligence" would be situated in the new South Africa. However, it was not the first time that "intelligence" had been placed squarely at the center of South African politics and society.[1] Rather, this was the continuation of the long history of such uses of intelligence throughout and even before the apartheid era. Similarly, it came to reflect the history of the post-apartheid era over the proceeding decades until today.

Throughout South Africa's entire modern history—as far back as the British colonial era and in both the apartheid and post-apartheid periods— "intelligence" was skewed to, if not outright intertwined with, the political drivers and motivations of the day by whoever was wielding it and in support of whatever entity or goal they sought. During the apartheid era, the government bent the intelligence developed by its security forces and its "securocrats" (the term used commonly to refer to those civil servants, intelligence, military, and police officials involved in driving the state's security policies, operations, and decisions) to fight a counterrevolutionary war against the liberation movements, no matter what the intelligence actually showed. At the same time, it was used to maintain an accepted position in the Western camp of the Cold War.

Similarly, the liberation movements in exile and in the internal insurgency—most particularly the African National Congress (ANC)—bent their own intelligence to maintain internal security and political cohesion among their cadres, as well as against their rivals in other liberation movements as much as against the apartheid government. During the 1990s transition to democracy, it was no surprise that "intelligence" was treated as a top-level issue by the negotiators, given its centrality to both sides. Even after the 1994 transition and the pronouncing of the new "philosophy of intelligence," this corrupting of intelligence continued and increased pace as the post-apartheid era moved beyond Nelson Mandela and the GNU into the era of sole ANC governance. It was in this period that the "battle over the intelligence brief" once again took off between different ANC rivals and factions and their reach into the different institutions of state, industry, and finance—ultimately bringing down Thabo Mbeki's presidency and seeing Jacob Zuma rise to the same, ushering in an era of utter corruption across South Africa's public sector, including with the intelligence services.[2]

Twenty-five years after the transition from apartheid to democracy, South Africa's intelligence dispensation remains in a state of seemingly never-ending crises since at least the Mbeki era at the turn of the century, but equally, most of the last five decades. In reconsidering South Africa's intelligence history and dispensation more recently, it has become increasingly clear that viewing South Africa's intelligence history through a traditional analytic lens of event, institution, structure, process, and law can only relate part of that story.[3] There have, however, been few analyses that have looked across the last seventy-five years thematically, starting with the end of the British colonial period and the beginning of the apartheid era in 1948. A wider lens is required to understand the role of intelligence in South Africa's modern history, throughout which intelligence has been used and misused for a range of state and personal purposes—consistently failing to play the "traditional" role as an independent, unbiased, and circumspect contributor of refined and analyzed information to support decision-making. Intelligence has been central to virtually every major event tied to that history, every societal change, every catastrophe small or large, every major personality on South Africa's national stage, and to the activities and decisions of virtually every leading political figure in that history. Ultimately, intelligence—as institutions and structures, as personalities, as societal touchstones and as insight-providing lubricant—has been the key currency to all sides in both the apartheid conflict and the post-apartheid transition over these decades. Indeed, it is the facilitator of South African history and the lubricant on which that history has flowed over the last century, used for both altruistic and corrupt purposes.

This chapter is organized into four chronological sections across which five prevailing themes are analyzed twenty-five years after the transition. The first section examines the intelligence of both the apartheid state and ANC during the apartheid era with attention to the "securocrats" and the changes in strategy. Next, it explores the transition of intelligence as it moved from the apartheid to democratic state by highlighting efforts to reform intelligence and instill transparency and prevent abuses. The third section describes the contemporary aspects of intelligence with an examination of recent corruption and the return of the politicization of national security. Last, the chapter provides an analytic conclusion that draws together the overriding themes of South Africa's intelligence history.

Within these eras, the first of the five themes addressed is "intelligence" as a constant, distinguishable thread running through the apartheid and post-apartheid eras, on all sides and in all debates about what kind of state South Africa should be. The second is intelligence as a currency, moving away from a traditional analytic lens of institution, structure, and process to one that appreciates the very fluid, lubricating nature of intelligence to all sides and players in South Africa's history. Third is the influence of key individuals on all sides of the intelligence dispensation, both during and since apartheid, which not only drove intelligence activities and evolutions but also had an outsized influence on these, often over the role of formal structures, laws, and processes. The fourth—resulting from the first three—is the corruption of intelligence in almost every way, including the privatization of intelligence toward personal as much as commercial gains. Finally, the historical context for South Africa's transition in the 1990s—happening at a time that many other autocratic states were transitioning away from their Cold War–induced or colonial structure, with similar impacts on their intelligence and security setups—can be recognized as having a notable influence on how South Africa positioned itself post apartheid and the role intelligence played in this posture.

INTELLIGENCE DURING THE APARTHEID ERA

Following the introduction of apartheid with the Afrikaner-dominated National Party's election victory in 1948 and up to the transition to democracy starting in 1993, both the state and its anti-apartheid opposition movements became structured around intelligence. Prior to 1948, the Union of South Africa was a dominion of the British Empire, governed with English interests dominating and without a formal intelligence service of its own. Security intelligence—the primary focus in this era—generally followed the traditional British model of colonial policing for controlling South Africa internally and was provided by the South African Police (SAP) that began developing a countersubversion intelligence capability in its Detective Branch in the 1920s; the British Security Service (MI5) retained responsibility for South Africa's external intelligence needs.[4] While a fledgling Department of Military Intelligence (DMI) was created within the Union Defence Force (UDF) at the outbreak of the Second World War, it notably played third fiddle in the dominant focus of union intelligence under Prime Minister Jan Smuts: the identification and countering of Afrikaner nationalism and militancy against British dominion. While the SAP was concerned secondarily with the political organizing and organizations of the black African population from a colonial policing perspective, it considered the threat from Afrikaner nationalism to be primary. This was reflected in Smuts's very real concern about Afrikaner nationalists and republicans infiltrating the SAP, which caused him to question the intelligence it provided him.[5] This was a clear demonstration of one of the main themes that wound its way through subsequent decades: the infighting and politicization of the intelligence functions allegedly serving the state.

Following 1945, both MI5 and its sister, Secret Intelligence Service (MI6), returned to their prime twin focus from before the war: countering both communism and Afrikaner nationalism with little concern for "native agitators."[6] This focus shifted dramatically after 1948. For the apartheid state, this centrality of the intelligence function to everything else was a tangible legacy of the British colonial period and institutions. The National Party government both leveraged it and learned from it as they took control of the state's institutions from the British between 1948 and 1961. During this period, the new government continued to employ and benefit from British intelligence support—whether from MI5, MI6, or military intelligence—largely because in their continued dominion capacity up to 1961 (the year that South Africa declared itself a republic and withdrew from the Commonwealth), the British did not allow the apartheid government to have an independent intelligence function.

After its breakaway from British dominion, this changed markedly. By the end of the 1960s, South Africa not only had a fully established intelligence capability in the Bureau of State Security (BOSS) but had also established the State Security Council (SSC)—and later its National Security Management System (NSMS)—as the governance mechanism for society. Through the SSC and the NSMS, with BOSS as its operational arm, the security state was established and driven by intelligence and the need to collect it at every level. Through these mechanisms, all recommendations and decisions that affected the governing of the country were made. Ultimately, bodies such as the SSC ran the policies of "Total National Strategy" and "Total Counter-Revolutionary Strategy" under which South Africa operated. The authority of the wider cabinet was not effectively restored until President F. W. de Klerk came to power in 1989.[7]

For the ANC, in its alliance with the South African Communist Party (SACP), intelligence also became fundamental to all its activities, whether in the field in the frontline states or abroad in exile. At the same time as the apartheid state was coalescing into a security state, the ANC launched its "armed struggle" in cooperation with the SACP following the Sharpeville Massacre of March 1960. It established *Umkhonto weSizwe* ("Spear of the Nation" or MK, the guerrilla army founded in June 1961 by Nelson Mandela) and later the National Intelligence Department (NAT) in 1969—including its internal security arm *Mbokodo* (a Xhosa word for the stone used to grind maize, used as a derogatory reference to the "harshness with which the Department treated its victims"[8])—to govern, manage and control the anti-apartheid revolutionary war and the ANC/SACP cadres. The NAT existed in a semiformal state until 1981 when it formally became a national director-ate within the ANC's National Executive Council under the leadership of Mzwandile (Mzwai) Piliso.[9]

By the end of the 1960s, both the South African state and the major libera-tion movement opposing it built their central pillars of governance, policy, and operation on security and intelligence capabilities. Intelligence in South Africa must be seen in light of the role it played in supporting and driving the counterrevolutionary strategies, structures, and operations of the apart-heid state, alongside the role it played for the exiled ANC-SACP's efforts to overthrow that state through revolutionary means. This centrality continued for the following decades—in warfare, in policy, with regard to internal secu-rity, in foreign policy, and in all dimensions of society—until the leadership of those same intelligence functions negotiated the end to apartheid and the transition to democracy in the mid-1990s.

Throughout this earlier era, a handful of personalities dominated and drove the entire intelligence dispensation. They loomed over all aspects, controlling everything from the creation and management of the intelligence function stra-tegically to its place within the politics and policies of the apartheid state or liberation movement to the ways in which intelligence was utilized. In Pretoria, starting in the 1950s and gaining in dominance throughout the 1960s under the successive leadership of Prime Ministers Hendrik Verwoerd and B. J. (John) Vorster, one man—Brigadier "Lang" Hendrik van den Bergh—controlled the state intelligence apparatus and was the single biggest intelligence-centered influencer on the premier and the state's direction. As leader of the SAP Secu-rity Branch and fully championed by these premiers, starting in 1961, van den Bergh swiftly created the architecture of what would become the State Security Council and the security system around it, while similarly moving the reformed and increasingly-powerful South Africa Defence Force (SADF)'s DMI—and its champion, Defence Minister Piet (PW) Botha—away from all state matters. He established new operational counterinsurgency capabilities within the Secu-rity Branch to rival and take control of the state's growing war against the liber-ation movements. While the DMI fought back, initiating reforms itself starting in 1962 to increase its weak capabilities, it was unable to contest the growing power and dominance of van den Bergh across all intelligence matters.[10]

That van den Bergh was able to act so swiftly was due to the weak nature of the state's intelligence structures in the wake of the restrictions placed on it by the British as well as his strong personal relationship with both premiers—most particularly Vorster (with whom he had been interned during the Second World War). Indeed, both men "made the matter of internal security their own and rapidly came to appreciate the reciprocal character of intelligence and counterintelligence."[11] Similarly, the Security Branch's influence and dominance within the SAP had a lasting effect on the direction of South African security policy formulation. Following 1960, all SAP commissioners either served as the head of the Security Branch or otherwise had Security Branch experience. Consequently, "in virtually every significant period of unrest, a former security branch head has occupied the post of Commissioner of Police."[12]

Under this troika of "big beasts"—Vorster, van den Bergh, and Botha—intelligence rapidly became the focal point of not only their personal political rivalries, but also that of the two major security arms of the state, which van den Bergh and Botha sponsored respectively—BOSS and DMI—competing for dominance and power. The increased rivalry and poorly delineated mandates led inevitably to infighting within the intelligence community, including incidents of spying on each other (an aspect that continued into the post-apartheid era). Important and relevant information was withheld by one side from the other; agents of either side were exposed by the other; and political backstabbing within the government arena grew. This happened as militant opposition to the apartheid government was growing from the ANC, SACP, and their joint armed-wing *Umkhonto weSizwe* and global opposition to South Africa was increasing in the aftermath of the 1960 Sharpeville Massacre and the 1964 Rivonia Trial of ANC leaders. With challenges to the apartheid state emerging domestically, regionally, and globally, institutional and personal infighting, increasing politicization, and outright discord in the state's security direction impeded the ability of the state's leadership to gain clear, independent strategic intelligence about threats and the potential opportunities to quell it.

If the republic was to develop the capability to defend itself independently, such problems would have to be terminated and a strong threat-assessment capability founded on strategic intelligence analysis. As a result, in 1969, the new Bureau of State Security—created from the Security Branch—and the State Security Council were given the mandate for strategic intelligence assessments independent of the operational considerations and machinations of the security apparatus. Yet this objective failed spectacularly because of the dominance of BOSS and its personnel over all security matters, taking this mantle from the Security Branch.[13] It also failed because of other factors that were repeated over the next three decades, including: the insufficient coordination of meetings for the heads of the security forces with each other and with their political customers, conflicting agency perspectives, the need to justify increasingly extensive operational and covert action arms with intelligence due to the rivalry between BOSS and DMI, and personality clashes between van den Bergh and others.[14]

This also did nothing to end the intelligence abuses for political, careerist, or other personal gains and leverage and did not stop the counterrevolutionary mindsets that developed over the course of the 1960s and hardened in the 1970s. While there is little evidence publicly of the focus and conclusions of intelligence assessments conducted in these decades and presented to policymakers, the outcome was evident. The South African security state increasingly focused on countering a domestic insurgency that in reality, and as openly admitted by the ANC by the mid-1980s, never really gained the operational traction nor the level of threat seen in the minds of the securocrats.[15] Indeed, by the 1976 Soweto Uprising, the ANC's MK still had "not fired a single shot within the country's borders;"[16] and by October 1986, the ANC was lamenting that "despite all our efforts, we have not come anywhere near the achievement of the objectives we set for ourselves."[17] In reality, countering an insurgency inside South Africa that was far less developed than the one inside neighboring South West Africa/Namibia could have been addressed by police action and brought to an acceptable resolution sooner through political negotiations. The need to counter a much wider, increasingly interconnected threat only became a significant military issue in the frontline states after the 1974 Portuguese coup that resulted in the collapse of Portuguese rule in Angola and Mozambique (see Sirrs in this volume), and it only really grew significantly in intensity after the end of white-minority rule in Rhodesia in 1979.

The conflicts were fed by the securocrats' mindsets, namely a mix of fears regarding the internal collapse of white-minority society in South Africa supported by a "Total Onslaught" of African militaries from the frontline states. It was also a desire to implement operational and strategic counterinsurgency and counterrevolutionary warfare tenets learned from the experiences of the Americans, British, and French during decolonization. Last, and perhaps the most alarming, was the dramatic increase in operational capabilities to justify their services' existence. The beast needed to be fed—and what it fed on supported its continued growth, power, and reach, even if the assessed realities did not align with this outlook.

The dominance of Vorster and van den Bergh was ultimately brought to a jarring close in 1978 with the "Information Scandal." It caused both the end of Vorster's premiership and the rise of Botha to the leadership in September 1978, a period also known as the "Battle for the Intelligence Brief."[18] With his succession, Botha brought in leading proponents of counterinsurgency and counterrevolutionary warfare from within DMI who drove the growth of DMI's operational capabilities in its new Special Forces and

Special Tasks units and ended the dominance of the Security Branch in strate-gic decision-making. Within this "battle," two trends were clearly discernible: the effort to centralize and coordinate national security intelligence and the DMI's growing dominance in the intelligence brief. While heavily political, especially as Botha brought about the resignation of van den Bergh, it also involved BOSS battling for its own survival.

There was little doubt about the outcome. The past rivalries combined with DMI's role as Botha's "pet thinking shop" on issues of national secu-rity meant it would become the central body. Meanwhile, this allowed new dominating securocrats, including the head of DMI, Brigadier G. P. "Joffel" van der Westhuizen; the head of Special Forces, Major General F. W. Loots; and the head of Security Branch, Brigadier Johan Coetzee, to make their marks on the overall approach to intelligence and security and dominate at both the operational and strategic levels. Following his succession, Botha dissolved BOSS and created the civilian National Intelligence Service (NIS), with BOSS's operational capabilities by and large terminated and the NIS's mandate limited to research and analysis of strategic issues.[19] It was led by a young academic, Niël Barnard, who was handpicked by Botha to become the first NIS director general, and his deputy, Mike (MGM) Louw. Both men later played central roles in the "intelligence wars" of the 1980s, but took a far less militarized view of the conflict. They also maintained distance from the counterrevolutionary warfare activities of both the DMI and Security Branch and later initiated the secret negotiations with the ANC's Department of Intel-ligence and Security (DIS) that led to apartheid's end.[20]

Botha also launched a Commission of Inquiry to examine options to ratio-nalize the intelligence functions and determine a future course for the strate-gic intelligence brief.[21] Again, unsurprisingly, this determined (many would argue this was already determined before the commission began its inves-tigations) that the strategic intelligence brief should be given to DMI as a precursor to the development of a new security architecture around it and the SSC. BOSS's covert functions were transferred to DMI, and the majority of its senior managers took early retirement. Having been deeply involved in the rivalries between the intelligence agencies and their champions throughout the 1960s and 1970s, Botha also divided responsibilities for the intelligence brief between the agencies (DMI, NIS, Security Branch, and Foreign Affairs), which contributed to the overall intelligence picture. DMI served as the lead agency in all respects, but the others would be responsible for clearly defined mandates in combating the "Total Onslaught."

While Pretoria witnessed these ongoing rivalries, growth and collapse in power bases, and misuses of intelligence, the ANC was not exempt from similar problems. Its military and political alliance with the SACP in the early 1960s meant that it became not only increasingly rigid in its approach to internal security, but similarly became ever more reliant on security and intelligence training from the Soviet Bloc and Chinese intelligence services.[22] It did so while trying to hold together an insurgency in the frontline states that was feeling increasingly detached from the struggle inside South Africa.[23] This led to internal security mechanisms becoming increasingly intolerant of dissenting opinions, while also seeking to identify apartheid spies in its midst, of which there were many: mostly "rehabilitated terrorists" known to the apartheid security establishment as *askaris*—the Swahili word for "fighters"—who were captured and turned against their former comrades by the Security Branch and DMI Special Tasks units. The ANC's *Mbokodo* security department was increasingly paranoid of these *askaris* "fleeing" South Africa to join the ANC and MK cadres in exile.[24] This often led to their murder by ANC security forces or MK leaders simply because of the suspicion that the people were spies or disloyal to the ANC/SACP-MK.[25] These issues regarding the paranoia about infiltration, the imposition of Soviet-style approaches to internal security and dissent, and the breakdown in relationships between the ANC and faraway exiles meant that the ANC's own intelligence was often as politicized and skewed as that of the apartheid state—factors that would last well into the post-apartheid period.

The ANC also had its "big beasts." These included Joe Nhlanhla, the secretary of the ANC/SACP Political-Military Committee (PMC), which oversaw all ANC/SACP activities, and who would later became the first minister of intelligence services in the post-apartheid government; Jacob Zuma, deputy to Nhlanhla (who later became deputy president to Thabo Mbeki, then a highly controversial president in his own right); Sizakele Sigxashe, deputy head of the ANC's DIS, and later, the first head of the new post-apartheid National Intelligence Agency (NIA); Mzuvukile J Maqetuka (a former DIS lead, who after the transition would serve as deputy director general of both the NIA and its sister South African Secret Service (SASS), then the national coordinator of intelligence, and later the first director general of the new State Security Agency in 2010); Joe Slovo, chief of staff of MK (who later became minister of housing in the new government, which was one of the most important positions under GNU's Reconstruction and Development Program); and Ronnie Kasrils, the head of MK Intelligence and Special Operations (who served as deputy minister of defence in the GNU, then minister for intelligence services under Zuma's presidency). Each person influenced the overall direction of the ANC/SACP, the revolutionary warfare program, and the later decision to engage in secret negotiations with the NIS to end the conflict.

ANC intelligence demonstrated a more independent mindset to the realities of the struggle, its position, and the opportunities to generate effective intelligence for operational use. In the mid-1970s, it had established the National Intelligence Department (NAT) through formalizing intelligence as part of an overhaul of the ANC's overall apparatus, which was further expanded in 1982 to include intelligence, counterintelligence, security (*Mbokodo*), VIP protection, and Central Intelligence Evaluation departments.[26] It was reformed in 1985 and again in 1987 to become the Department of Intelligence and Security (DIS). By all accounts, DIS's intelligence collection and evaluation capabilities were largely independent of *Mbokodo*, and over time, it generated highly effective intelligence, leading to its greatest success: Operation Vula (short for "Vulindlela," Zulu for "to penetrate"), a proper intelligence operations capability within South Africa itself.[27] "Vula" came into effect only in 1988, but was uncovered in July 1990 just as the negotiations between the ANC/SACP and the de Klerk government were getting started. Had it not been uncovered, "Vula" would have continued through the negotiations phase, as the ANC had decided that, in spite of the negotiations starting, "it was too difficult to trust a regime that had always acted with such duplicity; this was just another trick."[28] This view prevailed until February 1991 when it was determined by the ANC/SACP leadership that the National Party was negotiating in good faith. As Tim Jenkin, formerly of the ANC and a key architect of "Vula," explained: "So long as the regime maintained its arrogant attitude and the situation could not be said to be irreversible there was a need to maintain structures that could be aroused to carry on the struggle."[29] Alongside "Vula," the ANC also initiated Operation BIBLE—effectively the "Vula" intelligence and security apparatus, which succeeded in developing a significant number of "turned" sources of its own within South Africa's intelligence apparatus. This intelligence not only gave them insights into the security forces' apparatus, operations and decision-making, but also— crucially—the Security Branch's records on its moles within the ANC's ranks. BIBLE became sophisticated enough to even "recruit" false agents to improve the record of its Security Branch moles.[30]

INTELLIGENCE IN TRANSITION FROM APARTHEID TO DEMOCRACY

The transition period from apartheid to democracy between 1990 and 1998 is effectively the lynchpin to understanding the people, organizations, and events of South Africa's intelligence history. Indeed, everything that came before and since is filtered through the lens of personalities, power politics, decisions, and structures and statutes laid down in this era. During the transition period, the civilian spies from both sides, especially the leadership of both the apartheid-era NIS and the ANC's DIS, played an outsized role in shaping the negotiations, the drafting of first the interim constitution and later the full constitution, and ultimately the security structures of post-apartheid South Africa.[31] After all, it was the secret negotiations between the NIS and

DIS that started as early as 1986 in Europe—unknown to even Botha at the time—that paved the way for the changes after 1990 that formally ended hostilities, brought about the negotiated settlement, and launched the country into full democracy.

In most ways, but not all, the leaders of this transition attempted to bury most of what had come before in the history of South Africa's intelligence wars. Ultimately, this was an unsuccessful endeavor. Additionally, these leaders attempted to lay the ground for a new era in South Africa's intelligence history through new statutory, institutional, and mandatory approaches to intelligence. As with the failure to bury all the bad elements of the past, the inability—many would argue, impossibility—to establish a clean break with the past doomed the new dispensation to failure and with it the creation of a truly new dawn for South African intelligence.[32]

In this sense, a new "battle for the intelligence brief" ensued following de Klerk's 1989 succession to the presidency and leadership of the National Party. Eschewing DMI's and Security Branch's overwhelming influence on the state's overall policies and functions, de Klerk reined in all covert activities both inside and outside the country and increased the NIS's role in advising and influencing decision-making for the coming transition. Over the subsequent five years, DMI and Security Branch were broken up, but not without violent, consequential pushback from their covert units that almost brought South Africa to a state of civil war by 1993, leading directly to their severe diminishment in the post-apartheid era. The NIS, on the other hand, survived not only the transformation, but—under its Director General Barnard and his deputy, Louw—became the basis for the post-apartheid intelligence structures, including its central mechanisms, key leadership and structures.[33] Consequently, the civilian spies won the second and final "battle of the intelligence brief" of the apartheid era; unfortunately, this was not to be the last such "battle."

With the end of apartheid and the release of Nelson Mandela in February 1990, political reform became the state's primary interest. The Department of Constitutional Planning (subsequently, Constitutional Affairs) was supported by the NIS in its alliance with the DIS. Many NIS officials were transferred to the Department of Constitutional Affairs to "provide intelligence/policy support for [the] government negotiating team [as] their intelligence experience and linkages allowed them to be utilised as key planning assets."[34] NIS and DIS senior leadership as well as many staff were involved extensively in the day-to-day negotiations, which resulted progressively in the new political dispensation that came from the Conference on a Democratic South Africa (CODESA), the Transitional Executive Council (TEC), and—following the April 1994 elections—the Government of National Unity (GNU).

In this sense, the civilian spies guided in the new era.[35] The effort was led by Barnard (who was transferred to the Department of Constitutional Affairs in 1992 to oversee the negotiations), Louw (who took over as NIS director general), and Mauritz Spaarwater (chief director of NIS operations, who was also transferred to Constitutional Affairs to run a new directorate responsible for analyzing the political situation and the key players as well as for supporting the government's negotiators) on the government side.[36] On the ANC side, individuals such as National Executive Council members Mbeki, Zuma (at this time, the deputy director of the NAT), Nhlanhla (the head of DIS), and Rieaz "Moe" Shaik (the ANC's key strategic thinker on intelligence matters, one of the MK Intelligence leads of "BIBLE," and a key advisor to Zuma) led the negotiations with their NIS counterparts. Nhlanhla and Shaik later had leading roles in the post-apartheid intelligence structures, with the latter becoming increasingly controversial as Zuma ascended to the presidency.[37]

Most of the new intelligence policies and legislation emerged out of the NIS-DIS discussions in the TEC's Sub-Council on Intelligence, which became the forum for debates on the future structure of the intelligence community carried out prior to the establishment of the GNU. Its Joint Co-ordinating Intelligence Committee (JCIC) gave the TEC some oversight of the intelligence services' operations as well as an intelligence pipeline back to the TEC.[38] These bodies led the drafting of the sections in the new constitution that addressed national security, redefining it from its apartheid-era focus on the security of the state to instead reflect "the resolve of all South Africans, as individuals and as a nation, to live as equals, to live in peace and harmony, to be free from fear and want, and to seek a better life."[39] This same approach underpinned the "philosophy of intelligence" written into the 1994 *White Paper on Intelligence* and ultimately informed the drafting of new intelligence legislation that the GNU would pass in 1995. All this led to the dissolution of the NIS, DMI, and Security Branch and the establishment of the new National Intelligence Agency (NIA) for domestic security intelligence, the South African Secret Service (SASS) for foreign intelligence, the reformed South African National Defence Force's (SANDF) Intelligence Division, and the Crime Combating and Investigation Service (later the National Crime Intelligence Service) of the newly reformed South African Police Service (SAPS). Alongside these institutional changes, the National Security Council—de Klerk's revamped SSC—was dissolved and a new National Intelligence Co-ordinating Committee (NICOC) was formed. Finally, oversight was established with the new Joint Standing Committee on Intelligence (JSCI) in parliament and the new inspectors general of the intelligence services.[40]

This "philosophy of intelligence" centered around a number of key pillars that the new intelligence structures were required to uphold in the new era. These included allegiance to the constitution, subordination to the rule of law, a clearly defined legal mandate, budgetary control and external auditing, an integrated national intelligence capability, political neutrality, and the separation of intelligence from policymaking, a balance between secrecy and transparency, and the absence of law enforcement powers.[41] National security was extended to encompass nonmilitary security, threats to stability and development, the reality of international interdependence, the pursuit of democracy, sustainable economic development, and social justice; regionally, South Africa aimed to advance the principles of collective security, nonaggression, and peaceful settlement of disputes.[42] Significant reviews of the intelligence dispensations of Western democracies such as Canada, the United Kingdom, and the United States were also conducted to see what elements could be imported to South Africa.[43]

The *White Paper*'s creation and the related new legislation were important because the future scope and focus of South Africa's intelligence community was not covered in the interim constitution. The intelligence leaders convinced the constitutional drafters to leave the role, structure, and position of the future intelligence services out of the interim constitution even though those for the defense forces and police were established. Consequently, the future intelligence dispensation was not subject to the constitutional negotiations during the settlement process leading to the 1994 transition.[44] This was largely because the intelligence negotiators were not prepared to have their particulars carved in stone, but rather, desired to maintain flexibility in apartheid-era state security apparatus that could be "transitioned" to the post-apartheid state. This was an extremely important issue, given the parallel enshrining of the Truth and Reconciliation Commission (TRC) into the constitution for addressing the human rights violations and other crimes of the past by all sides. On top of all this, there was another extremely contentious issue: the intelligence that the apartheid intelligence services held on the ANC itself, including especially its recruiting of ANC/SACP and PAC personnel as spies in their comrades' ranks. When tabled during the TEC negotiations, the negotiators left the issue alone, as both sides had informers, and the launching of mole hunts would have been detrimental to the success of the transition and the incoming GNU.[45] This issue would come back to haunt the post-apartheid era time and again, with devastating consequences.

The new "philosophy of intelligence" was not mere lip-service either. The "philosophy" would be cited over the following decades, as the intelligence dispensation encountered increasingly troubling problems—most recently in the 2018–2019 review of state security, which was also but one of a number of recent demands for the 1994 *White Paper* to be updated to reflect the changed reality in the country's intelligence dispensation over the previous twenty-five years.[46] It was treated as remaining the touchstone for what South Africa's intelligence setup should reflect in terms of structures, operations, adherence to the constitution, and overall direction. As such, this era was the only period where South Africa's intelligence dispensation collectively was on the right path when measured against its own intentions and standards for transparency, independence, accountability, and operating within constitutional norms found in other democracies. However, it can be argued that, given how intelligence leaders attempted to put themselves above the constitutional process, as well as the continued covert operations by both sides against the other, the intention behind the "philosophy" was immediately undermined.[47]

By the time SACP secretary general Chris Hani was assassinated in April 1993 by a white right-wing radical—the point at which the country came closest to civil war during the transition—the apartheid security forces' covert elements were in the process of being shut down, although many analysts would observe that much of these units' personnel simply transitioned into the growing number of private military and security companies proliferating in South Africa at this time (such as Executive Outcomes, the most well known of these). The new constitution included a commitment to a Truth and Reconciliation Commission (TRC) in which potential amnesty for human rights violations committed during the apartheid era could be provided in return for full confessions to the crimes by the individual applicant and a clear demonstration of remorse and the desire for a peaceful reconciliation. Following the uncovering of several deeply covert elements of both the DMI and Security Branch between 1990 and 1992, it was clear that the TRC would be a powerful tool to identify human rights violators in the security and intelligence apparatus of both sides. The TRC's mandate not only addressed the apartheid forces, but also covered human rights violations by the liberation movements, which for the ANC raised particular concerns around both the activities of *Mbokodo* in internal security and of MK intelligence and special operations in some of its indiscriminate attacks against South African civilians.[48] Like the strategic pressures to reform, this impending demand for truth and transparency also brought significant pressure on the shapers of the new intelligence dispensation and those empowered to enact it from 1994 onward.

FAILING TO DELIVER: INTELLIGENCE, CORRUPTION, AND CRISIS IN THE NEW ERA

The transition era was the only period until today where South Africa's intelligence history briefly righted itself. Even still, the continued prevalence of both the apartheid state's and the ANC's covert intelligence capabilities throughout this transition may have doomed the transition to failure regardless of good intentions. After 1998, the early hopes that the intelligence dispensation would usher in a new era in intelligence—characterized by transparency, accountability, a lack of political or personal bias, and a binding to democratic principles and goals—were soon disappointed. By 1998, it was clear that several of the new pillars were creaking or had failed all together, leading to a new raft of intelligence-focused reviews, legislation, and reorganization.[49]

Between 1998 and 2005, no fewer than nine new intelligence-related acts were passed to address shortcomings in both civilian and parliamentary oversight (under the Intelligence Services Control Amendment Act, Act 42 of 1999; and the subsequent Intelligence Services Control Amendment Act, Act 66 of 2002—see below); creating a new minister of intelligence services and defining its role (under first the Intelligence Services Control Amendment Act, Act 42 of 1999; and later the National Strategic Intelligence Amendment Act, Act 67 of 2002);[50] enshrining employment terms, labor relations, and an Intelligence Review Board to oversee the post-employment disclosure of an employee's employment (under the General Intelligence Law Amendment Act, Act 66 of 2000);[51] clarifying the minister's responsibilities, the creation of a new National Academy of Intelligence, the creation of an Intelligence Services Council on Conditions of Service answerable to the minister and the president, and the defining of offences by employees of the intelligence services (under the Intelligence Services Act, Act 65 of 2002); and creating both an appeals panel process responsible to the minister of intelligence services and the further mandating of the Intelligence Services Council to oversee human resources and performance standards within the intelligence services and the academy (under the General Intelligence Laws Amendment Act, Act 52 of 2003).[52] The parliamentarians recognized there were problems not only with South African intelligence during the 1990s, but also with the original acts passed immediately at the end of the apartheid.

One notable step forward was also taken in creating both a statutory capability for the civilian oversight of signals intelligence (SIGINT) and the interception of communications by the newly-established National Communications Centre (NCC) and its Office for Interception Centres (OIC), responsible for these capabilities (previously the domain of DMI), and for electronic communications security by the Electronic Communications Security (Pty) Ltd (all under the 2002 Intelligence Services Control Amendment Act; the Electronic Communications Security (Pty) Ltd Act, Act 68 of 2002; the Regulation of Interception of Communications and Provision of Communication-Related Information Act, Act 70 of 2002 and its 2006 update; and the General Intelligence Laws Amendment Act, Act 52 of 2003).[53]

Many other challenges, issues, and failings were occurring around the intelligence dispensation in the country and continued through Jacob Zuma's presidency. Some were related to the GNU's inability to properly fulfill the terms of the new dispensation. A notable example of this was the consecutive failures to appoint the two new inspectors general (IG) of intelligence with any permanency, the reduction of the two roles to "one or more," and then subsequently to "one" (under the Intelligence Services Control Amendment Acts 1999 and 2002),[54] and further challenges in appointing an IG until 2004. This meant that between 1995 and 2004, the position was only briefly occupied twice with each incumbent resigning soon after taking office, resulting in a crucial lack of oversight.[55]

Most issues were connected to corruption in the post-GNU era. This involved financial corruption and personal gain exercised by many new securocrats and their political masters. Additionally, there was a growing distrust by the ANC leadership and its factions in the intelligence institutions and their public servants at the same time as there was a marked shift of intelligence and security professionals into the private sector. As a result, there was an increased use of "private" intelligence capabilities outside the state intelligence structures by the ANC, the National Party, and the Inkatha Freedom Party during the GNU period as well as by ANC factions during both Mbeki's and Zuma's presidencies to gain insights into their opponents.[56]

This new "battle for the intelligence brief" was corrupted less by personal drivers to dominate the security portfolio strategically and politically and more by the goal of enrichment and the need to ensure dominance and control in the internecine warfare between the different ANC factions that pulled the state's financial and commercial levers.[57] It was ultimately one such intelligence scandal—centered on continued rumors and accusations regarding ANC leaders who may or may not have been "apartheid spies"—and its investigation (the Hefer Commission) that led to President Mbeki's resignation and the rise of Jacob Zuma as president after a series of corruption and rape charges against him were quashed.[58] This led to what most observers saw as the total corruption of the highest office in the state and a tangible contagion effect on the intelligence and security institutions.

In recognition that things were going badly—and triggered specifically by another scandal when head of the NIA, Billy Masethla, was fired for criminal activities—then minister of intelligence Kasrils struck the Ministerial Review Commission on Intelligence under Joe Matthews in 2006.[59] The Matthews Commission concluded that the NIA was "politicized" and tainted by an "inappropriate focus on political activities" with the mixing of the NIA's covert intelligence capabilities and its role in "monitoring and reporting on transformation within government departments, on competition within and between political parties and on the impact of political policy decisions," all of which was considered to be "very troubling." This was due to the NIA's mandate under the 1994 National Strategic Intelligence Act—and the subsequent "interpretation" by the NIA of opposition to the ANC's governance as "subversion, treason and sabotage," which was determined to be "too broad and open to interpretation . . . impractical and unnecessary."[60] The commission's report provided many concrete and hard-hitting recommendations on cleaning up and improving the intelligence dispensation, especially concerning the elimination of corruption and misuse in the intelligence services, the primary raison d'être for the commission in the first place. The recommendations center around transparency, oversight, non-politicization, and public accountability of the intelligence services. However, most of these were not taken up by the post-Mbeki intelligence leadership under Zuma.[61] If anything, with the new intelligence leadership appointed in October 2009—all of whom had questions about their pasts—there was even more cause for concern. Equally, the reportedly disastrous internal collapse of the functions and capabilities of the NIA particularly and the SASS is also due to the fractious nature of the integration process and its history in the apartheid anti-liberation war.[62] While but one symptom of the failure, it called into question the degree to which the NIA is accountable to oversight.

This is just one reason for the decision in September 2009 to merge the NIA and the SASS into a new State Security Agency (SSA), a highly significant move that also amalgamated the South African National Academy of Intelligence (SANAI), the National Communications Centre (NCC), and the Office for Interception Centres (OIC), the Electronic Communications Security (Pty) Ltd, and the Intelligence Services Council on Conditions of Employment (ISC).[63] The new state security minister, Siyabonga Cwele, who himself appeared to suffer from some of the same problems that blighted some of his colleagues,[64] noted that this amalgamation would "centralise command and control of the intelligence structures [and] create greater efficiency and effectiveness, enhance cooperation between the various intelligence structures as well as effect savings."[65] In reality, this represented not only a continued failing of the state's institutions concerning the intelligence dispensation, but also a return to one of the themes of the apartheid era when the political leadership exerted the highest degree of control possible on the civilian intelligence service. It bent intelligence to political interests and viewpoints rather than allowing it to function as a truly independent provider of "truth to power." As scholar Laurie Nathan mused, "The Zuma administration had learned a lesson from the Mbeki experience—'ensure that your top spies are appointed above all on the basis of personal loyalty, never mind loyalty to the Constitution.'"[66] This was a similar observation made by one senior official early in the transition:

> No government can rule effectively without having the power to ensure that the leadership of the government departments will act according to the political will of the government. The old civil service was full of personnel who had no commitment to fulfil the will of the new government—should we have left them in an untransformed civil service?[67]

Little seems to have changed in the almost fifteen years since the Matthews Commission Report and the subsequent reorganization of the intelligence community under the SSA. This is largely due to the growth in corruption among the government and intelligence services under Zuma until his resignation in ignominy in February 2018. Moreover, this was the notable conclusion of the High Level Review Panel of the State Security Agency, established by new President Cyril Ramaphosa in June 2018 mere months after Zuma's resignation. Its recent *Report on the State Security Agency* noted starkly up-front that:

> our key finding is that there has been a serious politicisation and factionalisation of the intelligence community over the past decade or more, based on factions in the ruling party, resulting in an almost complete disregard for the Constitution, policy, legislation and other prescripts, and turning our civilian intelligence community into a private resource to serve the political and personal interests of particular individuals. In addition, we identified a doctrinal shift toward a narrow state security orientation in the intelligence community from 2009 in contradiction to the doctrines outlined in the Constitution, White Paper on Intelligence and other prescripts. . . . The cumulative effect of the above led to the deliberate re-purposing of the SSA [which] became a "cash cow" for many inside and outside the Agency.[68]

The report and its hard-hitting conclusions demonstrated that, truly, South Africa's post-apartheid intelligence dispensation was on the wrong path. Overall, there is no question that the ANC in the post-GNU period politicized and corrupted South Africa's intelligence dispensation, potentially—when reflecting on how a similar politicization occurred through the apartheid-era securocrats and the SSC/NSMS structures—to a degree not seen during the apartheid era given the levels of personal and financial corruption that has come with these new securocrats' politicization. With Zuma now removed from the presidency and Ramaphosa serving, the lasting effects of this damage in the post-Zuma era remains to be seen.

CONCLUSION

In the twenty-five years since the end of apartheid, the transition of South Africa's intelligence dispensation has clearly ended. In hindsight, it almost certainly ended when Mbeki fell and Zuma rose. The framers of the new intelligence era during the transition realized that they needed to either address the most difficult and contentious elements of the apartheid-era conflict on all sides, or willfully ignore them and hope that they did not corrupt the future intelligence posture of the country. They were successful in several strategic ways, such as integrating the institutions and organs of the conflict era into a new intelligence setup, confronting the worst excesses and human rights violations of the conflict by all sides, and eradicating the covert oppression arms of both military intelligence and police intelligence. However, they were unable to address some key factors that led subsequently to the descent of the intelligence dispensation into political and personal corruption. The power that wielding the state's intelligence capabilities offered to the individual was key to this. Indeed, as had been the case within the apartheid security structures as well as within the ANC, it continued to be a hallmark of the new intelligence era after 1998. The ANC's history also proved anathema to implementing the full mechanisms of transparency, accountability, and over-sight laid out in the constitution and the raft of intelligence-related legislation between 1994 and 2006. The failure proved a boon to the factionalism that came to the surface in the Mbeki era and led to his downfall.

South Africa's ongoing intelligence problems are due in no small part to the failings of its institutional and political leadership after 1998 to create the "culture of intelligence" that they so strongly committed themselves to during the previous decade. One of the transition phase's legacies has been the impact on the state of mind of the individuals responsible for intelligence and security matters. Notably, there has been a lack of trust inherent in the new dispensation: a lack of trust between individuals (not just "old guard" and "new guard," but also between the various individuals affiliated with one liberation group or party who now find themselves working together); a lack of trust in the institutions (including the disastrous internal collapse of the functions and capabilities of the agencies); and a lack of trust in the intelligence itself that perhaps worst of all, led to the politicization of the intelligence process. Notably, this included the intelligence product becoming politicized and the political leadership developing parallel, but independent, intelligence structures due to their own lack of trust in the state structures.

These and other similar legacies of the apartheid era undermined what should have been a new dawn in South Africa's intelligence history and the creation of a successful transition of an intelligence dispensation from authoritarianism to democracy. South Africa's new intelligence framers sought this new dawn and provided what was probably the best possible start to it; as such, this failure is a tragedy, with South Africa's intelligence falling victim to factionalism, corruption, mismanagement, and politicking—a failure that will hopefully be undone in the post-Zuma era.

NOTES

1. For the purposes of this chapter, the discipline of "intelligence" shall be used to mean, in all its aspects, a *process*, an *institution* (as seen through the lens of a Western formalised and bureaucratized approach), a *set of actions or activities*, and a *product*

to support decision-making (as taken from Sherman Kent, *Strategic Intelligence for American World Policy*, revised ed. [Princeton University Press, 1966], Allen Dulles, *The Craft of Intelligence* [New York: Harper & Row, 1963], and Harry Howe Ransom, *Central Intelligence and National Security* [Cambridge: Harvard University Press, 1958]). References throughout to an intelligence "dispensation" or "enterprise" should be considered to reference all four aspects collectively as an aspect of national power.

2. A short summary of this can be found in Sam Sole, "Jacob Zuma's Decade of Destruction," *Mail & Guardian*, November 2, 2012. https://mg.co.za/article/2012-11-02-00-jacob-zumas-decade-of-destruction/.

3. See: Kevin A. O'Brien, *The South African Intelligence Services: From Apartheid to Democracy 1948–2005* (London: Routledge, 2011) as well as (e.g.) Chris Alden, *Apartheid's Last Stand: The Rise and Fall of the South African Security State* (London: MacMillan Press Ltd, 1996); James Sanders, *Apartheid's Friends: The Rise and Fall of South Africa's Secret Services* (London: John Murray, 2006); Annette Seegers, *The Military in the Making of Modern South Africa* (London: Tauris Academic Books, 1996); Howard Barrell, *MK: The ANC's Armed Struggle* (London: Penguin Books, 1990); Stephen Ellis and Tsepo Sechaba, *Comrades against Apartheid: The ANC and South African Communist Party in Exile* (London: James Currey, 1992); and Daniel L. Douek *Insurgency and Counterinsurgency in South Africa* (London: Hurst & Company, 2020).

4. For a comprehensive examination of this relationship, see Jonathan S. Chavkin, *British Intelligence and the Zionist, South African, and Australian Intelligence Communities during and after the Second World War* (Unpublished PhD Thesis—Faculty of History, University of Cambridge, 2009).

5. O'Brien, 15.

6. Annette Seegers, *The Military*, 60–61, 76–77. Swaenpoel notes that this concern over "native agitators" was identified by the SAP intelligence arm in 1931—see P. C. Swanepoel, *Really Inside BOSS: A Tale of South Africa's Late Intelligence Service (And Something about the CIA)*, revised ed.. (Derdepoortpark, South Africa), 2008): 5–8.

7. Seegers, 126–32.

8. Stephen Ellis, "*Mbokodo*: Security in ANC Camps 1961–1990," *African Affairs* 93, no. 371 (April 1994): 285.

9. For detailed discussions of the ANC's intelligence and security apparatus, see Ellis, "*Mbokodo*"; African National Congress, *Further Submissions and Responses by the ANC to Questions Raised by the Commission for Truth and Reconciliation—Operations Report: the Department of Intelligence and Security of the African National Congress*. www.anc.org.za/ancdocs/misc/trc2d.html (downloaded 05/16/97); African National Congress, *Further Submissions and Responses by the ANC to Questions Raised by the Commission for Truth and Reconciliation—Appendix One: ANC Structures and Personnel, 1960–1994* (May 12, 1997). www.anc.org.za/ancdocs/misc/trc2a.html) (downloaded 04/08/10); ANC Submission, 6.3.2; and Tsepe Motumi, "The Spear of the Nation—The Recent History of Umkhonto we Sizwe (MK)"; J. K. Cilliers and Markus Reichardt, eds., *About-Turn: The Transformation*

of the South African Military and Intelligence (Midrand: Institute for Defence Policy, 1996), 92–93.

10. Much of this is outlined in Seegers, *The Military*, as well as at "A Short History of Military Intelligence Division." http://uk.geocities.com/sadf_history2/mihistory. html.

11. James Roherty, "Managing the Security Power Base in South Africa," *South African International Quarterly* 15, no. 2 (October 1984): 71.

12. *TRC2:3*, Appendix 12.

13. Seegers, *The Military*, 131.

14. Williams, 62.

15. By the mid-1970s, the ANC were "in danger of becoming irrelevant in South Africa." Ellis and Sechaba, *Comrades*, 6.

16. Sampson, *Mandela*, 264.

17. Alden, *Apartheid's Last Stand*, 216.

18. Roherty, 61.

19. Kenneth W. Grundy, *The Militarization of South African Politics* (London, 1986): 44.

20. See: Allister Sparks, *Tomorrow Is Another Country* (London: William Heinemann Ltd, 1995), 54–56, 109–19.

21. Grundy, 44; Rocklyn Williams, *Back to the Barracks: The Changing Parameters of Civil-Military Relations under the Botha and De Klerk Administrations* (Colchester: University of Essex, 1992), 130.

22. Such training facilities, financial, and materiel support were procured from China, the Soviet Union, East Germany, and Cuba primarily: Johns, "Obstacles," 277, 278. By the mid-1980s, it was believed by the U.S. government that the ANC was receiving 90 percent of its military aid and 60 percent of its overall aid from the Soviet Bloc (mostly the Soviet Union, East Germany, and Cuba): see P. Vanneman, *Soviet Strategy in Southern Africa: Gorbachev's Pragmatic Approach* (Stanford: Hoover Institution Press, 1990), 19–20; Daniel Kempton, *Soviet Strategy towards Southern Africa: The National Liberation Movement Connection* (New York: Praeger, 1989), 169.

23. For an assessment of the ANC's revolutionary war strategy and the intelligence capabilities that underpinned it, see Kevin A. O'Brien, "A Blunted Spear: The Failure of the ANC/SACP Revolutionary War Strategy 1961–1990," *Small Wars and Insurgencies* 14, no. 2 (Autumn 2003): 27–70; and Douek.

24. Gordon Winter, *Inside BOSS: South Africa's Secret Police* (London: Penguin Books, 1981), 568–569.

25. Ellis and Sechaba, 116.

26. See note 8.

27. The full tale of Operation Vula can be found in Tim Jenkin, "Talking to Vula: The Story of the Secret Underground Communications Network of Operation Vula," *Mayibuye* (May–October 1995).

28. "SANDF Chief of Staff testifies in De Kock trial," SAPA, November 23, 1995; "ANC leaders' arrests led to closure of Operation Vula," SAPA, November 24, 1995; Jenkin, "Talking to Vula."

29. Sparks, *The Mind of South Africa: The Story of the Rise and Fall of Apartheid* (London: William Heinemann Ltd, 1990): 400; Jenkin, "Talking to Vula."

30. Padraig O'Malley, *Shades of Difference: Mac Maharaj and the Struggle for South Africa* (New York: Viking, 2007): 267–70, 275–77.

31. This is covered extensively in Sparks, *Tomorrow Is Another Country*, 54–56, 109–19; Barnard, *Secret Revolution*, and *Peaceful Revolution: Inside the War Room at the Negotiations* (Cape Town: Tafelberg, 2017); Mark Shaw, "Spy Meets Spy: Negotiating New Intelligence Structures"; Steve Friedman and Doreen Atkinson, eds., *The Small Miracle: South Africa's Negotiated Settlement*. South African Review 7 (Johannesburg: Ravan Press, 1994), 259, 261, 262; Robert d'A Henderson, "South African Intelligence under de Klerk," *International Journal of Intelligence and Counterintelligence* 8, no. 1 (Spring 1995); Annette Seegers, "Current Trends in South Africa's Security Establishment," *Armed Forces and Society* 18, no. 2 (Winter 1992); and the author's *The South African Intelligence Services*, chapters 8 and 9.

32. For a full discussion of this transition and its implications for the subsequent two decades of South Africa's intelligence history, see Kevin A. O'Brien, "Fragmented Hydra: The Evolution of South Africa's Intelligence Community, 1960–2005," Mark Phythian et al., eds., *National Approaches* in Loch Johnson (series editor), *PSI Handbook of Global Security and Intelligence* (Santa Barbara: Praeger Security International, 2007).

33. This retention of senior personnel (not including those who voluntarily resigned) was mandated in section 2(b) of the 1995 Intelligence Services Act. Of the approximately 4,000 personnel included in the new NIA and its sister organization the South African Secret Service (SASS), 2,130 came from the NIS and 910 from the ANC-DIS, with the remainder coming from the intelligence services of the formerly independent "homelands" across South Africa. For the full summary of these changes, see O'Brien, "Fragmented Hydra".

34. Henderson, "South African Intelligence under De Klerk," 79.

35. Alden, 267. For a discussion of the secret negotiations, see Sparks, *Tomorrow Is Another Country*, 21–119 *inter alia* and 109–19 specifically concerning the initial secret negotiations in Switzerland.

36. Sparks, *Tomorrow Is Another Country*, 115; Henderson, "South African Intelligence under De Klerk," n66.

37. Shaik continued as a close advisor to Zuma as the latter became deputy president; Shaik's brother Schabir would also serve as Zuma's financial advisor and become embroiled in fraud, corruption, and related charges surrounding Zuma's role in the 1990s arms purchase scandal (see Jason Burke, "Zuma to stand trial on corruption charges relating to $2.5bn arms deal," *The Guardian*, October 11, 2019. https://www.theguardian.com/world/2019/oct/11/zuma-to-stand-trial-corruption-charges-arms-deal-south-african-president for a recent update on this scandal and Zuma's role in it). By the late 1990s, Moe Shaik had been appointed as deputy national coordinator of intelligence; then in mid-2009, the director of the NIA by Zuma, then subsequently chosen to lead the SASS in 2010. See "DA to oppose appointment of Mo Shaik as NIA head," SAPA August 30, 2009. www.mg.co.za/article/2009-08-30-da-to-oppose-appointment-of-mo-shaik-as-nia-head; "Moe Shaik's appointment angers

opposition parties," SAPA, October 3, 2009. www.mg.co.za/article/2009-10-03-moe-shaiks-appointment-angers-opposition-parties. A profile of Shaik can be read at Paddy Harper, "I Spy . . . a man born to be in intelligence," *Sunday Times* (South Africa), October 10, 2009, www.timeslive.co.za/sundaytimes/article145322.ece.

38. Participants in the discussions included the NIS, DIS, and representatives from the services of Transkei, Venda, and Bophutatswana. Initially, the ANC had asked for managerial control through this body over the day-to-day functions of the intelligence community; the NIS opposed this. This compromise was written into the mandate of the Transitional Executive Council Act: Republic of South Africa, Transitional Executive Council Act (Act 151 of 1993); see also Shaw, 263.

39. Republic of South Africa, *Constitution of the Republic of South Africa* (as drafted April 1996): s186(a).

40. See: Kevin A. O'Brien, "South Africa's Evolving Intelligence and Security Structures," *International Journal of Intelligence and Counterintelligence* 9, no. 2 (Summer 1996): 187–232 for a full overview and discussion of these reforms.

41. Republic of South Africa, *White Paper on Intelligence* (October 1994): 9–10, 13–14 [hereafter *White Paper*].

42. *White Paper*, 7.

43. See: Kevin A. O'Brien, "Controlling the Hydra: A Historical Analysis of South African Intelligence Accountability"; Hans Born and Loch K. Johnson, eds., *Who's Watching the Spies? Establishing Intelligence Service Accountability* (Potomac Books, 2005).

44. Shaw, 268–69.

45. Shaw, 265.

46. See: *Report of the High-Level Review Panel on the SSA and Related Matters* (2018), https://www.gov.za/sites/default/files/gcis_document/201903/high-level-review-panel-state-security-agency.pdf, as well as statements by successive state security ministers, e.g. Siyabonga Cwele in 2010 ("White Paper on Intelligence under Review," *defenceWeb*, May 7, 2010: https://www.defenceweb.co.za/security/national-security/white-paper-on-intelligence-under-review/) and Ayanda Dlodlo in 2019 ("Dlodlo undertakes to salvage the image of the State Security Agency," *African News Agency*, July 19, 2019, https://www.polity.org.za/print-version/dlodlo-undertakes-to-salvage-the-image-of-the-state-security-agency-2019-07-19) concerning such intentions, which as of writing are yet to be realized.

47. See: Douek, 350–51 summarizing this point.

48. The ANC would institute no fewer than four high-level investigations into the abuses alleged against *Mbokodo*—alongside mutinies by MK cadres—in its camps, including the Stuart (1984), Jobodwana (1990), Skweyiya (1992), and Motsuenyane (1993) commissions: see Ellis, "Mbokodo," 279–84, 292 for a discussion of both the commissions and their conclusions.

49. For a discussion of these, see O'Brien, "South Africa's Evolving Intelligence and Security Structures," 187–232.

50. Intelligence Services Control Amendment Act (42-1999): s7; and *National Strategic Intelligence Amendment Act* (67-2002): s6.

51. General Intelligence Law Amendment Act (66–2000): s18–22B.

52. These were the Intelligence Services Control Amendment Act (Act 42 of 1999) and its follow-up, the Intelligence Services Control Amendment Act (Act 66 of 2002); the Electronic Communications Security (Pty) Ltd Act (Act 68 of 2002); the General Intelligence Law Amendment Act (Act 66 of 2000); the Intelligence Services Act (Act 65 of 2002); the National Strategic Intelligence Amendment Act (Act 67 of 2002); the General Intelligence Laws Amendment Act (Act 52 of 2003); and the Regulation of Interception of Communications and Provision of Communication-related Information Act (Act 70 of 2002, updated in 2006) This is all summarized in O'Brien, "Fragmented Hydra."

53. The creation of the ECS(P)L was greeted by many as odd, as it created that body as a private company, governed—under ministerial direction—by a board and a CEO, and subject to parliamentary and ministerial oversight. Electronic Communications Security (Pty) Ltd Act (Act 68 of 2002): s7 and chapters 2, 3; Ronnie Kasrils, MP, "South African Intelligence Services: Towards Meeting the Challenges of the 21st Century—Ten Priorities for Immediate Action"—Speech on the Occasion of the Secret Services Debate (Cape Town, June 23, 2004). www.intelligence.gov.za/Speeches/BudgetVote2004.htm.

54. The 1999 Act, in watering down the original objectives and capabilities of the inspector generals, clarified that "one Inspector-General may be appointed with regard to some of or all the Services as long as the activities of all the Services are monitored by an Inspector-General": ISC Amendment Act 1999: s5a/b; and ISC Amendment Act 2002: s7(7).

55. Intelligence officials said that the process of establishing the IG's office had been hampered by the illness of former minister of intelligence Joe Nhlanhla, who was then replaced by Lindwe Sisulu: "SA Intelligence Boss Throws in the Towel," *ZA*NOW*, January 28, 2002. See also: "Care Needed in Selecting Intelligence IG: DA"—PARLIAMENT SAPA, June 17, 2003. www.anc.org.za/anc/newsbrief/2003/news0618.txt; Ministry of the Intelligence Services, *Inspector General*. www.intelligence.gov.za/OversightControl/inspector_general.htm.

56. In the mid-1990s, the existence of a subcommittee on intelligence and security attached to the ANC National Executive Committee was discovered (composed of Joe Nhlanhla, Joe Modise, Sidney Mufamadi, and Bantu Holimisa); additionally, an ANC document published in the mid-1990s analyzing the success of the GNU, recommended that a number of small, mobile, professional intelligence units be set up to "detour deficiencies within the official ranks of the NIA and the information flow that runs through NICOC to the government." There were also reported attempts by Inkatha to resurrect a paramilitary and intelligence capacity within both the IFP and the KwaZulu-Natal Police, using funds from Germany's Konrad Adenauer Foundation and, allegedly, the CIA: Paul Stober, Marion Edmonds, Eddie Koch, and Ann Eveleth, "Inkatha's secret German war chest," *Weekly Mail and Guardian* (September 15, 1995); Jeff Stein, "South Africa's Many 'Watergates' May Spill Over on the CIA," *Baltimore Sun* (March 20, 1996). In November 2001, Mbeki's office established a new presidential support unit in the Ministry of Intelligence to provide logistical backing to the presidency and former president Nelson Mandela: "'Spy unit' for Mbeki," *ZA*NOW*, February 22, 2002. See also: Stefaans Brümmer, "Inside the ANC's spy unit," *Mail & Guardian*, May 6, 2001. www.mg.co.za/mg/za/

archive/2001may/features/04may-spy.html. This issue is discussed in more detail in O'Brien, "South Africa's Evolving Intelligence and Security Structures," 208–211.

57. This is explored in detail in O'Brien, *The South African Intelligence Services*, chapters 9 and 10.

58. See: Basildon Peta, "ANC split threatened as leaders face spying charges," *The Independent* October 16, 2003. www.independent.co.uk/news/world/africa/anc-split-threatened-as-leaders-face-spying-charges-583511.html; the Commission's findings in *Report of the Hefer Commission of Inquiry into Allegations of Spying against the National Director of Public Prosecutions, Mr BT Ngcuka*, January 20, 2004. www. info.gov.za/otherdocs/2004/heferreport.pdf; Laurian Clemence, "Ngcuka was 'probably never' a spy-Hefer," SAPA, January 21, 2004. www.polity.org.za/article/ngcuka-was-x2018probably-neverx2019-a-spyhefer-2004-01-21; and the Commission's documents at "O'Malley Archives: Hefer Commission." www.nelsonmandela.org/ omalley/index.php/site/q/03lv03445/04lv04015/05lv04120.htm.

59. Masetlha was dismissed and prosecuted on two criminal charges: contravening the Intelligence Services Oversight Act by lying to intelligence inspector-general Zolile Ngcakani about the origins of the hoax emails and for committing commercial fraud by using NIA funds to pay "others" involved in the hoax emails. The "others" included the former NIA manager for electronic surveillance, Funokwakhe Madlala and IT salesman Muziwendoda Kunene. The NIA's counterintelligence manager Bob Mhlanga was transferred to the SAPS and Gibson Njenje, the NIA deputy director-general of operations, was suspended. Njenje was subsequently reappointed as head of the NIA in October 2009. See Seegers, "The new security," 274, n66.

60. *Intelligence in a Constitutional Democracy—Final Report to the Minister for Intelligence Services, The Honourable Mr Ronnie Kasrils, MP*. Ministerial Review Commission on Intelligence, September 10, 2008. www.ssrnetwork.net/document_ library/detail/4276/intelligence-in-a-constitutional-democracy-ndash-final-report-to-the-minister-for-intelligence-services-10-september-2008, 15.

61. Indeed, as the Institute for Security Studies (South Africa) notes, "Since then, nothing has been seen or heard of the Commission's Report nor of the recommendations for tighter controls on the use of special powers that are detailed therein"—ISS, "Spies, Lies And Secret Tapes," *ISS Today*, March 30, 2009. www.issafrica.org/ pgcontent.php?UID=18569. On the Commission, see: "Kasrils: Ministerial Review Commission on Intelligence," *Polity.org.za*, November 1, 2006. www.polity.org.za/ article/kasrils-ministerial-review-commission-on-intelligence-01112006-2006-11-01; and the Commission's final report *Intelligence in a Constitutional Democracy*, op cit. The ISS also began a project to review the future plans and priorities of South Africa's intelligence dispensation—see Lauren Hutton (ed.), *To Spy or not to Spy? Intelligence and Democracy in South Africa*. ISS Monograph Series No. 157, February 2009. http://www.iss.co.za/pgcontent.php?UID=2537; Lauren Hutton, "Intelligence and Accountability in Africa," Policy Brief Nr 2, June 2009, www.issafrica.org/uploads/ JUL09INTELLIGENCEACCOUNT.PDF; and all seminars and reports from this project.

62. Seegers notes the relationship between private intelligence companies and the NIA's inabilities—a symbiotic and self-sustaining problem: Seegers, "The new security," 276–77.

63. Nthambeleni Gabara, "SA's civilian intelligence structures to merge," *SA News*, October 4, 2009. https://www.sanews.gov.za/south-africa/sas-civilian-intelligence-structures-merge. Full details of the creation of the SSA and the merger of the various legacy agencies were contained in a series of Proclamations made by Cwele on September 17, 2009, under the Public Service Act 1994 (Proclamations 912–915)—see https://www.gov.za/sites/default/files/gcis_document/201409/32576912.pdf, . . . 913.pdf, . . . 914.pdf, and . . . 915.pdf.

64. Cwele's wife was arrested in drug-smuggling charges in January 2010: "S African minister's wife Sheryl Cwele on drug charges," *BBC News*, January 29, 2010. http://news.bbc.co.uk/2/hi/africa/8488355.stm; the minister claimed to have no knowledge of the activities.

65. Siyabonga Cwele, "Mobilising our resources to work together to do more to achieve National Security, State Security Minister," *South African Government Information*, October 2, 2009; "State Security Agency restructuring going well—Cwele," *City Press*, June 2, 2011: https://www.news24.com/citypress/SouthAfrica/News/State-Security-Agency-restructuring-going-well-Cwele-20110602.

66. Sam Sole, "Zuma's new spy purge," *Mail & Guardian* February 5, 2010. www.mg.co.za/article/2010-02-05-zumas-new-spy-purge. Laurie Nathan, an academic from University of Cape Town and formerly a member of the 2006 Ministerial Review Commission, also commented on many of these issues in his paper *Lighting Up the Intelligence Community: A Democratic Approach to Intelligence Secrecy and Openness*—Global Facilitation Network for Security Sector Reform Policy Paper, April 2009. www.ssrnetwork.net/documents/Publications/Intelligence/Intelligence%20Policy%20Paper.pdf.

67. Confidential interview, April 1996.

68. "Preface" and "Executive Summary," *Report of the High-Level Review Panel on the SSA*.

Chapter 10

The Challenge of Effective Intelligence in Nigerian Post-Military Rule

Ibikunle Adeakin

Nigeria's current intelligence framework is a result of military rule and was used by military regimes to perpetuate human rights abuses. From the military's first intervention in politics in 1966 led by Major Kaduna Nzeogwu, the military has played a pivotal role in Nigerian politics.[1] The military dominated the political process for nearly thirty years, and the country experienced six successful coup d'états.[2] Of these coups, the ones in January 1966, December 1983, and November 1993 were against civilian governments.[3] By the time military rule ended on May 29, 1999, it left a strong authoritarian imprint on the polity. Despite the transition to democratization, Nigeria's intelligence services continue operating in frameworks laid out during military rule, which provided them great latitude for carrying out operations with little or no civilian oversight. While the current literature on Nigerian democratization covers many political institutions and the challenges facing their operation under democratic rule, little research has been done on the country's intelligence services and how their traditionally unchecked privileges threaten the stability of the democratization process. This chapter argues that the operational effectiveness of Nigerian intelligence services is hindered by the legacy of "institutional prerogatives" that these services acquired under military rule and that remained virtually unchallenged post-military rule.

Effective and transparent political institutions are vital to both established and aspiring liberal democracies, especially those like Nigeria that are emerging from decades of authoritarian military rule. As states, strong civil institutions are the "decisive step towards . . . the devolution of power from a group of people to a set of rules."[4] For over two decades, political power in Nigeria was concentrated in the hands of a few military rulers, leaving many of the country's civil institutions weak, corrupt, and ineffective.[5] There are many theories as to why developing nations tend to have weak civil institutions.

Scholar Joel Migdal argued that in certain cases a country's geographic area is too large and its government too small for the nation to be effectively governed. This lack of effective control is in turn often a legacy of colonial rule and the introduction of the global capitalist system of trade.[6] In the sub-Saharan African context, this resulted in the imposition of exploitative taxation and forced labor (especially in Francophone Africa), with cash-crop agriculture for export being prioritized and the development of local government and institutions actively discouraged.[7] The development of new systems of taxation, land tenure, and transportation—such as railway lines to bring cash crops to the coast for export—transformed the administrative landscape of colonial societies.[8] The specifics of colonial administrative structures varied widely depending on what best served the interests of the colonizers. In certain cases, precolonial structures were left largely intact, such as in the case of Sokoto Caliphate in Northern Nigeria where colonial authorities carried out a policy of indirect rule whereby colonial mandates were delivered through emirs and the sultan, the region's traditional rulers.[9]

Similarly, James Wunsch and Dele Olowu explained that the failure of political institutions in virtually all African countries can be attributed to the "overcentralized" systems of governance adopted following the end of colonial rule. Having known nothing but centralized authoritarian rule for decades, following independence, most colonized countries fell back on similarly centralized systems of government.[10] However such systems, designed for the efficient extraction of resources, were not suited to providing adequate governance at the local level in remote, often agrarian, regions far from central administrative centers.[11]

Since the start of democratic civilian rule in 1999, there have been numerous reports, based on extensive interviews in conflict areas of Nigeria, by Amnesty International and Human Rights Watch that have accused Nigeria intelligence and security services of human rights abuses committed during campaigns against internal threats, such as Boko Haram.[12] Similar accusations of human rights abuses have also been reported by both local and international media outlets. Much criticism has fallen on the federal government for its lack of oversight over these services that have enabled these abuses to be committed with impunity. For democratic principles to thrive in Nigeria, it is necessary to build effective civilian oversight frameworks capable of reining in the excesses of the existing security and intelligence establishment.

The chapter uses document analysis by examining relevant records generated from government and nongovernmental institutions, such as from the National Assembly, Amnesty International, and Human Rights Watch.[13] Also archival materials of newspaper articles and editorials, news magazines, Nigeria's past constitutions, and military decrees are examined. Other data collected are sourced from relevant journal articles, books, contemporary news articles, and editorials from reputable local and international media outlets and newspapers.

This chapter takes a qualitative analytic approach with six different sections. It begins with a literature review about governance to understand how intelligence oversight is tied to broader governance issues. Next, the chapter looks at Nigerian history, highlighting the role colonialism had in shaping the intelligence services that was further reorganized and professionalized under military rule. Then it assesses three intelligence prerogatives that remain unchallenged post-military rule. These are inadequate articulated missions for the intelligence services in post-military rule that provides significant role expansion without civilian and then National Assembly oversight—the legal framework that provides intelligence services with broad legal justifications as well as responsibilities, but prevents legislative scrutiny. As for coordination, the present intelligence framework hinders interagency intelligence cooperation. Consequently, intelligence heads can act with impunity based on the malfunction of the coordinator of intelligence services, the national security adviser. Finally, it examines these intelligence services' operational struggles in dealing with the rise in ethnic and ethno-religious conflicts. The conclusion summarizes the chapter, finding that the legal framework's evolution since colonialism has prevented any meaningful civilian oversight and rectifying this would require significant political will that the country currently lacks.

THE HISTORY OF INTELLIGENCE SERVICES IN NIGERIA

The history of Nigerian intelligence services began during the period of British colonial rule. However, the service did not begin as a full-fledged organization, but rather evolved over time in response to the changing needs of the colonial administration. Initially, intelligence collection was not a significant issue for the colonialists, who established security services for law and order and also conducted limited intelligence activities. The most important of these security services established by the colonial government was the police force.

The Nigerian Police Force's origin is similar to that of the military, which was created like a militia.[14] This occurred when the British Council in-charge of Lagos Colony, ceded to Britain in 1861, created a quasi militia of thirty men commonly referred to as "Glover Hausa" or "Hausa Guard."[15] The thirty men numerically increased over time to about 600 men, and the militia was eventually regularized through the promulgation of an ordinance on October 8, 1863. In 1865, this security unit was renamed the Lagos Hausa Constabulary and was headed by an inspector general of police. After a protectorate was declared by the colonialist in 1885 over the Cameroons and Oil Rivers, a local force was created by the colonial administration, which was initially known as the Oil Rivers Irregulars. This force later became known as the Niger Coast Protectorate Constabulary. Similarly, in 1896, another group was established in Lagos that was known as the Lagos Police Force and had functions like the Hausa Constabulary.[16]

In 1888, the Royal Niger Company established the Royal Niger Constabulary in Northern Nigeria and had it headquartered in Lokoja. The constabulary's objective was to protect the Royal Niger Company's interests and installation along the River Niger, which was the main way of transporting goods from the north to the coastal port towns in the south.[17] By 1906, the Lagos Police Force and part of the Niger Coast Constabulary became integrated into the Southern Nigeria Police Force. On the establishment of the Protectorate of Northern Nigeria in 1900, the Royal Nigeria Constabulary was split into the Northern Nigeria Regiment. In 1908, the Northern Nigeria Police was established and was headed by an inspector general who was assisted by district superintendents.[18]

The merging of Northern and Southern Nigeria as a single political entity in 1914 did not stop the two police services from operating as two separate commands. By 1930, the police forces of the Northern and Southern provinces were fused to create a centralized Nigeria Police Force.[19] To enhance the country's internal security, in 1936, the Criminal Investigation Department (CID) was created, which later evolved into the Special Branch of the Nigerian Police. The structure and role of the CID was loosely based on a unit known as the Eastern and Western Preventive Service, established in 1931 as an anti-smuggling agency.[20]

The rise of nationalist and independence movements in the British Empire colonies following the Second World War made it necessary for colonial authorities to establish institutions and enact administrative reforms for eventual self-rule. However, due to Cold War fears of Marxist-Socialist ideology infiltrating colonial governments, these efforts placed great emphasis on bolstering intelligence and security institutions to combat left-wing political movements.[21] Prior to Nigeria officially gaining independence on October 1, 1960, the CID and Special Branch were officially separated as two distinct departments. CID became known as the "D Department," while the Special Branch and "Alien Branch" were merged to form the "E Department."[22] It was expected that the E Department would rely on the Native Authority Police for intelligence gathering, as the police possessed an intimate understanding of local affairs.

While most government institutions after independence fell under native control, British officers continued to occupy key positions within the security and intelligence apparatus, including serving as the heads of the E Department and Special Branch.[23] It soon became apparent, particularly to the general public in the south of the country, that these services were not impartial in their operations and largely served as instruments of the ruling political class.[24]

Among the Special Branch's most significant achievements during the Nigerian First Republic from 1960 to 1966 was the infiltration and exposure of a plot by federal opposition leader Obafemi Awolowo to overthrow the government. It was alleged during the subsequent trial that Awolowo and his Action Group party leaders lost confidence in the federal parliamentary political system, as it routinely delivered an absolute majority for the Northern Region. Awolowo organized men for a coup, sending them to Ghana to train in guerrilla warfare tactics. Awolowo and his associates admitted that they had sent men to Ghana for military training, but stated that this force was intended to counter the autocratic rule of Ladoke Akintola, premier of Nigeria's Western Region.[25] At the end of the trial, all but four of the twenty-five accused were found guilty, and Awolowo was sentenced to ten years in prison. The incarceration of Awolowo and his associates and the continuation of Akintola's unpopular premiership led to a series of violent ethno-political clashes that engulfed the First Republic, which only ended following military intervention in 1966.[26]

The Special Branch continued as the country's primary intelligence agency until 1976 when the Nigerian Security Organization (NSO) was created as an independent intelligence service separate from the police. This was enacted in response to the Special Branch's failure to uncover the failed coup attempt by Lieutenant Colonel Buka Dimka, which led to the assassination of then head of state General Murtala Mohammed in February 1976.[27] While the Special Branch alleged that they had uncovered a plot in 1975 to overthrow the regime of General Yakubu Gowon (1966–1975), it was instructed by the military to not act. Consequently, the government viewed the Special Branch as untrustworthy and removed its national intelligence mandate.[28]

Unlike the Special Branch that evolved gradually to meet the needs of colonial rule, the NSO was established hastily without any deliberate consideration as to the type of intelligence service Nigeria needed. According to scholar Jimi Peters, Decree 16 of 1976 established the NSO with the following functions:

> The prevention and detection of any crime against the security of Nigeria, the protection and preservation of all classified matter concerning or relating to the security of Nigeria and, such other purposes, whether within or without Nigeria, as the Head of the Federal Military Government may deem necessary with a view to a securing the maintenance of the security of Nigeria.[29]

Scholar Basil Ugochukwu described how the NSO, to achieve its tasks, needed:

> "to obtain by secret sources or other means accurate intelligence regarding persons or organizations, whether within or outside Nigeria, engaged in acts of

espionage, subversion, or sabotage against Nigeria or engaged in acts that may threaten the security of Nigeria;

   to identify and, where necessary, apprehend or assist in the apprehension of persons believed to have committed any crime against the security of Nigeria;

   to collect, collate, assess, and disseminate intelligence information affecting Nigeria's state security and the maintenance of public order;

   to detect and investigate all acts of subversion, espionage, and sabotage against the country;

   to maintain records of individuals and organizations engaging in subversive activities;

   to investigate the reliability of persons who may have access to classified information or material and who may be employed in sensitive or scheduled posts;

   to advise and assist in the implementation of protective security measures in government establishments and sensitive installations; and

   to provide personal security to very important personalities."[30]

Thus, the NSO was expected to combine the functions of the United States' Federal Bureau of Investigation (FBI) that primarily engages in domestic law enforcement and counterintelligence activities and the Central Intelligence Agency (CIA) that mainly focuses on gathering foreign intelligence.

Since the NSO was established hastily, there was a lack of adequate consultation and planning that resulted in numerous operational deficiencies. Part of this inadequacy is from the initial composition of the organization's staff drawn mainly from the External Affairs Ministry research department and Special Branch officers.[31] This led to the organizational structures, mandates, and operations of the NSO more closely resembling those of a police department rather than an intelligence service. In addition, the NSO competed directly with the Directorate of Military Intelligence (DMI) for dominance over intelligence operations, which persisted well into the Second Republic from 1979 to 1983.[32]

On December 31, 1983, a military coup ended the Second Republic and led to the installation of Major General Muhammadu Buhari as head of state. Under Buhari's regime, from 1983 to 1985, the NSO's activities were expanded to roles it was never intended to fill, including the intimidation and harassment of the regime's political opponents. This was achieved in two governmental decrees. The first, Decree No. 2, authorized detention without trial of anyone deemed a threat to the regime. The second, Decree No. 4, forbade any publication or broadcast that could embarrass the government. These laws led to the arrest and detention of many journalists.[33] However on August 27, 1985, Buhari was overthrown in a bloodless coup by his chief of army staff and third-in-command, Major General Ibrahim Babangida. The coup was partially justified by Buhari's overly draconian administration, and upon taking power, Babangida suspended Decrees 2 and 4, and released all political detainees.[34] To address operational deficiencies and its use by the Buhari regime for political repression, in 1986, the NSO was replaced with Nigeria's current intelligence framework. Three new intelligence services were created: the State Security Service (SSS), Defence Intelligence Agency (DIA), and the National Intelligence Agency (NIA).[35]

The SSS, also known as Department of State Service (DSS), is the main internal intelligence agency tasked with domestic intelligence gathering, internal security, counterterrorism, and the protection of senior government officials. It is headed by a civilian, the director general, and is a member of the Joint Intelligence Board (JIB), also established in 1986 following the NSO's dissolution. The JIB's role is to collect intelligence from the SSS, DIA, and NIA for the National Security Council, which is the highest security body in Nigeria and presided over by the country's president. The SSS/DSS is divided into national, state, and local commands with the national level consisting of eight directorates.[36] At the state level, the DSS operates commands in each of the thirty-six states of the federation and one in the federal capital territory (FCT) of Abuja. At the local level, each local government in the thirty-six state commands and Abuja are commanded by local government security chiefs (LGSC) who report to the state command heads and ultimately to the director general.[37]

In contrast, the DIA is headed by an active-duty military officer and tasked mainly with intra-military intelligence and producing comprehensive, contextual, and timely intelligence support to defense planners to effectively maintain national security. According to Jimi Peters, the DIA is charged with these responsibilities:

- the prevention and detection of crime of a military nature against the security of Nigeria;
- the protection and preservation of all military classified matters concerning the security of Nigeria, both within and outside Nigeria;
- and such other responsibilities affecting defense intelligence of a military nature, both within and outside Nigeria, as the president, commander-in-chief of the armed forces (C-in-C), or the chairman, joint chiefs of staff, as the case maybe, may deem necessary.[38]

Last, the NIA is tasked with overseas intelligence and counterintelligence operations. It is also headed by a civilian, and according to Peters, it is responsible for:

"the general maintenance of the security of Nigeria outside Nigeria, concerning matters that are not related to military issues; and such other responsibilities affecting national intelligence outside Nigeria as the National Defence and Security Council or the president, C-in-C, as the case maybe, may deem necessary."[39]

There were also provisions for the establishment of two advisory councils within the Office of the President with specific intelligence gathering functions. These are the National Defence Council, charged with responsibilities for the defense of the sovereignty and territorial integrity of Nigeria, and the National Security Council with public security responsibilities. Coordination of the three main intelligence services is managed by the Office of the National Security Adviser (NSA).[40] The NSA advises the president on the activities of the three services, including making recommendations regarding intelligence operations, analyzing intelligence reports relating to national security, and disseminating them to appropriate government departments.[41]

Throughout the period of military rule, the activities of the DSS did not differ from the defunct NSO. Indeed, it was perceived as an instrument of political oppression with allegations of human rights abuses. Perhaps the most noteworthy allegation brought against the DSS was its involvement in the assassination of Dele Giwa, a prominent Nigerian journalist who was the founder and editor of the influential *Newswatch* magazine. On October 19, 1986, Giwa was killed by a mail bomb in his home when he tried to open a parcel allegedly sent from the office of the "C-in-C" (commander-in-chief).[42] There was great suspicion from civil society that the DSS was responsible for Giwa's murder because it came two days after being interviewed by the service. Additionally, a few weeks after Giwa's death, the DSS deputy director, Lieutenant Colonel Kunle Togun informed some journalists at a security seminar organized for media executives and security services that the DSS had reached a compromise with editors of major Nigerian media organizations. In the supposed deal, key media organizations would inform the DSS of any news article that was perceived as detrimental to the government's interests. Togun further stated, "I mean we came to a real agreement and one person cannot just come out and blackmail us. . . . I am an expert in blackmail."[43] This statement suggests Togun's complicity in Giwa's murder.

The DSS also targeted several pro-democracy and human rights advocates, as they were constantly harassed, imprisoned, exiled, and denied rights. Prominent human rights lawyer, Gani Fawehinmi, was imprisoned and detained multiple times, and his passport was seized so that he could not leave the country.[44] Nobel laureate Wole Soyinka suffered a similar fate when DSS officials seized his passport when he attempted to leave the country in November 1994. Even though Soyinka was advised to report at the DSS headquarters on November 16, 1994, he disregarded the order and left the country clandestinely through the land border.[45] Patrick Wilmot, a professor of sociology at Ahmadu Bello University, Zaria, was known as a critic of the Babangida regime and had radical leftist beliefs.[46] Without prior warning, he was forcefully taken from Zaria in March 1988 and deported to the United Kingdom the following day by DSS officials. The official position of the regime was Wilmot was a spy for apartheid South Africa as well as a political radical and Marxist.[47]

Under the regime of General Sani Abacha from 1993 to 1998, agencies were created to undermine the power of the three main intelligence services and consolidate Abacha's power. These agencies included the Special Body-guard Services (SBS), created for the personal protection of Abacha, and the Strike Force and K-Squad, whose activities involved state-sponsored terrorism and assassinations of the regime's opponents.[48] However, following Abacha's death in June 1998, these two services were dissolved. Additionally, on the eve of the transition to the newly elected civilian government on May 29, 1999, the regime of General Abdulsalami Abubakar from 1998 to 1999 repealed many decrees used by previous military governments to suppress political dissent. The repealed decrees included Decree 2, State Security (Detention of Persons), that was enacted during the regime of Major General Buhari in 1984. It provided the now defunct NSO powers to arrest and detain indefinitely without trial any individual or group that was considered a security risk to the regime.[49] Another law repealed was Decree 29, Treason and Treasonable Offences Decree of 1993. Enacted under the regime of General Babangida, it gave the government the right to seize any publication within the country that the regime deemed likely to "disturb the peace and public order of Nigeria."[50] Journalists critical of the regime could be detained on a "treasonable felony" charge, which was punishable by long prison sentences and death. Additionally, Decree 35, Offensive Publications (Proscription), was enacted under the regime of Babangida and allowed the regime to shut down or suspend the operations of media organizations that published articles the regime deemed to be damaging or harmful. General Babangida's successor, General Abacha, used the decree to convict journalists Kunle Ajibade, Chris Anyanwu, George Mba, and Ben Charles Obi as "accessories after the fact to treason, for reporting on an alleged coup plot" in 1995.[51]

There were other important laws used to oppress dissidents that were repealed. Decree 1, Treason and Other Offences (Special Military Tribunals), was initially issued following the failed coup attempt by Lieutenant Colonel Buka Dimka in 1976 that led to the assassination of then head of state, General Murtala Mohammed. The first task of the Special Military Tribunal (composed of military officers) was to try all the officers who'd taken part in the failed coup.[52] Successive military rulers used the special military tribunal to try abortive coup attempts, such as Major General MammanVasta's alleged plot against General Babangida in 1986 as well as that of Major Gideon

Orkar against the same regime in 1990.[53] General Abacha expanded the provisions of this decree and used this tribunal to try serving military officers and civilians. Notable civilians who were arraigned under the military tribunal included Olusegun Obasanjo and Musa Yar' Adua, retired military officers involved in the alleged coup attempt of 1995. Environmental activist, Ken Saro-Wiwa and nine other Ogoni leaders were executed by hanging after their murder cases were heard by a military tribunal.[54] However, other decrees such as the 1986 Decree 19 (National Security Agencies Decree) that established Nigeria's current intelligence framework remained the law.

INSTITUTIONAL PREROGATIVES OF THE NIGERIAN INTELLIGENCE SERVICES

The reorganization of Nigeria's intelligence framework in 1986 had negative consequences in the post military–rule era. This included the establishment and retention of "institutional prerogatives" that have hindered institutional reform and the establishment of effective civilian oversight. The concept of "military prerogatives," outlined by scholar Alfred Stepan in the Latin American context, largely refers to "reserve domains" that the military acquired under authoritarian rule that granted it great latitude in carrying out security operations against civilians.[55]

Empirically, prerogatives acquired under military rule can be challenged post-military rule. Examples of such military prerogatives, as stated by Stepan, include guaranteed constitutional positions for senior military officers in the cabinet or parliament; the statutory role of the military under democratization; legislative oversight over the military, particularly its budget, weapons procurement, and force structure; and whether there is a process that guarantees the involvement of civil society and experts on military matters in military affairs.[56] Based on the context, it is conceivable that the military would resist attempts to limit its prerogatives by the civilian government. Under this scenario, if not strongly addressed, it could lead to another coup d'état. There might also be situations where the civilian government enacts policies that reduce or abolish such prerogatives, under which, it is likely that the military is committed to its full disengagement from politics, and this ultimately would lead to a process of re-democratization and, eventually, democratic consolidation. It is also possible that military prerogatives would not be contested by the political elites, perhaps due to the lack of an articulated/agreeable policy alternative to the status quo. This condition could cause political elites to accommodate the prerogatives, which may or may not be due to possible consequences, such as a coup d'état.[57]

The 1999 constitution retained the military and intelligence structures established under military rule, including their original military prerogatives and autonomy. Specifically, Section 315(5) c of the constitution left the military and intelligence apparatus of Nigeria without adequate civilian oversight, which led to many allegations of human rights abuses. Further, there is an inadequately articulated mission for the intelligence services: lack of legislative oversight and improper coordination of the security services.[58]

QUEST FOR INTELLIGENCE SERVICES MISSION

To ensure the rapid consolidation of democratic administration following the end of authoritarian rule, it is vital that an articulated security framework be laid out and implemented. Failure could risk elements of the former regime conspiring to overthrow the nascent democratic government. The law governing the operational use of Nigeria's intelligence services is derived from the 1999 constitution, but not debated by any elective representative body before adoption. Rather, General Abubakar's regime from 1998 to 1999 created a Constitutional Debate Coordinating Committee (CDCC) tasked with incorporating public comments made on the 1995 draft constitution introduced by Abubakar's predecessor, General Abacha.[59] The regime gave the CDCC just two months to deliberate and did not include public hearings, which had been the practice of other military regimes.[60]

Immediately following the swearing-in of the new civilian president in 1999, media outlets alleged that the new constitution had essentially been hijacked by the military. As the National Security Agencies Act (Section 315(5)c) originated as a military decree, critics questioned its legitimacy under the new civilian administration. However, it was entrenched within the constitution, which means the act can only be repealed with the support of two-thirds of the National Assembly at both the state and federal level. This effectively placed the Nigerian government at the mercy of a military and intelligence apparatus with vaguely defined powers and largely unfettered by civilian oversight. Under the law, ultimate power over military and intelligence operations lay with the national security adviser and, ultimately, the president.[61]

The National Security Agencies Act does not specify that the president must obtain approval from the National Assembly in directing the activities of the intelligence services. The only exception is the DSS, the main agency for domestic intelligence. The act states the National Assembly can assign other responsibilities outside of the DSS's legal duties regarding internal security. However, there is little evidence of any such actions being taken by the National Assembly after 1999, with the president enjoying de facto unlimited powers to direct the DSS, DIA, and NIA in carrying out internal and external operations.[62]

As a result of the continued legal framework, the intelligence services have the same limited civilian oversight in carrying out their operations as they possessed under military rule. This poses a significant danger to the stability and legitimacy of the current government, particularly as the state is embroiled in violent conflicts against ethno-political and religious insurgent groups, such as Boko Haram. In the course of counterinsurgency operations, the DSS has been accused of human rights abuses, including illegal arrests and detention of individuals beyond the legally mandated time period.[63]

ROLE OF THE NATIONAL ASSEMBLY

There is little, if any, tradition of civilian oversight of Nigeria's security and intelligence services.[64] Ideally major policy decisions concerning intelligence budgets, operational structure, missions, and weapons procurements would be closely monitored by the National Assembly. Top civilian appointees such as the national security adviser and director general, State Services (DGDSS), are also expected to appear before legislative committees in order to explain and defend intelligence policy initiatives and other issues such as alleged human rights violations. Yet, the National Security Agencies Act does not clearly specify that the National Assembly has oversight functions over the intelligence services. Rather, it allows the DIA and NIA to be assigned additional responsibilities of a military nature both within and outside Nigeria by the president, National Defence Council, or the chief of defence staff. Only the Department of State Services (DSS) falls under the direct control of the National Assembly.[65]

Another issue hindering legislative oversight of the intelligence services is extra-budgetary spending funds allocated to the intelligence services directly by the president or state governors. These funds are provided under "security votes" for certain federal, state, and local government officials to spend on security-related expenses. This allocation is not subject to any established budgetary review process, making audits nearly impossible. Additionally, contracts awarded using these funds are exempt from key provisions of the Public Procurement Act, meaning that contract tenders do not need to be publicly advertised and can be awarded at an individual's discretion.[66] Consequently, security votes have become synonymous with political corruption in Nigeria.[67]

COORDINATION OF THE INTELLIGENCE SERVICES

Though the law provides the national security adviser, principal officer within the Office of the President, with the authority to coordinate intelligence services' activities, in practice, the heads of the individual services have considerable autonomy in the use of monetary allocations and operational and technical operations. This autonomy has limited the role of the national security adviser to effectively coordinate intelligence. One might expect that the core of intelligence expertise would be the Office of the National Security Adviser, involving extensive participation of professional civil servants, academics, and civil society.[68] Yet, that is not the case in Nigeria.

There are currently several multiagencies engaged in intelligence gathering outside of the DSS, NIA, and DIA. This is partly as a consequence of the evolving challenges of the information technology age and the continuous multiethnic/multireligious conflicts that have forced traditional security agencies to create or enhance intelligence units for greater mission effectiveness. Agencies, such as the Nigerian military—primarily in counterintelligence activities in the northeast—and the Nigeria Police Force, have intelligence units that are used in their internal security operations.[69]

Along with the limitations of the national security adviser's office, there is a culture among the services, particularly the military, that makes it believe the military is superior to other intelligence and security services. This has created an unhealthy rivalry, as each service attempts to surpass others in their operations and justify their relevance and especially budgetary allocation, which have increased significantly since the escalation of the crises in the northeast. Perhaps, the most obvious lapse in the intelligence framework is the duplication of roles among the services. For example, while the DSS statutory mandate covers all aspects of domestic intelligence, the police have a similar unit, Force Intelligence Bureau (FIB), whose role covers national intelligence gathering and dissemination among the various police formations.[70]

The United Kingdom's Department for International Development, for example, lists principles that countries with decades of authoritarianism might adopt to assure democratic control of its security apparatus.[71] Expectedly, it states that there should be policy that provides for significant level of coordination between the Office of the National Security Adviser, the national and intelligence services, civil society, and civilian intelligence experts. Others are summarized as follows:

- Establish security sector organizations within security forces accountable to both elected civil authorities and the public at large.
- Mandate that these organizations operate in accordance with the international law and domestic constitutional law.
- Make information about security sector planning and budgeting widely available, both within the government and to the public at large.
- Adopt a comprehensive and disciplined approach to the management of defense resources wherein the public is regularly consulted on matters of security policy, resource allocation, and other relevant issues.

- Enquire that security personnel are adequately trained to discharge their duties in a professional manner consistent with the requirements of democratic societies.[72]

Yet, none of the security principles specified have been implemented within Nigeria's intelligence and security sector.

THE RISE IN ETHNIC AND ETHNO-RELIGIOUS CONFLICT

One of the striking features of Nigeria since the start of civilian rule in 1999 has been the emergence of violent ethno-political and religious militant groups throughout the country. These groups have been responsible for a rise in violent conflict and are key to understanding why authoritarian practices continue to persist within Nigeria's intelligence and security services.[73] While each militant group is currently active within the country, they have unique motivations and can be broadly characterized into three main categories:

- Groups that seek to preserve, expand, and consolidate their political power.
- Ethnically based associations who demand changes in governmental revenue allocation based on ethnic identity.
- Religiously inspired groups seeking to reform government according to religious doctrine.

The groups seeking to preserve, expand, or consolidate the political power of their ethnic group are the oldest such group in Nigeria. These originated as sociocultural associations in the 1940s and 1950s, which gradually evolved into full-fledged political parties. Their main objective is ensuring the ethnic group represented is not politically or socially marginalized at the federal level. Even though these groups are known for making inflammatory ethnic/ethno-religious remarks, their leaders normally do not have any confrontation with the DSS. However, it is logical to assume that these groups' activities are covertly monitored by the DSS. Examples of contemporary ethnic associations include the Igbo's Ohaneze Ndigbo, the Yoruba's Oduduwa People's Congress (OPC) and the Hausa-Fulani Arewa Consultative Forum (ACF).[74]

Other associations use ethnicity as a rallying point to demand changes in federal revenue allocation. These groups argue that geographical areas that have abundant natural resources and generate significant foreign exchange for the country should benefit from the royalties and taxes paid by extractive companies. The best known organization in this category includes the Niger Delta Avengers (NDA), Movement for the Emancipation of the Niger Delta

(MEND), and Niger Delta People Volunteer Force (NDPVF) which operate in the Niger Delta area of Nigeria.[75] These groups often employ violent tactics, and on several occasions, their leaders have been arrested or investigated by the DSS and other security agencies for violent acts, such as attacking and sabotaging oil infrastructure (pipelines, pumping stations, wells, and transport vessels) and engaging in fuel theft ("oil bunkering").[76] The vandalism is intended to place pressure on the federal government, Western countries, and multinational corporations—that depend on Nigeria's crude oil and gas—to effect changes to the country's resource-extraction policy, but the main effect has been the federal government paying financial settlements to the action groups. Ultimately, those settlements largely do not benefit the people these groups claim to protect from exploitation.[77]

The final category is religiously inspired groups. They believe that the current secular political system has failed to provide accountable leadership and good governance, arguing the only alternative is Sharia or Islamic religious law. Significantly, groups advocating for the implementation of Sharia law in Nigeria is not a new phenomenon. These groups have continually been under surveillance by intelligence and security services. The first notable group with such an agenda was Maitatsine, founded by Muhammadu Marwa in 1962. Marwa preached against those who owned products of modernity such as television, radio, wristwatches, cars, and bicycles and believed that any Muslim who read books other than the Quran was an infidel who should be killed or converted to Marwa's brand of Islam.[78] Marwa and many followers were killed by security forces in 1980 following religious riots in Kano. Yet his teachings served to inspire subsequent militant groups such as Boko Haram, whose name roughly translates to "Western values are sin." Boko Haram's primary goal is to undermine the current Nigerian government to establish an Islamic state.[79]

The main agency in-charge of domestic intelligence is the DSS, but since 1999, the agency has been largely unable to adequately respond to the rise of violent ethno-political and religious groups within the country.[80] Broad and ambiguous laws have led to numerous lapses and duplications in duties among the intelligence and security services. It is generally assumed, based on how prior military regimes employed the DSS that the service has the same powers as the Nigeria Police to arrest, search, detain, and interrogate individuals.[81] Yet, unlike the police, the DSS is not subject to any constitutionally mandated limits as to, for example, how long an individual can be detained without trial, and this lack of operational restrictions has enabled numerous human rights abuses.[82]

There are several significant examples of the DSS disregarding court rulings on individuals perceived as state security threats since 1999. Among the most notable of such cases is that of former national security adviser Sambo

Dasuki, who was arrested in November 2015 on corruption charges. Sambo was eventually released in December 2019 despite four different high court judges having granted him bail a full year earlier.[83] Similarly, African Action Congress (AAC) founder Omoyele Sowore was arrested by the DSS in 2019 agitating for revolution following that year's general election, which was won by incumbent President Muhammadu Buhari. On September 24, 2019, Sowore was granted bail by the federal high court in Abuja, but the DSS refused to release him from custody. It was not until December 24, 2019, following significant public outcry and another court ruling that Sowore was released.[84] Moreover, the leader of the Shi'a-inspired Islamic group, Islamic Movement in Nigeria (IMN), Sheikh Ibrahim Zakzaky, has remained in DSS custody with his wife, Ibraheemat since 2015, despite numerous court orders for their release. IMN's objective is to establish a Shi'a-inspired Islamic state in Nigeria modeled after the Islamic Republic of Iran. In December 2015, the IMN engaged the Nigerian military in a large-scale violent confrontation that led to the incarceration of Zakzaky on terrorism-related charges.[85]

In the light of these ongoing security crises, this chapter acknowledges that establishing perfect transparency and accountability between intelligence services and the civilian government is impossible on account of the sensitive operations involved in counterinsurgency work. Even the intelligence services of fully mature liberal democracies are not completely transparent to their governments, especially when dealing with ongoing hostile adversaries.[86] Nonetheless, most of the countries with stabilize democracies have some form of civilian oversight over its intelligence and security services. Nigeria has no such checks and balances. Furthermore, the intelligence and security frameworks of mature democracies were established to advance the rule of law, national strategic interests, and the cause of constitutional order. It was not to consolidate a ruling party's power as was the case in Nigeria. Consequently, the lack of accountability and transparency in Nigeria's security and intelligence apparatus poses a significant threat to the survival of democratic principles and institutions in the country.

CONCLUSION

The history of Nigeria's intelligence and security services framework highlights several broad aspects about the country, the role of colonialism in establishing the services and how military rule influences the current formation of the services. Most significantly, Nigeria's intelligence has typically served those in power, whether under colonial, military, or civilian rule. Indeed, Nigerian intelligence has been largely shaped by the impact of "institutional prerogatives" in which the contemporary legal framework they operate in is from an earlier period when successive leaders acted with impunity and used intelligence as a weapon against opponents. The preservation of the intelligence administrative structure after the end of military rule in 1999 has left the security and intelligence apparatus with broadly defined powers operating virtually free of civilian oversight, whose operations can be directed with impunity by the president. This allowed Nigeria's intelligence services—particularly the DSS—to commit numerous human rights abuses over the past twenty years.

This chapter highlighted four major issues surrounding "institutional prerogatives" that still shape Nigeria's intelligence community. First, it demonstrated how the legal framework that established the current intelligence services prerogatives—the National Security Agencies Act—emanated from a military decree and was entrenched in the 1999 constitution. This act can only be repealed by support of two-thirds of the federal and state legislative houses. Second, the chapter highlighted how post-military rule failed to provide adequate intelligence services' missions and frameworks that would operate within the polity with civilian oversight. Third, it explained how the act minimized legislative oversight of the intelligence services, particularly investigating internal security operations and monitoring funds. Last, the chapter explained how there is limited interagency intelligence coordination as the statutory coordinator of intelligence services—the national security adviser—lacks a meaningful role. Indeed, the intelligence services heads have significant autonomy in their internal operations with meaningful oversight from the national security adviser. For Nigeria's democracy to survive, it is imperative that measures be enacted to ensure proper transparency and civilian intelligence oversight. Without such robust measures, Nigeria's intelligence and security apparatus will likely be unable to effectively cope with the various internal security challenges faced by the nation.

NOTES

1. Adewale Ademoyega, *Why We Struck, the Story of the First Nigerian Coup* (Ibadan: Evans Brothers, 1981); D. J. M Muffett, *Let Truth Be Told: The Coups d'etat of Nineteen Sixty-Six* (Zaria: Hudahuda Pub. Co, 1982).

2. The successful coups happened on January 15, 1966; July 29, 1966; July 29, 1975; December 31, 1983; August 27, 1985; and November 17, 1993. In contrast, there were four unsuccessful coups, including in February 1976, which lead to the assassination of the then head of state, Murtala Muhammed. Two attempts were made on Ibrahim Babangida in December 1985 and April 1990. The two attempts against Sani Abacha in 1995 and 1997 are still very controversial. Abacha's second-in-command, Oladipo Diya, was arrested for the 1997 attempted coup and claimed that the allegations brought against him and other officers was a setup. See: Abraham

Useh, "Nigeria Held Hostage: Abacha's Years of Terror," *Tell,* November 20, 1995; Chris Anyanwu, *The Days of Terror* (Ibadan: Spectrum Books Limited, 2002); Dare Babarinsa et al., "The Day After, Death of Coup Plotters," *Newswatch Magazine,* August 3, 1990; S.K Panter-Brick, ed. *Soldiers and Oil; the Political Transformation of Nigeria* (London: Frank Cass, 1978).

3. The November 1993 "palace coup" by General Sani Abacha was against the Interim National Government (ING) of Ernest Shonekan, a body to which the regime of Babangida handed over power after eight years of military rule. This happened after the regime annulled the June 12, 1993 presidential election that was presumably won by Moshood Abiola. Larry Diamond, *Class, Ethnicity, and Democracy in Nigeria: The Failure of the First Republic* (Syracuse: Syracuse University Press, 1988); Ademoyega; Larry Diamond, "Nigeria in Search of Democracy," *Foreign Affairs* 62, no. 4 (1984); Max Siollun, *Soldiers of Fortune, Nigerian Politics from Buhari to Babangida 1983–1993* (Abuja: Cassava Republic Press, 2013).

4. Adam Przeworski, *Democracy and the Market: Political and Economic Reforms in Eastern Europe and Latin America* (Cambridge: Cambridge University Press, 1991), 14.

5. Adam Przeworski, Michael Alvarez, and Jose Antonio Cheibub, eds., *Democracy and Development: Political Institutions and Well-Being in the World, 1950–1990* (Cambridge: Cambridge University Press, 2000).

6. Joel S. Migdal, *Strong Societies and Weak States: State-Society Relations and State Capabilities in the Third World* (Princeton, NJ: Princeton University Press, 1988).

7. Walter Rodney, *How Europe Underdeveloped Africa* (London: Bogle-L'Ouverture Publications, 1972).

8. Migdal.

9. The Sultan of Sokoto is the supreme traditional leader of the Sokoto Caliphate in present-day Nigeria. The sultan is often regarded as the "Amir ul-Momineen" translated to mean the commander of the faithful or the leader of the faithful in Nigeria; See: Elizabeth Isichei, *A History of Nigeria* (Essex: Longman Group Limited, 1983); Mahmood Mamdani, *Citizen and Subject: Contemporary Africa and the Legacy of Late Colonialism* (Princeton: Princeton University Press, 1996); Toyin Falola, *Colonialism and Violence in Nigeria* (Bloomington: Indiana University Press, 2009).

10. James Wunsch and Dele Olowu, eds., *The Failure of the Centralized State: Institutions and Self-Governance in Africa* (San Francisco: ICS Press, 1995).

11. Philip Mawhood, ed. *Local Government for Development: The Experience of Tropical Africa* (Chichester: John Wiley, 1983).

12. See: Human Rights Watch, "Nigeria Events of 2019," 2020. https://www.hrw.org/world-report/2020/country-chapters/nigeria; Amnesty International, "Nigeria 2019," 2020. https://www.amnesty.org/en/countries/africa/nigeria/report-nigeria/.

13. For more on document analysis technique, see: John W. Creswell, *Research Design, Qualitative, Quantitative, and Mixed Methods Approaches*, 2nd ed. (Thousand Oaks: Sage Publications, 2003).

14. For history of the Nigerian military, see: Norman J. Miners, *The Nigerian Army 1956–1966* (Suffolk: Methuen and Co Ltd, 1971); C.N Ubah, *Colonial Army*

and Society in Northern Nigeria (Kaduna: Baraka Press and Publishers Limited, 1998); H.B Momoh, "Evolution of the Nigerian Armed Forces," in *Nigeria; A People United, a Future Assured Volume 1 a Compendium*, eds. H. I. Ajaegbu, B. J. St. Matthew-Daniel, and O. E. Uya (Calabar: Federal Ministry of Information, 2000).

15. See: I. James, "Security Agencies and Paramilitary Organizations," in *Nigeria: A People United, a Future Assured, Volume 1*, eds. H. I. Ajaegbu, St. Matthew-Daniel B. J., and O. E. Uya (Calabar: Federal Ministry of Information, 2000); Momoh, in *Nigeria; a People United, a Future Assured Volume 1 a Compendium*.

16. Charles Joseph Jeffries, *The Colonial Police* (London: Max Parrish, 1952).

17. James, in *Nigeria: A People United, a Future Assured, Volume 1*.

18. Ibid.

19. Jeffries.

20. Georgina Sinclair, " 'Hard-Headed, Hard-Bitten, Hard-Hitting and Courageous Men of Innate Detective Ability. . . ' From Criminal Investigation to Political and Security Policing at the End of Empire, 1945–50," in *Police Detectives in History, 1750–1950*, eds. Clive Emsley and Haia Shpayer-Makov (Abingdon Oxon: Routledge, 2006).

21. Ibid.

22. Ibid.

23. At the trial of Chief Obafemi Awolowo in 1962 an Irishman John O'Sullivan headed the Special Branch and was a key prosecution witness in Awolowo's trial. Another Irishman John Lynn was the head of the Criminal Investigation Department, CID.

24. Diamond, *Class, Ethnicity, and Democracy in Nigeria: The Failure of the First Republic*.

25. Ruth First, *The Barrel of a Gun, Political Power in Africa and the Coup d'etat* (London: Penguin Books Ltd, 1970).

26. Ademoyega.

27. Panter-Brick.

28. Max Siollun, *Oil, Politics and Violence: Nigeria's Military Coup Culture (1966–1976)* (New York: Algora Publishing, 2009).

29. See: Federal Republic of Nigeria: National Security Agencies Decree 1986. Decree No. 19-In: Supplement to Official Gazatte Extraordinary No. 38, Vol. 73, August 5, 1986, Part A, pp. A 111–14. Jimi Peters, "Nigeria's Intelligence System: An Analysis," *African Spectrum* 22, no. 2 (1987): 184.

30. Basil Ugochukwu, "The State Security Service and Human Rights in Nigeria," *Third World Legal Studies* 14 (1997): 73–74.

31. Siollun, *Oil, Politics and Violence: Nigeria's Military Coup Culture (1966–1976)*.

32. David Ashaolu, "Solving Security Challenges in Nigeria through Intelligence Gathering and Surveillance," Social Science Research Network, 2013. http://papers. ssrn.com/sol3/papers.cfm?abstract_id=2275986.

33. Ugochukwu.

34. Larry Diamond, "Nigeria Update," *Foreign Affairs* 64, no. 2 (1985).

35. Peters.

36. They are: Directorate of Operations, Directorate of Intelligence, Directorate of Security Enforcement (DSE), Directorate of Administration and Finance (DAF), Directorate of Technical Services (DTS), Directorate of Inspectorate (DINSP), Directorate of Training and Staff Development (DTSD), and Directorate of Economic Intelligence (DEI), and four strategic departments: The Base Command Lagos (BCL), National Assembly Liaison (NAL), Simulation and Crisis Management Centre (SCMC), and Independent National Electoral Commission Liaison (INECL).

37. Muyiwa B. Afolabi, "Nigeria's Major Internal Security Agencies and Their Statutory Roles," in *Unending Frontiers in Intelligence and Security Studies*, ed. Uju Edekobi (Ado-Ekiti: Intelligence and Security Studies Programme, Afe Babalola University, Ado-Ekiti, 2017).

38. Peters, 187–88. It should be noted that the original wording of the decree stated chairman, joint chiefs of staff; however, since that position was abolished under military rule, this responsibility is charged with the chief of defence staff.

39. Ibid., 188.

40. Ibid.

41. Nigerian Law Intellectual Property Watch Inc, "National Security Agencies Act," 2020. https://nlipw.com/national-security-agencies-act/.

42. Ndaeyo Uko, *Romancing the Gun: The Press as a Promoter of Military Rule* (Trenton, NJ: Africa World Press, 2004); Uduma Kalu, "Dele Giwa: Fond Memories for First Nigerian Letter Bomb Victim," *Vanguard Newspaper Nigeria*, October 22, 2011. https://www.vanguardngr.com/2011/10/dele-giwa-fond-memories-for-first-nigerian-letter-bomb-victim/.

43. Ugochukwu, 89.

44. Larry Diamond, Anthony Kirk-Greene, and Oyeleye Oyediran, eds., *Transition without End: Nigerian Politics and Civil Society under Babangida* (Boulder, CO: Lynne Rienner Publishers, 1997); Ugochukwu.

45. Ugochukwu.

46. Patrick Wilmot is originally from Jamaica and lectured at Ahmadu Bello University Zaria from 1970 to 1988.

47. See: "Prof Patrick Wilmot: The Abu Lecturer Deported by the Ibb Regime," TheAbusites, September 24, 2019. https://www.theabusites.com/patrick-wilmot-the-radical-abu-lecturer/; Ugochukwu.

48. Useh.

49. Wale Adebanwi, "The Radical Press and Security Agencies in Nigeria: Beyond Hegemonic Polarities," *African Studies Review* 54, no. 3 (2011): 45–69.

50. Uko, 196.

51. Ibid., 195–96.

52. Siollun, *Oil, Politics and Violence: Nigeria's Military Coup Culture (1966–1976)*.

53. Babarinsa et al.

54. The killing of Ken Saro-Wiwa and nine other Ogoni leaders significantly changed the dynamics of the Niger Delta and led to the creation of violent militant groups that continue to agitate for greater proceeds of the sale of crude oil to the region. See: Ed Pilkington, "Shell Pays out $15.5m over Saro-Wiwa Killing," *The*

Guardian, June 8, 2009. http://www.guardian.co.uk/world/2009/jun/08/nigeria-usa; Temitope Oriola, *Criminal Resistance? The Politics of Kidnapping Oil Workers* (Farnham: Ashgate, 2013); Mikail Mumuni, "Blood for Blood," *Tell Magazine (Nigeria)*, November 20, 1995.

55. Alfred Stepan, *Rethinking Military Politics, Brazil and the Southern Cone* (NJ: Princeton University Press, 1988).

56. Ibid.

57. Ibid.; Alfred Stepan, ed. *Democracies in Danger* (Baltimore: Johns Hopkins University Press, 2009).

58. Rollin F Tusalem, "Bringing the Military Back In: The Politicisation of the Military and Its Effect on Democratic Consolidation," *International Political Science Review* 34, no. 4 (2014): 482–501.

59. The 1995 constitutional conference that produced a draft constitution was a political farce. As General Abacha had no plans of relinquishing political power; rather, he had plans of succeeding himself.

60. Kayode J. Fayemi, "Entrenched Militarism and the Future of Democracy in Nigeria," in *Political Armies; the Military and Nation Building in the Age of Democracy*, eds. Kees Koonings and Dirk Kruijt (London: Zed Books, 2002).

61. Ibid.; Olusola Ojo, *The Nigerian Military: An Obstacle to Enduring Democracy?* (Jerusalem, Israel: The Harry S. Truman Research Institute for the Advancement of Peace, The Hebrew University of Jerusalem, 2000); Emmanuel Ojo, "The Military and Political Transitions," in *Nigeria's Struggle for Democracy and Good Governance*, eds. Adigun Agbaje, Larry Diamond, and Ebere Onwudiwe (Ibadan: Ibadan University Press, 2004).

62. Pita Ogaba Agbese, "Democratic and Constitutional Control of the Military in Africa," in *The Military and Politics in Africa, from Engagement to Democratic and Constitutional Control*, ed. George Klay Kieh and Pita Ogaba Agbese (Aldershot: Ashgate Publishing Limited, 2004).

63. Human Rights Watch, 2020.

64. Joseph Yinka Fashagba, "Legislative Oversight under the Nigerian Presidential System," *Journal of Legislative Studies* 15, no. 4 (2009): 439–59.

65. Nigerian Law Intellectual Property Watch Inc.

66. Matthew T. Page, *Camouflaged Cash, How 'Security Votes' Fuel Corruption in Nigeria* (Transparency International, 2018). https://ti-defence.org/wp-content/uploads/2018/05/DSP_Nigeria_Camouflage_Cash_Web2.pdf.

67. Ibid.

68. See Ashaolu; W. Omitoogun and Eboe Hutchful, eds., *Budgeting for the Military Sector in Africa, the Processes and Mechanisms of Control* (Oxford: Oxford University Press, 2006).

69. See: Eboe Hutchful, "Bringing the Military and Security Agencies under Democratic Control: A Challenge to African Constitutionalism," in *Constitutionalism and Society in Africa*, ed. Okon Akiba (Aldershot: Ashgate Publishing Limited, 2004); Narcis Serra, "Beyond the Threats to Democracy from the Armed Forces, Police, and Intelligence," in *Democracies in Danger*, ed. Alfred Stepan (Baltimore: The Johns Hopkins University Press, 2009).

70. Simon Gray and Ibikunle Adeakin, "The Evolution of Boko Haram: From Missionary Activism to Transnational Jihad and the Failure of the Nigerian Security Intelligence Agencies," *African Security* 8, no. 3 (2015): 185–211.

71. DFID, *Security Sector Reform and the Management of Military Expenditure: High Risks for Donors, High Returns for Development* (London: Department for International Development, 2000).

72. Ibid.

73. J. N. C Hill, *Nigeria since Independence, Forever Fragile?* (Hampshire: Palgrave Macmillan, 2012).

74. John Campbell, *Nigeria, Dancing on the Brink* (Lanham: Rowman & Littlefield Publishers Inc, 2011).

75. Temitope B. Oriola and Ibikunle Adeakin, "The Framing Strategies of the Niger Delta Avengers," in *The Unfinished Revolution in Nigeria's Niger Delta Prospects for Environmental Justice and Peace*, ed. Cyril Obi and Temitope B. Oriola (New York: Routledge, 2018).

76. Oriola.

77. Michael Peel, *A Swamp Full of Dollars, Pipelines and Paramilitaries at Nigeria's Oil Frontier* (Chicago: Lawrence Hill Books, 2010).

78. Elizabeth Isichei, "The Maitatsine Risings in Nigeria 1980–85: A Revolt of the Disinherited," *Journal of Religion in Africa* 17, no. 3 (1987): 194–208.

79. Gray and Adeakin.

80. Ibid.

81. Peters.

82. Ibikunle Adeakin, "The Military and Human Rights Violations in Post-1999 Nigeria: Assessing the Problems and Prospects of Effective Internal Enforcement in an Era of Insecurity," *African Security Review* 25, no. 2 (2016): 129–45.

83. Human Rights Watch, "Nigeria Events of 2018," 2019. https://www.hrw.org/world-report/2019/country-chapters/nigeria.

84. "Nigeria Releases Sowore and Dasuki after Ag Orders Bail," Reuters, December 24, 2019. https://www.reuters.com/article/us-nigeria-politics/nigeria-orders-release-of-sowore-and-dasuki-after-court-orders-attorney-general-idUSKB-N1YS14V.

85. Simon Gray and Ibikunle Adeakin, "Nigeria's Shi'a Islamic Movement and Evolving Islamist Threat Landscape: Old, New and Future Generators of Radicalization," *African Security* 12, no. 2 (2019): 174–199.

86. Florina Cristiana Matei and Carolyn Halladay, "The Role and Purpose of Intelligence in a Democracy, " in *The Conduct of Intelligence in Democracies: Processes, Practices, Cultures*, ed. Florina Cristiana Matei and Carolyn Halladay (Boulder, CO: Lynne Rienner Publishers, 2019).

Chapter 11

Meeting the Needs of the State: Intelligence, Security, and Police Legal Frameworks in East Africa

Christopher E. Bailey

The existing national-level intelligence, security, and police services in East Africa play significant roles in maintaining regional peace and security.[1] This chapter provides a comparative legal analysis of the roles and authorities of the intelligence, security, and police services in Kenya, Uganda, and Tanzania. It highlights the strengths and weaknesses of each service in combating a range of national security threats, with attention to efforts at increasing the legal accountability of public officials and compliance with human rights law. The chapter argues that the East African states generally have legally sound structures for the administration of the intelligence, security, and police services and an evolving institutional capacity to face certain serious transnational threats, such as al-Shabaab extremists and long-standing ethnic tensions. In practice, however, the regional intelligence, security, and police services operate with varying levels of legal regulation and accountability.

This chapter has three sections and is organized by country. This chapter provides a comparative legal analysis on the regional intelligence, security, and police services. Specifically, it examines the national-level constitutional and statutory law with an emphasis on legal accountability and institutional legitimacy in a political and social context. The first part explores Kenyan law on its intelligence, security, and police forces, showing a marked improvement in oversight structures—but with notable shortcomings—over the last twenty years. Next, Uganda law is reviewed by focusing on security and police forces, demonstrating an uneven application of the rule of law and significant human rights abuses. Last, Tanzanian law is analyzed, finding that the police force has a sound legal structure but has problems with institutional capacity that undermines its public legitimacy. The conclusion highlights the similarities and differences between the countries, describing challenges in legal accountability and shortcomings in institutional capacity.

SECURITY AND POLICE FORCES IN KENYA

Kenya enacted a 2010 constitution, as well as a new statutory law, that provides for reformed intelligence, security, and police services. Both Kenya's National Intelligence Service (NIS) and the National Police Service are established under the 2010 constitution and subsequently implemented legislation. Both the NIS and the National Police Service are executive branch organizations with specified functions and authorities operating under presidential control, but with a strong legal structure for parliamentary and judicial oversight. The changes provide an important starting point for overcoming a legacy of politicized intelligence (i.e., favoring the Kikuyu ethnic group over others), corruption in government, and abusive police practices that has supported regime security.[2] In part, Kenya's post-9/11 experience in combating terrorism indicates that the NIS and the National Police Service have continuing shortcomings in capacity and respect for international human rights law that undermine institutional legitimacy.

In August 2010, after multiple failed attempts at constitutional reform over a twenty-year period, the Kenyan people approved a new constitution—the first major reform since the 1963 "independence" (Lancaster) constitution and the December 1964 amendment that created a presidential form of government.[3] The 2010 constitution recognizes a three-part national structure involving a parliament, a national executive, and a judiciary as well as "devolved" structures at the county level that include legislative assemblies and executive structures. This new structure created an institutionalized system of checks and balances with limitations on presidential power, a bicameral parliament with oversight authority over the executive branch, increased autonomy at the regional level, and a judicially enforceable Bill of Rights.

In general terms, the 2010 constitution is a marked improvement in the structures, processes, and authorities necessary for the administration of justice in Kenya. In fact, the changes in constitutional and statutory law provide an important starting point in overcoming a legacy of government corruption (i.e., the 1991–1993 Goldenberg scandal involving senior government officials in a scam led by the newly retired intelligence chief), and the heavy-handed use of security and police forces.[4] First, the 2010 constitution provides for an independent judiciary, one that is "subject only to this Constitution and the law and shall not be subject to the control or direction of any person or authority."[5] Second, the 2010 constitution contains several important national security provisions, outlining certain important principles, defining organs and structures, and establishing the defense forces, the NIS and the National Police Service. Article 58, combined with Article 132(4) (d), gives the president the limited authority to declare a state of emergency only when "(a) the State is threatened by war, invasion, general insurrection, disorder, natural disaster or other public emergency; and (b) the declaration is necessary to meet the circumstances for which the emergency is declared."[6] A presidential declaration can be prospective only and is valid for fourteen days unless extended by the parliament.

Kenya's first statutory security service—the National Security Intelligence Service (NSIS)—was established by the parliament in 1998, replacing the earlier Directorate of Security Intelligence, better known as Special Branch (see Shaffer in this volume).[7] Subsequently, with the sweeping changes in the 2010 constitution, the NSIS was replaced by the NIS as a "disciplined civilian service" under a new 2012 statute with a civilian director general who is appointed by the president and confirmed by the parliament.[8] This 2012 statute is comprehensive, establishing an effective framework for accountability and, where possible, public transparency. The director general is responsible for the overall management and administration, as well as operational control, of the intelligence service. The director general reports to the president, the National Security Council, and the cabinet secretary on threats to Kenyan national security. The parliament has, however, explicitly retained oversight authority over the service and has also provided for an Intelligence Service Complaints Board that can receive, investigate, and make recommendations on complaints against the service or any of its members.[9] The statute provides that the public's right of access to information, as set out in the 2010 constitution, is limited in respect to classified information and that the cabinet secretary may issue security classification regulations.[10] The statute also criminalizes the unauthorized disclosure of the identity of a confidential source as well as the unauthorized disclosure of information.

The NIS is responsible for security intelligence, counterintelligence, and a range of other assigned functions.[11] The service has internal divisions responsible for domestic intelligence, external intelligence, and counterintelligence. However, it is precluded by statute from carrying out police functions or paramilitary activities, from committing violence against a person (i.e., torture or other cruel treatment), or from undertaking any activity that furthers the interests of a political party.[12] The service also lacks the power of arrest, but the director general, where "reasonable grounds to believe that a warrant . . . is required to enable the service to investigate any threat to national security or to perform any of its functions," can apply to the high court for a warrant.[13] This warrant can be used

(a) to enter any place, or obtain access to anything; (b) to search for or remove or return, examine, take extracts from, make copies of or record in any other manner the information, material, record, document or thing; (c) to monitor communication; or (d) to install, maintain or remove anything.[14]

Kenya has also made important efforts over the past fifteen years to reform its police services and practices.[15] Currently, the 2010 constitution provides that the National Police Service, including both the Kenya Police Service and the Administration Police Service, is supervised by an independent inspector general who holds office through a presidential appointment.[16] The inspector general has authority over the investigation of crime, enforcement of the law, and personnel management involving the National Police Service.[17] Article 246 established the National Police Service Commission, which is responsible for recruiting and appointing senior police officials, reviewing all matters of compensation and service, exercising disciplinary control, entering into performance contracts with senior officers, and liaising with oversight authorities with respect to complaints made against the police.[18]

The Kenyan Parliament subsequently passed two important statutes aimed at police reform. First, the 2011 National Police Service Act lays out the general roles, responsibilities, and authorities of police officials at all levels, to include disciplinary processes and procedures for offenses by officers.[19] The act also places the previously existing Criminal Investigation Directorate (CID) on a statutory basis, which is led by a presidentially appointed director, responsible for the collection of criminal intelligence and the investigation of serious crimes such as homicide, human trafficking, money laundering, terrorism, economic crimes, and organized crime.[20] Second, the 2011 Independent Policing Oversight Act provides civilian oversight of the police with an Independent Policing Oversight Authority (IPOA) conducting independent investigations, inspections, audits, and monitoring of the National Police Service, thus aiming to increase police accountability, enhance professionalism, and provide for independent oversight involving complaints against the service.[21] In general, the recent police reform efforts demonstrate that considerable effort has been devoted to changing the culture of the Kenya Police Service from an instrument of the ruling regime, largely through changes in legal structures, to an effective community-oriented service that would be accountable to the Kenyan people. In practice, however, Kenya still experiences considerable ethnic violence, the use of security and police forces to repress political and ethnic opponents during presidential elections, and widespread corruption involving public officials. Indeed, Amnesty International and Human Rights Watch report that the IPOA has not been effective in investigating cases about allegations of police misconduct.[22]

Nonetheless, the Kenya Police, including the specially formed Anti-Terrorism Police Unit (ATPU) and the paramilitary General Service Unit (GSU), have been used to combat a range of terrorist threats and repress ethnic violence—but often operating outside the law.[23] Both the ATPU and the GSU are apparently subordinate to the Kenya Police, but neither of these specially equipped organizations has been formally established by law. This raises issues involving parliamentary oversight and the legal accountability of police officials for human rights abuses.[24] In one 2008 case, for example, the High Court considered a claim of extraordinary rendition made by eleven petitioners—including eight Kenyan and three Tanzanian citizens—who had been unlawfully sent by the ATPU to Somalia and Ethiopia where they had been tortured.[25] The petitioners claimed that they were refugees from the civil war in Somalia.[26] The government agreed that all had been deported—without any judicial process—as threats to national security, but claimed that none of the accused produced identification documents or other proof that they were lawfully present in Kenya.[27] The High Court held that the arrest, detention, and removal of the petitioners violated their constitutional rights to due process and freedom from torture. The court explained that the

> state could not cite national security concerns to justify its acts, particularly at this point in time when the Constitution of Kenya 2010 clearly spells out at Article 25 that the right not to be subjected to torture and other cruel and degrading treatment cannot be derogated from.[28]

The High Court then made global awards of compensatory damages to the petitioners.

The transnational threats emanating from Somalia extend beyond terrorist attacks by al-Shabaab and its supporters to a wide range of criminal activity that can be used to finance regional terrorist operations. According to a 2011 study by the International Peace Institute (IPI), there are six types of transnational crime present in Kenya: drug trafficking, trade in counterfeit goods, trade in wildlife products, human trafficking, small arms trafficking, and money laundering.[29] The IPI reported that Somali militia groups have been involved in the trafficking of drugs, wildlife products, sugar, humans for prostitution and slavery, and small arms, with the laundered funds sometimes ending up with al-Shabaab.[30] This report also described the widespread corruption within Kenya, particularly in the Kenya Police, the Registrar of Persons, the judiciary, the Kenya Ports Authority, and the Department of Immigration.[31]

The transnational threat posed by al-Shabaab presents the government with important legal problems. Initially, to the extent that the Kenya Defence Forces (KDF) are operating on Somali soil in support of the current government in Mogadishu against an organized armed group (al-Shabaab), the KDF would be bound by international humanitarian and Kenyan military law in conducting its operations.[32] Yet, with respect to the spate of terrorist attacks and related criminal activity in Kenya, the government would likely be bound to apply the full protections of international human rights law and Kenyan domestic law—absent a declaration of a state of emergency by the

Kenyan president.[33] For crimes committed in Kenya, the government would be obligated to investigate and prosecute terrorism offenses committed by al-Shabaab and its supporters under its domestic criminal law.

Another national security threat to Kenya involves the use of its territory as a recruiting, training, and financial support base for Kenyan nationals and foreign fighters, who are typically ethnic Somali and Islamist in orientation and who support al-Shabaab. The organization has been effective at recruiting Somali-Kenyans and Muslim foreign fighters and garnering financial support in the region, often through radical clerics in Eastleigh mosques, using its key regional affiliate al-Hijra with its extensive ethnic connections in Kenya, and through recruitment videos that are prepared in both English and Swahili and released over the internet.[34] Al-Hijra, with active branch offices throughout Kenya and Somalia, has emerged as al-Shabaab's "most important regional ally," by hosting events, issuing publications, and maintaining an active Twitter account and website.[35]

The ATPU has led the counterterrorism effort against al-Hijra.[36] However, there have been numerous reports of human rights abuses made against the ATPU by the Muslim community, with extrajudicial killings of Muslim clerics and youth leaders that "have generated a climate of fear and anxiety amongst Muslim leaders of all shades of opinion: and it is difficult to avoid the conclusion that this is precisely the intention."[37] In fact, on April 2, 2014, the government launched a major security operation, Operation Usalama Watch, in a crackdown that resulted in the arrest and illegal detention of more than 4,000 persons in Nairobi's predominantly Somali Eastleigh district.[38] This operation—involving more than 6,000 security personnel—included indiscriminate house-to-house searches, nighttime raids, and widespread complaints of excessive force and looting, all reportedly done in search of terrorists and illegal Somali aliens.[39] Hence, many observers argue that such an operation, coming on the heels of recent high-profile attacks by al-Shabaab in Nairobi and Mandera County, "played into the hands of al-Shabaab by appearing to scapegoat ethnic Somalis and to alienate Muslims."[40]

The non-state groups are often well armed and are able to engage in sustained combat with Kenya Police, Kenya Police Reserve (KPR), and military units.[41] For example, on October 19, 2012, dozens of police officers were killed in an ambush by over a hundred cattle rustlers from the Turkana tribe, while in July 2004, at least seventy people—including twenty-five children—were massacred in fighting between cattle rustlers and local villagers.[42] Both incidents demonstrate the serious problems raised by the readily available arms and ammunition, some coming across Kenya's porous borders and some sold by corrupt police officers, combined with a lack of police capacity in rural areas, as rival domestic—some of which are vigilante—groups terrorize each other and local communities. Minimally, this also means that strong penal statutes must be combined with effective law enforcement operations and criminal prosecutions.

This raises issues for the Kenyan government in terms of addressing both the supply and demand aspects of its "gun culture" problem. First, there must be strong regional cooperation to eliminate international arms smuggling through strong border controls and to coordinate disarmament campaigns to reduce the cross-border supply to pastoral groups. Second, the Kenya Police, the KPR, and military units deployed in support of civil authorities must be trained to a high standard—to include the appropriate limits on the use of force—and available for local use, helping to reduce the demand for local groups to provide for their own security.[43] This means that police officers must be held accountable for human rights abuses, acts of corruption (e.g., the illicit sale of arms and ammunition to local clans and groups), and performance failures, likely through the IPOA. This also means that all government-owned arms and ammunition should be marked, a measure that should improve accountability and curb corrupt practices.[44] Moreover, with a boost in police resources—thereby enhancing investigations and prosecutorial effectiveness—Kenya could also increase its conviction rate, deterring more people from possessing or using illegal arms and ammunition.

In general terms, Kenya needs a greatly expanded security and police presence—either the Kenya Police or the KPR—in the outlying counties that were created in 2010 to replace the postcolonial provincial system. Locally recruited, community-based police officers would have many advantages over the use of national-level assets in response to a crisis situation (i.e., the slow response to the April 2015 terrorist attack on Garissa College). Locally recruited officers would have a better appreciation for the local security and cultural dynamics and would be better positioned to anticipate problems. Indeed, with a level of trust between the local police and the community, people would probably be more likely to report suspicious activity and feel less need for having privately owned weapons. Still, an expanded KPR should remain under the operational control of the National Police Service and the IPOA, which could address concerns that the expanded KPR, properly manned, trained, and equipped, could be dominated by local politicians (i.e., mitigating against conflicts of interest, the demanding of favors, politicization, and clan bias) or that it could use its weapons for criminal acts against rival groups. In any case, there is substantial evidence that the outlying counties are poorly staffed in police personnel and that much greater efforts are required to fund, manage, train, equip, and discipline the existing structures.[45] In the long term, a better staffed, trained, and equipped police service would have greater legitimacy with the people, enhancing its overall effectiveness and reducing insecurity.

SECURITY AND POLICE FORCES IN UGANDA

Unlike Kenya's efforts to reform its institutional oversight structure and define the roles and responsibilities of its security and police forces, Uganda has a weak legal structure, and the country's recent history has been marked by even more significant human rights abuses. This includes the notorious period of state terror under President Idi Amin and the subsequent Uganda-Tanzania war during which as many as 800,000 Ugandans may have died from 1971 to 1985 as well as current concerns over civil and political rights under the semi-authoritarian regime of President Yoweri Museveni and the National Resistance Movement (NRM).[46] Uganda has, nonetheless, made improvements in its human rights record since the NRM took power in 1986. While there have been advances in the rule of law and the role of the judiciary as a check on executive power, Uganda still has a semi-authoritarian government that is dominated by the Uganda People's Defence Force (UPDF) and a president who has been in office for over thirty years.[47] In fact, for many Ugandans and foreign observers, the security services and police forces in Uganda lack institutional legitimacy in that those organizations have been used for regime security and have engaged in repressive practices.

Uganda was a British protectorate until its independence on October 9, 1962. The country has since passed through several periods of military rule marked by human rights abuses. Eventually, in 1986, Yoweri Museveni seized power and established a new government. The 1995 constitution provides for the overall structure of the government and outlines a series of rights and freedoms. The constitution creates a legislature (the parliament), an executive (the president), cabinet (to include both an attorney general and a deputy attorney general), a director of public prosecutions (DPP) who directs police investigations and criminal prosecutions, and a judiciary.[48] The Ugandan judiciary is based upon the legacy of British colonialism: the English legal system, which includes a hierarchy of courts and English common law that has left an enduring imprint on the administration of justice. On national security matters, the constitution creates the UPDF, intelligence services, and the Uganda Police.[49] This basic government structure, particularly as it relates to the "movement" (a nonparty form of government, with compulsory membership), is unique and has been heavily criticized as a means of repressing political and civil liberties.[50]

The 1995 constitution authorizes national-level security services, but without any parliamentary controls. Article 218 provides that the parliament may establish intelligence services and that no other "intelligence service shall be established by the Government except by or under an Act of Parliament."[51] In fact, Uganda has two security services that have been created by a cursory

1987 statute: the External Security Organisation (ESO) is the government's foreign intelligence service, and the Internal Security Organisation (ISO) is the government's counterintelligence service.[52] The Uganda Penal Code also criminalizes several security-related offenses, to include treason, inducing soldiers or policemen to desert, the publication of information detrimental to security, sedition, and promoting sectarianism. However, several code sections are broadly written, allowing them to be a tool to repress political opponents.

The 1987 Security Organisations Act creates both the ESO and ISO as government departments, answering only to the president, and there is no provision for parliamentary oversight. The two organizations are mandated "to collect, receive and process internal and external intelligence data on the security of Uganda" and "advise and recommend to the President or any other authority as the President may direct on what action should be taken in connection with that intelligence data."[53] Intelligence officers may not take any action not sanctioned by the president, although

> either of the Directors General may direct the police to arrest and detain, in relation to intelligence gathered, any person for not more than forty-eight hours pending a report by the Director General under section 3(b) and a decision by the President.[54]

The ESO and the ISO have broad undefined authorities and are answerable only to the president. Unlike the Kenyan NIS, there are no limitations placed on the president's ability to appoint or remove its director general, no limitations on the conduct of intelligence activities, and no means for the filing/ investigation of complaints involving either organization.[55] Indeed, there is a very close relationship between the UPDF and the two security organizations, with military officers often serving on assignment in a security position.[56]

The parliament created the Uganda National Police as well as the Uganda Police Reserve by statute.[57] The Uganda police service consists of the regular police, the reserve, and special constables.[58] The force functions to protect the life, property, and rights of the individual; maintain security within Uganda; enforce the laws of Uganda; ensure public safety and order; prevent and detect crime; and "perform the services of a military force."[59] It is under the command of an inspector general of police (IGP).[60] The statute also establishes a code of conduct as well as a system of police disciplinary courts that provides "the basis for disciplinary control of all police officers and other persons employed in the force under this code of conduct."[61] The Uganda Police has two important directorates, the Directorate of Criminal Investigations and the Directorate of Crime Intelligence, that have responsibilities in domestic security cases.[62]

Uganda Police officers have broad authorities to conduct searches and arrests. For example, a search may be ordered by

> a police officer, not being lower in rank than a sergeant, [if the officer] has reasonable grounds for believing that anything necessary for the purposes of an investigation into any offence which he or she is authorised to investigate may be found in any place and [that] thing cannot in his or her opinion be otherwise obtained without undue delay.[63]

In addition, "a police officer may, without a court order and without a warrant, arrest a person if he or she has reasonable [not probable] cause to suspect that the person has committed or is about to commit an arrestable offence."[64]

Generally speaking, the Uganda National Police is a militarized force under presidential control and subject to limited parliamentary oversight. The UPDF and the Uganda Police have a close relationship with military officers often serving on assignment with the police. In 2001, Major General Katumba Wamala was appointed to serve as the IGP; four years later, he returned to the UPDF to serve first as chief, land forces, and then as chief of defence force.[65] In 2005, General Wamala was replaced by Major General Kale Kayihura who then served as the IGP until 2018.[66] The appointments of these senior officers to the Uganda Police demonstrate the close, effective collaboration between the police and military at the operational level in fighting domestic security threats. Additionally, this also raises serious questions about the independence of the police and the application of military law in a domestic setting.

There have been long-standing and substantial human rights complaints levied against the Uganda security services and Uganda National Police.[67] Both the security forces and the Uganda Police have been criticized for a wide range of human rights abuses including unlawful killings, torture, and abuses against suspects.[68] The Joint Anti-Terrorism Task Force (JATT) is a joint interagency organization that was formed in 1999 using personnel from the ISO, the UPDF, the Uganda Police, and intelligence organizations to combat a rebel group, the Allied Democratic Forces.[69] The JATT lacks a statutory mandate and has been under the operational control of the chieftaincy of military intelligence (CMI). Typically, JATT personnel operate in civilian clothes and drive unmarked cars, and each officer uses the statutory authorities from the person's home organization/command. According to Human Rights Watch, the JATT and other ad hoc units are "comprised of police, military, intelligence personnel, and sometimes other unofficial forces established to address particular security challenges, blur the boundaries between the codified mandates and roles of the military and civilian law enforcement."[70] This raises important questions about the UPDF's role in domestic security cases as well as the independence of the Uganda National Police from military control.

The JATT has been accused of the arbitrary arrest of suspected criminals. In particular, Human Rights Watch alleged it has held suspects in lengthy pretrial detention, waiting months, if ever, to bring a suspect before a magistrate; used "ungazetted" detention facilities (i.e., safe houses); employed torture and other abusive interrogation practices; and engaged in extrajudicial killings.[71] While the then CMI, Brigadier James Mugira, had promised in early 2009 to investigate all claims of human rights abuses made against the JATT, it is unclear whether and to what extent the government has addressed these abuses.[72] In fact, Human Rights Watch found no evidence that police and military personnel were held accountable for any prior abuses.[73] In any case, there are substantial issues regarding the impartiality and integrity of law enforcement investigations, including confused and overlapping police and military law enforcement authorities.

The treason case against Kizza Besigye illustrates the toxic role of politics in the administration of justice in Uganda.[74] Besigye, who had been President Museveni's physician during the 1980–1986 war to overthrow the prior government, retired from the UPDF in 2001. He subsequently became the leader of the largest opposition political party, the Forum for Democratic Change, accusing the government of corruption and pushing to end the "movement" system of "nonparty" government. President Museveni threatened prosecution in military courts, resulting in Besigye's arrest for treason and misprision of treason.[75] On November 16, 2005, while making bail applications at the high court, Besigye and several codefendants were seized by an armed team from the JATT and taken to a local prison.[76] He was court-martialed, after being charged with terrorism, rape, and the unlawful possession of a firearm. In December 2005, despite an injunction by the High Court ordering the stay of court-martial proceedings, the UPDF continued its own proceedings. On January 31, 2006, the constitutional court, acting on a petition from the Uganda Law Society, held that the court-martial proceedings violated the Uganda Constitution.[77] Nonetheless, he and the others were not released.

The treason trial commenced in the High Court and, at the same time, the government proceeded to amend the charges from the first court-martial proceeding.[78] On November 9, 2006, the government commenced a second court-martial, and several warrants were served on the Uganda Prisons Service to deliver the defendants to the constitutional court on various days in January 2007, but the defendants were never produced. Later, on March 1, the defendants were taken to the High Court for bail processing, but heavily armed security personnel again took control of the court.[79] The defendants were not told why they were being rearrested or where they would be taken. One advocate stated under oath: "The security personnel simply insisted that they had orders not to permit the bailed petitioners to go out on bail as ordered by the Court."[80] That same day after the defendants were turned over to the security forces, they were reportedly assaulted.

In October 2010, the Uganda Constitutional Court eventually held against the government in a unanimous decision, describing the evidence as largely not challenged and the government's actions as an affront to the constitution.[81] The decision gave a two-page dramatic, even poetic, recitation from a book by another judge called "The Rape of the Temple."[82] The court found that the defendants had been subjected to "humiliating, cruel and degrading treatment," that the defendants had been deprived of a fair hearing, and that unprecedented executive actions had illegally interfered with the exercise of judicial power. The court then stayed all criminal proceedings in all courts and directed the government to release the defendants. Furthermore, the court held that the court-martial proceedings as well as the treason and murder trials were null and void.

This case illustrates problems involving the UPDF and Uganda National Police's lack of accountability. First, it is unclear whether there was actual merit to any of the criminal charges that were filed against Besigye or any of his codefendants. Second, there was an apparent political component to the case. Besigye had been a former colleague of President Museveni, accusing the president of corruption and sought to replace him in office. Evidentially, the UPDF and Uganda National Police acted to repress one of the president's important political opponents. Third, the UPDF and the Uganda National Police used a heavy-handed approach that demonstrated a lack of respect for the judiciary. The executive actions in this case undermined the institutional legitimacy of the ISO, the UPDF, and the Uganda National Police, which demonstrates the lack of executive accountability under the law.

A December 2012 report, prepared by Uganda's Inspectorate of Government, concluded that the Uganda National Police, followed by the judiciary, is the most corrupt institution in the country.[83] Abusive police practices, particularly if biased toward the government, as well as excessive delays and costs in court proceedings, can lead to a situation conducive to corruption, with people trying to buy their way out of a bad situation.[84] Uganda does have two well-written statutes that can be used to combat corruption in government. Under the first statute, the 2002 Leadership Code Act, senior officials are obligated to submit a biannual declaration of income, assets, and liabilities to the inspector general of government (IGG). Furthermore, the IGG has broad powers to investigate and decide cases involving senior officials.[85] Under the second statute, the 2009 Anti-Corruption Act, the government can investigate and prosecute a wide range of cases involving corruption, bribery of public officials, conflicts of interest, sectarianism, nepotism, threats of injury to persons employed in public service, and fraudulent acts. While both statutes should be effective tools for use in investigating and prosecuting corruption cases involving security and police officials, neither statute has been effectively implemented—likely the result of a lack political will on the part of the government.

SECURITY AND POLICE FORCES IN TANZANIA

Like neighboring Kenya and Uganda, Tanzania has experienced unstable constitutional history since its independence in 1961, with Tanzania having five constitutions (for the country's intelligence in the first decade of independence, see Graham in this volume).[86] Initially, Tanzania adopted a "Westminster" Constitution, with the British monarch as head of state, a governor general, and an independent judiciary, but without an explicit Bill of Rights. This constitution was promptly repealed in 1962 and replaced with a new one featuring a republican government and an executive president. The current constitution was adopted in 1977 with a strong presidency, a dual-state structure (a union government and a second, largely autonomous, government for Zanzibar). The constitution has been amended multiple times since, with many amendments concerning the structural relationship between the union and Zanzibar, the 1992 transition to a multiparty political system, the method for presidential selection, and increasing the role of women in the parliament.[87]

The 1977 union constitution provides that Tanzania is one state and a sovereign united republic, consisting of the largely Christian mainland Tanzania and a semiautonomous, but almost entirely Muslim, Zanzibar.[88] Article 3 provides that the united republic is a "democratic, secular and socialist state which adheres to multi-party democracy."[89] The constitution identifies twenty-two areas that are union matters (e.g., foreign affairs, defense and security, police, emergency powers, citizenship, and immigration), while all areas not listed are non-union matters left to Zanzibar. This union structure creates an institutionalized system of checks and balances with limitations on union and presidential power, a unitary national assembly (parliament), Zanzibari autonomy, and a Bill of Rights that became judicially enforceable in 1987. The constitution is an improvement over the earlier versions, particularly with the Bill of Rights. However, there have been some acrimonious problems, leading to electoral violence, with respect to Zanzibari autonomy.

The Tanzania Intelligence and Security Service (TISS) was established by a 1996 statute as a "department of Government within the office of the President."[90] The TISS was tasked to "obtain, correlate, and evaluate intelligence relevant to security," to communicate with and advise ministers, to cooperate with other state and public authorities, and to advise the president on new national security threats.[91] The service cannot enforce security measures or institute surveillance on persons "by reason only of his or their involvement in lawful protest or dissent in respect of any matter affecting the Constitution, the laws or the Government of Tanzania."[92] The president has the authority to appoint a director general, as the chief executive officer for the service, for a renewable five-year term (not to exceed a total of ten years in office). The statute criminalizes the unauthorized disclosure of information or the identity of a confidential source.[93]

Some members of parliament have recently called for reform of the TISS citing a need to focus on economic intelligence and wanting to provide the agency with greater autonomy to stop it being used for partisan political surveillance.[94] Currently, the TISS cannot legally perform either task without a change in its statutory authorities. In other words, while the 1996 statute is silent on whether the TISS can collect economic intelligence, the statute specifically prohibits the TISS from conducting surveillance of lawful domestic political activities.[95] Such changes in statutory authorities would, however, raise problems: First, would the TISS be authorized to collect foreign and domestic economic intelligence, and would the TISS be able to share that information with nongovernmental business entities (thereby, allowing Tanzanian businesses entities a competitive economic advantage)? Second, would the statute be amended in such a way that could facilitate the surveillance of opposition political parties? The better view, proffered by human rights organizations such as the Tanzania Human Rights Defenders Coalition, the Collaboration on International ICT Policy in East and Southern Africa, and Privacy International (PI), is that the "lack of transparency and oversight of the TISS is compounded by the fact that there is no requirement of judicial authorisation for interception of communications."[96] This is a critical shortcoming in Tanzanian law: the TISS operates under the control of its director general, the minister for intelligence and security, and the union president, but there are no provisions in either the 1977 Union Constitution or the 1996 statute for parliamentary or judicial oversight over the TISS and its activities.

The police force was established by a 1965 statute, incorporating certain colonial ordinances, and is under the operational command of an inspector general of police.[97] The inspector general has broad authority to administer the force, consisting of the police force, a police reserve, and an auxiliary police force, subject to the approval of the minister of home affairs. The statute provides for a Criminal Investigation Directorate, responsible for crime intelligence and the investigation of serious crime, subordinate to the inspector general. The police officers' powers and duties have a broad range of limitations—including the use of force, arrest, and search and seizure—on law enforcement operations. The statute also details disciplinary processes and procedures that can be used to hold officers accountable for offenses against discipline. A 1990 statute created the Police and Prison Service Commission that advises the president on matters related to either service.[98]

While the Tanzania Police Force has a solid legal foundation, it has experienced shortcomings in institutional capacity that undermines public legitimacy. First, the president may order the arrest and indefinite detention without bail of any person considered dangerous to the public order or national security.[99] This broad authority, subject to challenge by a detainee at ninety-day intervals, is open to abuse against political opponents. Second, even though the 1977 constitution prohibits torture and other cruel, inhuman, or degrading treatment or punishment, there have been repeated reports that "police officers, prison guards, and soldiers [have] abused, threatened, and otherwise mistreated civilians, suspected criminals, and prisoners."[100] Third, Tanzania uses police officers with legal training, under the control of the minister of home affairs, as prosecutors in most criminal matters. This is a relic from British colonial law that raises questions about the independence of such prosecutors and a defendant's right to a fair trial, namely whether the police can investigate and prosecute a case fairly.[101] Investigative and prosecutorial roles should be separated, and all prosecutors should be employed by and under the control of the director of public prosecutions and the Ministry of Justice.[102] Finally, there is ample evidence that corruption is pervasive in the judiciary and the national police.[103] In 2019, the U.S. Department of State reported that the Tanzanian "government took steps to investigate and prosecute officials who committed human rights abuses, but impunity in the police and other security forces and civilian branches of government was widespread."[104]

Like Kenya and Uganda, Tanzania faces several different terrorist threats, often requiring regional collaboration and cooperation on law enforcement matters. Tanzania faces threats from foreign terrorist fighters transiting the country, from violent Islamic groups attacking foreign tourists and diplomatic interests, and from domestic groups with political and economic grievances against the government. In 2005, Tanzania established a National Counterterrorism Center (NCTC) within the Ministry of Home Affairs as an "interagency unit composed of officers from the intelligence, police, defense, immigration, and prison sectors who work collectively on counterterrorism issues."[105] Yet, according to the United States Institute for Peace, Tanzania has experienced significant shortcomings in its counterterrorism program. Notably, there is a "lack of trust between the community," which "prevents [it] from collaborating effectively on a joint response," while "communities are highly suspicious of police" believing people are "being subjected to enforced disappearances and extrajudicial killings by security forces."[106]

CONCLUSION

The East African intelligence, security, and police services share a common colonial background, inheriting legal structures, English common law, and policing traditions from the British. Each country did, however, travel a different road to and since independence, but leaving fertile grounds for ethnic animosity and conflict. In colonial Kenya, the British fought a bloody uprising by the Mau Mau in the 1950s, leaving the Kikuyu as the politically dominant ethnic group after independence, and, in colonial Uganda, the British favored the Baganda in state administration and the Acholi in the military (i.e., the King's African Rifles), leaving the different kingdoms and ethnic groups to compete for political and military power after independence. Tanzania has experienced post-independence problems with the union of Tanganyika and Zanzibar, including with a large Muslim presence on the mainland coast and on Zanzibar. The intelligence, security, and police services of all three countries have been used as a tool by the ruling regime to repress political opponents with limited accountability either in the parliament or before the courts.

The East African intelligence, security, and police services have a range of institutional strengths and weaknesses. Kenya has the strongest and most comprehensive legal mandate in terms of constitutional and statutory law, especially with its 2010 constitution and related statutes. The NIS and the National Police Force operate under comprehensive statutory mandates with clearly defined roles and responsibilities. In fact, Kenyan law imposes important restraints on government officials. This structure, along with its Official Secrets Act and a Freedom of Information statute helps promote public accountability and institutional legitimacy. Establishing the NIS as a "disciplined civilian service" and reforming police practices is a positive development. These changes are important steps to overcoming decades of distrust in marginalized ethnic groups. Still, the reports of police brutality in the aftermath of the disputed August 2017 presidential election show that Kenya has a long road to travel.[107]

In contrast to Kenya, Uganda has a cursory legal structure that fails to delineate the roles and responsibilities of its security services and the Uganda National Police. The Uganda ESO and ISO are executive tools that operate without effective judicial or parliamentary oversight. As a result, the lack of legal constraints on the intelligence, security, and police services as well as the close relationships among them create considerable risk of executive abuse. The evidence indicates that the system of presidential control allows for the repression of political opponents and human rights abuses. Uganda requires a thorough overhaul of the statutory law that governs its security services and the national police. Uganda law should clearly define the roles and responsibilities for the security and police forces, the appropriate jurisdiction of civilian and military courts, and provide for parliamentary oversight. Uganda should also have an independent oversight authority to investigate and prosecute wrongdoing by government officials. Moreover, security and police officials who violate the law should be held accountable before the courts for any misconduct.

Tanzania, like its neighbor Kenya, has a strong and comprehensive legal mandate that governs the TISS and the Tanzania National Police. Similar to both Kenya and Uganda, the Tanzanian intelligence, security, and police services have noteworthy shortcomings in institutional capacity and compliance with international human rights norms. Tanzania should revise its 1992 Preventive Detention Act to allow for greater judicial oversight. The use of police as prosecutors in its courts suggests a lack of qualified lawyers in the country. Expanding legal education in the country could help provide greater judicial oversight over the security and police services and help eliminate corruption by public officials and human rights abuses.

NOTES

1. Some parts of this chapter have been previously published in Christopher E. Bailey, *Counterterrorism Law and Practice in the East African Community* (Boston: Brill/Nijhoff, 2019). All statements of fact, analysis, or opinion are the author's and do not reflect the official policy or position of the National Intelligence University, the Department of Defense or any of its components, or the U.S. government.

2. Ryan Shaffer, "Following in Footsteps: The History of Kenya's Post-Colonial Intelligence Services," *Studies in Intelligence* 63, no. 1 (2019): 23–40.

3. Kenya has often been described as a politically polarized nation with ethnic groups competing for resources under successive autocratic and corrupt governments (i.e., under Jomo Kenyatta from 1964–78, Daniel arap Moi from 1978–2002, and Mwai Kibaki from 2002 to 2013). Daniel Branch, *Kenya: Between Hope and Despair, 1963–2011* (New Haven, CT: Yale University Press, 2011), 103–5, 217–18, and 252–57.

4. Michela Wong, *It's Our Turn to Eat: The Story of a Kenyan Whistleblower* (London: HarperCollins, 2009), 62–63. See also: Evelyne Kwamboka, "Kanyotu's secrets erupt from grave," *The Standard* (Nairobi), September 29, 2009, https://www.standardmedia.co.ke/article/1144025145/kanyotu-s-secrets-erupt-from-grave#.

5. Constitution of Kenya, 2010, art. 160(1).

6. Ibid., art. 58.

7. Republic of Kenya, National Security Intelligence Service Act (1998) (repealed). Wilson Boinett, "The Origins of the Intelligence System of Kenya," in *Changing Intelligence Dynamics in Africa*, eds. Sandy Africa and Johnny Kwadjo (Birmingham, UK: GFN-SSR and ASSN, 2009).

8. Republic of Kenya, National Intelligence Service Act (2012).

9. Ibid., art. 67(1).

10. Ibid., art. 37.

11. Ibid., art. 5(1).

12. Ibid., art. 5(3).

13. Ibid., art. 42(1).

14. Ibid., art. 45.

15. Yoshiaki Furuzawa, "Two Police Reforms in Kenya: Their Implications for Police Reform Policy," *Journal of International Development and Cooperation* 17, no. 1 (2011). Kenyan citizens who were aggrieved by human rights violations at the hands of Special Branch/police officials during the period 1982–1992 at the Nyayo House "torture chambers" have been able to recover judgments for monetary compensation against the government. KNCHR, *Footprints of Impunity: Counting the Cost of Human Rights Violations* (Nairobi, undated), available at http://www.knchr.org/.

16. The Constitution of Kenya, 2010, art. 244.

17. Ibid., art. 245.

18. Ibid., art. 246.

19. Republic of Kenya, National Police Service Act (revised ed. 2012).

20. Ibid., art. 35(b).

21. Republic of Kenya, Independent Policing Oversight Authority Act (2011), art. 5–6.

22. Amnesty International/Human Rights Watch, *"Kill Those Criminals": Security Forces Violations in Kenya's August 2017 Elections* (New York: Amnesty International/Human Rights Watch, 2017), 36.

23. Open Society Foundations, *"We're Tired of Taking You to Court": Human Rights Abuses by Kenya's Anti-Terrorism Police Unit* (New York: Open Society Foundations, 2013).

24. Human Rights Watch, *Deaths and Disappearances Abuses in Counterterrorism Operations in Nairobi and in Northeastern Kenya* (New York: Human Rights Watch, 2016), 4.

25. Salim Awadh Salim & 10 Others v. Commissioner of Police & 3 Others, Petition No 822 (2008), eKLR, at 2–3. See also Human Rights Watch, *Kenya: Killings, Disappearances by Anti-Terror Police*, August 18, 2014, https://www.hrw.org/news/2014/08/18/kenya-killings-disappearances-anti-terror-police.

26. Salim Awadh Salim & 10 Others v. Commissioner of Police & 3 Others, Petition No 822 (2008), eKLR, at 2.

27. Ibid., at 7–8.

28. Ibid., at 29.

29. Peter Gastrow, *Termites at Work: Transnational Organized Crime and State Erosion in Kenya* (New York: International Peace Institute, 2011), ix.

30. Ibid.

31. Ibid., 3–6. Kenya has two important tools for fighting corruption among security and police officials. First, Kenya has a 2003 Anti-Corruption and Economic Crimes Act that permits the government to suspend officials who are charged with corruption or economic crimes and to dismiss them from government service upon

conviction. Second, Kenya has a 2003 Public Officer Ethics Act that requires officials to file a biennial "declaration of the income, assets and liabilities of himself, his spouse or spouses and his dependent children under the age of 18 years." Ibid., art. 26(1).

32. Republic of Kenya, The Kenya Defence Forces Act, No. 25 of 2012 (as amended).

33. The Constitution of Kenya, 2010, art. 58.

34. Christopher Anzalone, "Kenya's Muslim Youth Center and Al-Shabab's East African Recruitment," *CTC Sentinel* 5, no. 10 (Combating Terrorism Center, West Point, October 2012): 9–11.

35. Ibid., 12.

36. David M. Anderson and Jacob McKnight, "Kenya at War: Al-Shabaab and Its Enemies in Eastern Africa," *African Affairs* 114, no. 454 (2015): 17–18.

37. Ibid., 18.

38. Ibid., 20–23. This security operation was immediately preceded by a series of three explosions on March 30—at two restaurants and a clinic in Eastleigh—that was then followed the April 1 extrajudicial killing of a radical Muslim cleric and rioting in Mombasa. Moreover, the Kenya Police was accused of, but denied any wrongdoing, with respect to the cleric's murder by unidentified assailants. Janelle Dumalaon, "Life in Eastleigh, Where a Bomb Attack Monday Means You'll Be Arrested Tuesday," *PRI Global Post*, April 9, 2014, https://www.pri.org/stories/2014-04-09/life-eastleigh-where-bomb-attack-monday-means-youll-be-arrested-tuesday.

39. Ibid.

40. Ibid., 21. One observer noted that the "[p]ublic support for the pogrom against Somalis was high; the atmosphere in the capital was vicious." Ben Rawlence, *City of Thorns: Nine Lives in the World's Largest Refugee Camp* (New York: Picador, 2016), 341.

41. The Kenya Police Reserve (KPR) is authorized under the 2011 National Police Service Act, and its officers typically serve as an unpaid locally selected civilian militia force, often operating outside centralized control and living with the tribes that they protect. Kennedy Mkutu Agade, "Changes and Challenges of the Kenya Police Reserve: The Case of Turkana County," *African Studies Review* 58, no. 1 (April 2015): 210–15. Thus, the local KPR officers generally have substandard training and equipment, and with reduced effectiveness and less accountability for human rights abuses.

42. Eric Matara, "Police officers killed in Baragoi were young, had no experience," *Daily Nation*, June 22, 2016. http://www.nation.co.ke/counties/nakuru/Baragoi-attack-case/1183314-3261338-agjw6q/index.html. Noor Ali and Garrick Anderson, "Kenya Seeks Bandits after Massacre in Rural North," *Reuters*, July 15, 2005, http://www.washingtonpost.com/wp-dyn/content/article/2005/07/14/ AR2005071401868.html.

43. This would, for example, include deployments taking place pursuant to a presidential decree made under articles 58 and 132(4)(d) of the 2010 Kenyan Constitution.

44. Manasseh Wepundi, et al. *Availability of Small Arms and Perceptions of Security in Kenya: An Assessment*, Special Report (Geneva, SZ: Small Arms Survey, 2012), 75.

45. Ibid., 202–4.

46. Human Rights Watch, *The Movement System and Political Repression in Uganda* (1999). Uganda adopted multiparty elections in 2005, but the NRM-dominated government has used repressive tactics, to include heavy-handed police tactics, arbitrary detention, and torture in secret and illegal facilities (i.e., safe houses), and charges of treason and sedition that can be used to detain someone who might be accused of promoting "sectarianism"—although that person might be later released without a trial.

47. Elias Biryabarema, "Uganda Seeks Constitutional Change That Would Let Museveni Extend Rule," *U.S. News & World Report*, July 14, 2017, https://www.usnews.com/news/world/articles/2017-07-14/uganda-seeks-constitutional-change-that-would-let-museveni-extend-rule.

48. The Constitution of the Republic of Uganda (1995), art. 120.

49. Ibid., art. 211–18.

50. Human Rights Watch, *Hostile to Democracy: The Movement System and Political Repression in Uganda* (1999).

51. Uganda Constitution (1995), art. 218.

52. Republic of Uganda, Security Organisations Act 1987. Haggai Matsiko, "Intelligence in crisis," *The Independent* (Kampala), November 8, 2013. https://allafrica.com/stories/201311111658.html.

53. Republic of Uganda, Security Organisations Act 1987, art. 3.

54. Ibid., art. 4(1).

55. The current director general of the ESO is former ambassador Joseph Ocwet. Charles Etukuri, "Museveni appoints new ESO boss," *New Vision* (Kampala), June 11, 2015. https://www.newvision.co.ug/news/1328140/museveni-appoints-eso-boss.

56. Derrick Wandera and Risdel Kasasira, "CMI raids ISO safe houses," *The Daily Monitor* (Kampala), July 11, 2020, https://www.msn.com/en-xl/news/other/cmi-raids-iso-safe-houses/ar-BB16C5lw.

57. Republic of Uganda, Police Act 1994 (amended 2006).

58. A special constable is a person appointed by the "officer in charge of an area in which an unlawful activity has occurred or is likely to occur" and is used to reinforce the local police. Republic of Uganda, Police Act 1994 (amended 2006), art. 64. In other words, a special constable could be someone appointed from the local community, lacking any prior training or police experience, but with the power and authority of regular member of the Uganda Police.

59. Ibid., art. 4(1).

60. Martin Okoth Ochola, a lawyer and career police officer, has been the IGP since March 2018; his two predecessors were both general officers in the UPDF. Andrew Bagala, "Ochola's long walk to become IGP," *The Daily Monitor* (Kampala), March 6, 2018. https://www.monitor.co.ug/News/National/Ochola-long-walk-become-IGP/688334-4330642-bkphrj/. Steven Candia, "Maj. Gen. Kale Kaihura takes over Police Force," *New Vision* (Kampala), November 3, 2005, https://web.archive.org/web/20150623073214/http://www.newvision.co.ug/D/8/12/464172.

61. Republic of Uganda, Police Act 1994 (amended 2006), art. 44.

62. Vision Reporter, "Police Intelligence arm to become a Directorate," *New Vision* (Kampala), June 13, 2014, https://www.newvision.co.ug/news/1341675/police-intelligence-arm-directorate.

63. Republic of Uganda, Police Act 1994 (amended 2006), art. 27.

64. Ibid., art. 23.

65. "Profile: Gen. Edward Katumba Wamala," *The Independent* (Kampala), February 7, 2017. https://www.independent.co.ug/gen-edward-katumba-wamala/.

66. "Uganda arrests ex-police chief Kale Kayihura," *Daily Nation* (Kampala), June 13, 2018, https://www.nation.co.ke/kenya/news/africa/uganda-arrests-ex-police-chief-kale-kayihura-54290.

67. Brooke J. Oppenheimer, "From Arrest to Release: The Inside Story of Uganda's Penal System," 16 *Indiana International & Comparative Law Review* 117, 120–136 (2005) (describing the corruption, incompetence and inefficiency in the Uganda Police, the court system, and the prison service).

68. "Uganda 2015 Human Rights Report," U.S. Department of State, 2019, http://www.state.gov/j/drl/rls/hrrpt/humanrightsreport/#wrapper.

69. According to Human Rights Watch, the government had intended that the JATT would be under the command of the inspector general of police, but—when it appeared that the police could not manage the organization—it was transferred to the CMI. The JATT's mission has since expanded to include treason cases and other terrorist threats to Uganda. Human Rights Watch, *Open Secret: Illegal Detention and Torture by the Joint Anti-Terrorism Task Force in Uganda* (New York, 2009), 20–22.

70. Human Rights Watch, *Open Secret*, 16.

71. The 1995 Uganda Constitution, art. 123 (4), requires that an arrested person be brought to court within 48 hours from arrest. The 1995 Uganda Constitution proscribes the holding of prisoners in "ungazetted" places, namely unacknowledged locations that are not published in the official gazette. Ibid., art. 23 (2). While police stations are typically gazetted, "legal" facilities, other places such as military barracks, "safe houses," and offices are not; and Human Rights Watch, *Open Secret*, 34.

72. Ibid., 58–60.

73. Ibid., 5.

74. Dr. Kizza Besigye & Others v. Attorney General (Const. Petition No. of 2007) UGCC (2010).

75. Ronald Naluwairo, "Military Justice, Human Rights and the Law: An Appraisal of the Right to a Fair Trial in Uganda's Military Justice System" (Nov. 2011) (unpublished PhD thesis, University of London), 212.

76. Dr. Kizza Besigye & Others. The dramatized court decision refers to this incident as the "First Court Siege." According to Human Rights Watch, this siege and a later one conducted in March 2007, were actually conducted by the "Black Mamba Hit Squad," a largely unknown military intelligence team. Human Rights Watch, *Open Secret*, 15–16.

77. Uganda Law Society v. Attorney General of the Republic of Uganda (Constitutional Petition No. 18) (2006) UGCC 10.

78. Dr. Kizza Besigye & Others.

79. Ibid. This incident is referred to in the record as the "Second Court Siege." Apparently, this siege also resulted in the unlawful confinement of the judges and court staff for over six hours.

80. Statement by Titus Kiyemba Mutale, para. 25, Besigye & Others v. Attorney General.

81. Dr. Kizza Besigye & Others.

82. Ibid.

83. Republic of Uganda, Inspectorate of Government, *The Third Annual Report on Tracking Corruption Trends in Uganda: Using the Data Tracking Mechanism*, December 2012, //www.igg.go.ug/publications/?page=3.

84. On its Corruption Perceptions Index for 2019, Transparency International ranks Uganda as 137th of the 180 countries in the world. Transparency International, https://www.transparency.org/en/countries/uganda.

85. The inspector general of government is created by the 1995 Uganda Constitution, art. 223.

86. Republic of Kenya, National Security Intelligence Service Act (1998) (repealed). Boinett, "The Origins of the Intelligence System of Kenya."

87. The Constitution of the United Republic of Tanzania (2005).

88. Zanzibar has a separate, 1984 constitution that addresses non-union matters. The Constitution of Zanzibar (rev. ed. 2006).

89. Tanzania Constitution (2005), art. 3.

90. Republic of Tanzania, Tanzania Intelligence and Security Service Act, 1998, art. 4.

91. Ibid., art. 4.

92. Ibid., art. 5(2)(b).

93. See also Republic of Tanzania, The National Security Act, 1970 (protecting classified information).

94. The Guardian Reporter, "Deputy Spy Chief Axed Amid Calls for Reform of TISS," *IPP Media*, April 22, 2018, https://www.ippmedia.com/en/news/deputy-spy-chief-axed-amid-calls-reform-tiss.

95. Republic of Tanzania, Tanzania Intelligence and Security Service Act, 1998, art. 5(2)(b).

96. The Tanzania Human Rights Defenders Coalition, "The Right to Privacy in the United Republic of Tanzania," Stakeholder Report Universal Periodic Review 25th Session —Tanzania, September 2015.

97. Republic of Tanzania, Police Force and Auxiliary Services Act, 1965.

98. Republic of Tanzania, Police Force and Prison Service Commission Act, 1990.

99. Republic of Tanzania, the Preventive Detention Act, 1962.

100. "Tanzania 2019 Human Rights Report," U.S. Department of State, 2019, https://www.state.gov/wp-content/uploads/2020/03/TANZANIA-2019-HUMAN-RIGHTS-REPORT.pdf.

101. Ibid., 10.

102. Laurean Mutahunwa Tibasana, "Effective Administration of the Police and Prosecution in Criminal Justice: The Practice and Experience of the United Republic

of Tanzania," 120th International Senior Seminar Participants' Papers (2003), in author possession.

103. For example, see: GAN, Business Anti-Corruption Portal, "Tanzania Corruption Report," https://www.ganintegrity.com/portal/country-profiles/tanzania/.

104. "Tanzania 2019 Human Rights Report," U.S. Department of State, 2.

105. "Country Reports on Terrorism 2017 - Tanzania, Sept. 2018," U.S. Department of State, https://www.state.gov/wp-content/uploads/2019/04/crt_2017.pdf.

106. Lillian Dang, "Violent Extremism and Community Policing in Tanzania," *Special Report* no. 442 (March 2019): 18–19.

107. Kamua Maichuhie, "KNCHR report exposes police brutality as perpetrators of sexual violence especially during political unrest," *Daily Nation* (Nairobi), December 3, 2019, https://www.nation.co.ke/kenya/gender/knchr-report-exposes-police-brutality-during-2017-polls-228664.

Index

Abboud, Ibrahim, 172, 173

Abdallah, Salah ("Gosh"), 177, 179, 180, 181

Abdullah, Sayyid Jamshid bin, 48

Abushouk, Ahmed Ibrahim, 171

African National Congress (ANC), 192, 210, 211, 212, 213, 214, 215–17, 218, 220, 221, 222, 223, 224, 226, 227, 232n56; Department of Intelligence and Security, 216, 217, 218–19, 219n33, 220, 220n38; National Executive Council, 213, 220, 224n55; National Intelligence Department, 213, 218; *Umkhonto weSizwe* (Spear of the Nation or MK), 213, 214, 215, 220, 222, 222n48, 225n65

African Union, 17

Afrikaner nationalism, 211, 212

Afro-Shirazi Party, 48, 54, 60

aid and trade narratives, 47, 61

Al-Hijra, 262

Alliance des militaires agacés par les séculaires actes sournois des Unaristes (AMASASU), 135–36

Amin, Idi, 12, 264

Amnesty International, 260

Andropov, Yuri, 75

Angola, 13, 69, 70, 76–77, 78, 81–82, 83, 105, 193; abuses of, 80, 81; armed forces of, 82; counter-subversion and, 79, 81, 85; culture of fear and, 80–81, 85; Directorate for Information and Security, 76, 79–80, 85; economy of, 83; elimination of, 76, 81–82, 85; factionalism of, 80–82; independence, 69, 78, 84; Information Service, 84; insurgency in, 77–78, 82–83, 84; intelligence organization and missions, 79–81; interior ministry of, 82, 83, 84; laws and, 80, 81; Ministry of Information and Security, 82–84; National Liberation Front of Angola, 77, 79; National Union for the Total Independence of Angola (UNITA), 77, 79, 82–83; Popular Movement for the Liberation of Angola, 71, 77, 78, 79, 83; security department in, 78, 84; South African conflicts with, 215

apartheid (South Africa), 209, 210, 211, 212, 213, 214, 217, 218, 219, 220, 221, 222, 223, 224, 225, 226, 227

Arewa Consultative Forum (ACF), 248

Asia, 22n46

askaris ("rehabilitated terrorists"). *See* South Africa, informers, use of in South African intelligence

Attwood, William, 32

autocracy, 34, 143, 144, 148

About the Editor and Contributors

Ibikunle Adeakin is a lecturer at Ajayi Crowther University in Oyo, Nigeria, and previously worked with an energy research team at the National Center for Energy Efficiency and Conservation in Nigeria. He holds a PhD in political science from the University of Waikato, New Zealand, and a master's in political science from the University of Lagos, Nigeria. Adeakin's research interests include civil-military relations, Islamism, African security, and comparative politics. Adeakin's work has appeared in journals, including *African Security*, *African Security Review*, and *Commonwealth and Comparative Politics*.

https://orcid.org/0000-0003-0099-364X

Christopher E. Bailey is associate professor at National Intelligence University in Bethesda, Maryland, where he specializes in national security law, international law, and professional ethics. He is licensed to practice law in California and the District of Columbia and is a member of the American Society of International Law. Bailey has a JD from the McGeorge School of Law at the University of the Pacific, an LLM degree in national security and U.S. foreign relations law as well as an SJD in international and comparative law from the George Washington University School of Law. He is the author of *Counterterrorism Law and Practice in the East African Community*.

Alex Bollfrass is a senior researcher with the Center for Security Studies at ETH Zurich. He was previously a Stanton nuclear security postdoctoral fellow with the Harvard Kennedy School's Belfer Center and an associate of the Davis Center for Russian and Eurasian Studies. Bollfrass was a nuclear weapons policy researcher at the Washington-based Arms Control Association and Stimson Center, before earning a PhD in security studies from Princeton

University's Woodrow Wilson School of Public and International Affairs. His archival research agenda compares how well intelligence agencies perform in assessing other countries' nuclear programs, with a focus on the East German Ministry for State Security. His parallel research also explores how climate affects civil wars and the ethical dilemmas of serving the security state.

Shannon Brophy is a graduate fellow at George Washington University in Washington, DC, where she joined the Middle East Studies program. She previously majored in language and intercultural studies and minored in global studies at Coastal Carolina University. Brophy completed an internship with the U.S. Department of State's Regional Security Office at the United States Embassy in Muscat, Sultanate of Oman. She has published her research on subjects such as international intelligence cooperation and the use of linguistics in intelligence, including in *The Intelligence Review*.

http://orcid.org/0000-0001-9125-0491

Glenn A. Cross is the founder of Crossbow Analytics LLC, a firm specializing in analysis of chemical and biological weapons (CBW) issues. He holds a PhD in biodefense from George Mason University in Virginia. Now retired from the U.S. government, he worked on CBW issues for several U.S. intelligence agencies beginning in the early 1990s. From 2008 to 2010, Cross was the deputy national intelligence officer for WMD & Proliferation, responsible for biological weapons issues. He is the author of *Dirty War: Rhodesia and Chemical Biological Warfare, 1975–1980*.

Joseph Fitsanakis is professor of Intelligence and Security Studies at Coastal Carolina University, where he teaches courses on intelligence analysis, intelligence dissemination, intelligence operations, intelligence in the Cold War, and the role of women in intelligence work, among other subjects. He has written extensively on intelligence policy and practice, intelligence collection, information security, communications interception, cyber espionage, and transnational criminal networks. His writings have been translated into several languages and referenced by media outlets such as the *Washington Post*, NPR, BBC, ABC, and *Newsweek*. Before joining Coastal Carolina University, Fitsanakis built the Security and Intelligence Studies program at King University, where he also directed the King Institute for Security and Intelligence Studies. He is also deputy director of the European Intelligence Academy and senior editor at intelNews.org.

http://orcid.org/0000-0003-0942-7505

Simon Graham is a postdoctoral researcher affiliated with the Laureate Research Program in international history at the University of Sydney and learning consultant for Sydney Living Museums. His work explores the intersection of intelligence history and international history on Central Europe, Eastern Europe, the Soviet Union, and the Global South. Simon has written extensively on intelligence collaboration and its influence on diplomacy throughout the Cold War. He currently leads an interdisciplinary research project titled *Spying on the World: The Stasi and the International Order*, examining how covert intelligence activities have shaped international institutions throughout the twentieth century. Simon's forthcoming monograph is *Stalin's Playbook: Collaboration, Conflict & Intelligence Cultures on Moscow's European Frontier.*

https://orcid.org/0000-0003-4576-4453

Tshepo Gwatiwa is a lecturer in the Department of International Relations at the University of the Witwatersrand in Johannesburg, South Africa. He is also a research associate at the African Centre for the Study of the United States at the same university. Prior to this, he was a lecturer at the University of Botswana and former adjunct at the Botswana Defence Force Defence Command and Staff College. His research interests are intelligence governance, foreign militaries in Africa, and African agency in international politics. He holds a PhD in International Relations/Political Science from the *Institut de hautes études internationales et du développement* (Graduate Institute of International and Development Studies) in Geneva, Switzerland. He is the co-editor of *Expanding US Military Command in Africa: Elites, Networks and Grand Strategy.*

John Burton Kegel has taught at the London School of Economics and Political Science and is a researcher at London Business School where he studies the colonial economies of Rwanda, Burundi, and the Democratic Republic of Congo. His PhD from the University of Kent, *The Road to Genocide: A History of the Rwandan Struggle for Liberation*, reevaluates our current understanding of the events leading up to the 1994 genocide by using previously untapped archival material and interviews collected during several stints of fieldwork. The work also combines his long-term interests in African and military history.

Kevin A. O'Brien is a senior visiting research fellow in digital intelligence and cybersecurity at King's College London as well as a consultant on security matters to governments and the private sector. He has previously held roles in RAND Europe and the Canadian government, served as a security advisor to a number of Western governments, and taught postgraduate courses in intelligence and security studies at King's College London and the University of Hull from where he obtained his PhD. He has written extensively about contemporary intelligence and security matters, including on South Africa's intelligence history, for more than twenty-five years.

Ryan Shaffer is a historian with expertise in extremism and intelligence. He holds a PhD from Stony Brook University in New York and was a postdoctoral researcher with the Institute for Global Studies. Shaffer has published over two hundred academic articles, reviews, and book chapters, including in *Intelligence and National Security*, *International Journal of Intelligence and CounterIntelligence*, and *Studies in Intelligence*.

https://orcid.org/0000-0002-6766-2194

Owen Sirrs is an adjunct faculty member of the Defense Critical Language and Culture Program at the University of Montana, where he teaches international security studies to the U.S. Army's Special Forces community. From 1998 to 2006, he served as an intelligence officer at the Defense Intelligence Agency in Washington, DC, where he specialized in the Middle East and North Africa. He is a graduate of Georgetown University's School of Foreign Service and received his master's in national security and strategic studies from the U.S. Naval War College and a master's in strategic intelligence from the U.S. Joint Military Intelligence College. He is the author of several books, including *Pakistan's Inter-Services Intelligence Directorate: Covert Action and Internal Operations*.

Benjamin J. Spatz is a fellow at the World Peace Foundation. He was previously a research fellow at Harvard Law School's program on negotiation. His research focuses on elite politics in violent, transactional political systems, conflict processes and conflict management, and targeted sanctions. Spatz has received many grants and awards, including from the U.S. Institute of Peace/U.S. Department of Defense and the Harry Frank Guggenheim Foundation. He has conducted extensive in-depth research in West Africa, and his professional experience includes, most recently, serving as a member of the United Nations Panel of Experts on Liberia. He received his PhD from the Fletcher School of Law and Diplomacy at Tufts University in Massachusetts and is a term member of the Council on Foreign Relations.

Lesego Tsholofelo holds a Master's in Intelligence and Security Studies from Brunel University London, the United Kingdom. He also holds a Master's in Defence and Strategic Studies from the University of Botswana. His areas of research include law enforcement and national security. He is also a former captain in the Botswana Defence Force.

www.ingramcontent.com/pod-product-compliance
Lightning Source LLC
Chambersburg PA
CBHW050630280326
41932CB00015B/2589